CANCELLED

MICHAEL GOVE

MICHAEL GOVE
A MAN IN A HURRY

OWEN BENNETT

Biteback Publishing

First published in Great Britain in 2019 by
Biteback Publishing Ltd
Westminster Tower
3 Albert Embankment
London SE1 7SP
Copyright © Owen Bennett 2019

ISBN 978-1-78590-440-0

10 9 8 7 6 5 4 3 2 1

A CIP catalogue record for this book is available from the British Library.

Set in Adobe Caslon Pro

Printed and bound in Great Britain by
CPI Group (UK) Ltd, Croydon CR0 4YY

For Alessandra

CONTENTS

ACKNOWLEDGEMENTS

This book, my third, was the most challenging to write. Boiling down a man's life to twenty-three chapters was a challenge, one that I did not truly appreciate until I was too deep into the research and writing to turn back. A constant throughout was my wife, Alessandra Pino, without whom this book would not have been possible. She provided support, tolerance, patience and love, as well as advice for when I was in one of many dead ends.

Thank you to my daughter Lucia for providing wonderful moments of light relief, such as showing me your ballet moves in one of your Disney princess dresses.

My mother, Deborah, and stepfather, Michael, also played supportive roles, as did my father, Nigel, my sister, Jennifer, and my brother-in-law, Steve. I also have to say *grazie mille* to my mother-in-law, Sandra and brother-in-law, Manuel, who provided ample distractions for Lucia and support for Alessandra as I pushed on.

Many thanks to all the people who agreed to be interviewed for the book. Some are named in the book, some are not – for obvious reasons – but I appreciate every scrap of information passed on to me. For ease of reference, it should be assumed that unless otherwise attributed all quotes and other pieces of information are taken from interviews conducted between March 2018 and May 2019. I am more than happy to admit that I have stood on the shoulders of giants in many parts of the book, and works by Tim Shipman and Harry Mount in particular informed the chapters on the Brexit referendum and the 2016 leadership contest.

I started this book at HuffPost UK, under the fantastic tutelage of Paul Waugh, and completed it while working at *City AM*. Christian May is a brilliant editor and a great man, and I thank him and the equally masterly Julian Harris for making me feel so at home there while I covered Cat Neilan's maternity leave.

If this book is in any way readable, coherent or entertaining, it is because of the forensic editing by Olivia Beattie, who must have been frankly gobsmacked at the state of the manuscript when it was delivered. Any errors remaining are mine and mine alone. James Stephens at Biteback was wonderfully patient with me, and a special mention must go to Iain Dale, who commissioned this book and promptly quit the publishing world a few weeks later out of what I imagine was sheer embarrassment.

I would like to say thank you to Michael Gove. He didn't ask me to write this book about him, and I'm sure he would rather I hadn't done so. However, he has always been unfailingly polite and professional with me, no matter the trouble I have caused for him.

This book was not designed to impact on Gove's career but to bring a greater understanding to the background and motivation of one of the most energetic, eloquent and, on occasion, surprising politicians of modern times.

Owen Bennett
Westminster, June 2019

CHAPTER 1

THE PARISH BOY'S PROGRESS

Life for Michael Gove did not necessarily begin on the day he was born. Indeed, on the day he was born, he was not Michael Gove at all – he was Graeme Logan.

On 26 August 1967, Graeme was born to an unmarried woman from Edinburgh. Up until 2019, Gove believed his birth mother was a student and that he was born in Scotland's capital city, but it can now be revealed that that story is not accurate. Baby Graeme was not born in Edinburgh but in a maternity hospital in Fonthill Road, Aberdeen. His mother was indeed from Edinburgh but was an unmarried 22-year-old cookery demonstrator at the time of his birth, not a student. His maternal grandfather was an optical frame maker, who himself was the son of a house painter. His maternal grandmother was a gelatin packer and the daughter of a French polisher. Baby Graeme would never know this part of his family, as he was put into care soon after he was born.

Living 140 miles north of Edinburgh were the couple who would become Graeme's adoptive parents: Ernest and Christine Gove. The Goves had been married since 19 September 1959, when Ernest was a 22-year-old working in the family fish business and Christine, barely out of her teenage years, was working as a despatch clerk. The pair were of solid Aberdonian stock, with their families' roots in the Granite City going back generations.

Ernest knew all about the importance of his name, as his father also shared the moniker. Ernest Sr was born on 13 November 1915 in Aberdeen. Like many in the city, situated in the north-east of Scotland, his trade was fishing. Aberdeen's harbour has been active as a business in its own right since 1136, and in 1900 some 200 fishing boats were working out of the city.[1]

Earning a living from the sea was in the Goves' blood. Michael's great-great-grandfather Hercules was a fisherman – a profession followed by his son, Andrew, born on 7 January 1883. While Andrew's name had less adventurous connotations than his father's, it did not hold him back. On 18 June 1911, Andrew saved the life of a girl who had fallen into the River Dee. A report from the time recounts how Andrew, 'accompanied by a lady friend' (presumably Sarah Ann Suckberry Phillips, whom he was to marry six months later), was walking over the suspension bridge when he heard the cries of a group of children as one of their friends had been borne away by the current. Removing his jacket, Andrew dived in, pulled the girl to safety and then promptly disappeared, 'without allowing any fuss to be made over his action', according to a report in the *Press and Journal* newspaper.

After being tracked down by a reporter the next day, Andrew explained why he fled the scene before being congratulated:

> I did not hurry away till I saw the child's life was sure, and after that I was naturally desirous of getting out of my uncomfortable clothes as soon as possible. A peculiar thing was that my watch stopped at one minute to eight – exactly the time I entered the water. It has refused to work since. That is nothing however, compared with the value of the child's life.

The girl's parents may not have replaced the watch, but they did give Andrew a gold medal out of gratitude.

Andrew married Sarah, a fellow fish worker, in December 1911, and the couple would go on to have three sons and a daughter. One son, born in 1915, was Michael's grandfather – Ernest Evans. Ernest Sr kept up the tradition of marrying a fish worker, wedding Williamina Webster in August 1936. The pair were both twenty years old at the time of the ceremony and in something of a hurry: Williamina was almost eight months pregnant with Ernest Jr when she walked down the aisle.

The Gove family were clearly of solid working-class stock, but the journey towards a more middle-class existence was begun by Ernest Sr. Whereas his father, Andrew, was a fish-market porter, Ernest Sr moved from worker to boss by establishing his own fish processing company. Based in Commercial Quay, and later Murray's Lane, in Aberdeen harbour, EE Gove and Sons would take the fish caught in the North Sea – primarily cod and whiting – gut the catch and smoke them before selling them on. At its peak, the business employed twenty workers, and it was passed on to Ernest Jr to run once Ernest Sr retired.

As well as sharing a business, the two Ernests had a joint love of sport. Ernest Jr enjoyed boxing as a youngster, and both men were avid football fans, with Aberdeen FC the object of their affections. They were also dedicated followers of the national side, and Ernest Sr would organise trips to Wembley to see the Tartan Army take on the Auld Enemy. But unlike thousands of other Scots who would make the trip down to London by train, Ernest Sr chartered a plane to take himself and other fish merchants to the match. He began running the excursions in the mid-1950s and carried on for more than twenty years.[2] Ernest Sr would have seen some memorable games, including when Scotland became the 'unofficial world champions' by beating the official holders of that title, England, 3–2 at Wembley in 1967. Ernest Sr had clearly decided that air was the only way to travel, as Gove Airlines took to the skies for domestic matches as well as international games. In February 1976, a plane was chartered to fly Aberdeen fans to Glasgow when the team played Rangers in the fourth round of the Scottish Cup. 'Those going are the same people who fly to Wembley every two years when we make a weekend of it,' he told the *Aberdeen Press and Journal*.[3] The journey back must have been somewhat muted, as the Dons lost to Rangers 4–1.

Michael's adoptive mother was born Christine Bruce on 24 July 1939. Her father, Charles, was a labourer, while her mother, Annie Thompson Melvin, was working as a waitress in a café when she got married in October 1938. The honeymoon was clearly a success, as Christine was born nine months later. Christine's paternal grandfather, Robert Bruce, was also a labourer, while her maternal grandfather, John Melvin, was a stonemason.

Both of Gove's parents left school at fifteen. While Ernest Jr was working with his father at the family fishing business, Christine started out working in a shop, before getting a job as a laboratory assistant.

Fishing, labouring, masonry. It was these jobs that had nurtured the oak trunks of the Gove and Bruce family trees, both of which had deep roots in Aberdeen. With the two families now linked, it seemed that no more branches would develop, as Christine and Ernest Jr were unable to have children. But the pair were determined not to see their desire to start a family thwarted, and they chose to adopt. And so it was that on 22 December 1967 Christine received a phone call that was to change not just the life of a little boy in care in Edinburgh but the entire direction of the Gove family tree.

'It was magic,' Christine later recounted, as she was told a baby boy was theirs to adopt.[4] The Goves travelled to the Scottish capital to collect their new son, and the baby that had arrived into the world as Graeme Andrew Logan was now Michael Andrew Gove.

There was a lot of him to love. Young Michael was a podgy infant. Early photos of him show him looking like a latter-day Les Dawson, with a round face sitting on top of an even rounder chin. 'He was just so cuddly, so chubby,' Christine remembers.[5] Christine gave up her job to care for her new son, and four years later the Gove family grew by one when the couple adopted Michael's sister, Angela. With another adoptee about to join the Goves, it was at this time that Christine explained to Michael the truth about his own origins. With words he would never forget, she said, 'You're different from other children because we chose you. You didn't grow under my heart, you grew in it.'[6]

Writing about that memorable conversation in 1998, Gove said,

When, and how, an adoptive mother chooses to tell their child about the past is one of the most delicate tasks she faces. My mother did so in such a way as to make me feel not rejected, but exceptional. I had been specially chosen by her and my father – a genuine love child.

He added, 'What son could not feel better equipped for life knowing how much he had been wanted by his parents?'[7]

Gove has always been open about his background, writing and speaking about it on numerous occasions throughout his careers as a journalist and politician. He once claimed he had 'lived a lie all my life' by being known as Michael and not Graeme, writing of the deception' in which he, his parents, his wife and even the Prime Minister were 'complicit'.[8] The underlying sentiment in the first-person articles, the interviews, and the profile pieces that appeared as Gove began to make the transition from journalist to politician all convey the sense of gratitude he feels towards his parents.

But there are, inevitably, two questions that Gove returns to again and again throughout his reflections on his origins: who are his real parents and does he want to find them? These are matters that Gove has clearly grappled with. 'I have never ... attempted to satisfy my curiosity on the mystery at the heart of my own story,' he wrote in *The Times* in 1998. His justification was simple: 'I have never tried for fear of offending the woman I have always called Mum, the woman in whose heart I grew.'[9]

It is a motive Gove has repeated numerous times, but it always carries with it a caveat: Christine has told him she would not be upset. Speaking to the *Daily Mail* in 2010, Gove said:

> My mother has always said if I want to [trace her] I should. She is equally clear there is no need for me to tell her if I do. I know, though, that she would take it as an indication that I did not feel my life or upbringing was fulfilled. It was. My mum and dad are fantastic.[10]

Gove put it even more starkly in an interview with the *New Statesman*, also from 2010: 'It's almost like saying to my wife that I needed to go out to dinner from time to time with another, single woman, just to be able to talk through my problems with her.'[11]

But while Gove has never attempted to find his birth mother, she was not completely shut out of his life; he revealed in 1998 that Christine kept her 'in touch with my progress through life'.[12]

So with his adoptive mother vowing that she and his father wouldn't stop him looking for his birth mother,[13] and his birth mother aware of how his life was progressing, there might be another reason for Gove's refusal to seek out the woman who had given him up when he was a baby. There was no way of knowing what his birth mother's reaction would be to hearing from the child she had put up for adoption, and there was of course the possibility that she did not want to be contacted – and could easily have rejected such an approach.

Back in 1971, the young Michael had other matters on his mind. Namely, his new baby sister. Angela Christine joined the Goves in their two-bedroom maisonette in 7 Erskine Street, in the Kittybrewster area of Aberdeen, and Michael would sit and watch as she was washed in front of the fire in the same old metal tub he had been bathed in years earlier.[14]

But within weeks a fresh challenge presented itself to the Goves. Angela was profoundly deaf, with total hearing loss in one ear and only 3 per cent hearing in the other.[15] It was a challenge Ernest and Christine approached with 'calmness, kindness and love', Michael wrote later.[16] As Angela grew older, Michael, his mother and one of his aunts learned the Paget Gorman system of sign language at the Aberdeen School for the Deaf. Christine was so taken with the school that she left her job as a laboratory assistant at Aberdeen University to become an assistant there, helping escort pupils, including her own daughter, on the bus that picked them up and dropped them home each day.

The Gove family was complete, and life settled into a routine. Ernest would set off for work early, often before dawn, to buy the cod and whiting brought in from the North Sea trawlers. He and his workers would skin and gut the fish and then smoke the catch over wood chips in the harbour.

It was not a world to which his son would take. Even as a child, Michael was more concerned with books than boats. Ernest tried to introduce Michael to the family business, but it was not a success. The boy was taken down to the fish house in Aberdeen harbour to see for himself how the family had earned its keep for generations. But it was clear that Michael would not be carrying on the tradition. Put off by the smell of fresh fish pulled out of the North Sea – let alone the act of cutting into the creatures – Michael turned to his father and said, 'Dad, this is no use for me. I can't do this.'

When Ernest asked what he wanted to do with his life instead, Michael replied, 'I'm going to get a job where it'll cost you money to speak to me.'[17]

It was clear very early on in Michael's life that that could well be the case. The boy was obsessed with reading and would continually absorb knowledge. 'He really just couldn't pass a bookshop. I had to get books for him all the time. He always carried a book with him, our Michael,' recalled Christine.[18] It wasn't just the typical adventure stories a young boy might read that occupied Michael – he would sit and devour encyclopaedias in order to cram as much information as possible into his expanding mind.

His appetite for learning only grew when he began to attend school. Gove's education began at Sunnybank Primary School on Sunnybank Road in 1972. Like most Aberdeen buildings, it was primarily made of granite, and had been founded in 1906. Situated a mile and a half from the city centre, the school's intake was a mixture of children from nearby council estates and those from the lower-middle-class background to which Gove himself now belonged. Sunnybank's headmaster was Ian Sharp, a 'no-nonsense' teacher in the 'traditional Scots mould', as Gove would later remember.[19]

After the Goves moved house in 1977, taking up residence in Rosehill Drive, Michael changed schools. He completed his primary education at Kittybrewster School – another institution housed in a sober granite building. The greyness of the architecture, which had all the warmth of a Victorian workhouse, was in contrast to the colourful and vibrant education taking place inside the stone walls.

Gove began putting his encyclopaedic knowledge to the test by taking part in inter-school quiz battles. His first appearance in the local newspaper came when the *Aberdeen Press and Journal* covered the 'Top Team' competition on 1 March 1979. A photograph shows a young Michael – complete with thick spectacles giving him the appearance of the schoolchild turned superspy Joe 90 – peering over the shoulder of quizmaster John Liddle. Alas, his team was knocked out in the semi-final stage by Broomhill Primary School a week later.

Michael was particularly inspired by two staff members at Kittybrewster: head teacher Robert Gillander, who had taken over the running of the school in 1975, and Eileen Christie, who taught him in his final year. He later reflected that Mrs Christie was akin to the titular character in the television adaption of *The Prime of Miss Jean Brodie*, broadcast in 1978 by Scottish Television. In the show, Brodie – played by Geraldine McEwan – injects her teachings with a degree of romanticism as she shuns the more formal style of the Edinburgh school in which she works. 'We were hardly the crème de la crème in Kittybrewster but Mrs Christie, like Miss Brodie, encouraged us to dream,' Gove later remembered.[20]

With primary school coming to an end, it was time for Michael to plot his next move. Mrs Christie was clear that his prodigious intellect should be nurtured in a suitably academic environment. She pushed for Michael to be sent to the independent Robert Gordon's College, located in the centre of Aberdeen. The Robert Gordon in the school's name was an Aberdeen merchant, born in 1668, who spent much of his life in Poland. Upon returning to his birthplace in around 1720, he had amassed a considerable wealth; with no wife or children, he decided to establish a 'hospital' to educate young boys. Gordon died in 1731, but his financial planning meant work on the building could continue, and the institution opened in 1750.

In 1881, it evolved into a day school, and in 1909 a separate adult education wing was established, eventually becoming Robert Gordon University.

Sending Michael to the school would not be cheap. Fees were set at £553 a year – almost £3,000 today. But with the boy already making it clear that he would not be able to earn a living with his hands, it was obvious to Ernest and Christine that investing in his brain was the way to go. Sacrifices had to be made, and the family avoided foreign holidays during the next seven years, while the family car remained the same clapped-out Datsun throughout Gove's time at private school. Michael passed the entrance exam and, with the Gove family tightening its collective belt to afford the fees, he was off to Robert Gordon's College in 1979.

The school – housed in another angular grey stone building – was a perfect fit for Gove. Indeed, he would go on to spend a considerable part of his political career trying to fill the entire country with Robert Gordon's Colleges. From his home in Rosehill Drive, he would travel south to the centre of Aberdeen to enter a world of blazers, academia and possibilities.

Gove's dominant features revealed themselves early in his tenure at Robert Gordon's. Polite, intelligent and outgoing, he seemed to arrive fully formed at a time when most boys on the cusp of manhood are searching for an identity – or at the very least trying a few out. 'When I see Michael on the television now, I can still see the eleven-year-old boy,' remembered his headmaster, George Allan, in 2012, adding, 'He didn't change his persona throughout his school career. Consistency – that's the word, consistency. We couldn't claim to be the authors of his remarkable civility. He created his own image.'[21]

It wasn't just the head teacher who was impressed by Gove. The school's head of English, Mike Duncan, who was also Michael's form tutor, remembers well his former student's precocious nature. 'He was one of the most inquiring pupils I ever remember teaching,' Duncan said in 2014, adding, 'At the start of every lesson a hand would go up and it would be Michael. The thought would go through my mind, "What is he going to ask me now and will I know the answer?"'[22]

The affection was reciprocated, and Gove has spoken about Duncan in lavish terms. 'My family apart, no other individual has had such a profound influence on my life,' he later wrote.[23] Duncan, who at thirty-one was the youngest head of department in the school, opened Gove's mind to a swathe of classic literature, helping him feast on the works of Jane Austen, George Eliot, Anthony Powell, Evelyn Waugh, Alexander Pope, Louis MacNeice, George Orwell and Lewis Grassic Gibbon. As per his tendency to couch his praise in literary comparisons, Gove described Duncan as 'like the teacher Hector in Alan Bennett's *The History Boys*, a lover of learning for learning's sake, intent on "passing the parcel" of knowledge to the next generation'.[24]

But it wasn't just the written word that Duncan helped Gove explore – it was the power of spoken English as well. Duncan helped stage school plays, and Gove was an enthusiastic participant in Robert Gordon's amateur dramatic productions. In 1982, he penned the annual report of the Vagabond Drama Club for the school's *Gordonian* magazine, and displayed the rhetorical flourishes which would become the hallmark of his career as a columnist some two decades later:

The Vagabond Drama Club has had to labour under the twin burdens of apathy and ignorance over the past year. However, Mr. Game's constant and unstinting support has inspired the Club to prepare for the showing of two short Scottish plays on the

Open Day. The standard of acting has been remarkably good with conspicuous performances from R. Berry and I. Head. The First Year section has been distinguished by youthful enthusiasm and excellent ability which augur well for Robert Gordon's College's dramatic future. Thanks are due to Mr. Gotts for the use of his room and facilities and to Mr. Gallie for his hard work, dedication and support.

Alongside acting, Gove found a natural home in debating, an activity also organised by Duncan. In 1981, he was one half of a two-man team that reached the regional final of the English Speaking Union Debating Competition. Alas for Gove, not only did he fail to win the Debater Trophy for his school, marking Robert Gordon's first loss since the competition's inception, but the award for best individual speaker was won by his partner, Martin Chalmers.

While Gove clearly relished the competitive element of debating, it was very much the taking part that seemed to count. He later reminisced about Duncan 'chaperoning us to debating competitions across Scotland and working out which chip shops might be open on the long drive back from Edinburgh so we could enjoy a late fish supper in the back of the bus after arguing the boys from Stewart's Melville College in Edinburgh into the ground'.[25]

Aside from am-dram and debating, Gove's plans for world domination also began at Robert Gordon's. He was part of the Wargames Club, which would see bookish boys play out doomsday scenarios thanks to games including Star Fleet Battles, Squad Leader and Third Reich. Gove's favourite was Kingmaker, a game created by Andrew McNeil, the father of his school friend Rupert. The game was set in the War of the Roses, and players indulged in diplomacy, alliance building and double dealing – essential skills for any future politician.

He also managed to fit in some music classes, taking lessons on that most unsubtle of brass instruments, the tuba.[26] Gove's musical tastes were more highbrow than low culture. While he was a fan of Simple Minds – with the 1982 album *New Gold Dream (81–82–83–84)* being one of his favourites – and an attendee of gigs by The Proclaimers, his true love was always opera. The Ring cycle by Wagner fascinated him, and it was a work he would return to again and again throughout his life.

The young Michael's lack of sporting ability – generously attributed to his hay fever by his mother[27] – meant most of his confrontations were always going to be solved theoretically rather than physically, but one former classmate told *The Guardian* in 2013 that Gove was unafraid to stand up for injustice where he saw it:

> He wasn't cool or fashionable, but he was very popular because he would always have a funny rejoinder, and could outwit the teachers. My childhood memories are peppered with laughter because of Michael. One of the things I valued him for was that he prevented me from being bullied. I had glasses and red hair, and I vividly remember being bullied in the changing room, and Michael tried to stop it.[28]

While the extracurricular activities seemed to help, rather than hinder, his schoolwork, the constant encouragement for Gove to engage in debates did have some downsides. Whereas Duncan enjoyed the verbal sparring with his pupil – including such games as Gove quoting the opening line of a novel and the English teacher having to guess what it was – other staff members were not as keen on the youngster's precociousness. 'I'm not sure he was universally liked by all teachers,' remembers Duncan, adding, 'I think some of them possibly felt a little bit, it seems bizarre to say, intimidated by him. He was so different and they didn't really know how to handle him.'

One way was certainly discovered by a few teachers: a sharp smack to the hand with leather belt known as a tawse. Gove was given this punishment on two occasions, once by his Latin master and once by his PE teacher. The reason, as he admitted in 2013, was simple: 'For answering back. For being cheeky.'[29]

Yet it was his old French teacher who would one day get an apology for past misdemeanours. In 2012, during Gove's battles with the teaching establishment while Education Secretary, he penned an open letter to Daniel Montgomery, the French teacher from his Robert Gordon's days. Gove admitted to indulging in 'pathetic showing-off' and posing 'clever-dick questions' instead of focusing on what was being taught. 'We were a cocksure crew of precociously assertive boys who recognised you were only a few years older – a rookie in the classroom – and therefore ripe for ragging. And because we misbehaved, we missed out,' he wrote.[30]

Montgomery, who was still teaching at Robert Gordon's when he received what a number of teachers craved – an apology from Michael Gove – plays down the disruption to his lessons. 'Even in those days, Michael stood out,' he says, adding, 'I remember the words of one of my colleagues at the time: "That boy is a future leader of the Conservative Party."'

The mention of the Conservative Party is worth noting, as up to that point in Gove's life the Labour Party had held sway over his beliefs. Inspired by the works of George Orwell, Gove was a typical teenage socialist, and in 1983 he became a fully paid-up member of Labour's Aberdeen North constituency branch, where the local MP was the anti-apartheid campaigner Robert Hughes. Labour was at that time led by Michael Foot, making the party the most left-wing it had been in its history – meaning the young

Michael Gove would have been quite at home in the company of 'Corbynistas'. The future Conservative leadership contender not only knocked on doors on behalf of Labour in the 1983 general election, he also represented them in his school's mock vote. Alas, Gove was unable to buck the national trend, and he finished bottom of the ballot.

Praised by teachers and respected by his peers, Gove was thriving at Robert Gordon's College. Scarcely could there have been a better fit for the boy, whose intelligence, wit, curiosity and bookishness were encouraged by those around him. The only question seemed to be just how high his star would rise.

Nor did Gove's education stop when he left the school gates at the end of the day. Every Sunday, his family would attend church services at Causewayend Church, now known as St Stephen's, a short walk from Erskine Street. The church minister was Douglas Sutherland, who helped instil a love of the works of Anthony Trollope. Gove went on to become a Sunday school teacher at the church, which mainly involved supervising a room of primary school-aged children, and it was while both learning and teaching the word of God that a seed was planted in his brain which would blossom later in life. Stories of the people of Israel were frequently recounted, and the young Gove found the tales moving. He was interested not only in the historical accounts, but in the perception of who were the ones really working for peace in the region and who were the ones posturing. Gove also started taking an interest in a land dispute much closer to home than the Middle East, with the conflict in Northern Ireland also piquing the boy's curiosity. Both disputes, centred in religion and territory, would help define his world view later in life.

Gove was thriving in and out of school, yet, as he approached his final two years at Robert Gordon's College, his father took a decision that would leave a lasting impact on the youngster. In 1983, the European Council signed off on the modern-day Commons Fisheries Policy. While the policy itself had been in operation since 1970, the changes saw the introduction of limits on the quantity of fish that could be caught, in an attempt to curb overfishing. Ernest Gove recognised that the changes could have an impact on his processing business and decided to sell up. EE Gove and Sons was bought by a man called Danny Cooper, who paid for the premises and the contract – but did not keep on the two dozen members of staff. With the business sold, the Gove family needed to make cutbacks – and with Michael's school fees now standing at £1,100 a year, that was the obvious area for savings. The encouraging teachers, the wargame-playing friends, the debating society, the amateur dramatics, the atmosphere of acceptance, the celebration of intellectualism above physical achievements – all at risk. How would Gove survive – let alone thrive – in the more rough-and-tumble atmosphere of a state school? For the second time in his short life, Gove's future was at crossroads. When he was a baby, given up for adoption by his birth mother, he had to rely on the kindness of strangers to give him a world in which he would be loved and nourished. Now he had to rely on his own intellect to stay in the world that he so relished. Gove needed to pass a scholarship exam to ensure he could remain at Robert Gordon's. The encyclopaedia-reading literary buff who regularly hit top grades in all his subjects, of course, passed. His future was secure.

Gove was a school prefect for two years from 1983, as well as school vice-captain in the 1984/85 academic year. Mike Duncan remembers that it was 'quite an achievement' for a boy so lacking in athletic ability to be awarded one of the top positions in the school hierarchy. His role as a prefect gave Gove an early opportunity to put into practice how he thought schools should operate. Duncan says, 'I remember saying to him once, "How do you deal with the cheeky boys?" "Oh," he says, "I just use large words that they don't understand and they are reduced to stunned silence." It's only Michael could have got away with that.'

Gove's debating skills continued to be honed and, along with his friend Duncan Gray, he finished runner-up in the Edinburgh University Bank of Scotland Debating Competition of 1985. He also reached the semi-final of the ESU Conoco Public Speaking Competition in the same year. Duncan was delighted with his star pupil, but did notice one slight flaw in Gove's approach to debating: an occasional lapse into getting completely carried away by his own arguments. Duncan says, 'When he was preparing for a debate and producing the arguments, he was usually pretty clear and logical, but then there would be occasions where I would say, "Michael," – maybe not said it to him, not in these words, but – "your judgement's gone out of the window here."'

It would not be the last time Gove would be accused of letting the desire to win an argument outweigh other considerations.

All good things must come to an end, and with the sun setting on his time at Robert Gordon's College, Gove turned his mind to another first for his family – a university education. The youngster had originally contemplated studying medicine, but when his enjoyment of English lessons began to drastically overtake that of maths and science, he decided to pursue his passion. While he was mulling over where to apply – St Andrews in Fife was initially the preferred choice – Mike Duncan suggested to Gove that he should consider the oldest university in the English-speaking world: Oxford. Duncan had established a relationship with the university's Lady Margaret Hall college after recommending another pupil three years earlier who had proved popular. When the English teacher flagged up another suitable candidate, he received an enthusiastic response from the college. 'I remember getting a letter back saying, "Well, if you can send any more like him, we'll be delighted to look at them" and that's how Michael ended up going there,' says Duncan.

Gove duly applied for Oxford, with St Andrews his second choice and Durham his third, and after completing an entrance exam was awarded a place studying English at Lady Margaret Hall. He wasn't the only Robert Gordon's pupil making the journey south, as his friends Duncan Gray, Rupert McNeil and Andrew Ross would join him in Oxford in the autumn of 1985.

The school's annual magazine marked the departure of the high-profile student in a manner befitting Gove's trademark love of words – and his distinctive dress sense. Next to cartoon of a smiling Gove, complete with a spotted bow tie, the following passage appeared in the Higher School Notes section:

MICHAEL GOVE. Orange's eventual entrance to Oxfam University has finally confirmed his place above mere immortals. All that now remains of his shady past is the nickname Raffles. He now earns his money by tutoring Mr Duncan in English. Naked without his tweeds, it is Colonel Fogey's ambition to be a listed building when he grows up.

Gove submitted his own poem to the magazine, titled 'An Essay on Teaching (with apologies to Alexander Pope)'.

> 'Tis hard to say, if greater want of skill
> Appear in learning or in teaching ill;
> It seems to be the teacher's twin offence
> To tire our patience and mislead our sense.
> Some few teach well, but may err in this,

They censure wrong and are in wit amiss.
A tutor ev'ry day must boys expose
To learning but too often his lack shows—
'Tis with our teachers as our leaderene,
The words o'erflow, the sense remains unseen
In class their wit is weak and knowledge rare
of taste in ties they have but little share.
They must alike from boys and head earn praise
Offend the Head and numbered are their days
The boys, tho' smaller, wield a greater pow'r
To displease them is not to last one hour.
For those who would a life of teaching lead
Remember this just as you plant the seed,
The soil of youth is fertile at the start
But want of care will have the bloom depart
So spare the boys the tedium of your talk
And let them in Parnassus' bow'r walk.

It would not be the last time Gove would lecture teachers on the best way to carry out their duties, and his literary effort provides further evidence – if it were needed – that the future politician was as sure of his own mind when he was at school as when he was in charge of them.

Before Gove completed the transition from school elder to university fresher, Robert Gordon's College was able to provide him with one more adventure. As the school's vice-captain, he was awarded the McKenzie Scholarship, a fund which enabled him to travel around Europe. Along with his friend and fellow soon-to-be Oxford student Rupert McNeil, the explorer took in Amsterdam, Munich, Salzburg, Vienna, Venice and Florence in a whistle-stop three-and-a-half-week tour before returning home, having run out of money. The young Gove was at his most pious when he delivered a report of his adventures to the *Gordonian* magazine the following year – an article he bizarrely began with the line: 'Like Hitler forty-five years before, all Europe lay at my feet last summer.' Amsterdam may have had 'delightful architecture' but was also home to 'unsavoury merchants in pornography and drugs', he revealed, also expressing anger that while 'immorality was so blatant, the church I visited was concealed behind the facade of a town house'. The 'impressively large, clean and efficient' Munich got a better review, even if its residents 'seemed to err on the side of smugness'. Salzburg was 'a little too tourist-oriented and pretty for my taste (or my pocket)', reported Gove, while Vienna – initially praised as 'pure sophistication' – soon received a black mark from the miniature Phileas Fogg:

> Much of Vienna is grim post-war bleakness and the Viennese are arrogant to the point of prejudice. When we were lost amidst the grandiloquent transport system, we were befriended by a Bengali newspaper-seller who heard us speak in English. Not only had the Viennese ignored our plight, it was quite clear from their attitudes and whispered comments that we had dropped in their estimation by talking to an Asian. The newspaperman confirmed that the euphemistically titled 'guest workers' were treated with scorn by the Viennese.

Thankfully for Gove, Venice ticked all the boxes. 'It is quite unlike anywhere else in the world,' he said, praising the 'crumbling facades' which 'hide beautifully appointed palazzos' and noting approvingly how 'every church seems to contain a priceless work of art'.

'The Italians obviously cared about these buildings; entry (unlike in the corrupted Amsterdam) was free and a sense of decorum (no bared limbs) was encouraged,' he added.

It wasn't just the architecture and sense of morality that appealed to Gove, but also the 'remorselessly well-dressed population'. 'Even pensioners wore smart and fashionable clothes with rare dash,' he gushed.

Gove had now learned something of the world, and now it was time for him to learn more of himself. The city of dreaming spires was waiting.

CHAPTER 2

BRAVE NEW WORLD

'I had a room overlooking the car park and we were just hanging around and staring out the window, and suddenly there was this bloke with a green tweed suit and a red tie. Of course, we fell about laughing.'

Gove's arrival at Lady Margaret College at Oxford was certainly memorable for Philip Hensher. The third-year English student and his pals were in full 'we've seen it all before' mode as they surveyed the new intake in October 1985, but even they were taken aback by this skinny kid from Aberdeen, dressed like a country gent in a £1.50 suit he had bought from a Salvation Army charity shop.

'You saw this process of people arriving at Oxford in ordinary clothes and then over the course of the next eight weeks they would sort of transform themselves into young fogeydom. It wasn't something that people would turn up wearing,' the novelist remembers.

Hensher and his friends decided to have some sport with the newest 'young fogey' on campus, and they immediately sought him out when they gatecrashed the freshers' drinks. However, they hadn't factored in two of Gove's greatest weapons, which he would deploy as often as possible throughout his life in order to get himself out of a variety of tricky situations: politeness and charm.

Hensher remembers, 'We went with the ambition of taking the

piss out of him, and that clearly wasn't going to happen. He's just an interesting guy. That's the thing: if Michael had never gone into politics, everybody would really like him.'

And so Gove continued at Oxford in just the same vein he had carried on at Robert Gordon's – at least initially. The tweed suits, the arch politeness, the self-deprecation – nothing had changed. He was practically fully formed – and in that self-possession lay a confidence which could easily come across as arrogance. While one contemporary describes him as a 'fucking phoney', others were fully signed up to the Gove persona from Day 1.

Like Hensher, the journalist Stephen Pollard has a vivid recollection of his first impressions of Gove. The former Mansfield College student says:

> He was very striking. He was one of those figures that people knew of within two days of his arrival, not least because of the way he dressed. He used to wear fogey clothes. For some people, like Jacob Rees-Mogg, it looks like an affectation somehow. With Michael it never seemed affected. That was just him. He always had charisma, but early on it was a slightly twee charisma. He gave the impression, I think, of being quite shy initially but he sort of overcame that and constructed this witty, charming persona, I think to overcome that shyness.

Gove's choice of Lady Margaret Hall (LMH) as the college in which to study for his English degree – at the recommendation of his school teacher Mike Duncan – meant he had avoided the political conveyor-belt colleges. Anyone with designs on reaching the top of the political tree would have been tempted to look at Christ Church, which has educated thirteen British Prime Ministers, or Balliol College, which has something of a reputation for excellence in political matters, being responsible for Tory Prime Ministers Harold Macmillan and Edward Heath, Labour Chancellors Roy Jenkins and Denis Healey, and Liberal Party leader Jo Grimond, among many others. As pro-European integration was a strain seemingly running through many of the Balliol alumni, however, perhaps Gove would not have enjoyed three years in that college.

Lady Margaret Hall was founded in 1878 and named after Margaret Beaufort, mother of Henry VII. It was the first Oxford college to educate women, and men were admitted only from 1979. Alumni included Josephine Barnes, the first female president of the British Medical Association; the future Pakistan Prime Minister Benazir Bhutto; and the actor Diana Quick, who appeared in the 1981 television adaption of *Brideshead Revisited*, which helped bring the aesthetic of young fogeydom to the masses (and clearly at least one teenage boy in Aberdeen). Alongside Gove in the 1985 intake were James Allen, who would go on to present ITV's and the BBC's Formula One coverage; Martin Giles, later to work at *The Economist*; and Samuel West, son of actors Prunella Scales and Timothy West, who would go on to tread the boards in his own right. What it lacked in a conveyor belt of Cabinet ministers, it made up for in the diversity of fields its alumni would go on to succeed in.

Conservatism was very much alive at LMH thanks to the presence of Dr Nicholas Shrimpton. The English tutor nailed his colours to the mast as that rare beast, a pro-Margaret Thatcher member of the higher education community, in the months before Gove's arrival at LMH. In January 1985, Oxford's governing assembly voted overwhelmingly not to award Thatcher an honorary degree, making her the first Prime Minister of the twentieth century educated at the university not to receive such an accolade. Many of the 738 dons and administrators who opposed the honour were from the medical and science departments, who were angry about the effect of cuts on their research.[1] Shrimpton, one of 319 who supported the honorary degree, labelled the blocking 'a futile, painless and self-congratulatory gesture'.[2] In an article for *The Times*, he suggested sexism was an underlying cause for many to want to withhold the honour, adding, 'Its absence is the badge of her radicalism, and some of us at Oxford salute her for it.'[3]

Gove may not have chosen his college with a future political career in mind, but his key goal at Oxford – even above his studies – was very much the ambition of someone preparing for high office. The Oxford Union is the zenith of student debating societies in the UK – and, some would argue, the world – and Gove, naturally, wanted to be its president. To reach such a position is to place yourself alongside some of the most prestigious and influential names in the world.

William Gladstone, H. H. Asquith, Edward Heath, Michael Foot and Tony Benn are just some of the former presidents of the Oxford Union, and Gove was set on joining that illustrious list. No sooner had he arrived on campus than he made a beeline for the union buildings in Frewin Court, a mile into town from LMH. He wasted no time getting stuck into the debates, and Anthony Goodman, who was president during Gove's first term, remembered being struck by the young Scotsman's debating abilities. 'He was one of the most gifted speakers I saw in the union,' Goodman said in 2012, adding, 'But he didn't generate any antagonism; he was confident, but not in a pushy, aggressive way. He just seemed like an old head on young shoulders.'[4]

In a 1987 collection of essays entitled 'The Oxford Myth', one former president of the union passed on advice to others who wished to ascend to the top of the debating society. A candidate needs 'a disciplined and deluded collection of stooges' who will persuade people in their respective colleges to back you, the essayist noted. Collecting and motivating these 'stooges' is a skill in itself. The presidential candidate must convince the stooge that there is something in it for them; that by so nakedly attaching themselves to his or her particular bandwagon the fruits of success will some-how trickle down. Yet, as the author of the essay pointedly revealed, 'The tragedy of the stooge is that even if he thinks this through, he wants so much to believe that his relationship with the candidate is special that he shuts out the truth. The terrible art of the candidate is to coddle the self-deception of the stooge.'[5]

In his first year at Oxford, Gove willingly became a 'stooge'. Indeed, to the student who wrote those very words: Boris Johnson.

Alexander Boris de Pfeffel Johnson was born in New York City on 19 June 1964 – three years before Graeme Logan entered the world in Scotland. While the young Johnson was brought up by his birth parents, it was Gove who had the more secure upbringing. Johnson's parents, Stanley, twenty-three, and Charlotte, twenty-two, had been married for a year when the little blond boy was born, and were living in the States, as Johnson Sr had won a fellowship to study economics after graduating from Oxford the year before. Charlotte was also a student, reading English at Lady Margaret Hall, but took a gap year in order to follow her husband to the new world. Little Boris spent the first few years of his life on the move, with his parents' work and studies taking him to Oxford, London, Washington DC, Connecticut and Devon. Meanwhile, after Gove's initial transition from Graeme to Michael, he only moved house once, and that was just to another part of Aberdeen.

Deafness was a presence in both Gove's and Johnson's child-hoods. But whereas young Michael learned sign language in order to communicate with his sister, Boris was the one with the affliction in the Johnson family. It wasn't until he was eight or nine, and after several operations to insert grommets into his ears, that the boy could hear. Both Gove and Johnson were privately educated, with Boris securing a scholarship to Eton, but where young Michael was the first in his family to receive paid-for schooling, Johnson's father had been a pupil at the historic Sherborne School in Dorset. Gove's adopted parents were present during his childhood – physically and emotionally – while Johnson's father would often disappear from his life for months on end as his work took him around the world. In 1974, when the Johnsons were living in Brussels, Boris's mother suffered a nervous breakdown and was sent to the Maudsley Hospital in London for nine months. Her bouts of depression – and hospitalisations – continued throughout the remainder of her marriage to Stanley, with the pair separating in 1978 and divorcing in 1980. Gove, of course, did not have to deal with the implosion of his family, although he did have to process the fact that biologically they weren't his family.

Johnson and Gove were both the eldest children in their families, but whereas Michael had just one sister to compete with for his parents' affections, Boris saw three siblings arrive on the scene within seven years. For the Johnsons, life was very much a competition, with the eldest child clashing most frequently with his sister Rachel, born little more than a year after him. His half-sister, Julia, describes how the atmosphere among the children was very much based on an 'academic rivalry of mind-numbing magnitude'. The atmosphere came from Stanley, with Julia remembering, 'If I came second in Latin, my father would instantly demand: "Who came first?" It became a standard catchphrase in our household and vigorous deterrent against being anything except top.'[6]

Michael had no such family rivalries to contend with or past academic milestones to measure his successes against. Both his parents had left school at fifteen, and while that is in no way a reflection of their intellectual abilities, it highlights how his passage to Oxford was truly a journey to a different world. Yet, for Gove, that brought a different kind of pressure. There was no safety blanket of seeing how this journey had been completed before; no previous examples of what worked and what failed. There was no context in which to place his achievements, no sense of what was truly a result of hard work or what was the by-product of natural talent. In Gove's case, this sense of the unknown was doubly intense compared to other youngsters who were the first in their families to go to university. Whereas some are able to look at their parents' natural abilities and infer which characteristics have been passed down – and therefore which areas of study or pleasure they might excel at – Gove did not have that genetic example before him. He was journeying into unchartered territories without a map, or even a compass.

By the time Gove arrived at Oxford, Johnson was one of the big figures on campus. His shock of blond hair, his larger-than-life persona, even his unusual name (he had shed 'Alexander' in favour of 'Boris' while at Eton) meant he was someone everybody knew. Johnson, who enrolled in 1983 to read Classics at Balliol College, had his sights set on the Oxford Union presidency in much the same way as Gove would in future years. He failed in his first attempt to get elected to the post in 1984/85, but had another crack at it a year later. This time, Johnson hatched a plan to reach out to more of the electorate than his Old Etonian demeanour had previously won over. He decided to mask his natural Conservative leanings with the trappings of the Social Democratic Party, the new political movement launched in 1981 and spearheaded by Roy Jenkins, another Balliol alumnus. American pollster Frank Luntz, an Oxford contemporary of Johnson, remembered well how Boris pivoted in order to win votes. 'He renounced his Conservative affiliation and fully embraced the SDP and the principles and people who supported the SDP to help him get elected. At that time being a member of the Social Democrats was the best thing to be at Oxford,' said Luntz.[7]

With the Tory wolf now dressed in SDP clothing, Johnson needed a flock of stooges to spread his many messages across campus. Gove was a willing member of the 'Boris cult', he later remembered, providing a vivid description of his first encounter with the man who would play such a key role in his life:

> The first time I saw him was in the Union bar. He was a striking figure with sheepdog hair and penny loafers, standing in a distinctive pose with his hands in his trouser pockets and his head bent forward. He seemed like a kindly, Oxford character, but he was really there like a great basking shark waiting for freshers to swim towards him.[8]

Gove was happy to be in the great basking shark's gang, and although he was taken with Johnson's debating skills ('He was quite the most brilliant extempore speaker of his generation'),[9] the canny fresher knew that helping a Balliol man secure the presidency was a useful political investment:

> The real reason why I became a stooge in the Boris machine was that Oxford politics was essentially a matter of the college that you found yourself in. I was in Lady Margaret Hall, which was a small satrap of Balliol, like a colony in Sicily aping the manners of our betters. Slates need balance, and an LMH debater fitted into the balance.[10]

Not for the last time, a Boris Johnson-fronted campaign with Michael Gove acting as willing stooge proved popular with the voters, and the future Mayor of London was elected to serve as Oxford Union president in the final term of the 1985/86 year.

Boris Johnson was not the only big beast at Oxford the same time as Michael Gove. There was also a future Prime Minister studying at the university – David Cameron, who began reading Philosophy, Politics and Economics at Brasenose College in 1985. Like Johnson, Cameron had been educated at Eton, but unlike his sometime friend and full-time rival, he was much more relaxed about 'getting on' in university politics, and shunned the Oxford Union – or any other overt political activity. Despite becoming great friends in later years, there is no evidence that Gove and Cameron interacted at all while at Oxford together. Other future political heavyweights on campus during that period included Ed Balls, David Miliband and Jeremy Hunt, but Gove moved in separate social circles to those who were more explicit in their political ambitions.

His living arrangements meant he was always in company. After staying on campus while a fresher, Gove moved to Iffley Road, south-east of the city centre, with nine other students for his second year. He moved to the north of the city in his final year, where he shared a house in Walton Street with, among others, Hugh Powell, son of Sir Charles, one of Thatcher's top foreign policy advisors.

Gove's enthusiastic support of Johnson, and his own performances in union debates, helped his notoriety grow on campus. He was anointed 'Pushy Fresher of the Year' by the Oxford student paper *Cherwell*, but it wasn't all bad press, as the same publication also dubbed him 'the best debater in the Union'.

His speeches at the union were full of Gove's trademark self-deprecation and wit, and it was there that he began to develop and toy with the notion that, far from being an adopted son of an Aberdeen fisherman, he was actually part of the Scottish aristocracy. Gove, along with his school friend Duncan Gray, would don a kilt when taking part in debates, and a regular refrain would be for Gove to apologise for his dishevelled appearance, saying that his Filipino manservant Pepe was on holiday so he had had to dress himself. Despite the joke, Hensher does not believe Gove was trying to mask his true background. Perhaps it would have been tempting, even on a subconscious level, to adopt the mindset of Pip in *Great Expectations*, who feels a degree of embarrassment when the world he comes from collides with that which he now inhabits. But Gove seemed completely at ease with his backstory. 'I don't think there was any question of him trying to hide his origins. That was a very common phenomenon at the time. One of the characteristic things was people got rid of their accent and he never did. He talked about his parents,' says Hensher.

Away from the union, Gove took well to the social aspect of university, but in a low-key manner. Friends remember him as more of a 'popping round for dinner' than a 'heading to a nightclub' kind of man. He was not part of the notorious Bullingdon Club, nor the Piers Gaveston Society, but did find himself invited to break bread at the Arnold and Brackenbury Society, a dining club organised by Balliol College. As Pollard remembers, 'It was basically an excuse to get drunk over dinner, and was all a bit pretentious, as you are supposed to make witty speeches.' The odd splash of pretension aside, there do not appear to be any tales of smashed-up restaurants or defiling the heads of dead animals in Gove's university closet. As one contemporary says, 'Believe me, if there were, I would tell you.'

That is not to say Gove did not get up to some mischief. One particular lark involved making prank phone calls – usually when drunk. One recipient of a Gove call was American politician Tom Kean. The then Governor of New Jersey was hotly tipped to be the running mate of George Bush in the 1988 presidential election. During a visit to London, the student Gove – egged on by his friends and buoyed by a large amount of alcohol – decided an early morning phone call was required to improve Anglo-American relations. Gove rang the hotel where Governor Kean was staying and, in his poshest English accent, demanded to be put through to the Republican's suite. The receptionist duly obliged, and Governor Kean was on the other end of the line within seconds. As Gove's friends tried to stifle their laughter in the background, Gove explained to the Governor what a fan he was of the politician and how he would be supporting him in the upcoming election. Indeed, perhaps Kean should run for the White House himself.[11] Despite the support of this unknown but incredibly well-spoken Englishman, Governor Kean did not put himself forward for the Republican presidential nomination. In the event, he didn't even get on the ticket, as Dan Quayle was chosen by George Bush to be his vice-presidential nominee.

Gove had proved he could do posh, so for another prank call he decided to mix it up a little. Author Colin Dexter – creator of Oxford police officer Inspector Morse – received a phone call one Saturday afternoon from someone who sounded like a stereotypical East End gangster. 'Oi, Dexter, I'm such a fan of your fucking *Inspector Morse*, it's fucking brilliant,' said the rather gruff Cockney, before putting the phone down. The well-educated Oxford student responsible for the call, and his rather drunk friends, found it hilarious.[12]

Gove secured the presidency of the union in his final year, and seems to have won support without resorting to dark tactics or masking his true beliefs. As one contemporary put it, 'He was just a brilliant debater.' Pollard remembers Gove's demeanour was very unpolitical. 'There were some people who would willingly stab their father in the back or their best friend in the back, but you never got that impression – and not just the impression, because it was true, Michael would never do that.'

Gove's fascination with the Oxford Union meant he played virtually no role in the other aspects of university life you would expect an aspiring journalist or politician to involve themselves in. He did not contribute to *Cherwell* and did not take an active part in any of the party-political associations on campus. It was while at university, though, that Gove completed his journey away from teenage socialism and joined the Conservative Party.

However, while friends remember him discussing politics in general, there was no sense that he was an overtly political animal. Pollard says, 'I don't recall having a single political conversation with Michael at university at all. It was obvious he was Conservative, and I was a member of the Labour Club, but I don't remember having any political conversations with Michael.' Hensher has the same memory of Gove, recalling that while 'he talked about political principles and how society would be, that makes him sound much too "leading forth". I have the distinct impression of a conversation consisting of a series of leading questions, a kind of general, unobjectionable sense of fairness, really.' Another university friend who would go on to become an MP agrees, saying, 'I don't remember Gove being overtly political.' While he was hardly donning a blue rosette and knocking on doors in support of Margaret Thatcher, it was clear, as Pollard says, where Gove's political loyalties lay. *Cherwell* even went as far as to describe him as having 'rabidly reactionary political views under a Jane Austen cleric-like exterior'.

But Gove did set out a manifesto of sorts as he kicked off his tenure as union president in January 1988. The union's magazine, *Debate*, set out the topics to be considered by the society in the upcoming term. The front cover of the magazine listed them as 'Money', 'Fear' and 'Sin'. In 2011, one of the magazine's editors, Samira Ahmed, who would go on to have a stellar career as a journalist for the BBC and Channel 4, recalled, 'The coverlines were

– Money about how most students seemed to be going into the City to become bankers, contrasted with mass unemployment, and poverty in many inner cities. Fear was about Aids, and Sin was about homophobia.'[13] But Gove used his 'President's Address' article to focus on a topic he was passionate about, and one he would return to repeatedly throughout his life: 'This House believes that Oxford and Cambridge are too elitist.'[14] The new union president described it as 'potentially the most important debate of the term' – although clearly not so important that he proofread the article before publication, as the word 'elitist' is misspelt as 'elist'. Reading the rest of the address, it is clear that Gove opposed the motion. He does not believe Oxbridge is too elite; rather, that it is full of the wrong kind of elite.

> The word is misused and wrongly applied with a frequently [*sic*] which makes me weep. Oxford may pander to privilege, it may be unjustifiably and insufferably smug and self-serving. It may be a creaking anachronism and bound together by too many old school ties but it is not truly elitist. It would be a better place if it was.[15]

Gove then went on to give a glimpse of exactly the mantra that would dominate his time as Education Secretary more than twenty years later – namely, that all schools should be in the image of Robert Gordon's College: 'If our state schools were a little more elitist, if they tested their pupils with greater rigour and frequency and brought home the difference between failure and success more forcibly they would have more pupils at Oxford.'[16]

The same objection may be levelled at Gove the student as at Gove the Cabinet minister, who would use the same language when promising to adopt an 'unashamedly elitist' approach: what exactly did this privately educated boy know about life in a state school?

He had been educated at Robert Gordon's College since the age of eleven. Many of his friends at Oxford had received a paid-for education. Was it the fact that his parents left school at fifteen that turned him into such a snob when it came to state education? He seemed to believe they are terrible places where even someone as bright as him would not be able to fulfil his potential:

> I am, as those who know me will bear out, cursed with arrogance and sloth in equal measures. If I had not been tested, cajoled, frightened by failure and stimulated by success I would not be at University. I was lucky. There are a great many in this country whose sloth, peculiar arrogance and distaste for privilege mean that they do not think of trying to come to somewhere like Oxford.[17]

Gove may have been keen to use the union to proclaim his burgeoning political views, but he was also alert to how he could use his position to get a leg up in the career that was becoming increasingly attractive to him: journalism.

During his tenure as president, he organised a debate on the future of the media, inviting then controller of BBC2 Alan Yentob and former economics editor of *The Times* Peter Jay to take part. Other high-profile figures tempted down to the union by Gove included Matthew Parris, the MP turned journalist, who was invited to debate 'homosexual law reform', and Secretary of State for Scotland Malcolm Rifkind, who took on Donald Dewar over the future of the United Kingdom.[18]

In an article for *The Times* on 14 February 1997, Gove engaged in some 'Weren't things better in my day' nostalgia as he berated the union for focusing more on attracting celebrity speakers such as OJ Simpson. 'It is no longer a surprise to see the Oxford Union invite individuals to speak who are famous only for being infamous,' he lamented.[19] Reflecting on his own period in charge, Gove allows himself some modesty, but clearly sees his tenure as in keeping with the traditions of Gladstone, Asquith and Heath. 'My own record as president hardly stands comparison with my distinguished predecessors. I presided over more than my fair share of catastrophes but at least we tried to make debating the heart and soul,' he wrote.

Aside from the more cerebral activities being union president entailed, Gove began to experience the sort of personal scrutiny that accompanies elected office. In an early example of the gossip that politicians are frequently subjected to, *Cherwell* printed details of a 'five in a bed romp', involving Gove and fellow union hacks during the 1987 Christmas holidays. According to the report, Gove, Anthony Frieze, Noel Sy-Quia and Murielle Boyd-Hunt 'decided to join' Flora McCullough in her bed after attending a ball at the Grosvenor Hotel. 'Since the evening in question, there have been many tight-lipped "No comments" about what they all got up to.'[20] When the story re-emerged in 2008, Gove told the *Mail on Sunday*, 'I had better get back to you on that' after being asked for a comment. Flora McCullough, now McClean, was slightly more forthcoming, telling the paper, 'Oh God, yes, I remember. I don't think we did all end up in bed. I don't think they even stayed with me afterwards. I think it was *Cherwell* making things up. He [Gove] always looked about twelve. They probably ran the story because it was so unlikely.'[21] When asked about it again in 2013, Gove admitted that the bed had been shared, telling the *Mail*, 'We all crashed there and then got up and went home the next morning. It wasn't like some sort of *Last Tango in Paris*-type affair.'[22]

The original *Cherwell* article speculates that the reason Gove was seeking the comfort of others that particular evening was because of an incident on Boxing Day 1987 involving Aberdeen football fans. Gove and his friend Duncan Gray were having a post-Christmas drink in Aberdeen city centre, taking in some of their favourite pubs, such as the Prince of Wales just off Union Street. Gove was in full young fogey dress when the pair came across a group of football fans celebrating Aberdeen's 2–0 victory over Falkirk. A skirmish developed and, as Gove took the punches, Gray ran away, according to one friend at Oxford who later heard the tale.

Gove was no stranger to seeking comfort in the arms of others. Describing him as a university lothario may be stretching his prowess, but Gove very much enjoyed the company of his female contemporaries. His first serious girlfriend was Marianne Gilchrist, a student at Corpus Christi alongside future Foreign Secretary David Miliband. Originally from Edinburgh, where her father was a Conservative councillor, she is described by a mutual friend of the pair as 'incredible fun'. The friend joked, 'She was one of these women who would drink twenty times more than the nearest man. Very Scottish in that respect.'

Gove and Gilchrist were an item for around a year, but it seems she broke off the romance in the spring of 1988 after taking a liking to Duncan Penny, a student who had helped campaign for Gove to be elected union president. According to *Cherwell*:

> Gove's jealousy got the better of him and he scrambled egg all over Penny's hair. He [Penny] managed to respond by reaching for his fridge and splattering the Honourable Gentleman with a tomato. In a fit of Hulkman rage Gove broke into Penny's room at two in the morning and fire-hosed his sleeping body. Unfortunately Gove somehow was unable to hit the mark and Penny wasn't aroused...[23]

Somewhere along the way, Gove picked up a rather saucy nickname while at university. 'Donkey' was the moniker bestowed on the tweed suit-wearing young fogey,[24] apparently a reference to a piece of anatomy that merited its own name. Perhaps his body confidence lay behind a skit at the Oxford Union in 1987, when Gove challenged the audience to ponder what he was wearing under his kilt. After he'd removed his boxer shorts and thrown them into the crowd, someone suggested the audience vote on whether he was truly honouring the Scottish tradition of wearing a kilt sans underwear. Gove, then aged twenty, told the audience he was more than happy to undergo an inspection, but only if the act was carried out by a 'nubile young girl'.[25]

When asked about his nickname in 2013, Gove played the innocent, saying, 'I don't recall being called Donkey, no. I don't know what that would refer to, so I don't remember.'[26] But it seems Gove was not always so reticent when discussing what God gave him. In 2000, *The Times* organised a photograph of its staff to mark the turn of the millennium. On a cold January day, journalists for the paper gathered on a grassy bank in Wapping to pose for the picture. According to one of those present, Gove was clearly feeling the cold more than most, as he quipped, 'It's a bit chilly, isn't it? It's so cold my cock has shrunk all the way up to my knee.'

Back in his student days, and Gove's notoriety for donning a kilt for debates travelled all the way to America. In April 1988, Gove, future Conservative MP Ed Vaizey and another student called Matthew Leigh were despatched to the United States by the university to show their American cousins that the Brits were still the best debaters in the world. The Oxford trio took on a team from the University of Rochester, New York, in front of an audience of 200, in a debate about whether NATO should be scrapped. 'This was no boring talk,' the *Democrat and Chronicle* newspaper wrote, adding, 'There were hisses. There were insults. It was what the Oxford team is used to.' Scott West, one of the debaters on the Rochester team, decided to hit Gove where it hurt during the battle. Reflecting on the Scotsman's decision to wear a tuxedo, not a kilt, West said, 'I'm told that the sight of his pale, scrawny and not very hairy legs is truly inspiring.' Regardless of the insult, the Oxford team – who were that arguing NATO should be abolished – won the contest by 105 votes to eighty-eight. To cement the goodwill, the Rochester team gave their opponents university-branded sweatshirts. The Oxford boys presented their American hosts with Oxford Union boxer shorts.[27]

The American trip marked the end of Gove's presidency of the union, but the crown wasn't passed too far. His old friend from Robert Gordon's College, Duncan Gray, was the next in line for the top job, meaning the kilt-wearing tradition would continue for at least another term.

With the Oxford Union presidency over, Gove had his final exams to focus on. He shunned writing a dissertation in favour of completing two special papers, one on Alexander Pope, a favourite since his days at Robert Gordon's, and the other on critical theory. He excelled at the latter, with an essay on feminist critical theory helping him get his best marks out of all his final assessments. His lowest mark came in his papers on William Shakespeare.[28] There was never any doubt that Gove would pass his degree, but unlike David Cameron, Ed Balls and David Miliband, who secured first class honours, he achieved only a 2:1.

By the summer of 1988, Gove's university days were over, and the young man was unsure what to do with himself after leaving Oxford. It didn't take long before he found himself getting back in touch with his inner socialist rabble-rouser.

CHAPTER 3

THERE AND BACK AGAIN

'**Y**ou're a scab! You're a dirty scab!'[1] The insult was spat out from the picket line towards a worker heading into the office. It was a regular occurrence, but the anger rarely boiled over into anything more aggressive.

Those manning the picket line, complete with their 'Official Picket – Don't Cross!' banners, were focused on keeping warm as much as hurling abuse at 'scabs'. Hands were stuffed into pockets of winter coats as those on strike tried to steal as much warmth as they could from the makeshift braziers. Striking workers gathering around naked flames was just as much of a snapshot of Margaret Thatcher's Britain as yuppies wielding Filofaxes or police clashing with miners. One of those on this particular picket in Aberdeen in 1989 must have thought he would play a different role in the story of Thatcher's premiership when he left university a year before, but, nonetheless, there was Michael Gove.

Many of his Oxford contemporaries had enjoyed gorging on the fruits of Thatcherism since graduation. Boris Johnson had had a very brief spell as a management consultant – he claims it was just a week – before tapping up a contact he had made at a New Year's Eve party to get a job in journalism. Frank Johnson (no relation) was working at *The Times* and promised to get his new friend in to see the paper's editor. Johnson landed a job as a trainee and, after a brief stint learning his trade on the *Wolverhampton Express and Star*, he was back in London to work on the national paper. He was sacked within months for making up a quote from a distinguished history don at Balliol College regarding the discovery of a long-lost palace of Edward II. Johnson's godfather, Dr Colin Lucas, was most perturbed to see his name in the article, especially as he had been quoted as saying the palace was the location where Edward II had cavorted with Piers Gaveston – a man who had been beheaded thirteen years before the palace was supposed to have been built.

On complaining to *The Times*, Dr Lucas received a reply saying the paper stood by the story. When an inquest was held by the *Times* editor, the truth was discovered and Johnson was dismissed. He wasn't unemployed for long, though; the *Daily Telegraph* promptly snapped him up and gave him a job as a leader writer. Within a year, he was despatched to Brussels, where he continued his habit of being completely lackadaisical when it came to small matters such as the accuracy of his stories. One rival correspondent described him as 'fundamentally intellectually dishonest', while another labelled him 'a complete charlatan'.[2]

While Johnson was developing a reputation in Brussels, David Cameron was building his own in London. After leaving Oxford with a First in Philosophy, Politics and Economics, the future Prime Minister mulled over his next step. He too considered journalism, and went for an interview at *The Economist*, but an advert spotted in his university's careers department piqued his interest: 'Conservative Research Department: bright graduates needed'.[3] A position in an elite department in the party of government was highly contested, but Cameron found his path to the door smoothed over somewhat by an anonymous phone call to the deputy director of the unit, Alistair Cooke. 'I understand that you are about to see

David Cameron,' the grand voice on the end of the phone said. 'I've tried everything I can to dissuade him from wasting his time on politics, but I have failed. I am ringing to tell you that you are about to meet a truly remarkable young man.'[4] Cameron was in, and without breaking a sweat.

Another Oxford graduate to get a job in the CRD was Gove's best friend from university, Ed Vaizey. The fellow Oxford Union hack had worked in the department on a voluntary basis during his gap year and was rewarded with a full-time job upon graduation.

Gove sought to follow the Oxford set to London. He floated the idea of becoming a barrister, but later admitted that 'it was a way of avoiding the discussion' on whether he would pursue politics as a profession.[5] He eventually applied for a job at the CRD, but without a mystery phone call or a backlog of voluntary hours to fall back on, he was rejected after being deemed 'insufficiently Conservative' and 'insufficiently political'.[6] With the London political set not opening their doors to him, he decided to focus on the career that had attracted him since he was boy at Robert Gordon's, when George Orwell almost tempted him to fully embrace socialism,[7] and try to earn his living as a journalist.

Gove sent out the usual begging letters to editors of the national newspapers, hoping his record as a debater and his Oxford University degree would land him a spot in a newsroom. The only outfit to take the bait was the *Daily Telegraph*, and the one-time Orwell wannabe was ushered in for a meeting with the paper's editor, Max Hastings, to assess his suitability. The interview focused less on Gove's abilities as a journalist and more on his knowledge of Scottish Presbyterianism and seventeenth-century military history.[8] Having passed the audition, he was handed a shift on the paper's diary section, known as the 'Peterborough' column, edited by David Twiston-Davies. Other hacks plying their trade in gossip suitable for a broadsheet at that time included Quentin Letts, Damian Thompson and James Delingpole, the latter becoming a lifelong friend to Gove. Despite his best efforts, Gove struggled to land more than a few shifts at the paper, and his confidence took a slight knock when Twiston-Davies informed him after he filed once particularly scurrilous piece about a prominent politician that while he did indeed have talent, it was actually for libel.[9]

Struggling to make a living in London, Gove decided to take a slight step backwards in order to leap forwards. He secured a place on the well-respected Thomson Regional Newspapers trainee journalist scheme, which meant a return to his hometown to learn his craft the old-fashioned way on the *Aberdeen Press and Journal*. With a history stretching back to 1747, the daily broadsheet covered the Granite City and wider news from the north-east of Scotland. In January 1989, after spending a few weeks getting a feel for the newsroom, Gove was sent to Newcastle to formally begin his apprenticeship at the Thomson training centre. He was one of around ten trainees from the *Press and Journal* and other papers in the Thomson Regional Newspapers group despatched to the city for a five-month course, where he was taught media law, public affairs and shorthand, as well as being sent out into the city to build up his portfolio.

Another young journalist on the course was Mike Elrick, a fellow Aberdonian who had landed a place on the *Aberdeen Evening Express*. A graduate from Strathclyde University, Elrick was the political opposite of Gove, and would go on to work for Labour leader John Smith and New Labour Cabinet minister John Reid. Despite their different views of the world, the pair got on well. Elrick remembers:

Michael was very much the young fogey. It was a bit more understated than the full tweed suit, but he had his corduroy trousers and his big glasses, and Michael does what Michael has been making a success of: hail-fellow-well-met. He's polite, he's courteous, he's friendly, he's funny, he's clever, so people warmed to him as a result regardless of their politics.

Gove and the other trainee reporters were placed in digs across Newcastle, usually in rented rooms in private houses. Gove was housed in the Gosforth district of the city, and treated it very much like a continuation of his student lifestyle – even repeating some of his old pranks. 'I remember one occasion late one night being in Gove's room when he phoned Jonathan Miller and pretended to be someone who wanted to get Jonathan Miller to direct either a play or an opera,' says Elrick, adding, 'Miller very quickly realised this was a studenty-type jape. Back then, although he was in his twenties, Michael probably was still in the Oxford-student mentality.'

Gove was still getting a regular hit of the Oxford lifestyle, travelling back to his old university town at weekends, as well as visiting friends in London. All of this would be done on public transport, as he had yet to pass his driving test. After five months of training, he returned to Aberdeen to begin his life as a journalist proper. He initially moved back into his parents' house in Rosehill Drive before sharing a flat with fellow hacks including Euan Ferguson, who would go on to be a TV critic for *The Observer*.

The life of a journalist seemed to do little to curtail Gove's desire to indulge his student side. One night after a few too many drinks in Aberdeen city centre, he took part in that most clichéd of student hijinks and started messing about with a traffic cone. Walking down Union Street, Gove decided a cone was located in the wrong place and the drastic action of throwing it off a viaduct onto a road below was taken. Unfortunately for Gove, the whole incident was witnessed by officers from Grampian Police. 'A police van turned up and the last thing I saw was Michael being taken into the back of the police van,' remembers Elrick. 'I obviously thought this was hysterically funny and couldn't wait to tell people subsequently.' Elrick did not always find it so amusing, as he has also described it as 'an act of hooliganism' and said that Gove was 'old enough to know better'.[10] When the incident found its way into the press in 2010, Gove claimed to have a 'hazy recollection' of the night in question, and another friend suggested the future Justice minister was given a dressing-down by police instead of being tossed into a van.[11]

Yet his career had barely begun when it threatened to grind to a halt completely. Gove joined the *Press and Journal* at a time of growing disquiet between workers and management. The row centred on plans to introduce personal employment contracts, thereby removing the collective bargaining power of the National Union of Journalists – and effectively removing union representation in the workplace. The dispute began in the summer of 1988 and, after a year of fractious talks between the NUJ and management, the decision to go on strike was taken in August 1989. Staff from the *Press and Journal* and the *Evening Express* walked out for nineteen days. The dispute escalated when the editor of the *Evening Express*, Dick Williamson, wrote to ten trainees warning them that if they did not return to work immediately, they could be sacked.[12] An attempt to restore relations failed, and at the end of September more than 100 journalists went out on strike again. This time, there was to be no rapprochement, and Aberdeen Journals Ltd, the subcompany of Thomson Regional Newspapers, fired 116 of those who had walked out. Iain Campbell, the head of the *Press and Journal*'s branch of the NUJ, seemed unfazed by the dismissals, saying at the time, 'Obviously people are concerned about being sacked, but you have to remember they've sacked us three or four times before, in fact in some cases five or six times, so it's not something new, they can't produce the papers without us.'[13] If Campbell thought this would be another brief stint of industrial action, he was wrong. The management – who succeeded in getting papers produced with a skeleton staff – dug their heels in and refused to offer any jobs back, despite the public seeming to side with the strikers. Some forty local authorities[14] withheld advertising revenue, readers cancelled their subscriptions and job adverts went unanswered.

Gove joined the picket line along with his striking comrades, and those who were gathered around the braziers with him remember he showed no indication he was opposed to the action. Speaking in 2013, Campbell said, 'We knew he was a Tory, and our concern was to have a united front. So we spoke to Michael, and he was happy to come on board. He wasn't a typical striker by any means, but he was very articulate.'[15]

Gove was certainly more than a passive participant in the action. The young Thatcherite joined his comrades on trips to the Conservative Party conference in Blackpool and the European Parliament in Strasbourg to lobby politicians and also took part in a march through Aberdeen city centre. Gove and his fellow picketers received strike pay from the NUJ, which shelled out almost £1 million during the year-long protest – a commitment which almost destroyed the organisation completely.

As any young journalist would be, Gove was restless during the strike and looked for ways to entertain himself when he wasn't on the picket line. He kept himself physically active in two ways. The first involved a spot of mountain walking near the grounds of Balmoral, the Queen's castle located in the Cairngorms National Park. Gove, Elrick and another trainee reporter, Ben Young, made the three-hour bus journey from Aberdeen to tackle Lochnagar, but before they reached the summit the snowfall became too much and they had to retreat. Elrick and Young lost Gove on the way down and spent anxious hours searching for him. It wasn't until a few days later, having returned to Aberdeen, that they learned what had become of him. 'We found out Michael had got down, had obviously come down a separate route and had just got on the bus,' Elrick recalls. 'At the time I kind of thought, "We were wandering round the estate trying to find you and you just got on the bus and headed back into Aberdeen." I thought then it was a slightly selfish thing to do.'

Gove's socialising was not confined to walks in the great outdoors. In a bid to keep up morale during a bitter strike with no indication of a resolution forthcoming, house parties and other social events would frequently be thrown. It appears that during these get-togethers Gove decided to ensure at least one of his fellow strikers was in a better mood, and he embarked on a relationship with a young female colleague. 'It was relatively short-lived,' remembers Elrick, adding, 'You would never have thought those two would have got together, would have hitched up. They were chalk and cheese and so unlike each other.'

Gove kept his brain active by signing up for a Grampian Television quiz show called *Top Club*. The programme, which had been running since 1971, featured teams of work colleagues or club mates, and Gove joined team captain Andrew Byrne, Andrew Craig and Lindsay Macdonald under the name The Wordsmiths. Macdonald remembered the initial plan was to be called the Dead Parrots Society, and when Grampian TV rejected that idea, they tried to plump for The Strikers – but that too was vetoed. Filming for the first two rounds took place on 19 February 1990, and Gove was given a suitably cheeky introduction by his team captain: 'Michael was born in Aberdeen, and his main hobbies are real ale and real women.'[16] The team sailed through the first two rounds and were called back for the semi-final and final recordings on 25 February. Having seen off teams from a rugby club and a retired naval association, The

Wordsmiths found themselves in the final up against a profession which would have a few more battles with Gove in years to come: head teachers.

Gove, a seasoned quizzer and debater, was his usual relaxed self during the filmings, and deployed his self-deprecating humour to elicit laughter from the studio audience. Macdonald remembers:

> He had a running joke in the second recording session. At one point he answered correctly a question about Archduke Franz Ferdinand and then said, 'He's my uncle.' In the final, one of the answers was about Teddy Taylor [a Conservative MP who had called for Nelson Mandela to be shot], and he said, 'He's my uncle too.'

The Wordsmiths emerged victorious, and a celebration party was thrown. Drink was taken, not only to celebrate the victory of The Wordsmiths but also to toast the departure of one of its members. Gove had landed himself a reporting job at Scottish Television, the ITV franchise for central Scotland.

Gove's departure was met with warmth, not hostility, by his fellow strikers, who understood that a young journalist would want to get their career up and running as soon as possible. The strike went on for another seven months after Gove left, ending on 14 September 1990. A handful of journalists got their jobs back; the rest had their possessions returned in black bin bags and were given a small payoff.[17] As the years went on, members of the group would reconvene to mark the dispute at appropriate anniversaries. Gove wasn't among them, though that is not to say the strike did not play a part in his life again. Indeed, events many years later would perhaps make him unwelcome at any such get-together. But in February 1990 Gove was very much looking forward, as he swapped braziers for broadcasting.

CHAPTER 4

BRIGHT LIGHTS, BIG CITY

L ike intercourse for Philip Larkin, television came rather late
to Parliament. It was not until 21 November 1989 that cameras
were permitted to broadcast the proceedings from the House of
Commons, when a six-month pilot began. Conservative MP for
Eastbourne Ian Gow was due to give the first televised speech from
the green benches – moving the Loyal Address to mark the state
opening of Parliament – yet before he got to his feet, Labour MP
Bob Cryer stood up and raised a point of order on how student
demonstrators who had travelled to Westminster were treated by
the police.[1] Cryer thus ensured he would become the answer to an
obscure pub quiz question many years later. In 1990, MPs agreed
the journey into television should continue, and the green light was
given to make the cameras permanent. Broadcasters began pumping up their political teams in order to make the most of this new
resource – and it was into this brave new world that Michael Gove
emerged.

Despite being qualified as a journalist for less than a year, and
with much of his early career spent on strike, Gove was talent-
spotted by STV to take part in this revolution in political reporting
and was swiftly hired, reporting to John Brown, brother of future
Labour Prime Minister Gordon. He was sent down to London to

begin work in Westminster, meaning his gamble of leaving the capital in late 1988 in the hope of later returning on a sturdier footing had paid off.

Needing somewhere to lodge, the new broadcast journalist turned to his old university friend Ed Vaizey. The Oxford contemporary had secured a job at the Conservative Research Department but was still living with his mother, the art critic Marina Vaizey, in Chiswick High Road, north London. Marina had a spare room and Gove became the Vaizeys' lodger.[2] After a few months, Ed and Michael moved into their own flat in Ledbury Road, Notting Hill, with Gove's old school friend Duncan Gray, who was working for the BBC London radio station GLR. It was through this living arrangement that Gove began making connections that would change his life. The most significant was with one of Vaizey's colleagues at the CRD, David Cameron.

Cameron was born on 9 October 1966 in a private hospital in London, the son of Ian, a stockbroker, and Mary, who would go on to become a magistrate. He was the third of four children and, like his father before him, was educated at Eton. While at the exclusive private school in Berkshire, Cameron was not marked out as one of the absolute top boys, with a school friend later describing him as 'good second-rate in terms of talent'.[3] It was at Oxford where Cameron hit his stride intellectually. He graduated with a First in Philosophy, Politics and Economics from Brasenose College, and contemporaries remember him as wanting to be a 'top-dog student'.[4] As we have already seen, he did not get involved in student politics – unlike future Cabinet colleague Jeremy Hunt – nor in the Oxford Union, where Gove was king. He displayed his political colours by throwing a party in his room to mark Margaret Thatcher's 1987 election victory,[5] but it was hardly a sign that he had aspirations to be Prime Minister. Outside of the lecture hall,

Cameron's spare time was spent on what he would later describe as a 'normal university experience'. There was plenty of sex, some mild drugs, and what would pass for rock and roll behaviour in the form of the Bullingdon Club. The 200-year-old society, which takes its members from the wealthiest sub-section of Oxford students, is famed for the trashing of restaurants and student digs at the culmination of a dinner. In 2009, Cameron said he was 'desperately, very embarrassed' about his membership of the club, adding, 'We do things when we are young that we deeply regret.'[6] After graduation, Cameron spent five years working at the Conservative Research Department, where he met Gove via Vaizey. Thanks to Gove's private school education and three years at Oxford, the adopted son of an Aberdeen fisherman was able to rub shoulders with an Old Etonian born into wealth and privilege with ease.

It wasn't just professional connections Gove was making. While working for STV, he also embarked on one of his most serious romantic relationships. Simone Kubes was the daughter of Czech-American Professor Jan Kubes and had been two years below Gove at university and in the same hall. The romance blossomed when Kubes moved to London to begin training as an accountant. Reflecting on the relationship in 2013, a mutual friend said, 'They were absolutely marvellous together. She, so bright, witty and larger than life, and he, the most entertaining man in any room.'[7]

The nature of the Westminster calendar meant Gove would spend summers away from London, working back in Scotland. In 1990, he returned to Aberdeen to work for Grampian Television for a month, and in 1991 he was sent to Edinburgh on behalf of Scottish Television.

While Gove was enjoying his life as a broadcaster, he was becoming frustrated with the annual redeployments and the local nature of the reporting he was undertaking. He craved to be at the heart of the Westminster action, and a job at the BBC offered just that chance. In the autumn of 1991, he moved into national broadcasting.

'Why have we appointed this child to be a reporter?' Sean O'Grady thought to himself as he surveyed the apparition in front of him. Gove was certainly nothing but consistent when it came to first impressions. 'He was this tallish chap, extremely polite, courteous, quite tweedy,' remembers O'Grady.

Luckily for Gove, having a slight air of the misfit about him was perfect for the BBC's *On the Record* programme. The politics show, broadcast on Sunday lunchtimes, was the brainchild of the corporation's deputy director-general, John Birt, who was also responsible for news and current affairs. Launched in 1988, *On the Record* had the goal of shaking up the BBC's political output. David Aaronovitch, who had worked on another Birt-instigated political programme from his days at ITV, *Weekend World*, was hired to be editor of the new show. While he had a background in television, many of the reporters brought in to make Birt's vision a reality had little broadcast experience. One of these was John Rentoul, hired from the *New Statesman* magazine. He remembers well the process of getting the hour-long show ready for broadcast each week. 'It was a comedy,' he says, adding, 'These print journalists trying to run a TV programme and the only thing that was professional about it was the title sequence, which was really distinctive and had good music.'

One of the main opportunities for the show to really break the mould was its choice of presenter. The programme it replaced was *This Week Next Week*, hosted by David Dimbleby. Who was the presenter of this new show, determined to shake things up? David's younger brother, Jonathan.

'He was fine, but nothing very exciting or different,' says Rentoul, adding, 'It was just a weird experiment. Everyone else in the BBC hated us because we were the new Birtist incomers who had been recruited in order to show the BBC how shit it was.'

It was into this atmosphere that Gove arrived. O'Grady, a researcher and producer on the show, may have been slightly taken aback by the sight of this tweed-wearing youngster arriving in the office, but it was very much in keeping with the 'shake it up' philosophy of the show.

It didn't take long for the typical first impression of Gove to move to the typical second impression of Gove. 'Very soon we discovered that he was quite precocious and quite mature in his outlook and a very intelligent man and very knowledgeable,' recalls O'Grady.

While O'Grady, Rentoul and others at *On the Record* were processing the young fogey in their midst for the first time, Gove found a familiar face in the team. On the staff roster that included future BBC political editor Nick Robinson and future *Today* programme presenter Martha Kearney was a Scottish journalist Gove had known since his student days: John Nicolson. Nicolson was one of the reporters who had helped launch *On the Record* and, despite being only twenty-seven when the programme started in 1988, he was already a TV veteran. While a student at the University of Glasgow in the early 1980s, Nicolson took part in the BBC Scotland show *Mr Speaker, Sir!*, in which undergraduates would take on politicians and other public figures in a debate. Nicolson so impressed the producers that he was asked to take over the hosting duties from legendary broadcaster Magnus Magnusson. It was on this show that Gove made his television debut while a student at Oxford. 'I remember him being very good and sharp and funny,' says Nicolson. The two hit it off, and Gove took it upon himself to play host to his new friend on his home turf of the Oxford Union. Nicolson was invited down to take part in a debate, and the evening before the event Gove appeared at his new friend's hotel, armed with a bottle of whisky, perhaps keen to learn some lessons from a man who at that point was a few years ahead of the young Michael in a career he was considering. As it was, Nicolson used the opportunity to attempt to persuade the Tory supporter to switch allegiance and back Scottish independence. The whisky drinking was successful; the conversion to independence was not.

The pair's friendship only grew stronger during their time at *On the Record*. Nicolson was certainly the more senior of the two in terms of experience and journalistic credibility, and Gove seemed to revel in his role as young mischief-maker alongside him. The two would often lunch together at various places around Notting Hill, with a tapas bar on Portobello Road being a particular favourite. But, being thrifty journalists, the pair would always keep an eye out for a bargain and after discovering that the Halcyon Hotel in Holland Park offered a cheap set menu they shifted their allegiance. One afternoon, the duo turned up to the hotel's restaurant to be told that unfortunately lunch was not being served as 1980s pop group Duran Duran were holding a press conference in the room. Michael and John looked at each other, and the younger of the two men whispered, 'That sounds like more fun than lunch, shall we stay?'[8]

After telling the man on the door that they were from the BBC and were of course there to interview the New Romantic icons, Gove and Nicolson were ushered into the press conference. It's fair to say that among the hacks from the *NME*, *The Face* and other music and fashion publications, the two men from the BBC stood out somewhat, especially as Gove was 'all tweeded up with his little round glasses', as Nicolson recalls.

As Duran Duran dealt with the usual questions regarding their latest album – the second they had released under the title *Duran*

Duran – Gove decided it was time to bring a hard political edge to proceedings.

'Yes, I've got a question,' said Gove, flinging his hand up in a theatrical fashion. After introducing himself, he addressed the group's lead singer, Simon Le Bon. 'Simon, can I just engage you about the meaning of some of your lyrics. "Hungry Like the Wolf" – who can fail to be impressed by that insightful commentary on Thatcherite economics? What inspired you for that devastating motif? Can you talk me through it?'

Le Bon looked perplexed. The words 'Thatcherite economics' or even 'motif' were clearly not ones he expected to be confronted with at the press conference. But Gove went on, quizzing Le Bon over more of his lyrics. Nicolson was simultaneously trying to hide his amusement at the unlikely line of questioning and also disguise his own surprise at Gove's apparent knowledge of Duran Duran lyrics.

'Everybody is turning round exasperated by this, but you could see Simon Le Bon suddenly thinking, "Really? Have I really written insightful, radical lyrics? That's not how I see myself at all,"' remembers Nicolson.

After a few minutes of being grilled on the socio-economic contents of his lyrics, Le Bon realised that perhaps the line of questioning was not entirely serious. 'When you say things like that to me, a shiver runs up my spine,' Le Bon said to Gove with a smile. 'And yes, right back down mine if I may say so, Simon,' Gove replied with a grin.

Another Scottish journalist was a regular dining companion of Gove and Nicolson. Sarah Smith, daughter of future Labour leader John, became friends with Gove and Nicolson through the world of debating. Like Gove, Smith appeared on *Mr Speaker, Sir!* while a student, and the pair struck up a friendship. They were so close that the tweedy Tory would sometimes stay in her house, prompting her father to proclaim, 'Oh God, is that right-wing young man sitting at the breakfast table again?'[9]

The bond shared by these Scots making their way in the media world endured long after two of the three threw off the shackles of journalism and embraced the world of party politics. When Nicolson was elected as MP for East Dunbartonshire in 2015, Gove gave his old friend 'something between a hug and a handshake'[10] upon his arrival in Westminster – much to the bemusement of many of Nicolson's SNP colleagues.

Aside from crashing pop stars' press conferences, Gove's main role at *On the Record* was to produce a video package on one of the leading political topics of the week. The short films, often running to around ten to twelve minutes in length, would contain a mixture of clips of politicians, case studies to demonstrate the relevance of the issue beyond the Westminster bubble, and that ever-present of broadcast journalism, a vox pop of the great British public. While Gove was more than competent at all aspects of the job, he thrived when he was able to focus on the goings-on in Parliament. As O'Grady recalls:

> He was very good at spotting the weakest link in a chain, the MP in any given party who is liable to let slip, is liable to rebel, is liable to be, as I say, a weaker link in an alliance or something like that. For a while I called him 'The Jackal' because he was able to spot this weak antelope at the back of the herd limping away. He'd pick on that one and go and interview them and get the soundbite and bring it back and we'd usually have a small story out of that. He was very good and thoroughly enjoyable.

With the footage recorded, Gove would retire to the editing suite to bring the package together in time for its broadcast on the

Sunday show. The editing work would often see Gove and colleagues locked in a room together on Friday and Saturday nights
and, as the videotapes whirled, the group would pass the time by
discussing politics. Gove made no attempt to hide his Conservative
and Unionist views in this forum, and would often end up debating
with a Trotskyist video editor about whether the country was on
the verge of a socialist revolution.

One of Gove's most memorable contributions to the programme
was a short film on the campaign to lower the age of consent for gay
sex from twenty-one. Over footage of a gay pride march through
the streets of London, Gove described the campaigners as 'out, loud
and proud' as he explained the issues facing the homosexual community.[11] O'Grady remembers some footage that didn't make the
film's final cut:

> We went round what was called Britain's biggest gay multi-store.
> It was a sex supermarket specialising in the sort of things you
> expect. I remember him looking round all the rubber dolls and
> sort of spanking implements and objects of that nature and being
> amused and bemused by them and giggling away. We were like
> a couple of schoolboys on a lunch break. It was pretty unprofes-
> sional, really, I suppose, but we did a very good job.

Another arena in which Gove thrived was the many meetings
that would take place during the week running up to the show.
'The thing that people loved more than anything else was having
meetings to talk about politics and show off how knowledgeable
they were. Michael Gove just absolutely loved that forum of just
holding forth with an absurd or outrageous theory about politics,'
remembers Rentoul.

Gove was comfortable at *On the Record*. The job allowed him to build up his Westminster connections while developing as a journalist. He was on the show during the 1992 general election, when John Major defeated the odds – and opinion polls – to lead the Conservatives to their fourth successive victory. Yet Gove faced the same problem he had encountered when working at STV: what to do in the summer when Westminster politics came to a halt and the political shows were taken off air? The answer came from an unlikely source.

CHAPTER 5

A COMEDY OF ERRORS

The bin bags were emptied out on to the floor, and Michael Gove began sorting through the rubbish. He was still wearing a smart black suit and dark tie but had at least made a nod to hygiene by donning a pair of dark red rubber gloves. Searching through the discarded items, Gove remarked, 'We notice that as well as being a bon viveur and a lover of wine, we're also visiting the household of a gourmet. We have genuine Parma ham here – £3.12 from Marks and Spencer's for six slices, obviously very good value.'[1] The rubbish bag belonged to David Attenborough, and the person going through it with Gove was Penny Walker from Friends of the Earth. The aim was to see just how environmentally friendly the TV naturalist was when it came to his own recycling. Once Attenborough's rubbish had been considered, the morality magnifying glass was applied to the bin bags of Body Shop founder Anita Roddick and musician Sting. This was not an early example of Gove's war on plastics, but a skit from the TV show he found himself co-presenting.

A Stab in the Dark was a late-night topical show broadcast on Channel 4 in the summer of 1992. It was designed to be 'a polemical, opinionated, anti-consensual blast of topical comedy',[2] according to one of those involved in the production. Seeing the success *Have I Got News For You* was having on BBC2, Channel 4 was keen to get in on a potential new satire boom – and wanted a show that would get to the heart of the political discourse as well as entertain.

TV executive Michael Wills was tasked with creating the programme, and he assembled a team of up-and-coming talent he believed would deliver the insightful and funny show the network desired. Paul Ross, elder brother of TV host Jonathan, was hired as editor, while researchers included Tibor Fischer, whose debut novel *Under the Frog* was nominated for the Booker Prize that year; Susie Gautier-Smith, who would go on to produce comedy classics such as *The Day Today*; and Franny Moyle, an art historian who became head of arts commissioning for the BBC. Providing some of the comic edge were the writing duo of Richard Herring and Stewart Lee. All that was needed to make the show a success was the right presenting line-up.

Comedian David Baddiel was recruited to ensure the show was, above all things, funny. The Cambridge graduate was finding fame with *The Mary Whitehouse Experience* on the BBC, where carefully crafted monologues on a topical theme were interspersed with sketches. His role on *A Stab in the Dark* was to replicate the monologues, but with a more polemical edge.[3]

Tracey MacLeod had experience of late-night presenting thanks to her stint as a host of *The Late Show* on BBC 2. She was involved in one of the most notorious incidents on the programme when the Stone Roses made their live TV appearance in 1989. A fuse tripped thanks to the volume of the band's amps, prompting the performance to be cut after just a minute. As Stone Roses singer Ian Brown shouted 'amateurs' at the BBC crew, MacLeod tried her best to deliver a link to camera about a photographer. Baddiel persuaded her to join *A Stab in the Dark*[4] after *Guardian* journalist Catherine Bennett dropped out with 'last-minute doubts'.[5]

The third spot wasn't originally earmarked for Gove, but, in an

example of his Oxford connections paying off, he was recommended for involvement by the boyfriend of his old English studying
partner, Lucasta Miller. Miller's partner, Ian Bostridge, was working
as a researcher for another Michael Wills project when he heard
they were on the look-out for someone who matched Gove's skill
set. Bostridge was immediately impressed with Gove, telling Wills:
'We invited him in and indeed he was brilliant and funny.'

Gove originally took part in the show's unaired pilot not as a host
but as one of the guests. After impressing during the trial run, he was
offered one of the top jobs. And so began Gove's brief foray into satire.

According to Wills, the remit was to be 'pretty counter-cultural'
and not have any sacred cows when it came to what could be
mocked. 'It was designed to challenge preconceptions,' he remembers. In order to achieve maximum authenticity, and add a height-
ened sense of danger, the show was to go out live, meaning no
laughter track could be applied to cover up where the jokes fell flat.
Each host would deliver monologues on a topical or controversial
topic, and there would be interviews and video packages to break
up the live show. One such video item involved Baddiel asking a
group of schoolchildren what they would like to do to those they
disliked. 'I'd like to hit her head across that lamppost,' was one girl's
response, while another said she wanted to hang her teacher and
a third admitted to pushing her younger brother down the stairs.[6]

The style of the show meant while the three hosts occupied the
same studio space, they would work independently. A weekly meeting was held where they, along with the rest of the production team,
would finalise what was going to be in that week's show, but other
than that there was very little interaction, either on or off screen.[7]
Writing about Gove in 2016, MacLeod recalled:

David and I did share the occasional canteen sandwich with our mysterious colleague, but we might as well have been lunching with a unicorn, so different was he from us or anyone else we knew. Apart from his politeness, and his apparent acid reflux problem, he didn't really register as an actual person.[8]

One reason the three may have not spent that much time together is because of Gove's digestive system. In 2013, Baddiel revealed his colleague had 'appalling flatulence', made worse by the occasional decision to eat beans for lunch.[9]

Ahead of the show's launch, Gove was chosen to front the advert for the programme. Walking through a tunnel in semi-darkness, he said, 'Most television programmes insult your intelligence. *A Stab in the Dark* is different: it's intelligent, and insulting. We're opinionated, vitriolic and poisonous – and that's only when we're being nice.'[10]

The programme went live to the nation at 11.10 p.m. on Friday 5 June 1992. The opening title sequence alone was enough to make anyone switch off. Against a soundtrack of a cat meowing and hissing, glass smashing and monotonous bass, silhouetted faces moved across the screen, interspersed with the words 'a stab in the dark'. Once that rather uncomfortable twenty seconds was over with, Gove appeared, walking down some concrete steps next to around twenty people who were presumably the audience. Before he could speak, the camera pulled back and up to reveal the full set. It resembled an underground car park, with scaffolding seemingly erected at random and staircases dotted around. The first words came from Baddiel, who delivered a monologue on lowering the age of consent for gay sex from a three-sided Perspex box.

Gove was up next, and his first monologue focused on penis enlargement surgery and led to a gag about Alison Halford, a high-profile female senior police officer who had brought a sexual discrimination claim against Merseyside Police: 'If Alison had the chance to take advantage of American micro-surgery, she could have moved her front bumps from her chest to her groin and then she would have had the necessary balls to succeed in the modern British police force.'[11]

After the clip of him going through the bins, Gove's other contribution to the first episode was to compare Prince Charles's interventions into the debate around nature and architecture to Adolf Hitler. 'There is one difference, however,' he said. 'When Adolf's wife tried to commit suicide, she succeeded.'[12]

The next week's episode saw Gove deployed as an interviewer for the first time. Former Northern Ireland minister Peter Bottomley was to be grilled, and Gove's aim was to wind the politician up until he snapped. The Conservative MP realised he was being set up in the green room before he went into the studio. He remembers:

> They offered me alcohol and I smelt a rat. I accepted, and poured it into a plant, twice – it was spirits. There was serious intent. Then I said, 'Could I go and see the studio?' and they said, 'No, wait.' I went to the loo and went and found the studio, and the warm-up person was saying something like, 'Michael's going to be pretty aggressive and you're supposed to be on his side and make the interviewee look a bit of a fool.' I'm not sure it was quite as explicit as that, but that was the sense of it. I went back to the green room and went out and we then did the interview.

The interview itself was tense to say the least. The topic was the government's Northern Ireland strategy, and Gove set it up with a long introduction listing what he deemed to be concessions by the British government after IRA acts of terror. 'Surely the message is: terrorism works,'[13] said Gove. Bottomley was clearly not in the mood to indulge this young upstart, and came out on the attack from the off, pointing out why he felt Gove was wrong. After a few minutes of going round in circles, an exasperated Bottomley said, 'First of all, we've agreed that the word "concession" is wrong … You might find it more difficult if I took your pad away because if all your questions are built on the idea of "concessions", that's a false basis for this discussion.'[14]

Gove wouldn't let it go, telling Bottomley his government was 'giving in' and 'appeasing' the IRA. 'I'm very tempted to knee-cap you – just kick you gently, there,'[15] said a smiling Bottomley, tapping Gove's knee. Bottomley admitted many years later that he didn't realise that threat had been broadcast.

Gove repeated the interview style every week in a bid to provoke a reaction from the person sitting opposite him. The technique led the young man into some very strange territory. An interview with the retired General Sir Anthony Farrar-Hockley on homosexuality in the armed forces was one of the most bizarre moments. Gove introduced the topic with a monologue so full of clichés and stereo-types it would have seemed outdated in 1992, let alone watching it back decades later. 'Everything about the army is designed to attract gays,' Gove said, adding, 'Gays attract each other by dressing in a certain way. Cropped hair, moustache and a peaked cap. Put them together and what have you got? Lord Kitchener.'[16]

He went on:

If you want to discourage homosexuality, you do not force thirty young men to sleep in the same room, encourage their aggressive instincts and deny them contact with the opposite sex. Banning homosexuality in the armed forces makes as much sense as outlawing it amongst male nurses, interior designers or Liberal MPs. It runs counter to everything natural. In fact, it's hard to conceive of an organisation more attractive than the army – apart, of course, from the navy. Indeed, far from punishing homosexual activity, the army ought actually to be encouraging it. From the dawn of time, the best soldiers have munched the mattress. Julius Caesar, Alexander the Great, Shaka Zulu and Earl Haig. It's no surprise, really. Homosexuals will fight better because they've got no family to worry about and all those men to impress.

Sir Anthony was just as insulting, claiming that one of the dangers of serving alongside a homosexual is: 'You don't want him suddenly putting his arm around you and beginning to stroke your hair. It's very distracting.'

Gove kept repeating the claim that gay men naturally belong in the army as they are well turned out and would want to impress other men. 'These are qualities that all homosexuals have and all homosexuals aspire to,' he said.

'I think you're being rather discriminating about homosexuals,' Sir Anthony replied. 'Homosexuals are people like the rest of us, and the fact of the matter is some of them want to be fit, but I guess quite a lot of them aren't fit and that's true of heterosexuals.'

The issue of homosexuality came back later in the series when Gove entered into a graphic conversation about anal sex with Judge Michael Argyle regarding the age of consent:

Gove: What is it about the homosexual act that you believe should lead to recriminalisation?

Argyle: The anus is designed physically to pass faeces downwards. It's not designed to have things rammed up it.

Gove: As far as I can see, explain why it is that you consider homo-sexuality wrong. You mentioned, for example, the anus. Now, while its prime purpose is the expulsion of faeces, if we can derive some pleasure from inserting things in it, what's wrong with that? It shows that man is using his intelligence and adaptability.[17]

When Argyle responded by saying that sodomy is banned in the Book of Leviticus, Gove hit back by pointing out that eating shellfish is also banned in that text. 'Why do you pick and choose from the Bible?' Gove queried.

'It's a health thing, it's unnatural, it's against the law of nature,' replied Argyle.

Sex was brought up again in a conversation with Conservative MP Jerry Hayes. Gove worked himself up over plans by the government to combat teenage pregnancies with a series of leaflets promoting contraception. After listening to Gove tearing into the plan, Hayes told his interviewer, 'Your knighthood has just bitten the dust, you realise that?'[18]

To laughter from the audience, Gove replied, 'I'll inherit the peerage from my father in due course, so that's not a worry.'

Gove also came into contact with some other future parliamentary colleagues on the show. Labour's Diane Abbott was called in to discuss whether the press should carry out exposés on the sex lives of politicians, while Labour MP Tessa Jowell was grilled over maternity benefits. If Gove was supposed to take the audience with him during the interview with the latter, his tactic of repeatedly claiming that motherhood is 'a lifestyle choice, and as such, shouldn't be subsidised by you or me'[19] failed to curry favour.

'I have to say, I think this is a rather ridiculous and old-fashioned view which puts you substantially to the right of most of this Tory Cabinet,' said Jowell. She earned applause from the audience when she told her young opponent, 'I think that this is becoming rather ridiculous and would seem rather ridiculous to all your viewers.'

Other interviewees included a retired armed robber known only as Dave X, who gave Gove his views on law and order while hiding his face with a balaclava.

Gove: Some people say that it's poverty and deprivation that have caused the increase in crime in the past few years. Do you think that's true?

Dave X: I actually think there's a lot of arseholes on the streets now and I actually think they'll just go for it anyway. It's nothing to do with society.

Gove: They're just wicked.

Dave: They're bastards. I'm a pro, I trained.[20]

Celebrity publicist Max Clifford appeared on the show to give his view on a kiss-and-tell story involving Conservative Cabinet minister David Mellor. After speculating that Mellor's lover might make half a million pounds from the story and subsequent publicity, Gove began asking women in the audience if they would consider such a career path. After one audience member said, 'I'd be prepared to earn half a million, but not with a Cabinet minister,' Gove jokingly propositioned her: 'So someone good-looking, a good-looking politician, say, or even a good-looking telly star who might one day be a politician?'[21]

The most intriguing moments of the show came when Gove made comments which take on a new light in the context of his subsequent political career. On Europe, he makes the case to pro-EU Conservative MP Hugh Dykes that the UK should merge with Germany as the country already controls 'our foreign, defence and economic policies'. 'Why don't we just go the whole hog, apply to become part of Germany, and get all the immediate benefits of being part of that immensely powerful country?' asks Gove.[22]

In a monologue on Scotland, Gove seems content to burn his

countrymen and women for laughs. 'Most Scots in London are not professionals,' he says, 'they are not in journalism, the law or in business, but in the London Underground, begging.'[23]

He goes on:

The Scots' ability to wheedle money out of the English isn't restricted to drunks on the Embankment. Drunks in Westminster have shown they are good at it too. A Scot rarely opens his mouth in Parliament without simultaneously extending an outstretched palm. Labour may have got it wrong in choosing John Smith. I like him because he looks like my dad. When the English hear his passionate appeal for a redistribution of wealth, they'll do what they always do when they hear a Scotsman ask for money: walk away.

In an interview with Conservative MP Sir Rhodes Boyson, the future Education Secretary put forward ideas on how schools should be run which are the complete antithesis of the policies he would later go on to extol. The monologue setting up the interview would certainly have raised eyebrows in the Department for Education some eighteen years later:

Last week, the government gave up responsibility for educating most British children. John Patten, the Education Secretary, announced parent power would improve schools in future, not him. Brute market forces will now determine education, like everything else. And now Mr Patten has linked how much money a school will get to how many parents decide to send their children there. Popular schools will grow; unpopular schools will close. Everything in the garden will be lovely. What a piece of nonsense. Are parents really the best judge of how good a school is? Parents will choose schools, if they can be bothered to exercise a choice at all, on all sorts of grounds, such as the number of Muslims, whether or not the headmaster has a beard, and its proximity to Sainsbury's so that collecting the kids after shopping is easier. Choice may all be very well when it's deciding whether you want lime or pink crazy paving, but education is too important to be left to parents. We need experts to decide where and how children should be educated.[24]

Sir Rhodes hit back, saying he would trust parents over 'so-called educational experts who are happy to experiment with other people's children'. Gove, in keeping with his *A Stab in the Dark* interviewing style, kept repeating his main point that experts, not parents, should be in charge of schools. With a sentiment echoed by Gove himself some twenty-four years later, Sir Rhodes said, 'This is the rule of the expert, which is a very dangerous thing.'

'Why is it? Is it wrong in medicine? Is it wrong with a doctor?' Gove responded.

The future Education Secretary did not confine his thoughts on schooling to his interview with Sir Rhodes. Gove also used his monologues to set out views intended to provoke a response, included this on truancy: 'Why should we waste money coercing pupils who chose to opt out of the education system? The truants, most of whom are over fourteen, have clearly decided they can learn more outside school.'[25]

He also took a swipe at the conversion of polytechnics to universities, saying that those who taught at such institutions are 'no more genuine university lecturers than Gazza or Crackers the Giraffe'. He added:

Polys aren't universities and they shouldn't try to be. They are admirable institutions which give people a couple of years to grow out of liking snakebite and prepare for a satisfying career in the lower rungs of local government. Universities are academic communities where the finest minds push forward the boundaries of thought and pass on their wisdom to our intellectual elite, which will always be, like all elites, small. It will not include the young men studying for a diploma in golf management at Kingston.[26]

The funniest interview, and the one which perhaps gets closest to the kind of show envisioned by the programme's commissioners, was with Alan Clark. The former Conservative MP – he had stood down ahead of that year's election – was on the show to defend the UK offering scholarships to Indonesian army officers while the Asian country was waging war on East Timor.

Clark was clearly not up for suffering any liberal guilt over the move, kicking off the interview by saying, 'I shouldn't think anyone in the audience knows even where East Timor is on the map. Well, do you?'[27]

Gove turned the boos to cheers as he replied, 'I have to say, Mr Clark, if they are ignorant of its whereabouts that's probably due to Conservative education policies.'

After discussing East Timor, Gove moved the interview on to how the UK had trained officers in the Iraqi army, then under the dictatorship of Saddam Hussein.

Clark responded simply, 'It was a friendly country.'

'A friendly country?' Gove exclaimed.

'It was a friendly country until we went to war with it, yes,' Clark replied, to laughter from the audience.

That laughter was, unfortunately, not an altogether common occurrence on *A Stab in the Dark*. The stark set and isolated audience contributed to a cold atmosphere, not helped by a lack of warmth between three presenters who barely acknowledged each other's presence. MacLeod recalled that Gove did his best to generate some sense of enjoyment by bringing along a group of friends who 'turned up to cheer him on from the studio audience, loudly applauding at the end of his sections and staying silent at the end of ours'.[28]

Viewing figures were low, and on the rare occasions it was noticed by critics it was given a kicking. 'It really didn't get the recognition its compulsive awfulness deserved,' David Sexton wrote in *The Independent* on 10 August 1992, after the show's ten-week run came to an end. Gove was described as 'bumptiousness caricatured', who 'might do better as a Jehovah's Witness, or as an estate agent in this difficult market'.[29]

The Stage proclaimed *A Stab in the Dark* one of the worst 'yoof' programmes of the year, describing it as 'an aptly named, live, late night show on which three smug lefties told each other how clever they were. Mind you, they probably had to, as virtually no one watched it.'[30]

The combination of critical derision and lack of an audience meant the show had no chance of securing a second series. 'There was no doubt about it,' recalls Wills. 'I didn't even talk to the commissioning editor about recommissioning it.'

In the hit-and-miss world of television, it can sometimes be difficult to explain why some shows soar and others fall. Wills is still as perplexed twenty-seven years on as he was at the time by its failure, saying:

I don't know ... I never know, really. Sometimes you are surprised by what gets traction. The title wasn't a great title, and it was a big mistake not to pad out with canned laughter the responses of a small studio audience to a live show. The studio audience did find most of it funny, it just didn't sound that way to the audience at home.

Baddiel is clearer in his view as to why it flopped, saying:

> The show didn't work because it wasn't clear what it was: it was kind of half a comedy show, half a politics show, half a series of polemical rants – and I'm aware the maths there don't add up: neither did the show. The addition of a laughter track would not have helped, would probably have made it worse. Having said that, I do think it had a few interesting and ahead-of-its-time things on it. But the style of it was kind of Channel 4 late-night show parody.

A Stab in the Dark quickly disappeared both from the airwaves and from the odd corners of the public consciousness it had managed to penetrate. Gove would very occasionally mention it in later years, once describing it as having a reputation as 'the biggest turkey to flutter on Channel 4'.[31] It was flagged up in the *New Statesman* in 2010, complete with the rumour that Channel 4 executives wore badges during its run reading: 'I had nothing to do with *A Stab in the Dark*'.[32] When Channel 4 launched its online streaming service in 2006, containing an extensive library of past shows broadcast by the channel, *A Stab in the Dark* was omitted.

It wasn't until Gove's Conservative leadership bid in 2016 that it once again reared its head. MacLeod penned an article for *The Guardian* in which she set out what it was like working with Gove, describing his 'famous courtesy and elaborate good manners' as being 'fully developed'.[33] Channel 4 decided to put the series up on its streaming service, allowing anyone to look back over the footage. Strangely, the show has dated well. Gove's interview style of trying to wind up the participant by repeating an outlandish notion at the very edge of credibility has echoes in some of the work of Sacha Baron Cohen and other comedy talk shows. Gove's best work on the programme was when he appeared to go against the grain and take on right-wing notions of education and law and order. His criticism of left-wing views just seemed too obvious coming from a man who was twenty-four going on fifty-four.

With his foray into satire over, Gove returned to *On the Record*. Yet, far from deciding to focus purely on his BBC job, the young man chose to embark on a project which he hoped would turn him from failed late-night provocateur to serious broadsheet journalist.

CHAPTER 6

GREAT EXPECTATIONS

July 1994 was a pivotal month in British political history. On the 21st, shadow Home Secretary Tony Blair was elected leader of the Labour Party, and the change he brought to his party was immense. Leading up to his victory, in which he defeated John Prescott and Margaret Beckett, Blair struck a markedly different tone to the Labour Party which had snatched defeat from the jaws of victory in the general election two years earlier. In an interview with *The Times* published on 6 July, Blair actually praised Margaret Thatcher's leadership style, and made it clear that with him in charge Labour would be the most-unashamedly pro-European it had ever been.

While Labour was renewing in opposition, the Tories were decaying in government. The sleaze era was in full swing, and in the same month that Blair was elected Leader of the Opposition, Tory peer Jeffrey Archer was investigated for – and subsequently cleared of – insider share dealing; two Conservative MPs were accused of accepting cash for questions in Parliament; and Prime Minister John Major carried out a reshuffle which saw more than a third of his Cabinet axed.

Also on the move in July 1994 was Michael Gove. After three years at *On the Record*, the 27-year-old had landed himself a job on the BBC's flagship current affairs show, Radio 4's *Today*. The editor of the programme was Roger Mosey, a rising star of the BBC who would go on to run BBC Radio 5 Live, become head of news across the whole corporation and direct its coverage of the 2012 London Olympics. Like Gove, Mosey was an Oxford graduate with a penchant for quizzes – he was part of Wadham College's *University Challenge* team in 1978 – and, also like Gove, he was adopted.

Gove was interviewed for the *Today* programme not by Mosey but by the show's deputy editor, Francis Halewood, and he was offered the job 'because he was the best candidate in the field and he was an extremely good reporter', Mosey remembers being told by his second-in-command.

The king of the *Today* programme in the mid-1990s was John Humphrys, a no-nonsense Welsh journalist who climbed to the top of the broadcast world the hard way. After leaving school at fifteen, he worked at local papers in Wales before joining the BBC in 1966. Humphrys became a *Today* presenter in 1987 and was no stranger to controversy, with his abrasive interview technique. In March 1995, Chief Secretary to the Treasury Jonathan Aitken accused Humphrys of 'poisoning the well of democratic debate' with his style.[1]

Mosey remembers that the famously polite Gove and the notoriously combative Humphrys developed an 'affection' for one another. The young reporter could very much hold his own with Humphrys and fellow presenter James Naughtie. 'Most reporters would sort of sit at Jim and John's feet and hear what they thought, whereas Gove was much more of a level participant in those conversations because of how well connected he was,' recalls their former editor.

In 1997, Gove wrote a stern defence of the interviewing styles of the two presenters. Naughtie and Humphrys were coming in for criticism for being too aggressive and indulging in 'verbal punch-ups', in contrast to the more pally interview techniques used on other radio channels. According to Gove, however, 'The average twentyish plasterer in Redditch, in so far as he exists, actually *prefers* Jim Naughtie to the laddish alternative a wrist-twist away.'[2] Gove did not detail how many twentyish plasterers in Redditch he had spoken to before reaching this opinion, but claimed his experience as an on-the-road reporter for *Today* meant he understood the listenership much more than BBC management. 'Humphrys and Naughtie are heroes. If anything, they weren't aggressive *enough* for the *Today* audience,' he concluded.

Despite it being the most influential political show on radio, *Today* programme reporters did not always cover politics. Mosey liked his journalists to report on a wide range of topics, something he admits was the 'bugbear' of some correspondents. 'They could be asked to do a political piece one day and another piece about why rap music is making its debut in the Top 40 the next day, and something about butterflies in Staffordshire the next day,' Mosey recalls.

The question of who would cover what was often decided less by an in-depth editorial discussion and more by who happened to be working a particular shift. Of the three shifts reporters were expected to work, one was focused on 'forward planning', which gave the reporter a week to do a story; another was as a day reporter, where the correspondent would turn up to work at 10 a.m. and be sent on assignment to produce a report for the next morning; and the third was the night shift, a fifteen-hour stretch which would see reporters producing a package on any overnight stories or recording two-way interviews with BBC correspondents across the world. This pot-luck approach to assignments did not suit Gove, who by both nature and experience was more at home covering the world of Westminster. 'I would say he was brilliant on politics, especially on Tory politics,' says Mosey. 'He was less good ... well, it wasn't the sort of thing he would most want to do if you asked him to do a piece about rap music in the Top 40. He would do them, and do them pretty well, but it wasn't where his interests lay.'

The upside to this fluctuating work pattern was that reporters would get four days off in a row – sometimes even six days if the rota was kind. Gove put those extended breaks to good use within weeks of starting on *Today*.

His first bout of extracurricular activity involved, bizarrely, a foray into acting. In the summer of 1994, two friends from his days at Oxford, Justin Hardy (whose father Robin had directed the cult horror film *The Wicker Man*) and Yoshi Nishio, began shooting a film in the grounds of Hawtreys Preparatory School near the village of Great Bedwyn in east Wiltshire. *A Feast at Midnight* was a gentle tale of a group of schoolboys rebelling against the imposition of a healthy food regime by forming a late-night eating society. Gove was recruited to play the school's chaplain. Indeed, according to Nishio, he was the only person they had in mind for the role. 'Michael was always quite theatrical – arguably, he still is – so it was a natural fit. We wrote the part specifically for him,' he recalled in 2011.[3]

So it was that Gove lined up alongside acting greats such as Christopher Lee, Robert Hardy (no relation to the director of the film) and Edward Fox. Also in the cast was another Lady Margaret Hall friend of Gove, the actor Samuel West, and Lisa Faulkner, who would go on to find fame in *Holby City* and *Celebrity Master-Chef*. Alas for Gove, his performance boiled down to three blink-and-you'll-miss-it moments. One involved making a high-pitched noise to express shock that Christopher Lee's character, Victor, is accidentally referred to by his nickname of Raptor; another was Gove looking concerned after Lee is hit in the testicles by a cricket ball; and finally he was filmed conducting the school's choir. His single line in the film is simply 'Amen'. At least all those years of Sunday school teaching had finally paid off.

Despite Gove's small role, Justin Hardy, the film's director, would later heap praise on his acting abilities: 'The man is, I would say, comedy gold!'⁴

The film was released in 1995, but it did not join the pantheon of British comedies that scored box office success in the 1990s, such as *Four Weddings and a Funeral* and *The Full Monty*. A two-star review by *Empire* magazine ruled: 'Nothing about it suggests it should have been made for the big screen, so modest is its scope ... Neither the conflicts nor the japes hold much drama or humour. Lee's tyrant provides a little spice to the soufflé, but it still doesn't rise.'⁵

The film may not have been the start of a glorious acting career for Gove, but it did mark the beginning of an unlikely friendship. Writing about the experience in June 2015, he recalled:

> The real joy of the whole enterprise for me was getting to know Christopher [Lee]. Over cast and crew lunches, during breaks in filming, over drinks in the evening, I and others listened spellbound to his stories. The secrets of Roger Moore's safari suit, the dry wit of Peter Cushing, the casting-couch antics of Hollywood moguls, and the seduction tips offered by JFK – his anecdotes were brilliant and compelling, and always delivered with a special, generous wit.⁶

The pair lost contact for many years, but the actor – by now Sir Christopher thanks to a 2009 knighthood – called Gove's office when he was Education Secretary to invite him for tea in his Cadogan Square flat. 'I hadn't imagined he would remember me, or my name, from among the scores of people who had populated the set of *Feast*. But I remembered just how scintillating his conversation was, so I had no hesitation in accepting,' recalled Gove.⁷ In Sir Christopher's drawing room, the two former castmates discussed 'history and politics, art and music, high and low culture, friendships and faith'.⁸

Aside from anecdotes collected from one of UK cinema's most respected actors, *A Feast at Midnight* left Gove with little to suggest a career on the silver screen was beckoning. He therefore returned to his preoccupation with politics.

His former *On the Record* colleague John Rentoul had mentioned to Gove that he was going to write a biography of the UK's next Prime Minister: Tony Blair. Gove admired the initiative but thought there was a flaw in Rentoul's logic. With John Major increasingly losing control of his party, Gove believed a Conservative leadership contest before the next election was inevitable, and the winner would be the next Prime Minister. The man deemed most likely to take the prize was Michael Portillo. Gove had met Portillo during his stint at *On the Record*[9] and was attracted by this dashing suave Thatcherite who shared a love of opera. Under the encouragement of Simone Kubes, he secured a literary agent in the form of Andrew Lownie and began pitching the book proposal around publishers in the summer of 1994.[10] In October, it was revealed that Fourth Estate was 'close to commissioning' the work[11] and Gove began writing in earnest soon after. He roped in his former *On the Record* colleague Sean O'Grady to help. 'It was a very jolly time,' O'Grady remembers. 'I used to basically do research. I looked through Hansard, went through cuttings, BBC archives, the famous Ribena ad.' (As an eight-year-old boy, Portillo had starred in a television advertisement for the drink.) Beavering away on the Portillo book helped expand Gove's contacts right at the top of the Tory Party, and that in turn led to him breaking the best story of his career to date.

On 22 June 1995, John Major decided to draw the poison from the Eurosceptic Tory snake by quitting as party leader and triggering a leadership contest. 'It is time to put up or shut up,' he told his opponents as he announced his high-risk strategy. All eyes immediately turned to the two Michaels: Heseltine and Portillo.

Heseltine, still bearing the scars of his successful assassination but failed succession plan against Margaret Thatcher in 1990, was at pains to show his loyalty to Major, helped by the promise of a promotion from Trade Secretary to Deputy Prime Minister. Portillo was seen as the man most likely to accept Major's challenge to 'put up', but he too calculated that the impression of disloyalty among his fellow MPs and grassroots activists could tarnish him in the same way as Heseltine had been undermined after Thatcher's fall. Seemingly, everyone was learning the lessons of Major in 1990: let other people bring down the boss and then enter in the second round as a 'clean' candidate.

However, a second round could only occur if a first round took place, and with the big hitters keeping their powder dry, it seemed perfectly possible that Major would not face a challenge at all.

Gove's cultivation of contacts at the top of the Tory Party paid off, and he was able to tell his editor that Major would indeed be facing an election thanks to the challenge of Welsh Secretary John Redwood.

Mosey remembers:

Michael really went out on a limb and it is that incredibly nervous moment when you are going with the opposite story on *Today* to what breakfast television is going with. Everyone else is saying Major runs unopposed and it was Gove through his contacts that got the fact Redwood was going to announce, and we trusted him on that and he was completely right. We did often use his political contacts to give us those kinds of stories which nobody else would have brought in, frankly.

His association with the Conservative Party was not going unnoticed in the Westminster bubble. On 22 February 1995, *The Guardian* identified Gove as part of a new breed of 21st-century Tories who were anti-John Major, anti-welfare state and anti-Europe. The BBC man was listed alongside his old university friend Matthew D'Ancona, future Tory MP Paul Goodman and the *Telegraph*'s Dean Godson.

With no name to assign to the bunch, *The Guardian* referred to them simply as 'The Group', describing them as being 'spread through history departments, journalism, advertising and, in one instance, radio'.[12] An interview with D'Ancona revealed that The Group had no time for the moralising 'Back to basics' agenda of Major's Conservative Party and was instead more concerned with further European integration. The article notes that 'like Churchill in the late '30s, they believe they are the only ones to see the dangers of a superstate with Germany at its centre'.[13]

Gove's 'outing' as a Conservative sympathiser could have caused problems for the BBC, whose reporters are expected to remain rigidly neutral when it comes to politics. Mosey had no concerns when it came to the integrity of Gove's work, saying, 'There was never a problem with impartiality with him; it was just good having his contacts and his contacts book.' Indeed, with the BBC often derided as being the centre of bleeding-heart liberalism, having a known Conservative on the books actually helped to counter accusations of institutional bias. 'If there are Tories in the BBC, which there are, of course, they tend to be nice liberal Tories and not particularly connected to the right, so that was why he had a special position I guess,' recalls Mosey.

Gove's 'special position' was confirmed with the publication of his biography of Michael Portillo in October 1995. Subtitled *The Future of the Right*, it details Portillo's life studiously and competently, but is hamstrung by the fact that it feels like – and is written very much in the style of – a prequel to another, more interesting, book in which the central character goes on to become Prime

Minister. The set-up is all there, but the pay-off is the 1995 Conservative leadership election, in which Portillo did not take part. Gove was generous in his assessment of why the man he had dubbed 'the future of the right' ducked the challenge, claiming that, for Portillo, 'running against the man in whose Cabinet he had been happy to serve for so long was wrong'.[14] The matter of the installation of forty phone and fax lines into a Westminster office owned by an ally of Portillo's friends – a sign he was readying an HQ in the event of a second round – was charitably written up as the work of the then Employment Secretary's advisor David Hart.

The theme of people embarking on embarrassing actions on Portillo's behalf without his knowledge runs through the book. Portillo was apparently 'genuinely shocked' that an extravagant party to mark his ten years in Parliament was due to be held in Alexandra Palace, of all places. Apparently his constituency agent Malcolm Tyndall was behind the plan, which saw invitations sent to hundreds, including Lady Thatcher.

The book provides useful little nuggets of Gove's feelings towards people who would one day be his colleagues. Future Commons Speaker John Bercow, then an ambitious young Tory very much on the right of the party, was described as 'a small, almost swarthy figure – not a naturally dominant presence – but he is a skilled platform performer ... Using mimicry and mockery, and pushing a passionately Thatcherite message, he warmed [the 1994 Tory conference] up perfectly.'[15]

One man who receives a large number of references in the text is David Cameron, popping up six times. When the book was written, Cameron was working for Carlton Communications, having previously served as an advisor to Chancellor Norman Lamont during Black Wednesday and to Home Secretary Michael Howard. Gove described Cameron as one of the 'brightest stars' to emerge from the Conservative Research Department[16] and he was considered a man on the up by many in the party.

Gove's praise of Cameron in the Portillo book signified a strengthening of relations between the two. They were part of a growing clique of young right-wingers progressing in the world of politics and journalism. As well as Vaizey and Cameron, there was one Steve Hilton, the son of Hungarian immigrants who also moved from private school to Oxford University. After graduating, Hilton joined the Conservative Research Department and was marked out as an advertising whizz. Another CRD high-flyer was George Osborne, a former school friend of Vaizey who had followed the well-worn path of private education, Oxford University and then national politics.

The book was released on 9 October 1995, and a launch party was held a few weeks later near Hyde Park, at the house of Lizzie Noel, a friend of Gove's then girlfriend Amanda Foreman.[17] Ex-Cabinet ministers Cecil Parkinson and Norman Lamont came along to offer support, but the book's subject did not make an appearance. Portillo later said he read the first 100 pages but set it aside after finding several inaccuracies. One claim which particularly angered him was that he had not joined the cadets while at school, as he was a pacifist. 'It is absolutely not right that I was a conscientious objector,' he said in February 1997.[18]

The reviews were lukewarm at best. Writing in *The Times*, future Conservative Cabinet minister Oliver Letwin, who had worked closely with Margaret Thatcher in the 1980s and would have known Portillo, praised Gove's professionalism but branded the book 'distinctly premature'.[19] Much of the review focuses on the various factions with the Tory Party, and Letwin uses the subtitle to make a none-too-subtle dig at Gove: '"Right" and "Left" are convenient labels, which help the lower sort of journalists to write articles without needing to engage in the uncomfortable activity of thinking.'

Conservative MP Julian Critchley, an ally of Michael Heseltine, wrote in the *Sunday Times* that it was 'tabloid journalism dignified by stiff covers',[20] while *The Guardian*'s Francis Wheen labelled the book an 'extended love-letter' showing that Gove had an 'infatuation' with Portillo.[21] Nick Cohen in *The Independent* was equally damning, claiming that 'there is little wit and not one flash of enmity in 344 pages' and adding that 'difficult questions about Portillo's politics and private life are evaded and sometimes not asked at all'. He chastised Gove for not tackling key issues, including the early '80s recession, the later '80s market crash and, most cuttingly of all, 'why Michael Portillo is suddenly the coming man'.[22]

It is that question of 'Why write a book about Michael Portillo?' – who at that point had not held any of the great offices of state nor stood in a leadership election – which hangs over the biography. In truth, political biographers who choose to write about a figure not yet at the end of their career are taking a gamble. When Gove started the project, Portillo was indeed seen as 'the coming man'. For a relatively young journalist wanting to build up his contacts in Westminster and be seen to have a degree of foresight as to the direction of travel in politics, penning a biography of a future party leader was a smart move. It was not Gove's fault that his subject did not keep up his end of the unspoken bargain and go on to be Conservative Party leader.

Portillo's ducking out of the 1995 leadership contest would have frustrated the young biographer, especially as the battle came at a time when most of the book had already been written. Had Portillo stood and won, an authoritative book on the country's new Prime Minister would have been out within weeks of him taking office, and the *Mail on Sunday* were already dangling a rather large sum for serialisation rights in front of Gove's eyes.[23] But biographers do not control their subjects, any more than those being written about can dictate what goes on the page, and the abrupt end to the book is perhaps indicative of a frustration that Gove would have felt that the gamble had not paid off. His subject going on to lose his seat in the 1997 election was really adding insult to Gove's injury, and it seemed the book, along with Portillo itself, would disappear without trace.

Interest in the text re-emerged in 1999, however, when Portillo used an interview with *The Times* to finally confront rumours about his sexuality. 'I will say what I want to say,' he told Ginny Dougray: 'I had some homosexual experiences as a young person.'[24]

On 10 September, the day after the interview was published, Gove opened his own article on the revelation with the most obvious question: 'Did I know?'[25]

In short: no. Gove had heard rumours, had been told about Portillo's homosexual past by 'a friend [who] knew a friend who knew a *very* close friend', but had never actually found anyone who could definitively recount sharing such intimacy with his biography's subject.

Gove argued that he did try to hint at the rumours 'without venturing into the territory of bald assertion'. The book references Portillo's time at Peterhouse College at Cambridge University as a place where 'fellows and undergraduates were given girls' names; parties were organised in meadows a little out of town and cross-dressing was encouraged'.[26]

Gove also described the Conservative Research Department, where Portillo worked from 1976 to 1979, as 'attractive to some homosexuals' where 'raucous talk about buggery' wouldn't be unheard of.[27]

The rumours were then tackled directly when Gove wrote:

As an opera-goer, Peterhouse graduate and party-lover, Portillo was assumed to share other tastes with some in the Research

Department, and there has been speculation about his past by political opponents anxious to suggest he could not have passed through Peterhouse and the CRD without being compromised. But, despite the best efforts of enemies, no evidence has emerged.[28]

As any biographer will admit, a large part of researching a book is separating the rumours from the reality. It is quite common for a friend of a friend to enthusiastically pass on something deemed to be scandalous, but after the wild goose is chased, the rumour dilutes and eventually disappears. Indeed, speculation about Gove's own past sexual behaviour has been brought up by numerous people in the course of writing the present book, but no one has been able to provide evidence that it is anything more than a rumour.

In truth, the desire to confirm such details has not been overwhelming. If Gove did indeed have same-sex relations in his younger days – and there is absolutely no evidence that he did – the level of importance in the story of his life, while potentially salacious, is minimal. Gove would not be open to the charge of hypocrisy – the usual justification for bringing a politician's personal behaviour into the public sphere – as he backed extending rights to same-sex couples when he was in Parliament, most notably on the equal marriage legislation. There are quite simply more interesting aspects of Gove's life and work to expend energy on.

Additionally, the public attitude towards such experiences is very different to when Portillo made his revelation. Whereas in the mid-1990s homosexuality was still something the Conservative Party mounted a determined resistance to, twenty years later the zeitgeist has changed entirely, and such rumours are now met more with a shrug than with a sense of shame. It would, quite simply, now be unremarkable if Gove had had same-sex relations at some point in his life.

The absence of Portillo's homosexual experiences in the biography became the butt of many jokes levelled at Gove in the following years. *The Guardian* in particular went to great pains to point out the book's failure to dig up that particular piece of what many still considered to be dirt. For his part, Gove reserved his famous self-deprecation for the book's subtitle. In an article for *The Times* predicting what the year 1999 held for politics, Gove wrote, 'The crystal ball is an incongruous addition to my desk. Anyone who has written a book entitled *Michael Portillo: The Future of the Right* cannot expect an easy ride as a forecaster.'[29] An updated edition of the book was mooted in 2000, due for release in spring 2001, but Gove pulled the plug, claiming he didn't have the time to complete the project.[30]

The Portillo book may have failed to generate big sales or turn Gove into the authoritative expert on the next UK Prime Minister, but it did demonstrate that the man known for his broadcasting abilities was capable of writing. By the end of 1995, Gove was looking to move again, and this time away from the constraints of BBC employment. It was time for Gove to find his own voice.

CHAPTER 7

SCOOP

Political jostling in Westminster dominated 1995, but that was soon dwarfed by the events of 1996. At one minute past seven on the evening of 9 February, a truck bomb was detonated in the heart of London's Docklands, the glass tower block-dominated area of the capital which had been rejuvenated under the guidance of Michael Heseltine in the 1980s. The explosion marked the end of a seventeen-month ceasefire by the IRA. It claimed two lives and left more than 100 injured.

For Michael Gove, the bombing was the obvious conclusion of the government's policy towards peace talks in Northern Ireland. He still held to the views he had expressed to an increasingly exasperated Peter Bottomley on *A Stab in the Dark* three years earlier: 'Surely the message is: terrorism works.'[1]

If the bombing had taken place a few months earlier, Gove would have had to restrict the broadcasting of his views to only his close friends, thanks to his role as a reporter, not a commentator, for the BBC. But the 28-year-old was a month into a new job as a leader writer at *The Times* when the bomb exploded, and the 10 February edition of the paper contained just his second bylined article. Under the headline 'Prisoners of their own violent creed', Gove argued that the collapse of the ceasefire was inevitable, as the concessions the UK government would offer would never be enough for a para-military organisation with the goal of reunification of Ireland:

> The decision to call a ceasefire and enter the political arena was not taken by a movement sickened by the slaughter nor one which lacked the stomach or resources to go on. Hardened IRA volunteers and a network of arms dumps across the whole island of Ireland could, and can, sustain years of violence. [Gerry] Adams persuaded republicans to abandon violence because he thought they could achieve their ends by other means. He detected a war-weariness at the heart of the British Establishment.[2]

Yet Gove also seemed to offer a sympathetic understanding of the problems facing Adams, suggesting that he was facing difficulty in persuading those on his side of the argument that peaceful means would lead to practical progress, even suggesting he 'may now be in danger of becoming the prisoner of those within republican ranks who wish to see war'.

The Irish issue would figure large in Gove's articles for *The Times*, the Troubles having fascinated him for many years. Sean O'Grady, the *On the Record* colleague who had helped him to research the Portillo book, remembers a rather eye-opening visit to Gove's Notting Hill flat in the early 1990s: 'It was lined with books all over the place, sort of political biographies, that sort of stuff, and he also had an enormous cartoon of the Ulster Unionist Party in Parliament – a great big Orange banner type of affair.'

O'Grady recalls that Gove's politics, as well as being 'firmly Thatcherite', were also 'quite Orange', referring to the Protestant creed originating from County Armagh in 1795 which is firmly opposed to the break-up of the United Kingdom. The infamous Orange Order parades often led to violence throughout the

Troubles, as the marching routes were disputed or the police tried to stop the events entirely.

While it should be no surprise that a Conservative and Unionist Party supporter should support a unionist cause, O'Grady describes Gove's enthusiasm as 'a bit odd', saying, 'He'd be perfectly happy to sing along with Orange songs – "The sash my father wore", all that sort of stuff.' O'Grady is not the only person to have witnessed Gove belting out such tunes. Mike Elrick, who trained with Gove in Aberdeen, remembers his colleague was 'very, very strongly supportive of Ulster Protestantism, and very much sided with the Protestant political parties'. He adds, 'On one occasion in my company I remember him singing various Ulster songs. Partly in jest, but he knew the words.'

Gove was given ample room by the *The Times* to focus on the Troubles. He was helped by the IRA's determination to keep the conflict at the front of people's minds. The organisation followed up the Docklands attack with an even larger bomb, this time in the centre of Manchester, on 15 June. The weapon was three times bigger than the device used in the Docklands and caused £700 million damage. Amazingly, no one was killed thanks to the rapid evacuation of 75,000 people by the emergency services.

In July, Gove was despatched to Northern Ireland to report on the row over the marching route of the Orange Order in the town of Portadown. The parade traditionally goes through a largely Catholic area of the town on its way to and from Drumcree Church, often leading to tensions between residents and marchers. In 1995, hundreds of Catholics staged a sit-in at the Garvaghy Road, blocking the parade as it returned from a church service. The Orange Order refused to take a different route, leading to a stand-off between the residents, the marchers and the police. When Gove visited the town the following year, his article focused on the frustrations felt by Orangemen. 'Only a couple of years ago Sinn Féin were murdering innocent people; now they're treated like film stars and lords of the manor. It proves violence works. Of course we're angry,'[3] one Protestant told Gove.

Gove would return to the Northern Ireland issue with even greater vehemence throughout his period at *The Times*, but there were other issues besides home-grown terrorism for the young man to focus on. He had joined the paper during the death rattle of the John Major government, taking over as a leader writer from his old university friend Matthew D'Ancona. The editor was Peter Stothard, a soft-spoken Oxford graduate who had been at the paper since 1981. Like Gove, he was a Eurosceptic who had precious little time for Major's pro-Brussels policies, and he was also a lover of literature and debating. As editor, his days centred on crafting the paper's leader columns. 'There would be a meeting just after the main conference, just before lunch,' Stothard remembers, adding:

> They were really the main point of my day. The leader writers, some of whom would have been at the news conference because they could, they would sit around in my office for about an hour or so in the morning – it could be longer – working out what we were going to say about the things that seemed important.

With D'Ancona gone, Stothard was in the market for a young Tory dipped in Euroscepticism and passionate about the Northern Ireland issue to add to his menagerie.

Gove was at that point looking to escape his own cage at the BBC. While his role at *Today* carried with it a certain level of prestige, Gove felt his career was losing traction as opposed to gaining momentum. 'I never bought this idea that he had been sort of relegated to the backwaters of the *Today* programme because he was a right-winger,' a close friend says. 'Talking to him, I got the feeling it was more that it's a very slow-moving business getting ahead in the BBC and frankly, in those days at least, if you were as talented as he was you could fly faster and more effectively in print than at the BBC.'

Stothard had no knowledge of Gove's work before interviewing him for the job as a leader writer, but he was instantly taken with the Scotsman after meeting him. One former *Times* journalist was not surprised the pair hit it off, agreeing that both men are big characters but in different ways. 'Peter's a very intellectual, cerebral character – as is Michael. I think that well-mannered intellectualism is what they had in common,' the source said.

The leader-writing team Gove was stepping into included noted economist Anatole Kaletsky and fully paid-up Blairite Mary Ann Sieghart. Every day, a miniature Oxford Union would be recreated in Stothard's office as the team thrashed out what the paper's line would be on the key issues. Sieghart well recalls the 'very high-grade arguments' that would take place. 'I remember once looking round the room and thinking, "Bloody hell, every single person here has got a First from Oxford or Cambridge."' Despite having a 2:1, Gove held his own.

Stothard was particularly pleased with his new debater, who quickly marked himself out as one of the best the editor had come across. 'The most striking thing about Michael from the first few years, and I think it alerted me early that he could have a political future, was that he was able to sway the undecided,' he says.

Stothard goes on:

Leader writing is not politics, but politics is hugely about motivating not the people who agree with you but the people who are close to agreeing with you and, if you're really good at it, people who don't agree with you at all but think you're somehow trust-worthy. In the early days, you could see it in leader conferences: Michael had that skill.

For those crossing swords with Gove, it was a lesson in debating. Sieghart says:

> Michael is the most brilliant arguer. Often he's wrong, but he can argue so well. He's terribly good at slightly twisting what you say, slightly distorting the argument, making it into a straw man – all that sort of thing. He was trained up at the Oxford Union and used these great rhetorical flourishes. We would laugh, it was brilliant, but it was a show.

Outside of the leader debates, Gove began forging a career as a national print journalist. His first byline came on 1 February 1996, when he reviewed pamphlets by the philosophers Roger Scruton and John Gray. The Northern Ireland-focused articles followed, but it wasn't long before Gove got his teeth into the subject that would come to define his later political career: the European Union. On 24 April, he mused on the implications of leading Tory Eurosceptic John Redwood meeting with Sir James Goldsmith, the millionaire businessman behind the Eurosceptic Referendum Party. Gove was clearly impressed with Sir James, and in a profile essay on him on 19 October, he gushed over the man who was seeking to help destroy the Conservatives at the next election:

> Some 6ft 4in, with chilling blue eyes, a bald dome which looks as though it was designed for the laurel leaves of a Caesar, and the physique of a rangy mountain lion, he seems eerily like the millionaire man of destiny from fiction to be true. His clothes,

understated and international, convey the quiet assurance of the first-class departure lounge with only the slight nod towards true plutocracy in the cashmere socks and cufflinks.

It is the voice that is truly singular. Dark chocolate with occasional descents to the guttural and curious, idiosyncratic pronunciation which renders Maastricht as Mystrict and Forsyth as Vorsyte, it exercises a hypnotic power, effective on the platform yet faintly unsettling in person.[4]

The love seemed to have waned by February 1997, as, with just three months before the general election, Gove remembered which side his bread was buttered and urged Goldsmith to call off his referendum dogs. On 10 February, under the headline 'Time to pack up, Sir James, The Referendum Party has done its work', Gove wrote, 'Sir James's insistence on contesting the general election is a tribute to his doggedness, but it reflects poorly on his judgment.'[5] Just to make sure the man he had compared to Caesar just four months earlier got the message, Gove added, 'It would be more dignified for Sir James to claim an intellectual victory now than to endure an electoral massacre this spring.' He also used the article to criticise the very notion of holding a referendum on the UK's involvement with the EU:

The other nations of the EU are bent on integration, and whatever might stop them in their tracks, it will not be a referendum in Britain. They know what we think. The question for Britain is which parts of the process it wants to join, which ones it wishes to opt out of, and which powers we want to repatriate as the price of allowing the others to advance. That can't be put on a ballot slip with room for only one tick. Questions like that require negotiations by a party sceptical in its sinews, such as the likely Tory party of the next decade.

Gove's own views were clearly Eurosceptic, although not yet with-drawalist. In an article on 14 June 1996 headlined 'Is there life out-side? British withdrawal from the EU need not be suicidal', Gove set out the case for the UK leaving the EU, but stopped short of actually endorsing that view himself. With arguments that fore-shadowed those of the 2016 referendum, Gove talks up the cost of being part of the project ('Britain contributes £7.7 billion gross and £3.5 billion net to the EU budget'); cites the economist Patrick Minford, a key figure for Brexiteers in the run-up to the 2016 ref-erendum; and talks of the UK being part of a 'wider world' once it leaves the EU. He weighs up, and then dismisses, the idea of the UK following the Norway model of relationship with Brussels, and, after considering Swiss and American options (what twenty years later would be classed as 'no deal'), he arrives at a conclusion not too dissimilar to Theresa May's Chequers proposal, created in 2018: a trade deal with full freedom of movement of goods – although Gove also backed free movement of EU citizens.

He writes:

> There is ultimately no reason, according to free thinkers, why an independent Britain should follow any established path. Britain is in a unique position. It has leverage. It has a trade deficit with the EU and our partners would fight hard to preserve their access to the British market ... Abandoning the veto would allow other nations to integrate without hindrance. In return for the freedom to go their own way, they might concede full freedom of move-ment in a federal Europe to British goods and citizens.[6]

But any suggestion that this is an early example of Gove calling for what would later be known as 'Brexit' is scuppered in the piece's final paragraph: 'It is still in Britain's interest to stay in the EU, to prevent, if possible, a profound upset in the balance of power in Europe and to make co-operation easier on matters of mutual interest.'

Gove, like much of the Conservative Party of the time, seemed content to bang on about Europe, but that wasn't where the public was in the mid-'90s. The topic of most political conversation was the seemingly imminent coronation of Tony Blair as at the next Prime Minister. When it came to New Labour, Gove – like many critics of the project – struggled to get a handle on what Blair and his allies actually stood for. It was a strange turn of events that many Conservatives who often reject the notion of adhering to an ideology were so focused on discovering what Blair's was. Gove was no different, and in an article on 1 February 1996 he accused the Labour leader of using the word 'community' with 'the enthusiasm of a Keith Floyd adding wine to a casserole, providing a sophisticated flavour and disguising the lack of beef'.[7]

His initial and instinctive hostility to Blair soon began to erode. Mary Ann Sieghart, who had known the Labour leader since the mid-1980s, remembers well a lunch at the Reform Club in Pall Mall organised by Peter Stothard where Blair was set to charm the paper's political staff. 'Blair, of course, is another man who shows elaborate courtesy; he has incredibly good manners,' says Sieghart, adding:

Although he was talking for most of the time, every time one of the waitresses would come and put some sort of soft boiled vegetables on to his plate he would look up, smile and say 'thank you' even while he was talking. Michael was bowled over by this. It was partly politeness but he was actually saying amazingly sensible things for a Labour leader. I think Michael's love affair with Blair began at that lunch.

While that might have been the moment Gove began to see the light, Blair had been on a charm offensive of the Rupert Murdoch-owned press since he became party leader. In June 1995, Stothard had contacted Blair to ask if he would meet with his proprietor the following month at the News Corporation conference on Hayman Island, Australia. Blair – to the horror of many in his party – accepted the invitation, and so began a relationship with Murdoch that would prove endlessly controversial.

Even inviting the Labour leader to the gathering showed the tectonic plates were shifting, but Gove, for one, was not publicly declaring his growing feelings for Blair just yet. Indeed, Gove was still in a political relationship with a certain Michael Portillo, and having stood by him during his non-challenge to John Major in the 1995 leadership contest, he was hardly going to switch allegiances now.

On 14 March 1997, with the Tories more than twenty-five points behind in the opinion polls, Gove tackled the inevitable question of who would succeed Major as Conservative leader. He flagged up eight potential replacements, with Portillo as the 3/1 favourite. Listing his advantage as 'Eurosceptic' and his disadvantage, rather bluntly, as 'Spanish', Gove wrote: ·

> Mr Portillo is known to enjoy the support of some of her [Thatch-er's] closest allies in the Commons, including her former political secretary John Whittingdale, but recently he has been earning warm notices from centre-left MPs such as Nick Soames, Robert Key and Tim Yeo. By trying to stick to his brief, Mr Portillo has made himself acceptable to mainstream figures, but his reluctance to put clear blue water between himself and Mr Major could allow him to be outflanked on the Right.[8]

The others on the list were Home Secretary Michael Howard at

3/1 ('Advantage: shoots to kill. Disadvantage: often misses'); Welsh Secretary William Hague at 4/1 ('Advantage: done nothing wrong. Disadvantage: done nothing'); and Health Secretary Stephen Dorrell at 6/1, with Ken Clarke, Michael Heseltine, Malcolm Rifkind and John Redwood all considered and dismissed.

It wasn't just the next Tory leader Gove was trying to predict. On 1 April, he took a stab at prophesying future Cabinet ministers, modestly avoiding chucking his own hat into the ring. Steve Hilton, an Oxford graduate who came from humble beginnings, had already picked up a reputation as a political messaging guru through his work at the Conservative Research Department. Gove described him as 'meaner than a two-bit dog' and 'all energy and aggression'.[9]

Another one to watch, according to Gove, was Daniel Finkelstein, described as 'the very model of a Tory moderniser' and 'a politics nut with an intellect larger than Norfolk and twice as fertile, his views are centre-right but his style is Wilf Lunn on E'.[10] Finkelstein was the head of the CRD, but he hadn't always been a Tory, having once stood as a candidate for the Social Democratic Party. He travelled over to the blue side after the SDP merged with the Liberal Party in 1988. The pair became friends in the early 1990s, and one mutual acquaintance describes the two as having 'Champions League final levels of banter'.

Getting references to his friends in the pages of *The Times* was something of a regular occurrence for Gove. In 1996, the paper carried two mentions of gatherings of the Roy Jenkins Appreciation Society.[11] Held at the Boisdale restaurant in Belgravia, Gove would join friends and fellow journalists such as Matthew D'Ancona, Adrian Lithgow and Hywel Williams for a boozy meal and much mockery of the former Labour Home Secretary. Stothard remembers:

I think the whole point was you had to communicate to other

members by means of quotations and quips by Roy Jenkins. 'The first time I met the Pope and he mispronounced my name' or 'The first time I turned down a dukedom'. I think you got more points for real Roy Jenkins quotes.

Getting it referenced in *The Times* so that it appeared to be a real society was part of the gag, and a write-up of its 'Winter Cocktail Party' in the 4 February 1997 edition of the paper reveals an impressive cast list for a not-very-elaborate joke. Cabinet minister Peter Lilley; Exchequer Secretary Philip Oppenheim; and Lord Strathclyde, the Chief Whip in the upper chamber, were all in attendance. Rising stars including Tom Bradby, who would later become ITV's political editor, and Tom Baldwin, the future chief spin doctor for Ed Miliband, also turned out.[12]

As well as the spoof societies, Gove was a member of some more serious dining clubs. The Fellow Travellers was a club run by the *Sunday Times* deputy editor Martin Ivens. It would meet at the Travellers Club – hence the name – in Pall Mall, and among the bright, right, young things setting the world in order were Gove and David Cameron.[13]

The pair were seeing plenty of each other throughout the mid-'90s, with the friendship growing thanks to a group holiday to Tuscany. Also present on the trip were Ed Vaizey, Simone Finn, Matthew D'Ancona, Robert Hardman, Jane Hardman, Marcus Kiggell and Lizzie Noel.[14] Gove attended Cameron's stag do in May 1996, which saw around thirty guests attend an afternoon at the races and then dine in a marquee in a field in Lambourn, in Berkshire. Again, Vaizey was present, as well as Steve Hilton and *Telegraph* leader writer Dean Godson.[15]

As we have seen, Gove was not averse to plugging his friends in the pages of *The Times*. On 23 December 1996, he speculated about what the Conservative shadow Cabinet might look like after the next election. John Redwood was installed as leader in Gove's fantasy Cabinet, with Michael Portillo as shadow Foreign Secretary, and Cameron, who was contesting the seat of Stafford, as shadow Chief Secretary to the Treasury.[16]

Rachel Whetstone and Catherine Fall – who would become key players in what was eventually dubbed the 'Notting Hill set' – were likewise flagged up by Gove in an article on 2 April 1997. Under the sub-headline 'They're spin doctors with sex appeal', Gove wrote:

Laddishness is, however, de rigueur at Tory Central Office, where breeding, in both senses, matters. While the boys tend to be *Loaded* meets P.G. Wodehouse, the girls are all real Wooster women. The most accomplished Conservative coquettes, such as Catherine Fall and Rachel Whetstone, all come from thorough-bred stables like Cobham and Roedean.[17]

Gove even managed to squeeze in a mention of his then girlfriend Amanda Foreman in a 22 October 1996 article on the return of political hostesses, in which he referenced her upcoming biography of Georgiana, the Duchess of Devonshire.[18]

One person who did not benefit from Gove's patronage was his best friend from university, Ed Vaizey. There is no mention of the man who was standing for the Tories in Bristol East in any of Gove's predictions of greatness. Perhaps it would have been too close to home – literally – as the pair had continued their living arrangement from when Gove had first moved to London. The duo shared a place on Golborne Road, in north Kensington, and as well as enjoying the upsides of London life, they also had to contend with some of the negatives. One evening, the pair came home to see their front door open and two burglars run past them. They gave pursuit – Gove slightly more enthusiastically than Vaizey, according to a friend – and the police eventually apprehended the felons, who had stolen watches and other valuables.

Gove's predictions for greatness received their first test in the 1997 general election. Facing an unprecedented lack of support in the opinion polls, Major opted for a long campaign, and on Monday 17 March the Prime Minister confirmed the vote would be held on 1 May, giving the Tories six weeks to turn around Labour's 25-point opinion poll lead. *The Times*, who had been severe critics of Major's leadership style and policies, particularly on Europe, held back from endorsing the Tories when the starting gun was fired. A leader column the day after the election was announced read, 'This newspaper, alone among its competitors, still has an open mind about the result of the election ... When polling day is near, we shall declare a preference; but not until we have seen how soundly each party stands up to the people's test.'[19]

In truth, Stothard was unsure of which way to go. Major was clearly a busted flush, and offering support to a man he had so relentlessly attacked would look bizarre. Yet the other option seemed equally unpalatable. While Blair had plainly moved Labour towards the centre of British politics, his enthusiasm for the European project was a genuine cause of concern.

To clarify his thinking, Stothard convened his leader-writing team at the Reform Club and, in homage to the Oxford Union, asked Gove and Sieghart to argue the respective causes. Sieghart recalls that her case was slightly easier to argue than Gove's. 'I think Michael admitted afterwards I got the better of him in the argument, but it wasn't hard because those were the facts, frankly, and it would have seemed very, very weird for us to continue supporting the Tories, especially after everything we'd been saying since the ERM debacle,' she remembers.

Yet, even with a weaker case, Gove did manage to put some doubts in Stothard's mind about fully coming out for Blair. Stothard says:

> By that stage he had done what quite a lot of Conservatives had done which is, 'We may think Major is no good, we may have been saying for years that Major's hopeless, but actually we've got an election coming up so we've got to vote Conservative.' He did that rather brilliantly.

The meeting broke up with no clear decision having been made, but Sieghart was certainly left with the impression that an endorsement for Blair – albeit heavily qualified with concerns about his Europhile pursuits – was on the cards.

On Tuesday 29 April, two days before the election, *The Times* showed its hand with the headline 'Principle not party. A vote for Members who will defend Parliament.' The paper was coming out for neither party but, instead, for a policy: Euroscepticism. After noting the 'fresh air and fresh leadership' of Blair, and reminding Major that he had lost the support of the paper in the 'chaos' of Black Wednesday, the leader reads: 'For *The Times* today – and for *The Times* in the spirit of its best past – the European future is the fulcrum of public policy ... Our endorsement in this election, therefore, falls not on a party slate but on individual candidates whose European ideals we can support.'[20]

Gove's Reform Club pitch had helped Stothard make up his mind, and he was drawn in by the editor to help write the decisive article.[21]

The leader would hardly have come as a shock to readers of *The Times*. The day before, the paper had printed a list of which Eurosceptic candidates they should vote for in their constituencies in order to get the most anti-EU parliament possible, with then relatively unknown backbencher Jeremy Corbyn flagged up as deserving of a vote.

If Stothard had hoped *The Times*'s endorsement of Eurosceptic Tories would help them survive the Labour tsunami, he was wrong. On 1 May 1997, the Conservatives lost 178 of the 343 seats it had secured five years earlier. Among the high-profile casualties were Foreign Secretary Malcolm Rifkind, tabloid favourite David Mellor and former Chancellor Norman Lamont. Gove's friends fared no better, with Ed Vaizey and Dean Godson failing to get elected.

At just after 3 a.m., the most striking result of the night was announced. Michael Denzil Xavier Portillo saw his thirteen years as MP for Enfield Southgate come to an end as a swing of 17.4 per cent installed Labour's Stephen Twigg in his place. The notion of a 'Portillo moment' – when a high-profile MP loses his seat – entered the political lexicon.

In the 2 May edition of *The Times*, it was, of course, left to Gove to pen Portillo's political obituary.

'The maybe man now won't be,' he wrote, arguing that the 'charismatic standard bearer of cavalier Conservatism' had 'lost any chance' of becoming Tory leader.[22] Gove listed Portillo's flashpoints while serving as an MP – his backing of the poll tax, the fall from office of his mentor, his rise as Defence Secretary – but it was the battle he ducked out of, standing against John Major in 1995, which meant he had 'lost credibility' among his colleagues.

In a prediction that proved to be wrong in the medium term but accurate in the long run, Gove concluded, 'His future is unlikely to be in politics.' It would not be the last time Gove would compress his biography of Portillo into a eulogy.

Now, for the first time in his professional life, Gove would be scrutinising a Labour government.

CHAPTER 8

THE IMPORTANCE OF BEING EARNEST

'**D**ifficult as the Conservatives' position is, it could still get worse,' warned *The Times* in a leader column on Saturday 3 May 1997. It was hardly an outlandish view. The election result had been such a total and utter rejection of the party that it was hard to know where to start the rebuilding work. John Major surprised no one by announcing his resignation as party leader just hours after the result was confirmed. In a linguistic throwback to his father's career as a music hall performer, Major said, 'When the curtain falls, it is time to get off the stage, and that is what I propose to do.'[1] A new leader was needed, and *The Times* wasted no time in going through the perspective candidates. The now ex-Chancellor, Kenneth Clarke, was dismissed for his pro-European views and inability to motivate Tory activists. Michael Heseltine was ruled out for being too closely linked to the 'election debacle', yet Michael Howard was spared from being tarnished with that brush and, although he was acknowledged as a 'controversial figure', he won praise for having 'combined loyalty with a strong sense of purpose'. John Redwood had 'proved his courage and his European colours', while the only virtue in a leadership bid by William Hague was that, at the age of thirty-six, he was younger than Tony Blair. The most positive comments were saved for Peter Lilley, who was deemed to have 'the intellectual power to map out a new path for Toryism in the future'.[2] Peter Stothard confirms that Lilley 'was the person I admired most' in the leadership election.

The first out of the blocks to declare was Clarke, who told the BBC's *World at One* the day after the election that he was going to put his name forward. The next day, Heseltine ruled himself out after being admitted to hospital with heart problems, and on Sunday 4 May Lilley threw his hat into the ring.[3]

On Tuesday 6 May, John Redwood joined the race, using an article in *The Times* to claim that he was a unity candidate. Michael Howard was next to stick his hand in the air, but his campaign got off to a terrible start when William Hague went back on a pledge to support him. Howard had offered Hague the deputy leadership in exchange for his backing, and the pair had met in London on Monday 5 May to toast the agreement with Bollinger champagne. With echoes of another a leadership deal which broke down nineteen years later, a close friend then urged Hague to go for the top job himself. Brooks Newmark, a future Conservative MP, who had known Hague since their student days at Oxford, turned up at his flat in the wee small hours of the morning to tell Hague this could be his only chance. At 6 a.m. on Tuesday 6 May, Hague picked up the phone and called Howard.[4] Unlike events nearly twenty years later, the man about to be knifed answered the phone, ensuring that the stabbing was in the front, not in the back.

Hague seemed to garner praise, not cynicism, for his move. The champagne pact had been leaked to the press, possibly by the Howard camp in a move to smear Hague as disloyal, but instead it portrayed the young politician as able to stand up to senior figures and not be overridden. By the time Hague launched his campaign on Wednesday 7 May, he was already installed as the bookies' favourite.

In the first round of voting on 10 June 1997, Clarke came top with forty-nine votes; Hague second with forty-one; then Redwood, twenty-seven; Lilley, twenty-four; and Howard on twenty-three. Lilley and Howard withdrew and supported Hague, and on 19 June the former Welsh Secretary beat the ex-Chancellor to become Conservative Party leader.

For Gove, Hague's election as leader was hardly inspiring. With Portillo unable to stand, and Lilley defeated early, the Yorkshire-man was perhaps the most in line with his Thatcherite principles, with the *Times* leader declaring the day after his victory, 'The Lady's lamp is still burning.' But, like many Conservative thinkers in the aftermath of the 1997 election catastrophe, he felt the wrong lessons were being learned from the defeat.

One senior figure in what would become known as Cameroon-ism says:

> After 1997, the initial thesis, which I'm sure Michael held, was that the problem with the Conservative Party was it had had this clear strong leadership and had won several elections and now it was diverting from the path of the truth. I don't think Michael would ever have expressed it as crudely as that, but certainly the idea that the Conservative Party had become insufficiently robust and that explained its decline was very widespread.

The desire for the Tories to have a strong leader manifested itself in strange ways. On 4 August 1997, Hague decided that the best way to begin the revitalising of the once great party was to be photo-graphed going down a waterslide in a Cornwall theme park while wearing a baseball cap with his own name stitched into the front. Another attempt to be seen to be 'down with the youth' involved Hague and his fiancée Ffion going to the Notting Hill Carnival and drinking from coconuts. To say the plan to paint Hague out as 'one of the people' was a failure is to put it mildly. On just his ninety-seventh day as leader, he issued a 'back me or sack me' plea to the growing list of dissenters in his own party.

It's little wonder that Gove was becoming increasingly disillusioned with the Tories. On 24 September 1997, he set out where he believed the party was going wrong. Taking a machine gun to the philosophy that underpinned the last Conservative administration, he wrote:

> A Conservative Prime Minister has no business trying to create a classless society. It is as offensive to Tory principles as claiming you have no 'selfish strategic interest' in keeping your country One Nation. For a Conservative to believe in classlessness is like a panther living on vegetation – so contrary to nature that it will lead to extinction.[5]

Gove blasted Major's introduction of the National Lottery, describing it as an 'exquisite device for exploiting the poor and subsidising the amusements of the rich'. He added, 'Short of drug pushing, there is no process where the failings of the disadvantaged are used so transparently to subsidise the wealthy.'

Reflecting on his own education background, he declared, 'The class system made Britain great. The public schools, far from holding the nation back, have been a priceless asset. It is the desire to send his son to Eton, for prestige as much as qualifications, that drives the man in the Midlands to build a better mousetrap.'

He continued:

> There is nothing wrong per se in ever-greater inequality. The real test of equity, in law and in society, is the process not the

outcome. A fair society is one where barriers to progress, not divisions between individuals, are as small as possible. To object to growing disparities in income is, ultimately, immoral, a genuflection to envy. Envy is a prejudice, as ugly as any, which seeks to punish another when no injury has been sustained. Snobbery, which drives man to excel and encourages the cultivation of taste, is, by contrast, a deeply moral impulse.

While Gove was tearing into Major, he was beginning to praise Tony Blair. In a *Guardian* article on 31 July 1997, he spoke of how some of the pragmatism of the New Labour project was appealing to those who were Tories by decision, not birth. 'For those not tied to the Conservative party by sentiment, but by certain ideas, by Margaret Thatcher rather than Party institutions, Blair has done enough ... It's important to keep open lines of communication with whoever's in power,' he wrote.

This crisis of confidence in the party he had joined as a student apparently almost led him to return to his first political love. At the Conservative Party conference in October 1997, Gove was seemingly making the most of the free alcohol laid on at the numerous fringe events taking place in and around the Winter Gardens venue in Blackpool when he made a startling admission. According to Atul Hatwal, a former Labour Party press officer who was at the Tory conference, Gove was still in a state of starry-eyed wonder over the Labour Party conference he had attended a week earlier. 'He had seen the light. The light had a name. And that name was Tony,' Hatwal wrote in 2012.[6] He went on:

[Gove] luxuriated in the company of Labour lobbyists who had worked for the party in the recent campaign, quizzing them on their campaign methods and the political faith of their master.

In one exchange at a reception, Gove laid bare his personal theo-logical struggle. Temperamentally he was a Conservative, but for him, Tony Blair was a game-changer. A politician who redefined the rules and offered hope of a new way. Dare we say it, a third way. Young Michael was dazzled and, as the gathered throng of ex-Labour staffers looked on, professed that he was seriously thinking of joining the Labour party. In fact, he was going to look into it and get the forms the following week when he was back in London.

Gove did not carry through his conversion to the Church of New Labour, and a friend suggests he was most likely either drunk or joking – or both – when he professed his love for Blair.

If there was any hint of doubt about his political allegiance, sal-vation from the cult of Tony came in the form of his fallen idol. Later at that same Conservative conference, Michael Portillo set out a strong defence of the eighteen years his party had spent in power. Speaking at a Centre for Policy Studies event, the deposed MP said:

> There is much for the Conservative Party to learn and to put right. We shall do it. But that is not to say that everything that we did in the past was wrong. Very far from it. We have many achievements of which we can be proud. The Conservatives did things in the last eighteen years that were imaginative, radical and good for our people. They were copied by many abroad and by our opponents at home.[7]

Portillo's speech wasn't just about defending what the Tories had got right, but about flagging up where the party needed to change. The key area was social attitudes.

Our society has changed. For good or ill, many people nowadays do not marry and yet head stable families with children. For a younger generation, in particular, old taboos have given way to less judgemental attitudes to the span of human relationships. There remain many other people to whom the new norms seem all wrong. The Tory Party is conservative and not given to political correctness. Still, the party never rejects the world that is. Tolerance is a part of the Tory tradition. I believe that the Conservative Party in its quiet way is as capable as any other of comprehending the diversity of human nature.

Had the party moved too far from Thatcherism, as Gove seemed to be suggesting? Was it more about the attitudes to society and personal choice, as Portillo identified? Or was it both? It was difficult to listen to what voters had told them in the 1997 election defeat when no one could agree on what had been said.

Initially, it seemed that Hague was picking up on the need for modernisation. While his baseball cap-wearing antics were prompting ridicule, he was trying to drag the party towards the twenty-first century when it came to social attitudes. In his first conference speech as leader, Hague used the word compassion or compassionate eight times – the same number as Blair in his address a week earlier.[8]

But this embrace of the new world seemed superficial at best. On 23 June 1998, the party showed its true colours. MPs were given a free vote on whether to lower the age of consent for gay sex to sixteen, bringing it into line with the age of consent for heterosexuals. Only sixteen Conservative MPs backed the move.

Gove's frustration spilled out in the pages of *The Times* through a leader article published on 6 July 1998. Under the headline 'Mods and Rockers', the editorial warned Hague that the biggest split in the party was not between 'Left and Right, Europhile and Eurosceptic', but between 'liberals and reactionaries'. It thundered: 'The most important argument the Conservative Party still needs to have is between those sensitive to changing times and those inclined to nostalgia. It is a battle, we believe, between Tory Mods and Rockers.' The paper made clear which side it was on with the pledge: 'In this conflict, *The Times* is a committed supporter of those who lead the liberal charge.' Gove and his fellow leader writers would not have to wait long to see whether Hague was going to lead as a Mod or a Rocker.

The future of the Conservative Party may have been of interest to Gove, but he also had his own career to worry about. Stothard was impressed with his leader-writing abilities, and he was given adequate room in the paper to branch out with non-political articles. On 27 December 1997, Gove dialled up his contrary side with an attack on that most traditional of festive films, *It's a Wonderful Life*. Not only is it deemed a 'truly terrible film', Gove blasts it as 'propaganda'. 'It should be a testament to self-sacrifice. It is, however, a hymn to mediocrity, a paean to protectionism, an assault on the best of America and a celebration of suffocation.' It is not clear what prompted this anger, but barely buried in the tirade is an anger which Gove may well be directing at his own family.

> [James] Stewart's character, George Bailey, yearns to do 'something big', but instead of lassoing the Moon he devotes his energies to running the family firm. Rather than making his mark on the biggest canvas available he prefers to doodle in the margins. This is not just a squandering of spirit, but an unfortunate endorsement of the gentlemanly rentier at the expense of the genuinely wealth-creating buccaneer. George Bailey is a Baring without balls.

Gove, of course, has never been content to 'doodle in the margins', and he took the opportunity afforded by *The Times* to tackle a manner of topics. One of these involved being a chef for the day at the Oxo Tower Brasserie for a TV show on the Carlton Food Network. The two-page write-up on 26 January 1998 was more the sort of article hard-pressed local journalists are asked to rustle up ahead of the slow Christmas news period than a piece you would expect to find in a national newspaper. Amid the 'Gosh, this is much harder than I thought it would be' schtick, Gove revealed his own dinner party delight was cooking 'pommes dauphinoise'.

The oeuvre of 'Gove trying things he's not very good at' continued on 25 July 1998 with a double-page spread on his inability to pass his driving test. 'I have a degree, a mortgage, a pension, wine club membership and am developing a curious interest in golf,' Gove sighed, 'but I still can't drive.'

Next to a large picture of Gove leaning out of the driver's side of car, pulling a cartoonish face of confusion, he lamented:

I have tried to learn to drive in Aberdeen, Oxford and London. I have taken lessons from my father, independent instructors, the Automobile Association and the British School of Motoring. I have tried Fiestas, Fiats and Ford Escorts. I have taken four driving tests. And at the end of the fourth I registered more black marks than at the end of the first.

Gove would eventually pass his test at the seventh attempt.

Reward for Gove's endeavours came in the form of a weekly column, beginning on 9 June 1998. The first topic was, somewhat strangely, the potential sell-off of the Royal Automobile Club, a private members' club which has a house in Pall Mall. His second regular column was much more in his usual vein, and focused on bashing the Chancellor, Gordon Brown.

His articles became, predictably, mini-Oxford Union speeches. Gove would pick an extreme view on a controversial topic and hold forth, desperate to argue the seemingly unarguable. On 23 June 1998, the future Justice Secretary went into bat for the rights of 'paedophiles, racists and soccer hooligans' in an attack on Labour Home Secretary Jack Straw. He accused Straw of pushing forward with making Orwellian 'thoughtcrimes' a reality, as the Home Secretary had floated the idea of extending the prison sentences of those 'who cannot control their criminal habits'. Gove hit back at the plan, stating:

> At the end of their allotted time, 'indeterminate custodial sentences' would allow these men to be incarcerated if it was thought they might reoffend. In as long as it takes to call a tabloid editor, one of the sacred principles of British justice was crushed under Jack's boot. We imprison people for what they do, not what they might do, or what they think.

He then went on to argue that racist violence should not warrant a harsher punishment than other violent crime. 'Why is one sort of hatred more deserving than another? Do I bleed more if my assailant's skin has more or less pigment than mine? How, in any case, can we prove and then punish more severely racist intent, other than by creating a new class of thoughtcrime?'

His attack on Straw prompted a response from the man himself, with the Home Secretary writing to *The Times* to say, 'What makes racist violence so horrendous is that it is not only a physical attack on the individual victim but an attack on the liberties and rights of a particular actions group as a whole.' He added, 'Mr Gove falls into a trap which Orwell always avoided, namely, reaching a conclusion before finding an argument.'[9]

That same critique can be levelled at another article on law and order published in the summer of 1998. On 30 July, the murder conviction of Derek Bentley, the nineteen-year-old who had been hanged in 1953 for his part in the death of a police officer, was quashed. The case had long been a black mark against the British justice system, as Bentley was sentenced to death not for firing the gun which killed PC Sidney Miles but for telling his accomplice in a failed burglary, 'Let him have it' when another officer demanded the weapon was handed over. The overturning of Bentley's murder conviction inspired Gove's column on 31 July, with the opening lines: 'Derek Bentley's vindication after forty-five years will incline us all to review our attitudes to crime and punishment. As a liberal on criminal justice it confirms my views: we were wrong to abolish hanging.'

He does not explain why the overturning of a death sentence after it has been carried out has prompted him to believe capital punishment should be restored. Indeed, the Bentley case does not get another mention at all in the piece. Instead, Gove argues that since the death penalty was abolished in the 'teeth' of public opinion, politicians have been trying to make it up to the mob ever since. 'Like a husband who has been caught in an adulterous affair, and who tries to repair his marriage with ever more extravagant gifts, the relationship between politicians and people has become demeaned.'

Gove then lists the concessions that he believes have tainted the justice system, including requiring the defence to disclose its case to the prosecution, and the change to the police caution meaning that a person who did not volunteer evidence at the earliest opportunity could have that used against them at trial. He claims that the prison sentences handed to Myra Hindley and the killers of James Bulger were influenced by public opinion, not legal arguments. 'They are, in a literal sense, political prisoners,' he argues.

Gove's conclusion is that the justice system has been so taint-ed by politicians trying to make up for the abolition of the death penalty that it no longer guarantees justice will be served. 'Were I ever alone in the dock, I would not want to be arraigned before our flawed tribunals, knowing my freedom could be forfeit as a result of political pressures. I would prefer a fair trial, under the shadow of the noose.'

The article is a perfect example of Gove's desire to argue the un-arguable: not the return of the death penalty – which is an argument many may choose to make – but that a 'liberal' can be in favour of capital punishment. Yet the article struggles to hold together, with the central claim seeming to be that a time machine is needed to go back to the 1960s to stop the death penalty being abolished. Mary Ann Sieghart remembers this series of articles well, saying, 'I was just aghast a lot of the time at how right-wing he was for someone so young. How could you be that right-wing at that age, especially at that sort of thing?'

Nor was Gove afraid to stir up a hornets nest in his own back garden. On 30 June 1998, he made the case for Scottish independ-ence from the UK – or rather, that England should cut adrift the country of his birth. After remarking that he had felt 'scared' upon seeing the prevalence of the St George's Cross on display during Euro '96 two years earlier, Gove reflected on what he believed were increasingly difficult arguments to rebut from his English friends who no longer believed the union worked for them. 'As long as the English Exchequer underwrites Scotland's politicians they will never be properly accountable,' he warned. The article also con-tained a line likely to raise the eyebrows of many an anti-Brexit voter in Scotland some eighteen years later: 'What would happen if Scottish votes in a referendum tipped the balance in favour of a single currency while England voted against? In a close-run contest, overwhelmingly pro-European Edinburgh might tip mildly sceptical Exeter into monetary union.'

Another article penned by Gove in the summer of 1998 deserves examination. In July, the Children's Society led the charge on reforming adoption laws, namely so that birth mothers would be able trace the children they had given up. The campaign had obvious resonance for Gove, who used the opportunity to talk about his life as an adopted child. On 24 July, he wrote of how he had curbed his natural curiosity as a journalist to avoid seeking out his birth mother, repeatedly falling back on the thought that it would cause pain for his adoptive mother. Gove reveals that his birth mother has been kept abreast of his 'progress through life' by his adoptive parents, suggesting that if the woman who brought him into the world really did want to make contact, it was possible. She hadn't, of course. She hadn't when Gove went to Oxford University; she hadn't when he had become president of the union; when he had starred in a television show; when he had worked for the BBC – all fantastic achievements for the boy she knew as Graeme. She would have known what her son was doing but had not sought to establish contact. And Gove would have known that too. He used the article in *The Times* to deliver a message to his natural mother: please stay away.

I would not want my [adoptive] mother to feel that another woman came between us, but I would feel powerless to resist any attempt by my birth mother to establish contact. Faced with this judgement of Solomon in reverse, I would only wish that I had not been thrust into this position.

Not all Gove's articles were doused in controversy. On 7 November 1998, he managed to squeeze out a whole column on snapping a shoelace and struggling to buy a replacement.

He returned to his contrary ways on 22 December with a bizarre poem looking back at some of the figures who had hit the headlines in the previous twelve months. With verse more appropriate to his Robert Gordon days than his position as a national newspaper journalist, some of the selections from the poem include:

> Robin Cook
> should have thought before he took
> a mistress called Gaynor,
> who, compared to his wife, is
> considerably plainer.
> *
>
> Ron Davies
> should have been christened Mavis,
> then no one would have thought him a wrong 'un
> for chatting to strangers on Clapham Common.
> *
>
> President Clinton
> thought he could get away with a bit on the side,
> but he reckoned without Senator Henry Hyde.
> *
>
> Monica Lewinsky
> got far too frisky
> and discovered that DNA
> is a devil of stain to wipe away.
> *
>
> Ulrika Jonsson
> has an unfortunate penchant

for uncivilised brutes
who connect her face to their football boots.[10]

Gove was clearly having great fun passing comment on the private lives of others, perhaps unaware that he now had someone in his life who would one day reveal a great many details about his. Thanks to the person he met in Waterloo Station earlier that year, the world would one day know that Gove dons lederhosen-style swimming trunks, tried to learn the ukulele, and once joked about the size of Mick Jagger's penis while standing next to the Rolling Stones singer at the urinal.[11]

CHAPTER 9

LOVE IN A COLD CLIMATE

At the beginning of 1998, Gove had agreed to go on a skiing holiday to Méribel in the French Alps with a group of friends, including Ed Vaizey. As the group prepared to board the Eurostar from Waterloo Station,[1] he was introduced to a late addition to the trip who had been invited after another person had broken their leg.[2] The pair both worked for *The Times*, but in his role as comment editor Gove had yet to come across the arts editor, Sarah Vine. It was not love at first sight for Vine: 'He wrote leaders and knew about politics. I liked movies and knew about handbags. Damn, I thought, I've come all this way to let my hair down (i.e., get pissed); now I'll have to stay sober and pretend to understand the long-term situation in the Balkans.'[3]

When the group arrived at the destination, it very quickly became apparent that it was Vine who had the advantage. Gove had never been skiing in his life, while Vine had picked up the skill during her slightly more nomadic upbringing.

Sarah Vine was born in Swansea on 16 April 1967. Her parents were Roger and Rosemary (née Parry), twenty-year-old university students, who had married young. Vine would go on to describe her mother as a 'nice, well brought up middle-class woman' who worked as a librarian, translator, model and magazine editor.[4] Her father was an accountant.[5] The family moved to Stourbridge in the West Midlands, and then Garsington, just outside Oxford, as her father was studying for a PhD.[6] A holiday to Italy when Sarah was five prompted a more dramatic change of scenery.[7] The Vines relocated to Rome and then Frascati, a small town twelve miles south-east of the capital city. There was a brief return to the UK, staying in Bromley, before the family settled in Turin in northern Italy when Sarah was eight.[8] It was there that young Sarah received what Gove never had – skiing lessons.[9] While she may have enjoyed the piste, she did not feel the same about the Italian way of life, which she saw as too chaotic and unpredictable. In 2016, she reflected on her time in the country:

> Each year, school would break up early, lessons cut short, because of another collapsed government. Politicians were forever being brought down by huge corruption scandals. Roads remained half-built, houses sprung up like jagged teeth where they ought not to be. Nothing mattered except who you knew and how much you could pay them. Everyone had a price, and if they didn't they'd probably end up in a coffin.[10]

She also felt physically different from the local children. 'All the Italians were teeny-tiny, and I was this great strapping English girl with big thighs and massive feet,' she remembered in 2013.[11] Her childhood ambition to become a small, blonde, delicate ballet dancer called Alice was never realised.[12]

The chaos in Vine's life wasn't only caused by the Italian culture. Her young parents were also a cause of instability. In 2006, she wrote about some of the more difficult aspects of being born to parents who were barely out of their teenage years:

> Having a baby when you're 20 is tough. You've hardly begun to

have fun; you can't possibly be ready to swap parties for nappies, kiss goodbye to your social life in favour of cosy evenings at home with baby. You're practically still a child yourself, and what you have in strong bones and firm thighs you lack in wisdom and experience. Routine, which all children thrive on, is anathema to a 20-year-old, as dull as a weekend's DIY, or washing the car on a Sunday afternoon.[13]

The lack of structure only got worse as Vine entered her teenage years, and she recalled that her house became full of 'tantrums, walkouts, angst-ridden heart-to-hearts. Sometimes I felt more like the parent than the child. I longed for some boundaries to be set, some consistency, some logic to it all.'[14]

That order was sought in a Sussex boarding school, and Vine remembered the sense of relief she felt about returning to the UK: 'I know it sounds ridiculous, but I remember coming off the ferry at Dover and seeing all these little houses, and just loving the neatness. Italy is all chaos. Everything's just so regular about Britain, it feels very safe.'[15] Her time at the boarding school did not last long, however – partly due to her being bullied, and partly due to 'a misunderstanding involving a nightclub in Piccadilly, a 4 a.m. trip on the milk train from Victoria and the theft of some Penguin biscuits',[16] she later revealed. Her education was revived briefly at Hammersmith and West London comprehensive ('where being able to spell your own name was considered a mark of genius,'[17] she later claimed), and then Holland Park School.

Like many teenage girls, Vine spent far too much time focused on trying to be thin. She tried 'every rubbish silly diet', but it was soon not her body that she was worried about, but her hair. When she was fourteen, a friend commented that her centre parting was looking a little wider than normal. While the issue was initially downplayed by her mother, Vine soon realised that her hair was indeed shedding. She wrote in 2015:

> It seemed to come in waves: sometimes my hair looked completely normal, other times it seemed more sparse and fly-away. Around the age of 16, I had it cut much shorter and wore it in a messier style, which made it much easier to conceal the bit at the front where it was thinning.[18]

Vine tried numerous treatments to help stop the thinning and was told by a doctor that the condition was likely stress-related and possibly hereditary. 'Even the name of my condition stressed me out. I had male pattern hair loss, I was told. Male pattern. At least these days they have the courtesy to call it female pattern,'[19] she later said.

At the age of sixteen, Vine finally received the stability she craved. She moved in with her grandmother in Bickley in Kent. 'She knew about my life, understood my dilemmas. She responded by cooking regular meals and making sure I got to bed early,' she would later recall.[20]

Having got sub-standard O-levels at Holland Park, Vine resat the exams at Lewes Technical College,[21] now known as Sussex Downs Lewes College, before being fast-tracked through three A-levels. 'Dear old Lewes Tech,' she recalled in 2014. 'It scooped me up, dusted me down and, somehow, squeaked me through three A-levels, which in turn got me into university by the skin of my teeth.[22] That university was University College London, where Vine studied French and Italian.

Despite describing her time in state education as both 'scary' and 'bloodcurdling', Vine seemed to enjoy the breadth of life at the schools and college she attended. Reflecting on her education in 2014, she wrote:

In their own way, they also provided me with a broad education. Not so much in, say, mathematics (I never managed more than a Grade 1 CSE); but in life. And in the realisation that you shouldn't judge people by their clothes, or where they live, but by who they really are; that kids studying to be hairdressers deserve as much respect as those wanting to be rocket scientists.[23]

Vine went off to university a self-confessed 'square' child, who had experimented with being a Goth (but wore too much blusher)[24] and did not have her first proper drink until she was eighteen – two glasses of Newcastle Brown Ale.[25]

Her first job after university was working in customer service for the women's clothes and fashion store Hobbs, but she kept her education going with an Apple Mac course. That tuition proved useful when a friend who worked for the *Daily Mirror* remarked to her in the pub one Sunday in 1991 that the paper was switching to Macs – and people were struggling to get to grips with the new computers. 'I wasn't an IT genius. I basically knew how to use a mouse, so they asked me to do a shift,' she recalled in 2017. That shift turned into a permanent role as a TV listings sub, and roles followed at *The Guardian*, the *Mail on Sunday*, the *Daily Express* and *Tatler*. She joined *The Times* as deputy arts editor in 1997, eventually being promoted to arts editor.[26]

And so it was, when she was 'going through a good hair patch', she arrived at Waterloo Station for a holiday that would change her life. After watching Gove spectacularly failing to get to grips with skiing, despite spending 'about a billion francs' on lessons from a 'a very tall, sexy handsome French ski instructor',[27] she took the gangly Scot under her wing and taught him some of the basics. 'It's the only time in my life I have actually been better at something than him,' she later recalled.[28]

In the chalet as well as on the slopes, the pair hit it off, and although there was not so much as a kiss on that holiday,[29] there was certainly a frisson, created somewhat by Gove's choice of nightwear. Amid the 'general mayhem' of the trip, Vine remembered that Gove 'maintained an admirable high standard of pyjama-wearing'. She went on, 'While other members of the group would stagger down to breakfast wearing last night's wine-stained shirts, he would appear in full Turnbull & Asser cotton piped. There was even, I seem to remember, a matching dressing gown.'[30] (Gove's recollection is more modest: 'Maybe they were Marks & Spencer pyjamas and I was passing them off as something more,' he suggested in 2010.)[31]

A smitten Gove invited Vine for a drink at Claridge's when they returned to England ('"Claridge's!" I thought. "This is my kind of man."'), but the romantic vibe was somewhat ruined when Ed Vaizey turned up as well, believing it to be a holiday reunion.[32]

The next date was organised at the River Café in Hammersmith. This time, Vaizey didn't show up, but then neither did Gove for the first hour and a half. He had got stuck in the *Times* office, but Vine refused to allow herself to be stood up. 'Luckily, I'm very greedy, so I thought, "I'm not leaving until he gets here,"' she recalled in 2017.[33]

The courting continued, and Gove was keen to show his alpha qualities to impress his new beau. On one of their early dates, a man walked past the pair and spat in front of Vine. 'Excuse me,' bellowed Gove. 'What do you think you're doing?'

'What's your problem, mate?' replied the spitter.

'My problem is that you spat in front of my girlfriend. I think you should apologise,' said Gove.[34] Fortunately for the man whose previous encounters of violence included getting beaten up in Aberdeen and throwing scrambled egg into the hair of a love rival, the run-in concluded with the exchange of strong language, not fists.

In a sign of their strengthening relationship – and perhaps

another attempt to escape the attentions of Vaizey – the pair took a holiday to the Seychelles in June 1998. In a write-up for the paper a few months later, Gove recalled how the tennis coach in the resort left 'Sarah more exhausted after half an hour than she's ever been with me'.[35]

As the calendar ticked over into 1999, it was apparent that it wasn't just Gove's relationship with Vine that was strengthening, but his love for *The Times* as well. On 12 January, he penned a column in defence of the paper's proprietor, Rupert Murdoch. Gove accused *The Guardian*'s editor, Alan Rusbridger, of being infatuated with the 'global media phenomenon' that is Murdoch. 'Of course, *The Guardian* protests that it hates the dark prince of print. It really detests him. Oh God, can't stand the vulgar creature,' Gove wrote, 'but it won't stop mentioning his name.'[36] He went on: 'The reason for *The Guardian*'s fascination with Mr Murdoch is that he encourages what it claims to promote – free thinking. His newspapers, like the Net itself, are driven by public demand and the creativity of chaotic, cock-snooking, individuals.' Gove even goes as far as to claim that 'the greatest godfather of mischief in print is Mr Murdoch'.

Such naked flattery only stirred up rumours that Gove – who was now comment editor – was positioning himself for the very top job should Stothard wish to move on to pastures new. His loyalty to *The Times* was demonstrated even more keenly by his role in a war between the paper and Michael (now Lord) Ashcroft. The billionaire was a year into his role as treasurer of the Conservative Party when *The Times* began probing his business empire and links to Belize. The first story, headlined 'Massive donations make Tories "the plaything of one man"', was published on 5 June 1999 and claimed Ashcroft was meeting a third of the costs of keeping the party going through £4 million in donations. Ashcroft later described the story as 'inaccurate and misleading', as the true level of money he was pumping in was £1 million.[37] *The Times* continued to run articles about Ashcroft and his links to Belize – where he was a naturalised citizen – throughout the summer, culminating in Labour MP Peter Bradley using a speech in the Commons to seek to link the Tory treasurer to enquiries into drug trafficking and money-laundering that the DEA were carrying out. Ashcroft was outraged, describing the claims as scandalous and an abuse of parliamentary privilege. On 21 July 1999, he issued a writ against Peter Stothard, *The Times* and two reporters at the paper. The man sent out to defend the paper on Radio 4's *Today* programme the next day was Michael Gove. He had been on message when it came to attacking Ashcroft, using a column a week earlier to pose the questions:

> What sort of man allegedly threatens his own country's diplomatic interests in order to open a bank in an offshore tax haven? Is it the sort of man who should be treasurer of a potential party of government? Or the sort of devil-take-the-hindmost, I'm alright Juan, wherever I pay no tax that's my home opportunist who gave the Tories such a bad name?[38]

When lines from the article were read back to Gove on *Newsnight* in 2011, he brushed them off by saying he was 'paid to entertain' while at *The Times* and was seeking to 'amuse and provoke'.[39]

He was actually required to defend and attack, and was put up to appear on the *Today* programme despite knowing little about the ins and outs of the story.[40] The battle came to a close just before Christmas 1999. On 4 December, Ashcroft met with *Times* owner Rupert Murdoch for secret talks to thrash out a truce. Five days later, a front-page article appeared under the headline '*The Times* and Michael Ashcroft'. It read: '*The Times* is pleased to confirm that it has no evidence that Mr Ashcroft or any of his companies have ever been suspected of money laundering or drug-related crimes.'[41] The businessman and the paper had agreed to draw a line under the matter and discontinue the libel action – and bear his own legal costs of pursuing it – in exchange for the correction. Although a truce had been declared, Gove still felt compelled to launch an attack on Ashcroft after the latter was awarded in a peerage in March 2000. In a no-holds-barred comment piece, Gove attacked Ashcroft and Hague – who had secured the peerage – in equal measure. 'Surely a party determined to make patriotism and tax its salient issues would not have as its paymaster a man, like Michael Ashcroft, who was Ambassador for one foreign country and a tax exile in another?' asked Gove.[42] Nevertheless, a great deal of time has since passed and relationships today between Ashcroft and Gove are reported to be cordial.

As Stothard remembers, though, 'The Ashcroft Affair', as it was dubbed, placed a strain on the *Times* newsroom:

> It was a pretty awful time as it forced a lot of people to take sides. Michael was brilliant then. He was in an awkward position then because Michael Ashcroft was extremely important for the Conservative Party at a very low point in its fortunes, so he could have been important to Michael's future. He was certainly important to keeping the Tory show on the road. Equally, a lot of people thought he was a bad thing. Michael was very deft and very supportive of *The Times*. I was very grateful to him then.

Stothard showed his gratitude in an unusual way. Gove, who had excelled as a leader writer and as comment editor, was shifted at the beginning of 2000 to become home affairs editor. Gone were the days of helping to formulate the views of the paper through college of cardinals-style musings in the editor's office. Now Gove was expected to prepare a daily news list, manage a team of reporters and contribute more to what went in the front of the paper.

Stothard claims the move was part of a plan to train Gove as a potential successor. 'When was Captain Gove going to take over from General Stothard?' was the question on the lips of many industry gossips, according to Stothard, who adds, 'He couldn't have been a successor unless he'd shown that he could do more dirty-handed jobs in the newspaper.'

An article in *The Spectator* on 5 February 2000, penned by the magazine's media correspondent, Stephen Glover, was much more cynical about the move: 'Some may say, indeed Mr Gove's friends are saying it, that this represents promotion. One might easily think that, but it is not so. Though being news editor is, of course, a tremendously important job, in the world of the *Times* it is less prized than being comment editor.' Glover speculated that far from training Gove as a successor, Stothard wanted him a on a shorter leash:

> My own reading is that Mr Stothard, still hoping for that 'one last push against the *Telegraph*', wanted to give Mr Murdoch the impression of meaningful activity – hence the transfer of Mr Gove and other changes. He also knows that a news editor is chained to his desk and unable to plot over long lunches. The promotion to the deputy editorship of Ben Preston shows where Mr Stothard's preferences really lie.

The Guardian had just as much fun with the news of the job change, and took the opportunity to remind readers of the biggest story Gove had missed in his career: 'Gove's fabled nose for news is such that his admiring biography of Michael Portillo contains not a word about Polly's student frolics.'[43]

Gove's shift to home editor provoked some uneasiness in the *Times* newsroom, with one journalist remembering, 'This was a guy who was perceived not to know anything about news, other than politics, and was perceived to have "opinions" – which they didn't like particularly.'

It is fair to say that home editor was not a job which Gove thrived in. Much like his tenure at the *Today* programme, he was simply not able to muster as much enthusiasm for news stories as he was for the world of politics. One reporter claims that Gove delegated much of the work to deputies, remembering:

> You'd hear his laugh booming around the newsroom just talking big-picture stuff. Occasionally he would sort of go into confer-ence and sort of tokenly read out the list, but he wasn't doing the job. He was basically immersing himself in the wider politics of the paper. He saw himself already either as editor or a Cabinet minister. You could see that; no one really doubted that trajectory.

One of Gove's main problems wasn't he couldn't bring himself to do the dirtier parts of the job. Delivering a dressing-down to a reporter for filing late copy, getting facts or spellings wrong, or even missing a story entirely is expected of an editor. Yet the famously polite and courteous Gove didn't have that in his locker. As Stothard puts it, 'You can't be a news editor without screaming quite a lot.'

His move to the home news beat did not mean that Gove was no longer to give his views. Since 1997, he had been beavering away on a pamphlet about the Northern Ireland peace process. Gove was given the not insignificant sum of £8,000 to pen 'The Price of Peace', after winning the Charles Douglas-Home Award.[44]

A year later, and Tony Blair delivered a speech satirists dream of as he arrived in Belfast on 7 April 1998 to push the peace talks over the line. 'A day like today is not a day for soundbites, we can leave those at home, but I feel the hand of history upon our shoulder with respect to this, I really do,' he proclaimed.

The Prime Minister had made securing a deal in the province a priority since his election almost a year earlier, and now, with inroads having been made by the energetic Northern Ireland Secretary Mo Mowlam, an agreement was within reach. On Friday 10 April, a deal was struck. A Northern Ireland Assembly would be created, and the composition of the executive would be decided using a form of proportional representation which encouraged power-sharing. As part of the deal, paramilitary organisations would decommission their weapons, and prisoners serving sentences for offences related to the Troubles would be considered for early release. It was the last point that provoked anger in Gove. While *The Times* had been supportive of the agreement, and maintained a pragmatism-over-purity approach to the talks, the man who knew the words to the songs of the Orange Order was in a state of incredulity. On Sunday 10 May, four IRA terrorists known as the Balcombe Street Gang were given special parole to leave the prison where they were serving life sentences to appear at the Sinn Féin conference in Dublin. They were given a triumphant reception, with Sinn Féin leader Gerry Adams describing them as 'our Nelson Mandelas'. This was too much for Gove. In an article two days later, he wrote that he was 'revolted' by the 'adulation' the four killers received. Describing the Sinn Féin conference as a 'Nineties Nuremberg', he asked:

What sort of peace can be built on the elevation of squalid, conscienceless gangsters to rock star status? Those of us disposed to anger are asked to think of the greater prize. We are told our feelings are understandable but misguided. I am afraid they are not. The disquiet and disgust are amply justified. Far from safeguarding lives and liberties, the Government is undermining the rule of law.[45]

Gove then returned to his familiar claim that the UK government was too weak in its negotiations with Sinn Féin and the IRA, adding, 'If the republicans who met on Sunday were really repentant, then where were the apologies to the dead and disappeared? Gerry Adams did not put on a sackcloth. He organised a gala for gunmen. And this Government facilitated the garlanding.'

He then turned his ire on the Conservative Party for not doing more to 'defend the rule of law', posing the question: 'If the Tories cannot articulate the honest, principled anger of the British people at the repulsive spectacle of terror triumphant, then who will speak for them?'

Yet Gove was not speaking for them either. Indeed, the daughter of Dr Gordon Hamilton, one of the men murdered by the gang in London in 1975, was in Belfast four days after the Sinn Féin conference to campaign for 'Yes' in a referendum on the Good Friday Agreement. Dr Diana Hamilton-Fairley said:

> They are alive and my father is dead. Nothing can change that, nothing will bring him back. But I am prepared to give these people the benefit of the doubt if it means that no one else will ever again have to go through the pain and suffering of having someone snatched away because two communities cannot find a way to live as one.[46]

She added that both sides would have to give up 'some of their most precious tenets' in order to secure peace in the province.

Dr Hamilton-Fairley was not the only one who had lost relatives at the hands of Republican terrorists to support the Good Friday

Agreement: Alan McBride, whose wife was killed by a bomb in 1993; John Maxwell, who lost his fifteen-year-old son in 1979; and Beryl Quigley, whose husband Bill McConnell was shot dead in 1984, all backed the peace deal.[47] Yet Gove did not share the conciliatory nature of those who had lost loved ones in the Troubles, and his rage at the Good Friday Agreement seemed to intensify over time.

In July 2000, Gove published the essay for which he had been awarded the Charles Douglas-Home Award, entitled 'The Price of Peace'. From the opening line, Gove pulled no punches. 'Criticism of the Northern Ireland peace process has become the closest thing in our secular society to blasphemy,' he opined. His rhetoric only scaled up from there. Gove argued that the Good Friday deal was akin to the Munich Agreement as he humbly elevated himself to the stature of Churchill warning of the gathering storm: 'Those who warned of the consequences of appeasement in the Thirties were derided as glamour boys, renegades and war-mongers. But if it were not for their opposition then who would there have been to rescue the nation from folly?'[48]

It wasn't just the appeasers at Munich that Gove drew comparisons with when considering the peace process. Accepting that terrorist groups would not disarm before engaging in talks was likened to accepting paedophilia as a legitimate sexual desire:

The deliberate amoral calculation of terrorists was now elevated to a 'reality', like gravity or the weather, which was a simple fact of life. By this token, the desire of paedophiles to ensnare children is a 'reality' which must be accepted rather than confronted. The criminal is absolved of all moral responsibility for his actions and the law-abiding must alter their behaviour, and expectations, to accommodate him.[49]

Gove didn't limit himself to the Good Friday Agreement itself, but went on to argue that New Labour was using Northern Ireland as a 'laboratory animal' for a 'vision of human rights which privileges contending minorities at the expense of the democratic majority'. In pushing for a police force which was more representative of the Northern Irish community, Blair had turned the Royal Ulster Constabulary into a 'political plaything' more focused on 'fashionable social theories and precise ethnic composition' than upholding the law.

Gove's criticism of the Northern Ireland Human Rights Commission went even further.

> Creating new rights to eradicate 'disablism' would mean that institutions such as the police, fire service or army would no longer be able to discriminate in favour of the able-bodied. Campaigners against sex discrimination have already ensured that the fire service cannot discriminate against women. The price, however, of this equality, has been that those in danger are forced to depend on firefighters who lack the physical strength to discharge their duties. It is a situation which can only get worse.[50]

He also turned his mind to what was then termed transsexual rights, stating, 'Creating new rights for transsexuals again allows common sense to be supplanted by legal intrusion. Will new rights to marry, adopt and enter any job of their choosing be extended? And if so, at what cost to the dignity, stability and durability of our tested notions of married life?'[51]

Having torn down the Good Friday Agreement, Gove argued that there are only two solutions to the Northern Ireland issue: 'Ulster's future lies, ultimately, either as a Province of the United Kingdom or a united Ireland. Attempts to fudge or finesse that truth only create an ambiguity which those who profit by violence will seek to exploit.'[52] As a dedicated Unionist, Gove did not support the reunification of Ireland, instead opting for a strong approach to security in the province. No representation for Sinn Féin unless the IRA decommissioned all its weapons, no special status for Catholics in any of the institutions, and a reformed Assembly that would not force rival parties into coalitions. 'It might be argued that such a policy would trigger an upsurge in terrorist, especially republican, violence,' Gove conceded. 'But this only reinforces the point that Britain is in danger of transforming the government of part of our democracy to appease a terrorist threat.'[53]

The essay is classic Gove. Find an argument and take it to the extreme. Use deliberately controversial rhetorical flourishes to essentially shock the reader into agreeing with you. It was a technique he had developed while a student at Robert Gordon's College (much to the chagrin of Mike Duncan), honed at the Oxford Union and despatched on numerous occasions since – and would do again throughout his political career. However, the discussion of paedophiles, female firefighters and trans people apart, the thrust of the essay's argument is the same point Gove had expressed to Peter Bottomley in *A Stab in the Dark* back in 1992: 'Surely the message is: terrorism works.'

On 25 July 2000, Gove used his column in *The Times* to flag up the release of his pamphlet. To ensure the article had a current edge, the first third of the piece centred on the murder of eight-year-old Sarah Payne, whose body had been found in a field in West Sussex eight days earlier. 'If, as we all pray, Sarah Payne's killer is caught and convicted then there is no doubt what punishment we should exact … The killer should be imprisoned for life,' he wrote. Gove then contrasted the moral outrage to Payne's death from liberals such as the *Mirror*'s Brian Reade and *The Guardian*'s Jonathan Freedland to the response to the early release of IRA terrorists: 'Those, in liberal newspapers and Government, who can clearly articulate our moral revulsion towards one murdered seek to smother it when directed towards others.' He concludes by saying the IRA and their allies are now 'dancing on the graves of children'.

The argument, unsurprisingly, proved controversial. Indeed, *The Guardian* dedicated a leader on 29 July to directly taking on Gove's accusations of moral hypocrisy:

> As Michael Gove, the *Times* columnist and author of a new pamphlet on the peace process, argued this week, we would not let Sarah Payne's killer walk free after four years, so why James McArdle? His error is to pretend that Northern Ireland is West Sussex: it is not. Whether it was the shoot-to-kill policy of the 1980s, Diplock courts or internment, Northern Ireland has not enjoyed the same rule of law as the rest of the United Kingdom. That is because a war has been fought there.

As well as taking a battering ram to what was viewed as one of the Labour government's crowning glories, Gove also used his weekly column in *The Times* to muse on the goings-on of the Conservative Party. At the end of 1999, the question of whether Hague was leading the Tories as a Mod or a Rocker became clear. In December, the government put forward plans to repeal Section 28 of the Local Government Act 1988. The notorious piece of legislation instructed local authorities – and the schools under their jurisdiction – not to 'intentionally promote homosexuality or publish material with the intention of promoting homosexuality' or 'promote the teaching in any maintained school of the acceptability of homosexuality as a pretended family relationship'.

Getting Section 28 repealed became a touchstone for gay rights campaigners throughout the 1980s and 1990s, and Labour were determined to see it wiped from the statute book. For the Conservatives, backing its repeal would have been a sign that the party was starting to learn the lessons from the 1997 general election defeat. It would show that Tories, as Portillo had put it, are 'as capable as any other of comprehending the diversity of human nature'.

The leadership took a different view. Hague instructed his MPs and peers to vote against any attempt to repeal Section 28, and sacked frontbencher Shaun Woodward for refusing to toe the line. Woodward, who later defected to Labour, wasn't the only Conservative angry with the party's position on the issue. Ivan Massow, an insurance magnate who specialised in offering cover to the gay community, was mulling over whether to stand as the Conservative candidate for the Mayor of London in the inaugural election in 2000. Hague was keen on the idea, as having an openly gay, metropolitan young man representing the party would be a visual representation of how progressive the Tories were. In an article in *The Times* on 9 July 1999, Ed Vaizey called for Massow to be selected as 'it would signal the long overdue demolition of the cramped Victorian quarters in which the Tory party has confined itself'. The article came only a few months before Portillo made his own revelations about his past, and it seemed for a brief moment as if the Tories truly were becoming the tolerant and open party the Mods had hoped for. However, Hague's support for Section 28 was a symbol that the Rockers were very much still in charge of the party. Massow lost out in his bid to be the party's mayoralty candidate, and in August 2000 he quit the Tories and defected to Labour. Massow refused to go quietly, telling *The Independent* that the Conservatives under Hague were now 'less compassionate, more intolerant and just plain nasty'.[54] He added, 'The Tories have exploited … Section 28, to stir up prejudice and fear … They ignore the facts and pander to hatred.'

Massow's outburst would not normally have caused any great

problems for Gove, but the matter was somewhat close to home as up until a few weeks before his defection the pair had been sharing a flat in Mayfair, along with Westminster City Councillor Nick Boles. The arrangement was described by Massow as 'like Tory *Friends*', in reference to the popular sitcom. In truth, it seems Gove and Boles were the Chandler and Joey of the flat, with Massow a more distant Ross figure. Massow would allege in 2009 that his chances of becoming a Tory councillor had been deliberately scuppered by Boles. 'In floods of tears, he told me he was jealous of all my other successes, and wanted something for himself that was better than me, which was why he'd ruined my chances,' Massow claimed.[55]

It was clear that any attempt to modernise the Tories was going to fail under the leadership of Hague, and Gove was starting to realise it. In February 1999, he had accompanied Hague on a trip to North America aimed at boosting the statesman credentials of the Tory leader and picking up some tips from conservative allies on how to take on Tony Blair's 'third way' rhetoric.

In what proved to be an influential moment for the future Education Secretary, Gove reported on Hague's visits to schools in New York's East Harlem district, where standards had drastically improved. The school visit was the brainchild of Daniel Finkelstein, the former head of the Conservative Research Department who had been promoted to Hague's chief policy advisor. Gove wrote glowingly of the schools he encountered. Gone were the metal detectors and weapons searches apparently commonplace a decade before. 'Now parents from Manhattan's most prosperous districts fight to have their children enrolled. In London terms it's as though Chelsea mothers were scratching their eyes out to send little Jasper to state school in Harlesden,'[56] Gove cooed, before putting into print a reflection he would eventually turn into policy:

The reason for the turnaround, Mr Hague discovered, was wrapped up in a word with which the Tories have had their difficulties – devolution. Teachers and parents had grabbed powers from the New York Central Board of Education to run their schools in their ways. They worked imaginatively and reinvented the whole idea of what a school was.

While the trip may have opened Gove's eyes to a new way of structuring the education system, it did not offer him the same insight into the Tory leader. 'Mr Hague is a very difficult man to get the measure of. Although I swigged Heineken with him at 30,000ft, followed in his footsteps around Harlem schools and shot the stratospheric breeze with him about Conservative philosophy, my conclusions about his character are still, just, provisional,'[57] Gove reflected.

The main takeaway for Gove seemed to be that Hague and his wife, Ffion, were genuinely in love. He notes how, on one flight, 'Ffion gently massaged the Tory leader's shoulders before settling into the seat opposite and coiling her calves around his.' He added, 'I suspect that the protective arm, and unfurrowed brow, the qualities which we were once unafraid to call manly, are more attractive to many woman than the feeble emoting of the New Man. Ffion certainly seems to think so.'[58]

But that 'feeble emoting' seems to cut to Gove's main criticism of Hague: 'In an emotionally literate age persuasion is more than a matter of logic. For compassionate conservatism to make sense, it must have passion at its heart,' Gove continues.

'Compassionate conservatism' was the very thing Massow accused the Tories of lacking when he quit the party, but ahead of the October 2000 conference, Gove seemed reluctant to echo the criticism from his former flatmate.

Fuel protests that had gripped the country the previous month had seen the Tories ahead of Labour in the opinion polls for the first time since 1992. While Labour had regained pole position by the time the conference season kicked off, Gove appeared to be convinced that Hague was doing a sterling job as leader. In an article on 3 October 2000, Hague was deemed to be reaching out 'to all those voters Mr Major left behind', despite the row over Section 28. As Gove saw it, all the leader had to do was chose whether to embrace the politics of his shadow Home Secretary Ann Widdecombe or shadow Chancellor Michael Portillo to further increase support.

Widdecombe was a favourite with the party faithful thanks to her no-nonsense approach to law and order. The former Prisons minister did as much as Hague to destroy Michael Howard's chances of winning the 1997 leadership contest, infamously describing her former boss at the Home Office of having 'something of the night' about him. Her opposition to abortion, support for the death penalty and votes against equalising the age of consent for gay sex put her firmly in the category of 'Rocker', but that didn't stop Hague from promoting her from shadow Health Secretary to shadow Home Secretary in 1999. Gove described her appeal as having 'all the qualities of a cheap hock – it makes the party go with a swing, but is designed primarily to appeal to older customers and over-indulgence renders one increasingly ridiculous'. He suggested Widdecombe had an 'Old Testament opposition' to homosexuality and abortion, leaving her 'out of touch with the complexity of human choices'.[59]

The other ideological future, as Gove saw it, was epitomised by the 'Spanish fizz' of Portillo. According to his biographer, Portillo had 'been on a journey' since losing his seat in 1997, and was now pushing for a post-Thatcher conservatism that was 'economically emancipatory, socially progressive, rhetorically modest'. Gove maintained that Portillo 'articulates a Toryism framed for a younger, more metropolitan Britain.'[60]

The article leaves the reader wondering where it is exactly that Gove thinks the Tory Party needs to position itself. It's all very well claiming that Hague was 'relaxed about sexual or ethnic difference', but having argued that Widdecombe's views left her out of touch with modern values, there is surprisingly little recognition that making Widdecombe his shadow Home Secretary leaves Hague open to accusations of failing to practise what he preaches.

Perhaps it is because, for all his hints otherwise, Gove was as guilty of 'Old Testament' thinking as Widdecombe. Was he drinking 'cheap hock' two years earlier when he used his *Times* column to call for the return of the death penalty? That was no reactionary one-off, as in May 2001 he penned an article which harked back to the days when the Tories were perceived as demonising single parents. After claiming that Labour's tax policy 'favoured illegitimate births' and could be seen as 'anti-family', he wrote:

> [The government] takes taxes from us to fund baby bank accounts and more generous child benefits. The money is allocated irrespective of parents' marital status, so that every child sees the State, not wedded parents, as its provider. Not only is our money taken, but more will be needed to deal with the social costs of subsidising children raised outside wedlock, where their life chances are diminished.[61]

The 2000 conference was indeed dominated by Portillo and Widdecombe. Portillo used his speech in Bournemouth to urge his party to show respect for all, telling activists, 'We are for all Britons – black Britons, British Asians, white Britons – we are for people whatever their sexual orientation.'[62]

Yet even if that was the face Hague wanted the Conservative Party to show the world, it was masked within hours as Widdecombe announced a hardline drugs policy. She called for anyone possessing even the smallest amount of cannabis to face a minimum fine of £100 – a policy which hit the newspapers before Hague was aware of it.[63] Police chiefs struck back against the plan, saying it would impact resources, and a conference that was supposed to be about showing that the Conservatives were ready for government instead descended into whether Cabinet ministers had ever smoked cannabis.

A *Times* write-up of the conference described it as 'Mods and Rockers fight for power', arguing that while Portillo has 'substantially reinvented himself as a man of compassion', Hague has 'gone in the opposite direction'.[64] Gove's assessment of the conference was that the cannabis row had done the party more good than harm. Yes, the spectacle of the shadow Cabinet arguing in public was not a good look to the voters, but the reaction against Widdecombe's policy – with eight shadow Cabinet ministers admitting they had smoked the drug[65] – showed that some in the party were willing to challenge 'Rocker' views.

'It seems clear that the momentum is with the party's liberal wing,' Gove wrote, adding, 'The applause for Portillo's message of respect for minorities, Francis Maude's argument for social inclusion and John Bercow's apologia for past prejudice may not have been as clamorous as Ann Widdecombe's conference ovations, but it's lasted longer.'[66]

He then went on to predict, 'The effect on perceptions of the Conservative party will endure beyond the drugs row.' In the world of Gove, or at least the window he provided through his articles in *The Times*, the flowerbeds in the Conservative garden were about to spring forth with the flora of victory.

His apparent optimism did not last. In February 2001, Gove appeared to finally wake up to the fact that the British public had not done a dramatic about-turn on the verdict it had delivered on the Tories just four years earlier, and it would take more than a few Cabinet ministers admitting they once smoked a spliff to truly show that the party was fit for the twenty-first century. 'Their unpopularity has nothing to do with Mr Hague's lack of hair, children, or even a plausible rival to Alastair Campbell,' he surmised.[67] Instead, it was a lack of ideology. Gove, who seemed to have forgotten his attack on Blair's lack of ideology five years earlier when he accused the Labour leader of using the word 'community' with 'the enthusiasm of a Keith Floyd adding wine to a casserole, providing a sophisticated flavour and disguising the lack of beef', suggested the Tories needed to ape the current government and develop a coherent framework for its policies. He cites the Conservatives' education policy, which would see the development of 'free schools' acting outside of government control. 'The Tories have failed to articulate how their policy would give parents the schools they want,' he warns, bluntly, adding, 'All the Tories offer on education is process, not vision.' He ends the article on a despairing note: 'I may be wrong. I hope I am. But I can hear the distant rumble of another deluge. And time is running precious short to steer a better course.'[68]

Gove was right, and the Tories were indeed set for another battering in the coming election. Yet, unlike in the aftermath of the 1997 defeat, Gove was adamant he wanted to play a part in the party's revival. The Notting Hill set was about to break out of west London cafés, but it would be a maverick from Durham who would have the first stab at rebuilding the Conservatives – a man who many years later would almost cause its destruction. And Gove would be the man to unleash him upon Westminster. But first, he had some personal business to attend to.

CHAPTER 10

THE MARRIAGE PLOT

To celebrate Sarah Vine's 34th birthday, Gove took her for dinner at the Connaught Hotel in the heart of London's plush Mayfair district. The couple had been together for three years, and stowed on the dessert trolley was an extra-special birthday present.[1] After discovering the engagement ring, Vine said yes, and the upcoming nuptials were announced in *The Times* on Friday 4 May 2001.

Before Gove's mind could fully turn to wedding preparations, there was the small matter of the 2001 general election to contend with. Alas for Conservative supporters, it was déjà vu all over again on the morning of 8 June: another landslide defeat for the Conservative Party, another leader quitting at the earliest opportunity. 'It is vital that the party be given the chance to choose a leader who can build on my work and also take new initiatives,' said William Hague as he announced his resignation.[2] *The Times* declared his departure as 'in the best interests of his party' in a leader on 9 June, as it called for a new philosophy from whoever succeeded him. Despite an almost identical result to 1997 – the Tories had managed a net gain of just one seat – *The Times* seemed in a more buoyant mood than it had four years earlier. In 1997, the paper proclaimed, 'Difficult as the Conservatives' position is, it could still get worse.' Despite having almost been proved correct, the 2001 leader article said, 'The Conservative Party is not dead, nor even in a deep coma, but it has to be willing to change in order to have any chance of returning to office quickly.'[3]

Gove used his weekly column in which to carry out his own post-mortem on the Conservatives' election campaign:

> The elevation of Section 28 into a talisman protecting family life, the suggestion that the war against drugs should be fought in middle-class teenagers' bedrooms, the estrangement from the difficulties women have juggling work and family, all distanced the Tories from significant sections of our country. It denied them not just support but even a hearing.[4]

The election result wasn't all bad for Gove: a smattering of his friends had found success at the ballot box. David Cameron was elected MP for Witney in Oxfordshire – succeeding Shaun Woodward, the shadow minister who quit William Hague's frontbench over Section 28 and subsequently defected to Labour. George Osborne had won Tatton in Cheshire from independent Martin Bell, while Paul Goodman – a former comment editor at the *Telegraph* who had met Gove on the right-wing drinks circuit – was the new MP for Wycombe.

While these new parliamentarians were held in high regard by the Westminster bubble, there was another entrant in the class of 2001 who had already shown he could reach parts of the electorate others could not. Boris Johnson was the new MP for Henley, having succeeded another blonde bombshell, Michael Heseltine. Since his shaky start as a journalist at the end of the 1980s, Johnson's career had gone from strength to strength, culminating with him being named editor of *The Spectator* in 1999.

He had originally promised the magazine's proprietor, Conrad

Black, that he would not pursue a career in politics, but, having also set himself the personal goal of becoming a Cabinet minister by the age of thirty-five, Johnson went back on the pledge. (Not that getting elected in 2001 helped him deliver on his own personal promise: the election was twelve days before his thirty-seventh birthday.)

Johnson had the beginnings of a national profile before he entered Parliament, largely thanks to an appearance on *Have I Got News For You* in 1998, and much of the focus on the new batch of MPs centred on his bumbling persona and whether he would continue as editor of *The Spectator* while serving as an MP. Prior to the election, Johnson had invited four potential successors for the top job for lunch – Stephen Glover, Alice Thomson, Matthew D'Ancona and Gove. It was, of course, not a serious attempt to gauge which one would replace him, but just a way of fuelling rumours. As Gove later explained, it was Johnson's way of saying, 'I know what you buggers are up to – I can have a laugh at your expense.'[5] Johnson stayed as editor.

When Gove profiled the stand-out new MPs elected in 2001, he warned that while Johnson's ascent had been swift thus far, Parliament was a different beast to any he had encountered before: 'The Commons tends to be suspicious of those who have enjoyed conspicuous success before entering and Boris may have to tread carefully to ensure that his talents flourish.'[6]

Other MPs picked out by Gove included, unsurprisingly, David Cameron and George Osborne, as well as Paul Goodman, Mark Francois and Mark Field.

Seeing his friends and colleagues enter Parliament, combined with yet another landslide defeat for the Tories, seemed to stir something in Gove. While he had spent the past four years throwing grenades at both Labour and the Conservatives from the pages of *The Times*, he had offered very few constructive ideas in terms of what policies the country's politicians should be pursuing. In a bid to remedy that shortcoming, he clubbed together with his old friend Ed Vaizey and former flatmate Nick Boles to produce a book aimed at kick-starting a debate about what the Conservative Party needed to do to return to power. The book would take the form of a series of chapters written by different thinkers within the movement, with Gove, Vaizey and Boles acting as editors.

While the project was under gestation, there was the small matter of the Conservative leadership contest to deal with. There was of course no doubt where Gove's loyalties lay, and it seemed that surely this time the chalice, poisoned or otherwise, was there for Michael Portillo's taking. The shadow Chancellor had successfully rebranded himself from a headbanging Thatcherite Rocker into a socially liberal 21st-century Tory Mod since his return to politics in 1999.

The first ballot of Tory MPs saw Portillo finish first, with forty-nine of the 166 votes on offer. Second was shadow Defence Secretary Iain Duncan Smith, a candidate very much to the right of Portillo on social issues and Europe. His thirty-nine votes put him three ahead of Ken Clarke in third place, while Michael Ancram and David Davis tied in fourth place with twenty-one votes each.

The ballot was rerun two days later to establish a genuine last place so a candidate could be eliminated. Davis had eighteen votes, compared to seventeen for Ancram, meaning the latter was out of the race. Worryingly for the Portillo camp, of the seven Tories who switched their votes during the rerun, only one opted for him. While he still came out on top, Duncan Smith and Clarke secured three more votes each. The momentum was disappearing from Portillo's campaign.

Ahead of the third ballot, Davis withdrew his candidacy and

announced his support for Duncan Smith. Ancram also urged his supporters to back the shadow Defence Secretary. Heading into what would be the final vote of MPs before the top two candidates went before the party membership, Portillo's biographer tried his best to knock down the support for Clarke to help get his man over the line. On the day of the final ballot, Gove published an article under the headline 'Why Ken Clarke is Blair's Trojan horse'. He then gave an absolute kicking to the former Chancellor. 'If the Tories vote for Clarke today they will have proved that the gods do wish to destroy them, for they will have gone mad,' he claimed, going on to explain his reasoning. 'For, despite the claims of his wilfully blind supporters, there can now be no doubt that a Clarke candidacy taken to the grass roots will reignite Tory passions over Europe. Any Clarke leadership that might follow would see the Conservative party consumed by warfare on the issue.'[7]

Wanting to avoid the Tories being torn apart by Europe was of course an important consideration, and, for Gove, the other two men in the race would avoid that fate: 'Neither Portillo nor Duncan Smith wants to reopen the European row. They thought it was settled by the referendum [of Conservative members on the UK joining the euro] William Hague held which confirmed that 85 per cent of the party wanted to hold the sceptical line.'

His conclusion was as brutal as it was clinical: 'A vote for either is a vote for a future, a vote for Clarke is a dash to the rocks.'

Conservative MPs chose not to heed his advice. Far from losing support, Clarke topped the third ballot, winning fifty-nine votes. Duncan Smith came second with fifty-four. Portillo finished third, just one vote behind Duncan Smith, and was eliminated. Gove watched the announcement of the result on a television in the *Times* office. Peter Stothard remembers Gove being 'really upset about it',[8] while another colleague recalls seeing him getting a text message within seconds of the news that Portillo was out. It simply read: 'Fuck'.[9]

Reflecting on the leadership contest, Duncan Smith says:

> Portillo destroyed himself ... He fought a terrible campaign. He fought a campaign that was based on winning the next election, not winning the leadership campaign. So what he did was he refused to talk about any of the subjects that anybody wanted to talk about – taxation, economy, Europe. He wanted to talk about social liberalism and everything else, which at that stage was a tough road to push. His thinking, whoever was advising him, had said, 'You've got to reach out beyond the Conservative Party, forget about the MPs.'[10]

In yet another profile piece of his fallen idol, Gove speculated on what the one-time 'future of the Right' would do with his days now his frontline political career was over: 'There is a strong service ethos in Portillo's make-up which could lead him to take up a prominent public-sector position, possibly on the international stage ... A more rounded and cultural figure than most politicians, he could play a role in the arts. Opera beckons where he has an expert's appreciation.'[11]

Portillo's exit from the leadership race wasn't all bad for Gove. Duncan Smith was a contact he had cultivated during the Maastricht rebellion days of the Major government. The pair had met a year before the 2001 election to discuss the future of the party. 'We'd had serious conversations about where we thought the leadership was going, not in a conspiratorial way but simply on the basis of me trying to pick his brains and him me,' Duncan Smith remembers.[12]

While Clarke and Duncan Smith spent the summer locking horns, Gove was putting the final touches to his wedding plans.

With his bride's parents now residing in Monaco, it was decided that a ceremony in the south of France would be appropriate, and Notre-Dame de la Nativité, in the town of Vence – located an hour's drive west of his future in-laws – was selected. In August 2001, Gove and Vine flew into Nice Airport to see family and finalise the wedding preparations. The flight was not an easy one. The plane encountered turbulence as it circled the airport preparing to land, prompting a sharp acceleration which left children crying and other passengers shrieking.[13] The incident had a long-lasting effect on Gove. 'I thought that I could put that experience behind me,' he later wrote, 'but something had been implanted in my mind which grew.'[14]

Having survived that not particularly near-death experience, the groom-to-be turned his mind to his stag do, planned for the weekend of 15 and 16 September 2001 at Cliveden House, a luxury hotel in Berkshire.[15] It was set to be a busy week, with the result of the Conservative leadership contest due to be announced on 12 September.

On Monday 10 September, Gove retired to an office in the corner of the *Times* newsroom to pull together his weekly column, a process which usually took no more than an hour. That week's article focused on the need for military action in the Middle East. 'The West should support democracy, not more concessions to terrorism' was the sub-heading, as he hit out at the West's insistence that Israel should enter into peace talks with Palestine – a land he described as a 'terrorist state'.

The day the article was published, 11 September 2001, the question of Middle East-facilitated terrorism sensationally moved from Gove's column on page 14 of *The Times* to the top of the international news agenda.

When the first plane hit the World Trade Center in New York, at 1.45 p.m. UK time on 11 September, the *Times* editor, Peter Sto-thard, carried on with his lunch. 'You knew the newspaper could handle that,'[16] he reflected. When news came through of the second plane fifteen minutes later, it was all hands on deck.

As those footage of the attacks played into the *Times* newsroom, and reports of a plane hitting the Pentagon and another crashing in Pennsylvania came through, speculation was rife as to who was behind the attack on America.

Mary Ann Sieghart remembers that when she first heard the name of the terrorist group which would within hours be known around the world:

> First of all they thought it was the Popular Front for the Libera-tion of Palestine or something, and I remember Michael saying, 'It's Al-Qaeda' and I said, 'Al who?' I'd never even heard of them then. No one was talking about them. You had to be incredibly well informed to have even heard of them.[17]

Gove had made it his business to be well informed about such mat-ters. Ever since hearing tales of the Holy Land while a parishioner at Causewayend Church in Aberdeen as a child, the geopolitics of the Middle East had fascinated him. He drew parallels between the wars involving Israel and the conflict in Northern Ireland, believ-ing that in both cases the Goliaths were more sinned against than sinners.

He first mentioned Osama bin Laden in the pages of *The Times* in the summer of 1998, with an almost throwaway reference during a discussion about the government's attempt to set up a Race Re-lations Forum.[18]

Gove had also written about the rise of Islamic fundamentalism long before the 9/11 attacks. An article on 19 January 1999 began with a fairly weak rant about the experience of shopping at IKEA, before branching off into a surprisingly sympathetic exploration of the appeal of anti-Western Islamists:

> For Britain's young Muslims, the reality of our professed multiculturalism is a consumerist monoculturalism. They already endure unemployment and discrimination. They are denied the protection in law offered to other minorities. But the real offence is neither economic nor legal, but cultural. Britain affects respect for other cultures, but seeks to suffocate them. We are not living in a patchwork society but under a continental quilt.

After setting out why young British Muslims might feel suffocated, he contended that Western interventionism had let down Muslims across the world: 'If an Islamic state offends, such as Iraq, then the B52s scramble. But when Muslims are the victims, as in Kosovo, then we pass by on the other side.' His blunt observation was that the West was happy to deploy forces to protect commodities such as 'Kuwaiti oil or African diamonds', but not to protect 'liberal principles'.

He added:

> It is therefore easy to understand why an initial distaste for the consumer culture of the West may harden into something altogether harsher. Where is the moral superiority in our anodised culture of consumption? For young Muslims seeking an identity which confers a sense of dignity, the appeal of fundamentalism is regrettable, but understandable. The Mujahidin of North Yemen and the Kosovan hills can capture young Muslim imaginations now as powerfully as the Republican figures of the Spanish Civil War inspired idealist youth in the Thirties.

Gove's desire for the West to protect 'liberal principles', and therefore provide a 'sense of dignity', underpinned his repeated calls for
the assassination of Iraqi dictator Saddam Hussein. 'The only satis-
factory means of ensuring that Iraq's weapons of mass destruction
are not used is to kill Saddam and his Takriti clansman,' he wrote
on 17 November 1998. On 16 January 2001, he urged Tony Blair to
align himself with the incoming US President, the 'proper jingoist'
George W. Bush, to deal with Hussein, and a month later he again
spoke of the need to 'get rid of him'.[19]

Gove was very much a hawk, and the 9/11 attacks were, in his
mind at least, a validation of his almost Churchillian 'gathering
storm' rhetoric. His view on the atrocity was published in *The Times*
on 13 September, and was clearly bashed out in something of a hurry
without undergoing the usual editing process – it keeps referring to
the events of 'yesterday' despite the fact that the attacks had taken
place two days earlier. With a leap to judgement that George W.
Bush would have welcomed, Gove pointed the finger at the states
which must be held responsible for sponsoring, facilitating and
organising Islamist terror: 'Syria, Sudan, Iran, and, above all, Iraq'.

Gove argued, 'Action against Iraq is … the most important step
the free world can take to safeguard its security.' He set out examples of links between Baghdad and Bin Laden, claimed Iraq was at
the 'apex' of work across the Middle East to help Islamic terrorists,
and, perhaps most worryingly of all, added that the country had
'continued to develop its stockpile of nuclear, chemical and biolog-
ical weapons of mass destruction … which, whether delivered by
suitcase, suicide bomber or missile, could transcend even yesterday's
death toll'.

The next day, Gove was appealing for Blair to become Bush's
advocate-in-chief for any military action the US would take in
response to the attacks. Under the headline 'Blair's experience of

Kosovo conflict gives him unique access to Bush', Gove waxed lyrical about the Prime Minister's seemingly unparalleled skills on the world stage. 'Uniquely among Western statesmen, [Blair] is a leader who has seen through a war and emerged with his international reputation enhanced,' he wrote, referring to the UK's intervention in the Balkans in the late 1990s.[20] 'Whatever position one takes on the wisdom of the initial intervention, once Nato took the collective decision to face down Slobodan Milosevic, it was Mr Blair who emerged as the coalition's strongest link.' Gove called on the Prime Minister to use his 'privileged position' with Bush to 'influence the shape of any response', but not to heed the calls from those on the 'Labour Left' to 'counsel caution'. 'Mr Blair is at his best when he leads from the front,' he concluded. Over the next few months, every word of Gove's advice would be – indirectly – heeded.

Gove took a break from talking up the burgeoning Blair–Bush relationship to focus on the object of his own desires: his stag do went ahead as scheduled, despite the dramatic increase in the news agenda, and some five weeks later, on Saturday 20 October, Michael and Sarah were married. Ed Vaizey was best man, and the sixty or so guests included David and Samantha Cameron, the latter then pregnant with the couple's first child; George and Frances Osborne; and feminist writer and *Times* colleague Caitlin Moran.[21] ('He's the most charming person I've ever met. He's incredibly funny, incredibly clever,' she said of Gove in 2014.)[22] The honeymoon was a two-week jaunt to Mexico, but Gove was not entirely looking forward to the holiday. The turbulent ending to his flight to the south of France earlier that summer had developed into a full-fledged fear of flying – a condition not helped by four planes being hijacked in America a few weeks later. The return journey was even worse than the outward trip and, after staying awake the entire transatlantic flight, he found himself clinging to Sarah 'with an intensity that seemed almost unseemly in front of a few hundred others' as the plane came in to land.[23] His aversion to aviation persisted for many years, and he eventually resorted to seeing a hypnotist to cure him of the fear.[24]

Aside from his wedding, the honeymoon and the deadliest terrorist attack in world history, there was another event that occupied Gove's mind in the autumn of 2001.

On 13 September, Iain Duncan Smith was announced as the leader of the Conservative Party. He secured 61 per cent of the membership vote compared to the 39 per cent won by Kenneth Clarke. His leadership unveiling, coming just two days after the 11 September attacks, received little attention.

Gove, of course, paid it a great deal of thought. Having watched the Conservatives stumble and fumble through the previous four years as the New Labour juggernaut rumbled on, he was not prepared to sit on the sidelines this time. His friends Cameron and Osborne were in Parliament, but as new backbenchers they had little influence over the direction of the party.

One way Gove and others on the periphery of the party sought to turn the fortunes of the Conservatives around was through the book *A Blue Tomorrow*, the project initiated by Gove, Boles and Vaizey. It was published in time for the party conference and contained contributions from, among others, future Cabinet minister Justine Greening; Kit Malthouse, who would become an MP in 2015; and the newly elected Mark Field. Greening's chapter focused on the NHS, arguing it was worth 'pursuing' private sector involvement in some aspects of the health service in order to improve delivery.[25] Malthouse called for all direct taxes to be abolished, while Field argued that one of the ways to win back young, urban voters was by providing affordable housing for key workers.

The book was seen as Portilloist document – not just because of

Gove's association but because Portillo's former chief press spokesman Malcolm Gooderham was another contributor. It generated
some minor press interest, with *The Guardian* focusing in on Gooderham's claim that under Hague's leadership the Tories focused
on traditional Conservative issues like Europe and asylum and had
nothing to say on social concerns such as drugs, deprivation and
poverty of ambition.[26] On 23 November, Hywel Williams, Gove's
friend from the Roy Jenkins Society, gave the book a fuller, but
mostly damning, review in *The Guardian*. 'Conventional complaints
about failure to listen leap from these pages with a persistently
shrill tone,' he claimed, adding later, 'They talk the talk of elec-
torally-enforced humility but walk a walk which is betrayed by its
swagger. They want Toryism to be virtually normal again – and so
contentious issues have to be presented as if they were just common
sense.'[27] However, Williams recognised that with a book such as
this, the people who are writing it is as important as what is being
written. He acknowledged the book as 'an important political
event', adding, 'Some can write; all are ambitious for a toehold on
a future which might belong to them. What they think matters –
their words are the graffiti on the Tory wall.'

Having helped set out a blueprint of ideas, Gove now wanted to
have an influence right at the top of the party. And he knew just
the man to help.

CHAPTER 11

CHANGING PLACES

It was a breakfast at the Royal Automobile Club in 1998 when Gove first met Dominic Cummings. The meal had been organised by Rodney Leach, a Conservative-backing businessman who was bringing Eurosceptics together in opposition to the single currency.[1] He had recently founded Business for Sterling, a lobby group featuring a thousand chairmen and chief executives, to help make the case for the UK to retain the pound. Cummings was being tapped up by Leach to become the group's campaign director. Born in Durham on 25 November 1971, Cummings was the son of an oil rig project manager and a special needs teacher. After attending a state primary school, he was educated at the fee-paying Durham School before studying Ancient and Modern History at Exeter College, Oxford. After graduating in 1994, Cummings shunned the typical route of launching a career in the City, politics or further academia and instead moved to Russia. According to a ConservativeHome profile in 2014, 'He helped set up a new airline flying from Samara, on the Volga, to Vienna. The KGB issued threats, the airline only got one passenger, and the pilot unfortunately took off without that passenger. Cummings is a Russophile, speaks Russian and is passionately interested in Dostoyevsky.'[2]

In 1999, Cummings joined Business for Sterling – initially as head of research – and it wasn't long before his unconventional methods were making the papers. On 1 November 1999, Cummings was accused of instigating a 'fracas' with the pro-euro chairman of the CBI's Small and Medium Enterprise Council. According to *The Times*, Colin Perry 'told friends he had been threatened and held against a wall' by Cummings after a 'heated head-to-head debate' on Radio 5 Live. Cummings's defence was the pair had 'stumbled into each other'.[3]

Despite a complaint to Leach, Cummings kept his job, and he would pop up sporadically in reports about the campaign to stop the UK joining the single currency. On 10 March 2000, he hit out at planned expenditure by Chancellor Gordon Brown on upgrading IT systems in Whitehall to cope with a shift to the euro. 'Almost 90 per cent of businesses have rejected the government's call for "intensive euro preparations" which would cost the country the whole NHS budget for a year,' he said. 'People would rather spend the money on health or the development of the internet.'[4]

After Cummings moved from head of research to campaign director, the lines coming out of Business for Sterling became even more antagonistic, and not just to those on the opposite side of the debate. In the run-up to the 2001 election, in which William Hague focused his campaign on stopping the UK joining the euro, the group refused any attempts to join forces with the Tories. Cummings's explanation was simple and, like his NHS argument a year earlier, would echo all the way to 2016: 'I have lost count of the number of times I have said that if the No Campaign were to be right-wing and based on sovereignty and the Union Jack – while the other side focus on jobs and living standards – we will lose.'[5]

Further seeds of the 2016 EU referendum campaign can be seen in a stunt orchestrated by Cummings in September 2001. Anti-euro beer mats and posters were placed in 500 Wetherspoons pubs in a bid to reach out to voters through non-traditional tactics. 'Thirty per cent of the public are strongly hostile to the idea of replacing the pound but the next 30 per cent, though on our side, do not know enough about the euro. It is this 30 per cent we are now talking to,' Cummings said at the time.[6]

Gove had been instantly taken with Cummings. The pair had much in common. Both were privately educated, widely read, avowed Eurosceptics and Conservative by choice, not by instinct. 'What they have in common is an almost Leninist belief – almost Trotskyite belief, perhaps – that you have to permanently revolutionise,' comments one friend of Gove's, adding, 'Institutions have this incredibly strong drag effect and unless you are zealously fighting to push through your reforms they will die.'

But whereas Gove is famously polite, courteous and – when needed – deferential, Cummings is none of those things. The word many use to describe him – both in praise and in criticism – is anarchist. For Cummings, there are no cows too sacred to be spared from slaughter, and the more blood, the better.

Impressed by his friend's zeal, clear thinking and innate self-confidence – amply displayed by his work at Business for Sterling, Gove decided to pitch him to the new Conservative leader as the man who could help reform the party. A meeting was set up between the two, and Cummings made it clear what he believed the Conservatives needed to do start winning back voters. 'We've got to get off Europe,' he told Iain Duncan Smith.

It was, perhaps surprisingly for a Maastricht rebel who had hammered his leadership opponent over his pro-EU views, a diagnosis Duncan Smith shared, and in January 2002 he appointed Cummings the Conservatives' director of strategy. Yet far from this being match made in heaven, the relationship quickly turned sour. Cummings's unconventional methods riled up the party. 'What I hadn't been prepared for was he'd turn up in clothes that hadn't seen an iron, he was shambolic, and this upset a lot of MPs,' recalls Duncan Smith.

One journalist remembers well the dynamic of briefings involving Cummings and the Tory leader: 'You'd go along to these lunches for IDS at which Dominic would sit furiously at the other end of the table with his shirt progressively becoming undone, furiously denouncing people either present or absent, as IDS sat with his head down like an embarrassed vicar.'

With Cummings starting to run riot at Conservative Central Office, Gove became involved in yet another outlet seeking to influence the political discourse. Portillo was no longer the king-in-waiting, but his followers were still keen to bear his standard. Chief among them was Francis Maude, the former Europe minister who had managed Portillo's unsuccessful leadership campaign. Having served as shadow Chancellor and shadow Foreign Secretary under William Hague, Maude was on the back benches in the new regime but keen to push forward his modernising views. Along with fellow Portillo-backing MP Archie Norman, the pair established a new think tank called Xchange. ('That's all one word,' Maude said in an interview to promote the enterprise in December 2001. 'It's frightfully modern.')[7]

The pair needed a forward-thinking director to ensure the venture would do more than just reheat Thatcherism, and they turned to Nick Boles, Gove's former flatmate, who had failed to be selected for a seat in the 2001 election. The first thing Boles suggested was changing the name from XChange to Policy Exchange ('less "clever-clever"' he said in 2002).[8] Maude used an interview with Sir David Frost on 3 February 2002 to soft-launch the organisation, calling on Duncan Smith to ensure the Conservative Party 'is seen to be generous and broad and not too narrow'. A launch event was held at the Tate Britain gallery on 29 April 2002 with a call for elected mayors in every major UK city, as well as directly elected police chiefs.[9] Gove was involved in the conversations throughout its establishment and became the think tank's first chairman. The line between Gove the political commentator and Gove the political activist was becoming increasingly blurred.

The catalyst for this shift was not just a desire to see a Conservative Prime Minister installed in Downing Street but also the result of Gove's career at *The Times* plateauing. His move to home editor had not been an unqualified success, and in the race to be Peter Stothard's preferred successor he was falling behind. A clear indication that he was no longer the person to beat came in March 2000. Stothard was diagnosed with pancreatic cancer and took an indefinite leave of absence from the paper to receive treatment. It was not Gove who was appointed to steer the ship while the captain was away but the paper's deputy editor, Ben Preston. In April 2001, Gove was moved from his position as home affairs editor – having been in the post for little more than a year. He was given more of a free role under the title assistant editor and contributed articles to the T2 section of the paper as well as his weekly opinion column. Although it was spun as Gove becoming No. 4 in the paper's hierarchy,[10] it was an indication that he lacked the skills required to organise and discipline a team of journalists. Stothard returned from his cancer treatment at the end of 2001, but in February 2002 he decided to leave *The Times* for good. Yet, far from the Michael Gove versus Ben Preston bout to replace him that Stothard had envisaged, the paper's proprietor, Rupert Murdoch, opted for an outsider to shake up the newsroom. Robert Thomson, the Australian-born managing editor of the US edition of the *Financial Times*, was handed the gig.[11] 'Robert was in his early forties he wasn't massively older than Michael. I think at that point Michael realised it isn't necessarily going to happen,' a former *Times* colleague remembers.

Thomson was charged with reversing a perceived dumbing-down

of *The Times*, and there was speculation that Gove would be one of those forced out to make way for a new team.[12] In a bid to show that he was, first and foremost, a thinker, Gove began appearing on two BBC shows where he could display his cerebral nature. On 29 May 2002, he was announced as one of the regular pundits on the BBC Radio 4 show *The Moral Maze*, which saw a panel of journalists and commentators grill a 'witness' on a particular subject, decided only a day before transmission.[13] His second bid at displaying a hinterland came on 8 June 2002, when he joined BBC 2's *Newsnight Review*, broadcast around 11 p.m. on Friday nights. Gove would muse over the week's cultural highlights – be it art exhibitions, theatre productions, films or television shows. His most memorable moment on the programme came during a discussion of *Love Again*, a drama based on the life of the poet Philip Larkin. With a comment journalists would describe as 'turning the air blue', Gove said, 'Philip Larkin is portrayed as an emotional fuckwit.'[14]

It was fortunate for Gove that he was pursuing interests away from politics, as his attempts to have any sway over the direction of the Conservative Party were proving increasingly futile. While Policy Exchange was trying to make itself heard outside the party, the man Gove had helped install on the inside was struggling to win support for his ideas, in part due to his increasingly chaotic style of working. According to a report in *The Times*, Cummings

> wore sunglasses in the style of Jackie Kennedy, perched high on top of his head, but never wore ties. He drank whiskey on top of wine at lunchtime and fell asleep at his desk in the afternoon. He smoked cigarettes and swore in front of Iain Duncan Smith, then went out with his metro-chic friends.[15]

Matters were made worse by an interview Cummings gave to *The*

Independent in June 2002, in which he claimed that the Tory leader would have to take a backseat in any single currency referendum because his party was so unpopular. 'The biggest potential threat to the pound's survival is the Conservative Party,' said Cummings, adding, 'If the Conservative Party were to define the anti-euro campaign and articulate its message as it has in the past, then Blair has a real opportunity to win a referendum.'[16] Suffice to say, Cummings's stark intervention did not go down well with the party faithful, and Conservative chairman David Davis took to the airwaves to describe the comments as 'just plumb wrong'.[17] The pair carried on feuding and Davis was eventually sacked as chairman in July 2002.

Cummings followed him out of the Conservative Central Office door soon after. Former Tory chairman Lord Tebbit demanded his sacking in an article for the *Sunday Telegraph* on 18 August, attacking the 'spotty youths, researchers, assistants and party apparatchiks' in Central Office, naming Cummings directly.

A month later, Cummings quit. He had lasted eight months as the party's director of strategy, and his insistence that the Tories should focus on standing up for the vulnerable rather than invoking more traditional Conservative touchstones such as business, the economy and Europe had won him few friends – as had his destructive nature. Reflecting on Cummings's departure, Duncan Smith says:

It just didn't work and he knew it just wasn't working because the expectation of the Conservative Party and the hierarchy didn't work for him at all. Dom is essentially an anarchist really and that's how he works, and when he does that kind of stuff, that's what makes him successful. When you are in a party structure, that's incredibly difficult, and he took no account of that. You have to carry MPs with you on things. Of course, he was hacking them off left, right and centre.

With Cummings gone, Gove found himself directly caught up in the Mods *v.* Rockers battle still raging at the heart of the party. Along with Dean Godson, he had proposed that the Tories should take a much more interventionist approach to increase the diversity of its candidates for the next election. Women, ethnic minorities and LGBT candidates should be given preference for safe-seat selection, even if a white male applicant would be a better MP, according to a report circulated in Tory HQ. In order to ensure this bout of positive discrimination was not detected, if several women in a row were selected, it would 'be advisable to put a couple of white men on the next shortlist to allay suspicions of a feminist agenda. One can safely assume that the associations will snap up the men!'[18] The document was leaked to *The Observer* on the eve of the 2002 Conservative Party conference and managed to achieve what Gove had longed for: it united the modernisers and traditionalists. Unfortunately, it was a unity based on fury, not support. 'If this is the basis on which the party is seeking to deliver Iain Duncan Smith's bid for a genuinely representative party, it is doomed to failure,' said former party vice-chairman Steve Norris.[19]

The reaction to his ideas for diversifying candidates showed that Gove's influence on the Conservative leadership – which had never exactly been Peter Mandelson-esque – had fallen drastically. His position as heir apparent to Stothard had completely disappeared, and it seemed, for the first time since he had joined his fellow journalists on strike at the *Aberdeen Press and Journal*, that his career was drifting.

The same could not be said for his friends who had won seats in Parliament in the previous year's election. David Cameron in particular was keen to raise his profile, and no sooner had he been elected than he started writing a regular column for the *Guardian* website detailing the life of an ambitious backbencher. He then

secured a spot on the influential Home Affairs Select Committee
in July 2001, where he vehemently defended a report produced by
the group in 2002 calling for ecstasy to be downgraded from a Class
A drug to Class B and proposing the introduction of 'shooting gal-
leries' for heroin users. George Osborne also landed a spot on a
committee – in his case, Public Accounts. Boris Johnson was not
yet giving Parliament his full attention, as he was still editing *The
Spectator* – a position which gave him far more influence over the
party leadership than most backbenchers enjoyed.

Perhaps it was this combination of losing access to the Tory
leadership, having his name dragged into a row over candidate selection, and seeing his political friends pushing forward with their
own careers instead of coming to his defence that prompted Gove
to pen a rather vicious article in *The Spectator* on 12 October. Headlined 'The Maggie, Tony and Iain Show', Gove claimed it was the
Labour Prime Minister who was learning the right lessons from
the Iron Lady's legacy, not the Tories. 'Margaret Thatcher's initial
electoral breakthrough was a consequence of new breadth and new
allies, and openness to changing times, circumstances and popular
aspirations,' he wrote. By contrast, the current Conservative Party
represented 'the retired residents of southern seaside towns, those
in Britain's last great nationalised industry, agriculture, and all those
Englishmen seeking refuge from the modern world in homes that
aspire to be castles'. Gove then got personal, turning his frustration
directly on his elected friends:

> Even the youngest recruits, the 2001 intake which includes the
> editor of this magazine, practise their own form of retreat from
> the modern world. The pleasing rituals of parliamentary life,
> the easy charm of Home Counties cocktail parties, the club-
> bish camaraderie of the House, all conspire to make the current

generation of new Tories surprisingly complacent with their lot. Their speeches defending hunting and Gibraltar or deprecating spin and glitz find a warm response among those who are still listening in South Barsetshire.

But they are increasingly detached from the concerns of those whom Tories once naturally represented in seats such as Swindon, Slough and Surbiton. Many of them are agreeable, but their posture is post-prandial; flush with pleasure at having secured a berth in the members' smoking room, they seem to have no particular appetite for power. If the Tories in Parliament were really hungry for office, then they would be behaving as every previous Conservative party has done when positioning itself for government. They would be flexible, diverse, open and setting themselves to catch the winds of change. They would be doing what Tony Blair did last week in Blackpool.

If the attack was designed to provoke a reaction, it worked. Three days after it was published, David Cameron used his column on *The Guardian*'s website to respond. Reflecting on the hatchet job, Cameron wrote:

> Nevermind [*sic*] the brass neck of all this coming from a comfortably upholstered commentator, who has the luxury of a weekly column putting the world to rights without having to worry about voters, surgeries, elections, whips, parliamentary procedure and all the rest of it: I'll come on to that later. The fact is that he is plain wrong.[20]

After listing the merits of a selection of his fellow new MPs, Cameron went public with a lobbying effort he had been carrying out in private for many years:

Give up the journalist's expense account and cast aside ambitions of editing the Thunderer. Gird up your loins and prepare for late nights sitting on uncomfortable green benches. Instead of dashing off 700 words at your PC that will flow effortlessly into the op-ed page of the *Times*, you may have to wait seven hours to make a 10-minute speech that few newspapers will ever report. In short, Michael, become a Tory MP.

The put-up-or-shut-up message seemed to fall on deaf ears. Gove had no intention of standing for a party which seemed to stagger two steps backwards towards the Rockers as soon as it tried to take a step forward with the Mods.

Besides, Gove had matters closer to home to be concerned with. Sarah was pregnant with the couple's first child, and so while Cameron, Osborne and Johnson were climbing the greasy pole in Parliament – the three were summoned by Iain Duncan Smith to help with his preparations for Prime Minister's Questions – Gove was processing having something new in his life for the very first time: a blood relative.

Beatrice was born on 7 May 2003, and Gove would later describe fatherhood as 'elation battl[ing] with exhaustion as you begin to realise how much your life is going to change.'[21]

It wasn't just life at home that changed in May 2003. Gove was handed a new job at *The Times* at the same time as Beatrice came into the world. He was appointed Saturday editor in a move that, while billed as a promotion, was more of a step sideways. The job had been vacant since 2001 and had been part of deputy editor Ben Preston's remit before it was shunted off to Gove. Speaking to the *Press Gazette* when the announcement was made, editor Robert Thomson sought to instil the move with a sense of gravitas by proclaiming that a 'truly extraordinary' amount of marketing money would be pumped into the revitalised Saturday edition. 'We want someone to "own" Saturday,' he said, adding, 'Michael's purlieu will include all the Saturday sections and just generally lifting the profile.'[22]

The truth was somewhat different. According to a journalist who worked under Gove in this period, the new Saturday editor barely had even the illusion of power. The source remembers:

On Friday itself the editor and the deputy editor would come in and usually chuck out everything that hadn't been printed. Ben Preston was particularly adept at doing this. You'd have someone working on a project for three days and he'd say, 'I'm not sure about this. What I really want to do is…' and 'Can we get some-one to do this?' Michael realised this was going on. It really did defeat him. He stopped caring.

It was against this background that Cameron again pressured Gove to join him in the Commons. Instead of lambasting him on the internet, he wooed him over lunch in his constituency home in the summer of 2003. 'Dave did more than anyone to persuade me to apply to go on the candidates' list … He would have sensed my initial crumbling,' Gove later remembered.[23]

The notion of becoming an MP was indeed starting to sit easier with Gove, but the slight misgiving in his mind centred on his personal politics. In a further sign of just how far he had drifted away from the party he had championed for nearly twenty years, Gove penned an article for *The Times* on 25 February 2003 headlined: 'I can't fight my feelings any more: I love Tony.'

This was not a case of a mischievous editor wanting to oversell a piece offering qualified support for Blair; it was a full-throated declaration of adoration for the Prime Minister. The backdrop was the ever-quickening drumbeat to war in Iraq which had started sounding in the wake of the 11 September attacks. As we have seen, Gove had been banging out that particular rhythm for years and was more than delighted that his calls for intervention were being echoed by the occupant of 10 Downing Street.

The gushing article was published the same day as the UK and US submitted a draft resolution to the United Nations arguing that Iraq had missed its 'final opportunity' to disarm peacefully. 'You could call it the Elizabeth Bennett [*sic*] moment,' the article began.

It's what Isolde felt when she fell into Tristan's arms. It's the point you reach when you give up fighting your feelings, abandon the antipathy bred into your bones, and admit that you were wrong about the man. By God, it's still hard to write this, but I'm afraid I've got to be honest. Tony Blair is proving an outstanding Prime Minister at the moment.

The spark for this emotional U-turn was not just Blair's Middle East strategy, but a range of domestic policies:

The Prime Minister has been right, and brave, to introduce market pressures into higher education by pushing through university top-up fees in the teeth of opposition from egalitarian Chancellor. He's been correct in conceding, to the annoyance of his wife I'm sure, that the European Convention on Human Rights gets in the way of a sane asylum policy. In dealing with the firefighters, and their absurdly selfish strike, he's been satisfactorily resolute.

It was, of course, the Iraq strategy which was the most attractive of Blair's qualities, and it was for that action that Gove delivered what was, from him, the highest praise imaginable: 'He's behaving like a true Thatcherite. Indeed, he's braver in some respects than Maggie was. The Falklands war took courage. But Thatcher had most of the country, and her party, behind her. In dealing with the Iraq crisis, Mr Blair has neither.'

Gove's justification for sticking up for Blair despite his own Conservative sympathies was simple: 'As a right-wing polemicist, all I can say looking at Mr Blair now is, what's not to like?'

Gove's defence of Blair extended into attacking his fellow journalists who were either less than sympathetic to the Prime Minister's foreign policy or simply more inclined to scrutinise the actions of the government. *Newsnight* presenter Jeremy Paxman was held up as one of several broadcasters who seemed 'determined to never give the elected head of our Government the benefit of any doubt'.

In August 2003, around the same time Cameron was pushing him hard to stand as an MP, Gove launched another defence of the Blair government – this time over the Hutton Inquiry into the death of David Kelly. The weapons expert was found dead – later ruled a suicide – two days after he appeared before the Foreign Affairs Select Committee, which was investigating a report by BBC journalist Andrew Gilligan into the use of intelligence in the run-up to the Iraq War. Gilligan had claimed that following a conversation with a 'senior official' – later identified as Kelly – it was clear the government inserted into an intelligence dossier a warning that Iraq could deploy weapons of mass destruction within forty-five minutes of an order being issued despite 'probably' knowing it was wrong. After Kelly's suicide, a judicial inquiry was ordered by the government.

As far as Gove was concerned, the inquiry was a 'grave misdirection of public resources, attention and thought'. He wrote:

The inquiry provides a chance for those in the shallow end of journalism and politics, who prefer cynicism to argument, to

indulge their endless, pointless search for another Watergate ...
From the Liberal Democrats to the *Daily Mail*, a gallery of op-
portunists will be hunting for 'killer' evidence of misbehaviour.
They are the unspeakable in pursuit of the unprovable.[24]

Gove argued that the Hutton Inquiry was the latest in a long line
of investigations – Scott into arms sales to Iraq; Macpherson into
the murder of Stephen Lawrence; Savile into Bloody Sunday –
which was about appeasing 'those on radical Left, or the cynical
fringe'. This was not an article by a man in love with journalism,
by someone whose gut was telling him to find out what was being
whispered behind closed doors. Gove was becoming more of a de-
fender of the government – a Labour government – than a critic,
holding the government to account. Perhaps his friend Dave was
right; perhaps it was indeed time for him to swap his column for
the Commons, where he could make his arguments from within
the corridors of power.

There was, however, the problem of the Conservative Party leadership. Despite Gove professing his love for Blair, it was only ever a
midsummer night's fling. He would never truly leave the Conservative home, even if he did not agree with how it was currently being
run by Iain Duncan Smith.

At the same time as he was extolling his love of Blair, Gove was
sticking the knife into the Tory leader. Indeed, three days before the
'I love Tony' article, Gove compared the Conservatives to a 'diseased
and weakened body' after another round of dismissals at Tory HQ
sparked yet more infighting. '[Duncan Smith] has decided to reject
the broad-based course that he tried to follow since being elected
and return to the traditional Tory message, people and postures
with which he is instinctively more comfortable,' wrote Gove.[25]

Speculation about Duncan Smith's future rumbled on throughout

2003, with talk very much focused on when not if he would be ousted by his MPs. His keynote speech at the party conference in Blackpool on 10 October contained attacks on Labour and his own critics. He called for the Tories to 'destroy this double-dealing, deceitful, incompetent, shallow, inefficient, ineffective, corrupt, mendacious, fraudulent, shameful, lying government once and for all' but warned, 'To those who doubt and to those who deliberate, I say this: Don't work for Tony Blair. Get on board or get out of our way. For we have got work to do.' That jibe could also have been written specifically for Gove – although the *Times* man was just one of many critics.

Two weeks later, and Gove's old friend Dominic Cummings decided to break his year-long silence on what it was like working for Duncan Smith. On 26 October 2003, he threw as many grenades as he could at both his former boss and the Conservative Party at large. Writing in the *Telegraph*, Cummings said:

> Mr Duncan Smith is incompetent, would be a worse prime minister than Tony Blair, and must be replaced. He is, however, the symptom rather than cause of a party desperately short of the political essentials: understanding, talent, will and adaptation … The party is a joke – around the country, people increasingly laugh at 'the Conservative Party'.

On 28 October, the threshold of twenty-five letters from Tory MPs calling for a change of leadership had been reached, and a confidence vote followed the next day. Duncan Smith lost by seventy-five votes to ninety.

Not wishing to embark on a fourth leadership contest in eight years, the party coalesced around shadow Chancellor Michael Howard as the person who should take over the top job. He was elected unopposed on 6 November. The former Home Secretary, famously described as having 'something of the night about him' in 1997, would be the one to finally put the Tories on course for an eventual return to government. As part of that mission, he turned to the bright young things in the party. Enter the Notting Hill set.

Four days before Howard was anointed as leader, Michael Portillo tried his very best not to say 'I told you so' in an article he penned for *The Observer* reflecting on Duncan Smith's disastrous leadership. Trying to accentuate the positives, he flagged up two up-and-coming Tories who could be his party's answer to Tony Blair and Gordon Brown. 'We have George Osborne and David Cameron, but they aren't ready. The party is in no mood to take risks again,' he wrote, before concluding the piece: 'If Howard guarantees our survival, the Osbornes and Camerons will reveal our long-term future.'[26]

Howard was clearly of the same mindset: he made Cameron deputy party chairman and appointed Osborne as an advisor to help him prepare for Prime Minister's Questions.

With the two men becoming the focus of media attention, the as-yet-unnamed world in which they operated also came under scrutiny. On the morning of Howard's coronation, *The Guardian* carried a two-page feature profiling the pair, including a hint at the upper-class, dinner-party aspect of the relationship between the two. 'If Evelyn Waugh's *Vile Bodies* had been written about political bright young things ... David and George's kind of circle might now have been on screens all over Britain in Stephen Fry's recent film adaptation.'[27]

That circle featured Ed Vaizey, who, through his time in the Conservative Research Department in the early 1990s, had become close friends with Cameron, whom he had already known through university. Also working at Conservative Central Office, where the

CRD was based, was Steve Hilton, who would go on to marry another colleague, Rachel Whetstone. Whetstone served as an advisor to Michael Howard when he was Home Secretary and was brought back into his inner circle in 2003 as the opposition leader's political secretary. She and Hilton were godparents to Cameron's first child, Ivan, born in 2002. Osborne was, of course, another alumni of the CRD, where he worked alongside Catherine Fall, a friend of Cameron's from university.

Conservative MP Derek Conway is often credited with coining the phrase 'Notting Hill set' – based on the shared postcode of most of the key players – in an attack on the group in July 2004. The moniker was supposed to be derogatory; it was used during a row over a list of twelve MPs deemed to be 'bed blockers' reportedly drawn up by Chief Whip David Maclean.

In fact, the first mention of the 'Notting Hill set' was in *The Guardian* on 13 November 2003, when a small profile of Whetstone described her as a 'leading light in the "Notting Hill" set of young modernising Tories.'

That term was further bolstered by an article in *The Spectator* on 19 June 2004, with Peter Oborne writing, 'Cameron is unmistakably the leader of these Notting Hill Tories.' While the focus on the shared geography of the group was understandable, a more apt name was the 'Smith Square set', according to Daniel Finkelstein, as that was where the key players all drew their first political blood.[28]

Howard's embracing of the group was the final push Gove needed to swap the news desk for the green benches. His friends and contemporaries were slowly but surely inserting themselves into key positions within the Tory Party, and Gove had to make a choice. He could, as Cameron had said in his *Guardian* blog, carry on enjoying the journalist expense account, restrict his political musings to a newspaper column and bash out the odd travel feature to keep himself interested. But Gove is a man who has always seen his life as a compelling autobiography in the making, and at this moment would the main character really pass up the opportunity to take a seat in the House of Commons?

Gove began working the Conservative Party drinks circuit in a bid to secure a seat. Party chairman Liam Fox held a series of informal events to sign up recruits ahead of the next election, and Gove found himself rubbing shoulders with many future MPs as he considered where he should launch his political career.

The answer presented itself in April 2004, when the plum seat of Surrey Heath became available. The incumbent Conservative MP, Nick Hawkins, was deselected by the local members – partly because they found him not to be a 'team player',[29] but mainly because the richest association in the country wanted to be represented by someone who could be a big-hitter in any future Conservative government.[30]

Gove was one of 200 who applied for the seat and in the last weekend of June 2004 he and twenty-three other hopefuls travelled to the village of Windlesham to undergo the selection process.[31] He was, unsurprisingly, facing tough opposition.

Nick Hurd, son of former Foreign Secretary Douglas Hurd, was seen as an early favourite, while Charles Elphick, a former advisor to Michael Howard, was also in contention. Alternatively, Nadhim Zahawi, a Kurdish-born former aide to Jeffery Archer, would have made Surrey Heath the first truly safe Conservative seat to select an ethnic minority candidate. Gove was not the only hopeful with a connection to *The Times* to put himself forward, thanks to Jacob Rees-Mogg, son of the paper's former editor William, throwing his top hat into the ring. Indeed, Gove wasn't even the sole representative from the Notting Hill set: Steve Hilton, who had voted for the Green Party in 2001 out of sheer disgust with the Conservative

leadership, was hoping his return to the blue team could be cemented with a seat in Parliament.[32]

Each of the twenty-four were given a twenty-minute grilling by
a panel of twenty, followed by the association's top brass whittling
the candidates down to a list of three. Hurd, Elphicke and Zahawi
were all culled, although they would all go on to be Conservative
MPs in the future. Hilton also failed to make the final three and
never fulfilled his ambition to sit in Parliament. Rees-Mogg, Gove
and Laura Sandys, daughter of former Defence Secretary Duncan
Sandys, were the three chosen to go through to a membership
ballot.

On Monday 5 July, Gove's victory was announced, and he gave
a humble speech to party members at a leisure complex in Frimley.
'You have placed your trust and confidence in me and I know how
precious that quality is,' he said. 'I will do my best as your candidate
to repay that trust and confidence and to ensure that I do not let
you down.'[33]

If the Surrey Heath Conservatives were hoping they had selected
a future big hitter in the party, they would have been reassured by
Michael Portillo's verdict on their new MP. Writing in the *Sunday
Times* on 21 November 2004, the former leadership contender
passed on the baton to his one-time biographer:

> If the party were a business it would instruct headhunters to
> find leadership material: 'Young, charismatic and clear thinking,
> amusing but not a comedian, media experienced but not celeb-
> rity obsessed, family person, reliable, preferably from a humble
> background, educated in a state school, must believe in sweeping
> change in the party. Candidates with origins in the southeast
> need not apply.' Luckily one person who fits most of the criteria
> will enter parliament at the next election. Like [Boris] Johnson

he is a journalist, but unlike him he would never be late for a meeting. His name is Michael Gove, who long ago wrote a kindly biography of me. He survived that lapse of judgment and climbed the ladder. He has given up the prospect of editing *The Times* to become a humble backbencher in a party whose fortunes are at a low ebb. That is what I call serious.

Gove was not overly enthused by the endorsement. 'This might be the kiss of death in every regard,' he said. 'If I lose the election, I might be the only person anointed future leader of the Conservative party who was never even an MP.'[34]

Gove was indeed taking things seriously, though – so seriously, in fact, that he was prepared to actually move to the constituency he had been asked to represent. The family let out their two-bedroom Notting Hill home and rented a five-bedroom house in Camberley. The extra space was useful as Vine was pregnant with the couple's second child, William, born in November 2004.

Writing about the relocation in *The Times*, Gove painted a fairly provincial picture of life in the suburbs, stating that his wife was a city girl who 'likes her manicures and lattes'. He bemoaned the commute into London, labelling South West Trains' timetable 'as reliable as a Tony Blair dossier'. After acknowledging his family was indeed happy in the world outside London, he concluded, 'All we need now is to find a good local manicurist, and our lives will be complete.'[35]

As if changing careers, moving house and becoming a father for a second time weren't enough for Gove, he decided to embark on another project in 2004. It had been nearly ten years since his biography of Michael Portillo had been published and Gove was itching to get another tome under his belt. He had learned the lesson from the Portillo book and chose to write about a politician whose career was already over. Long over. In fact, the subject of the biography had been dead since 1751. Henry St John, 1st Viscount Bolingbroke, would get the Gove treatment, and publishing house HarperCollins stumped up an advance of £40,000 – a third of which Gove received when he signed the contract, with another third to be handed over when the manuscript was delivered and the final sum paid out when the book was published. As of 2019, the manuscript has not materialised, with Gove saying his subsequent political career means he has yet to find the time to carry out the required research.[36]

Unlike Gove, Boris Johnson had never found it difficult to mix politics with personal pursuits, but just as Gove's star was on the rise at the end of 2004, Johnson's was threatening to burn out. Michael Howard had appointed him a shadow arts minister and vice-chair of the party, but he was sacked from these positions after being caught lying about an extra-marital relationship with *Spectator* columnist Petronella Wyatt. Michael Portillo went as far as saying that Johnson's political career was 'over' as a result of the scandal.[37] Johnson retreated to focus on his journalism duties – he was still *Spectator* editor – just as Gove was preparing to relinquish the majority of his. At the beginning of 2005, Gove left his staff job at *The Times* to focus on his political career. However, his nine-year association with the paper was not completely over, as he was kept on as a weekly columnist for the not-at-all-shabby sum of £60,000 a year. Gove would now spend his time writing speeches for Michael Howard alongside his old friend Ed Vaizey as he prepared for the election.

On 23 January 2005, it was made abundantly clear how the Conservatives would approach the election expected to take place later that year. Under the heading 'I believe we must limit immigration', Howard used a full-page advert in the *Sunday Telegraph* to set out his stall. 'There are literally millions of people in other countries who want to come and live here. Britain cannot take them all,' he wrote. He vowed to place a limit on the number of asylum seekers, and in an interview on ITV said, 'Community relations are at risk because under this government immigration is unlimited and out of control.'[38] Howard was pitching himself as speaking up for the quiet majority of Middle England who felt cowed by political correctness on such issues but were finding a voice through outlets such as the UK Independence Party, who had secured twelve seats and 2.7 million votes in the 2004 European Parliament elections.

In March, Howard again provoked controversy by calling for tougher action against illegal travellers' sites. One Labour MP said the plans and rhetoric from the Tories had the 'whiff of the gas chamber'. The tactics deployed by Howard were clearly not in keeping with *A Blue Tomorrow*, the book Gove had helped bring together three and a half years earlier. The campaign was once again focusing on asylum seekers and a sense of fear of the other. Yet, far from taking Howard to task for it, Gove defended the Tory leader in the pages of *The Times*:

The residents of Whitehall, and their extended family in the commentating classes, have reacted with anger to the recent arrival on their doorstep of some proposals from Michael Howard. The Leader of the Opposition has outlined a series of policies which should go a considerable way to helping resolve the tensions created by a minority of individuals who have been flouting the law. Mr Howard's proposals are intended to ensure that planning laws apply fairly to all. They are colour-blind, background-neutral, non-discriminatory and driven by a belief in the central principle of equality before the law. But because the Conservatives are unveiling these plans after a series of open breaches of the law by some travellers, Mr Howard has been accused of pandering to prejudice.[39]

By the time the election was called on 5 April, the Conservative campaign boiled down to six areas, summed up in eleven words: 'More police, cleaner hospitals, lower taxes, school discipline, controlled immigration, accountability.' The overarching slogan was 'Are you thinking what we're thinking?'

Down in Surrey Heath, Gove was trying his best to get across that message to anyone he met – including children at a local primary school. 'Do you think we need more aliens here, or should we control the number of aliens entering our country?' he asked one six-year-old boy who claimed his classmate was an extra-terrestrial.[40] The exchange was reported by Gove's friend from *The Times* Tom Baldwin, who had been despatched by the paper to chronicle the wannabe MP's campaign. Baldwin let Gove know he had been given responsibility for trailing him for the paper by ringing him up and saying, 'Michael, it's Tom. There's an easy way to do this or a hard way to do this, the choice is yours.'[41] It seems Gove picked the easy way and allowed his former colleague to follow him as he campaigned.

As Big Ben rang out at 10 p.m. on 5 May, the Dimbleby brothers – David on the BBC and Jonathan on ITV – told the country that Tony Blair would remain as Prime Minister but with his majority cut from 167 to sixty-six. The exit poll was spot on, meaning that while the Conservatives were going in the right direction, the party was facing yet another period in opposition.

Watching the exit poll announcement in the constituency he was hoping to represent, Gove was nervous. His inherited majority of 10,819 seemed bulletproof, but as the biographer of Michael Portillo was only too aware, election nights can throw up unpredictable moments.

It wasn't until about 3.30 a.m., when the piles of ballot papers were stacked up on the trestle tables, that Gove started to relax.[42] The Conservative bundle was obviously larger than that of the second-placed Lib Dem candidate, and Gove was soon announced as the new MP for Surrey Heath. He had secured 24,642 votes – representing a 51.5 per cent share – and even managed to increase his majority by twenty-six ballots. Michael Gove was now a Member of Parliament.

He was one of fifty-four new Conservative MPs, making up over a quarter of all Tories in the Commons. Among the class of 2005 were Justine Greening in Putney, Jeremy Hunt in South West Surrey, Douglas Carswell in Clacton, Theresa Villiers in Chipping Barnet and Peter Bone in Wellingborough. Michael Howard compared the new cohort to the surge of 101 new faces in 1950: 'Just as the 1950 intake ... absolutely transformed the House of Commons and set the scene for the next Conservative victory of 1951, so I am absolutely convinced that this splendid new intake, brimming with talent, is going to set the scene for the next Conservative victory.'[43]

Another new face on the Tory benches was Gove's good friend Ed Vaizey. Having failed in Bristol East in 1997 and sat out 2001, Vaizey was elected MP for Wantage in Oxfordshire. A friend who would not be joining him on the green benches was Nick Boles, who came within 420 votes of winning Hove from Labour. 'In politics, like war, no advance comes without the loss of brave and good people,' Gove wrote about Boles in *The Times* rather dramatically two days after the election.[44]

The battle to enter Parliament was now over, and it was now down to Gove to see how high he could rise in the ranks. But first, a change of general was required.

CHAPTER 12

HOWL

The Conservatives had a rich tradition of turning party leaders into Prime Ministers. Indeed, it was only Austen Chamberlain in the early 1920s who failed to marry together the two posts in the party's history – and he was only in charge for eighteen months. Then Tony Blair came along. Blair saw off William Hague in 2001; he didn't even need to see off Iain Duncan Smith; and on 6 May 2005 Michael Howard confirmed that his defeat at Blair's hands was effectively the end of his frontbench political career. In keeping with recent tradition, he announced his intention to resign as leader of the Conservative Party after their defeat at the ballot box. Speaking to activists in Putney, the 63-year-old said he would be too old to lead the party into next election. 'It's better to stand aside sooner rather than later so that the party can choose someone who can,' he said.[1]

That 'sooner' would not be imminent. Howard wanted to allow time for the Tories to re-examine its leadership selection process, which, for all its merits, had left the party with the unpopular Iain Duncan Smith in charge the last time it was properly enacted. Indeed, the contest would not officially begin until 7 October.

That meant plenty of time for prospective candidates to put themselves in the shop window. Shadow Home Secretary David

Davis was seen as the man to beat, and Ken Clarke was expected to throw his hat into the ring for the third time. While more experienced heads pondered the leadership contest, new MPs began getting settled into Westminster.

On 7 June 2005, Michael Gove delivered his maiden speech in Parliament. For a man so well versed in the art of public speaking, it was a low-key effort. The speech contained the usual praise of those who had spoken before him and the requisite platitudes to his predecessor in as MP for Surrey Heath – 'I have met many constituents for whom Nick [Hawkins] was an indefatigable champion; he set a standard that it would be difficult to match.' In praising his constituency, he quoted from Sir John Betjeman's poem 'A Subaltern's Love Song': 'Nine-o'clock Camberley, heavy with bells / And mushroomy, pine-woody, evergreen smells.'[2]

The policy issue Gove chose to expand on in the speech was national security. 'One area where I believe that public investment continues to be more necessary than ever is in our security,' he told the Commons, as he praised 'Britain's contribution to extending the cause of liberty'. Gove added, 'I pay tribute to this government for their role in defending the cause of freedom in Sierra Leone, Kosovo and Iraq.' Gove did not speak again in Parliament until October, but that did not mean he wasn't playing a key role in Westminster.

Even before Howard announced that he was going to stand down as Conservative leader, the Notting Hill set had been quietly working on a succession plan. David Cameron, George Osborne and Steve Hilton were at the centre of the manoeuvres, but it was not yet clear which of the two MPs should go for the top job. Gove met Cameron for a drink in Soho about a week after the election and was left with the impression his friend wasn't completely sold on standing. Gove rang Hilton to let him know that Cameron was undecided, but the pair agreed it had to be him, rather than Osborne, who stood.[3]

While Cameron was wrestling with the decision, Michael Howard was doing his best to make sure someone from the modernising wing of the party stood a chance against David Davis. His decision to delay his departure from the top job was designed to ensure that a new face had time to garner maximum exposure, something Howard assisted by inviting both Cameron and Osborne to join his shadow Cabinet. Cameron was lined up for the shadow Chancellor role but instead lobbied for the shadow Education brief. Osborne then accepted the job of taking on Gordon Brown, and mused on whether he should put himself forward for leader of the party. After consulting widely, including with former leader William Hague, Osborne concluded that at thirty-four he was too young to stand for the leadership.

In June, Cameron called a meeting in his office for a select band of followers to get a measure of his support for any leadership bid. Gove was one of the fourteen in attendance, along with Boris Johnson, Ed Vaizey and Osborne.[4] He spoke of the party needing a shake-up, but didn't actually go the whole hog and announce he was going to stand.[5] The rumours rumbled on, and a speech set to be delivered at Policy Exchange on 29 June was expected to be the scene of Cameron's declaration. In the event, the address, which Gove had helped write, was underwhelming and focused on the importance of family life and tax breaks for married couples instead of setting out his stall for modernisation. There was one line, however, which would later play a central part in the early days of Cameron's premiership: 'We are all in this together.'[6]

The speech failed to entice any more Tories to flock to Cameron's flag and, with the number of MPs supporting him hovering around the fourteen mark, Oliver Letwin decided to give the campaign a shot of adrenaline. In an opinion piece for the *Sunday Telegraph* on 3 July, the former shadow Chancellor set out why he was backing Cameron for the top job:

> To judge by my experience of working with David, he is some-one who lives the message, someone who actually believes in free markets, a stronger society, a more civilised Britain and a more civilised politics. I hope that he will stand. If he does, despite my admiration for other colleagues, I shall back him.

The intervention, coming from someone very much not part of the Notting Hill set, raised eyebrows in Westminster, but Cameron's not-yet-existent campaign was still regarded as the party's young bucks having a practice run ahead of a future election. That view was even echoed by some in Cameron's camp, remembers someone close to numerous members of the team: 'The question was "how far could Cameron get" and I remember in mid-summer one of Cameron's team came to me and said, "I guess the question is at what point do we draw stumps and say it's gone on long enough?"'

Despite those moments of doubt, Cameron stayed at the crease, and his team – with Gove playing a key role in speechwriting – spent the summer setting out his view of what was dubbed 'modern compassionate Conservatism'. To some, it seemed modern Con-servatism involved reheating aping Blairism. Writing in The Spec-tator, journalist Peter Oborne had no doubt who was responsible for 'David Cameron's Tories' embracing the Labour leader's style: '[Cameron's] speeches, said to be drafted by the Tory MP and Blair apologist Michael Gove, have been laboriously modelled on the Prime Minister's early efforts. They are so close in style as to be almost identical: the same piety of tone, staccato delivery and mania for verbless sentences.'[7]

On 29 September, Cameron held his leadership bid launch at the Royal United Services Institute in Whitehall – complete with free strawberry smoothies and chocolate brownies for journalists, many of whom had already attended the official unveiling of David Davis's bid to be the next Conservative leader earlier that day. Cameron spoke without notes as he warned the Tories that just waiting for the public to grow sick of Labour was not a viable election strategy. 'The problem at the last election was not that people trusted the Labour Party – they didn't. They got the lowest level of support for a government in our political lifetime. The problem was that people don't yet trust the Conservative Party, and it's we who have got to change,' he said.[8]

A week later and Cameron repeated the no-notes trick in his speech to the Conservative Party conference in Blackpool. He received rapturous applause from party members, extended by the appearance on the stage of his wife, Samantha, visibly pregnant with the couple's third child.

The conference speech changed the dynamic of the leadership race. Cameron went from being the outsider with little perceived support to the favourite who could offer a true break with the past. He wasn't the only member of the Notting Hill set to receive plaudits at the conference by presenting a forward-thinking vision of conservatism. The day before his speech, Cameron, in his role as shadow Education Secretary, appeared at a fringe event organised by the National Union of Teachers. Gove was also on the bill, and in a six-minute speech he put forward a blueprint for a Conservative education policy that was, according to the journalist David Aaronovitch, 'genuinely radical':

The Tories, he said, had been seen as a 'pressure group for the middle classes' and their pupils' passports policy had been rightly perceived as simply helping the bourgeoisie with their school fees. Also the Conservatives had been wrong to oppose variable tuition fees and wrong to oppose the expansion of higher education (look at China, look at India). Instead he wanted a system of school vouchers, 'weighted emphatically in favour of the poorest', the introduction of a baccalaureate, a look at childcare in Scandinavia and lots more. It was exciting stuff.[9]

The only way to ensure these 'genuinely radical' positions had a chance of becoming party policy, Gove implied, was if Cameron won the leadership contest. In the first ballot of MPs on 18 October, Cameron received fifty-six votes out of a possible 198, with Davis on sixty-two. The second ballot, held two days later, saw Cameron leap out in front, picking up ninety supporters, while Davis's numbers actually fell to fifty-seven.

The two men spent the rest of October and November wooing Conservative members across the country. On 3 November, the pair went head-to-head in a special edition of the BBC's *Question Time* show from Nottingham. Preparations for the contest saw Gove assuming the role of Davis, and the former *Stab in the Dark* presenter reverted to that aggressive and slightly malicious persona in the warm-ups to recreate how he believed the senior politician would treat Cameron. As it was, Davis treated the young challenger with respect, and even passed up an opportunity to punch what could have been a serious bruise in Cameron's campaign. At a fringe event at the party conference, Cameron was asked whether he had taken drugs while at university. 'I had a normal university experience,' he replied, adding after being pressed, 'There were things that I did then that I don't think that I should talk about now I'm a politician.'[10] During the *Question Time* show, an audience member threw the words back at Cameron, asking the panellists: 'Do you believe in today's Britain that drug-taking at university is all part of an ordinary university experience?'

Davis, who had previously suggested that anyone who had taken cocaine was not fit to run for high office, confined himself to saying that his views on drugs were a matter of public record, adding, 'This contest is going to be decided on policy, personality and delivery, not on media witch-hunts.'[11]

Cameron repeated the line he had put out during previous questions about this topic, that politicians deserve a private life before entering politics, and won a round of applause from the audience.

With that potential banana skin avoided, Cameron went on to easily win the ballot of party members. On 6 December, he was crowned leader, with 134,446 votes compared to Davis's 64,398. The Notting Hill set were in charge of the Conservatives.

Although Gove had helped Cameron throughout his campaign, he was not awarded a seat in the shadow Cabinet. Having been in Parliament only seven months, such a rapid promotion would have put too many noses out of joint. Instead, he was handed the role of shadow Housing spokesman in 2006, a topic he had previously shown little interest in. However, he did win recognition for his part in the campaign, with judges at Channel 4's Political Awards giving him the rising star award in February 2006, where Celebrity Big Brother winner Chantelle Houghton presented him with the gong.

Gove's first appearance at the despatch box came on 1 February when he asked the Minister for Housing, Yvette Cooper, about a proposed new tax on housing developments. At the end of March, Gove began probing the rollout of home information packs (HIPS), a set of documents that sellers had to provide before a property could be put on the market. The Labour government believed the extra information provided in HIPS would help stop property deals falling through at the last minute, while the Tories saw it as more red tape and an extra expense of up to £500 for house sellers.

With HIPS unpopular among many in the conveyancing and estate agent industries, Gove realised that this issue, though un-glamorous, was a perfect opportunity to attack the government for intervening in a market seemingly for the sake of it.

Gove's former Times colleague Alice Miles flagged up the battle brewing between the Surrey Heath MP and Labour's Yvette Cooper, writing, 'Both she and Mr Gove being clever, passionate and equally determined, it is rather a pleasure to watch them grap-ple with one another.'[12]

Gove pursued Cooper with his Oxford Union debating zeal across all forums available to him: in the Commons chamber, through written questions, appearing in Westminster Hall debates. His attacks centred on two themes: nobody wanted HIPS, and, even if they did, the government couldn't roll them out properly.

'The Minister is fond of saying that consumer groups favour the home information pack. Will she tell us which groups – in the plural – actually favour the pack? As far as we can see, only one organisation representing consumers has made representations in favour of the pack,' he asked Cooper in a Westminster Hall debate on 24 May 2006. The Labour minister was able to cite only a survey carried out by just one group – the Consumers' Association, other-wise known as Which? – while Gove referenced numerous industry bodies opposed to HIPS.[13] As he said in the Commons on 16 May 2007, 'Let us listen to the experts.'[14]

On 22 May 2007, just ten days before HIPS were due to become mandatory for all property sales, the government announced a delay to the project. Gove lapped up the apparent U-turn when the Secretary of State responsible, Ruth Kelly, came to the Commons.

After thanking her for her 'grace and courage' for coming to the House, Gove dispensed with the faux niceties:

> May I ask why, after being warned more than a year ago that they were comprehensively mishandling this issue, Ministers have seen fit to retreat only now – with eight days to go before home information packs were due to be implemented? Why did ministers not take the opportunity that we offered last week to think again? Was it stubborn vanity or sheer incompetence?

'I am absolutely delighted to see the hon. Member for Surrey Heath enjoying himself and in his place,' Kelly replied, adding, 'Indeed, only this morning the right hon. Member for Witney [Cameron] asked the Conservative Party whether it wants to be a serious force for governmental change, or whether it wants to be a right-wing debating society. Today, we have had our answer, and there he is, the honorary president.'[15]

Gove would have been pleased with the 'honorary president' jibe. After all, he had been in Parliament just two years but his HIPS campaigning had shown an effortless move from entertaining commentator to effective politician – a transition which had eluded Boris Johnson.

That's not to say that Gove had given up his commentariat role completely. As well as his regular column in The Times, Gove spent the first year in Parliament working on his second book. Not the biography of Viscount Bolingbroke that he had originally planned, but a polemic on an issue he had been grappling with long before it dominated the news cycle: Islamic fundamentalism.

Published in June 2006, Celsius 7/7 was conceived in the aftermath of the 7 July 2005 terrorist attack on London, which left fifty-two people dead when four suicide bombers struck during the morning commute.

As we have seen, Gove had been writing about Islamic fundamentalism since the late 1990s, and the short book – for which he received an advance of £40,000 from the publisher Weidenfeld & Nicolson[16] – echoed many of the ideas he had already put forward.

In the book, Gove argued that Western powers have to shoulder some of the blame for the rise of jihadists because of their selective use of force and the ease with which they back down in the face of military or cultural confrontation. The failure of European countries to intervene to stop the ethnic cleansing of Bosnian Muslims in the Srebrenica massacre allowed fundamentalists to preach that the West could not be relied upon to protect followers of Islam. 'Many British Islamists have dated their radicalisation back to the time of the Bosnian conflict,' Gove claimed, although he offered no evidence to back this up.[17] He went on to highlight the failure of the Western coalition in the first Gulf War to depose Saddam Hussein, 'to remove any doubt as to who was the victor of this exchange', as another sign of weakness which could be exploited by fundamentalists.[18]

Gove argued that the West was not just militarily weak but culturally cowardly when it came to confronting Islamic fundamentalism. He repeatedly cited the furore over the publication in a Danish newspaper of cartoons portraying the prophet Muhammad. The act had angered those Muslims who believed that depicting Muhammad was highly blasphemous, prompting protests across the world, with the Danish Embassies in Beirut and Damascus torched during demonstrations. At the time, UK Foreign Secretary Jack Straw had condemned the publishing of the cartoons, a move which Gove argued 'gave Islamists exactly when they had been asking for – a validation of their belief that the West lacked both the strength and the will to defend its core values when they came under sustained attack'.[19]

The former journalist bemoaned that no British newspaper had been brave enough to publish the cartoons, and 'thus we advertised our weakness to the world'.[20] There was nothing to stop Gove publishing the cartoons himself, of course, on his website, or even in the very book in which he was decrying the lack of courage of his peers to step up to the plate and show solidarity with their Danish counterparts.

Much of *Celsius 7/7* focuses on a tension which had fascinated Gove since his Sunday school days in Aberdeen – that between the State of Israel and the Arab world. Gove accepts that the relatively young country has a crucial role in the debate around Islamic fundamentalism, but rejects any suggestion that resolving the Palestinian issue would see an end to jihadism.

Gove believes that to the terrorist groups and their sympathisers, 'Israel's greatest crime is simply to exist at all.' He adds:

Israel's existence as an openly plural, explicitly Western, conspicuously successful democracy in the heart of the Islamic world is just too much to bear … Israel's success is a standing rebuke to so many of the assumptions cherished by the region's other leaders and the West's own radicals that it inspires a hatred that can, and does, lead to irrationality.[21]

Finally, on the issue of home-grown jihadis, such as the four suicide bombers behind the 7 July attacks, Gove is critical of the media for giving too much airtime to extremists like Anjem Choudary but contests the suggestion that those with extremist views represent little more than a 'tiny' minority of Muslims.

However reassuring it may be to work on that basis, it would be fatally misconceived … Those jihadists who make the case for violent action now are the militant vanguard of a wider movement. There are many Muslims, across the globe, within Europe and in Britain, who share the basic ideological assumptions behind the jihadist worldview.[22]

The book concludes with a vague chapter titled 'What is to Be Done' but offers very few practical suggestions. Gove calls for UK and US troops to stay in Iraq, not just to help stabilise the country but also because departure will, 'in the most important front we have in the War on Terror, fatally signal our own lack of stomach for the long haul'.[23] Indeed, the Western roll-out of democracy should not end in Iraq, Gove argues, as the power of the ballot box would see an end to nuclearisation of rogue states, thwart fundamentalism and ultimately deliver a better quality of life to those currently living under dictatorships. He does not go so far as to say the ballot should be delivered by the bullet, but the implication is clear:

> If we believe in the superiority of our way of life, if we believe, as the anti-apartheid movement and civil rights movement believed, that freedom knows no boundaries and every human being is precious, then we should believe in, and want urgently to work for, the spread of democracy across the globe.[24]

On the domestic front, Gove speaks in more philosophical terms, calling for 'a truly inclusive model of British citizenship in which divisive separatist identities are challenged, and rejected'.[25]

'Challenged and rejected' certainly summed up many of the negative reviews of the book. Writing for the Sunday Times, historian William Dalrymple savaged the text. After decrying Gove for having 'no knowledge of Islamic history, Islamic theology or Islamic culture', he said:

Gove's book is a confused epic of simplistic incomprehension, rid-dled with more factual errors and misconceptions than any other text I have come across in some two decades of reviewing books on this subject. Many are mistakes of the most basic sort that even a little experience on the ground could have disabused him of.²⁶

Damian Thompson in the *Telegraph* accused Gove of having a 'black-and-white approach' to his arguments, adding, 'His chapter on [Israel] could have been dictated by that country's ministry of information. One looks in vain for any recognition that Israel's for-eign policy is motivated not only by legitimate self-defence but also by vengeful (and distinctively Middle Eastern) tribal hatred.'²⁷

In a review on the ConservativeHome website, Brian Jenner at-tacked Gove's reliance on 'irritating overstatements', his frequent lapses into 'tendentious theorising', and his 'lazy sentences like "Clearly, the Palestinian people deserve a brighter future." ... Well that's very generous of you Michael,' noted the reviewer.²⁸

Gove brushed off the criticism, later saying, 'It wasn't intended to be a work of academic weight' and adding, 'You don't write a book that has a polemical twist to it without expecting that some people will have a go at you.'²⁹

There was some support for Celsius 7/7, however. Robert Halfon, political director of Conservative Friends of Israel and a parliamen-tary candidate, claimed it 'gives a clarion cry for moral relativism to be replaced by moral clarity about our values and what we stand for',³⁰ while Stephen Pollard, Gove's old friend from university, de-scribed it as 'a book which should be read by anyone who cares about the future of freedom and our civilisation'.³¹

The book was even reported to have been read by staff inside Nos 10 and 11 Downing Street, with the Telegraph claiming it had become 'an unlikely Christmas stocking filler for Labour ministers'.³²

Gove was not content just for members of the British government to consider the text; he wanted it to make a mark on the other side of the Atlantic as well. When Senator John McCain visited the Conservative Party conference in Bournemouth in 2006, Gove made sure he gave a copy to the man who was set to be the Republican Party's next challenger for the White House.[33]

Gove's first two years in the Commons had certainly marked him out as a competent performer who was not only able to think big on issues like Islamic terrorism but also to act forensically, as shown in his work on HIPS. A call-up to the shadow Cabinet was an inevitability, and in July 2007 David Cameron appointed him to a role which for many years looked as though it would be his legacy: education.

CHAPTER 13

ON THE ROAD

Gove's appointment came amid a furious row over the Conservatives' education policy. In May 2007, then shadow Education
and Skills Secretary David Willetts gave a speech at the CBI on
public services reform in which he took a wrecking ball to that
most cherished of Tory institutions: grammar schools. Willetts
argued that the schools were the bastion of the middle classes, with
wealthier parents able to provide extra tuition to their children to
ensure they passed the entrance exams. 'Just 2 per cent of children at
grammar schools are on free school meals when those low income
children make up 12 per cent of the school population in their areas,'
said Willetts.[1] Having argued that grammar schools entrench, rather
tackle, social immobility, he reaffirmed the long-standing policy of
the Conservatives not to introduce any more selective schools in
the state sector.

The speech provoked an immediate backlash from within the
party. Shadow Minister for Europe Graham Brady said new grammars should be introduced in inner cities, while the Conservative
MP for Thanet North, Roger Gale, described Willett's speech as
'bizarre'.[2]

Cameron relished the fight and seemed more than happy to
turn it into his own personal Clause IV moment. He accused those

advocating more grammar schools of 'splashing around in the shallow end of the educational debate'[3] and being guilty of 'ideological self-indulgence'.[4] He claimed the row would show whether the Tories were now 'an aspiring party of government' or whether they were to be a 'right-wing debating society'.[5]

Instead of new grammars, Cameron wanted the Conservatives to be enthusiastic supporters of academy schools – institutions which are either sponsored or receive funding directly from the government and operate outside of local authority control.

Gove had seen the merits of devolving power to teachers and parents during the visit to Harlem, New York, with William Hague in 1999, but in 2001 he had offered only a lukewarm endorsement of the Conservative policy on 'free schools' – the precursor to academies. 'The "free schools" policy at the last election was a passionless exercise in structural design, correct as far as it went, but bled of any vision of what education was for,' he wrote.[6]

His argument was that the Conservatives should be unashamed in their criticism of the current education system and carry out a root-and-branch reform of the sector. In July 2003, under the headline 'Let's unleash a working class revolution in our schools', Gove let rip. 'The biggest traitor to the working class was Shirley Williams … for presiding over the biggest betrayal ever endured by the education's poor. Comprehensive education,' he wrote.[7] According to Gove, the then Education Secretary Charles Clarke was just as culpable, and on his watch there was a 'further dilution of academic standards'. Working-class children needed to be taught maths, English, science, history and languages to 'compete in the modern world', according to Gove – who clearly did not think vocational training was as important as these 'bread and butter' subjects. For Gove in 2003, the key to improving the attainment of working-class children was to introduce the market into the education system:

Every parent in Britain should be given a scholarship for their child, worth broadly the amount currently wasted by the State on their schooling. This scholarship could then be used to buy a place at schools, which would have to compete for parents' money just as vigorously as airlines now compete for their holiday custom … If scholarships or vouchers were tied to household income, working-class parents could be given larger sums than their bourgeois neighbours. Their children would enter the market in a superior bargaining position.

Such an unqualified embrace of the market could be deemed ultra-Thatcherite, a term also applicable to his views on tuition fees in 2003:

The first point that needs to be made about the so-called deterrent effect of a £21,000 loan is that anyone put off from attending a good university by fear of that debt doesn't deserve to be at any university in the first place … Borrowing £21,000, at preferential rates, to secure twenty times that sum [in future earnings], is an offer you'd have to be a fool to turn down. And if you're such a fool that you don't want to accept that deal, then you're too big a fool to benefit from the university education I'm currently subsiding for you.[8]

When David Cameron carried out a reshuffle of his shadow Cabinet on 2 July 2007, he decided to embrace Gove's love of school reform but keep his tuition fee zeal at arm's length. Gove was appointed shadow Schools, Children and Families Secretary, while Willetts was handed the higher education brief, becoming shadow Secretary of State for Innovation, Universities and Skills.

After just two years in Parliament, Gove had made his way to the

Conservatives' top table, and he was determined not to let the opportunity go to waste. In his first Commons appearance as a shadow Secretary of State, Gove challenged Labour's numeracy strategy, class sizes, the use of streaming within schools, disciplinary powers available to teachers, and the relationship between academies and local authorities, all in the same question to his opponent, Ed Balls. He even managed to fit in a jibe found in the recently published diaries of Alastair Campbell: 'Ed Balls – no good on message – all he does is repeat what Gordon Brown has said.'[9]

Gove was not the only one who had been trawling the archives for attack lines. Balls cited Gove's call for school vouchers from 2003 as an example of where there would be no consensus between the front benches, and then issued him with a warning about how Willetts had been axed by Cameron over the grammar schools row: 'My advice to the hon. Member for Surrey Heath is this: next time the Leader of the Opposition declares a Clause IV moment in education, be afraid – very afraid.'[10]

Being one of Cameron's closest political allies – indeed, he helped prepare him for his weekly Prime Minister's Questions clashes with Blair and then Gordon Brown – Gove had no fear of being ousted from his position. Indeed, he worked hard to make him himself indispensable to the party leader. He used an article in The Observer on 1 July 2007 – the day before his appointment to the shadow Cabinet was announced – to insist that, far from Cameron aping Labour, the opposition was now defining the mainstream of UK politics. He cited Cameron's policies on the environment, the end of 'top-down targets' in the NHS, and the need for fewer laws emanating from Westminster as proof that the opposition leader had 'correctly identified and first occupied this new centre ground'.[11]

He added:

As one of his earliest supporters, I vividly remember the criticism which David faced at the time, when Westminster's old hands said he wouldn't get anywhere with this stuff and needed to get back on to traditional territory. But he stuck to his convictions, kept to the new centre ground, won the argument and then convincingly won the leadership election.

As well as seeking to drum up public support, Gove worked hard to ensure the parliamentary party were onside. Along with Bexhill & Battle MP Greg Barker, Gove established a pro-Cameron dining club called the Green Chip group. It was modelled on the Blue Chip group created by ambitious Tories in 1979, which counted John Major and Chris Patten as members. The 2007 version held its first meeting in a curry house in Ealing, west London, as Cameron's leadership hit choppy waters.[12] The grammar school row, together with a honeymoon bounce secured by Gordon Brown replacing Tony Blair as Prime Minister at the end of June, saw Labour leap ahead of the Tories in the opinion polls for the first time in more than a year. The mood in the Tory camp was further dampened by a third-place finish in the Ealing Southall by-election on 19 July. Like Hague and Duncan Smith, Cameron was coming under pressure from more traditional voices in the party to row back from his modernising agenda, with the focus on environment and social issues replaced by campaigns on the economy and Europe. The Green Chip group was an attempt to shore up support for Cameron's agenda and did not contain any MPs elected before 2001, meaning that while William Hague, David Davis and Liam Fox were excluded, George Osborne, Jeremy Hunt and Boris Johnson were invited to the monthly get-togethers, more often than not held in a Commons dining room.[13]

If the Green Chip group was about controlling the mind of the party, Gove was well aware that the hearts needed to be capture as well. In his speech to the Conservative Party conference in Blackpool on 1 October 2007, he avoided any mention of grammar schools or selective education, and instead threw as much red meat as possible to Tory activists. Francis Drake, Walter Raleigh, Captain Scott, Ernest Shackleton, Benjamin Disraeli and Winston Churchill all received namechecks, the strengthening of school discipline was talked up, and the word 'rigour' – long a hallmark of Gove's vocabulary – was deployed, with the shadow Secretary of State calling for every child to be given 'access to the best of what has been thought and written'.

'Under a Conservative government we'll have a curriculum that delivers on the basics, equips the next generation for a world of change and gives them back the chance to take pride in our country's history. Anything else would be a betrayal,' Gove added.14

If those sections of the speech were Gove by numbers, there was one part of the address that was slightly more off-kilter. 'We are on the brink of breakthroughs in particle physics which could lay bare the secrets of the universe,' said Gove, adding, 'Scientific innovation is driving improvements in every sphere of our existence.' These were not words which usually came out of Gove's mouth, and instead reflected the passion of his new advisor, a man known to the Tory hierarchy and who had already unsuccessfully tried to get the party to embrace new messages some six years earlier: Dominic Cummings.

Gove had brought Iain Duncan Smith's former chief of staff back to the fold after a period of self-imposed exile. After quitting Conservative Central Office in 2002, Cummings had helped launch the anti-EU New Frontiers think tank (which lasted only fifteen months); led the campaign against a north-east regional assembly in 2004; and then disappeared off the grid, spending two and a half years in a bunker on his father's farm, 'reading science and history and trying to understand the world.'¹⁵ Gove brought him back into the sunlight, as he needed someone by his side who would share his radical instincts and not be daunted by the processes and traditions of Westminster.

Gove would hold meetings of his team, including press office Alan Sendorek, policy advisor Jamie Martin and shadow minister John Hayes, in his cramped office in Portcullis House – the building next to Parliament which houses a third of MPs. Among the piles of papers and books, Gove honed his efforts to present himself as a true reformer in education policy, while painting Balls and Labour as more concerned with appeasing the teaching establishment than improving the lives of children. In short, Gove was the heir to Blair, and Balls was a reactionary conservative.

On 21 November, Gove used an opposition day debate to chastise the government for appearing to cool its enthusiasm for the academy programme. 'One of the most worrying aspects of the Secretary of State's tenure is a crab-like inching away from the proper reform programme, which began under Tony Blair,' said Gove, adding, 'In recent weeks, that process has taken on the aspect of a full-scale invertebrate retreat.'¹⁶

Gove was so keen to clothe himself in the garb of Blairism, he even took umbrage with the suggestion by Labour MP Tom Levitt that the Tories would axe a public spending scheme designed to rebuild or renovate schools across the country. 'I am afraid that he is completely wrong in his idea that we would abandon the building schools for the future programme,' said Gove, decisively.¹⁷

Just in case anyone had missed the memo on Gove's love of Blair, he penned an article in The Spectator in February 2008 under the headline 'I admired Tony Blair. I knew Tony Blair. Prime Minister, you are no Tony Blair'. Gove gushed over the former Labour leader as a 'genuine moderniser' who 'changed his positions as the world changed around him'.

'What Blair came to recognise, and what Brown still rejects, is that reform requires constant application of pressure to the accelerator,' wrote Gove approvingly.[18]

The love of the former Labour Prime Minister was beginning to prove too much for some Conservatives. Lord Tebbit, one of Margaret Thatcher's staunchest allies during her eleven years in Downing Street, issued a stern rebuke via The Spectator's letters page. 'I had hoped that David Cameron's claim to be 'the heir to Blair' was just a silly mistake springing from inexperience,' he wrote, adding, 'It is more worrying to find that Blair worship is now the doctrine of modern compassionate Conservatism.'[19] After listing what he deemed to be Blair's failings – immigration, identity cards, the 'despoliation of the family' – Tebbit concluded, 'In biblical terms, Blairism is the poisonous tree which can give forth only poisonous fruit and must be rooted out.' Little did Tebbit realise the true depth of the Blairite takeover at the top of his party. The Notting Hill set referred to Blair as 'The Master', so enamoured were they with the manner in which he had reversed Labour's electoral fortunes. Gove would even go on to pose for a photograph reading a well-thumbed copy of Blair's autobiography *A Journey* – 'I have never read a book like it,' he said in 2010.[20] It was all a long way from Gove attacking Ken Clarke in 2001 for being Blair's 'Trojan horse'.

In truth, Gove's political philosophy was even more controversial than the mere dash of Blairism. His belief in constant reform was more in keeping with the permanent revolution envisaged by Karl Marx. As one friend puts it, both Gove and Cummings have 'an almost Leninist belief – almost Trotskyite belief, perhaps – that you have to permanently revolutionise. Institutions have this incredibly strong drag effect and unless you are zealously fighting to push through your reforms they will die.'

Gove spent 2008 developing a multi-faceted approach to his

politics. The day job of a shadow minister is to scrutinise their opposite number, and his first move was to continue his approach of selective criticism of Labour policy. The plan to increase the age someone had to stay in a form of education was opposed, but he did speak out in support of the Educational Maintenance Allowance given to sixth-formers from low-income families. The quality of exams and the type of A levels being taught were a ready touchstone for Gove, who argued that subjects such as film and media studies, travel and tourism, home economics and dance attracted little respect from businesses or universities.[21]

After attacking the status quo, Gove began developing policies which the Conservatives would implement if they were in government. In a speech on 25 March 2008 to the Centre Forum think tank, he moved to outflank Labour on the roll-out of academies by arguing that organisations with a track record of running successful schools should be allowed to take over failing local authority-led institutions: 'Why not get every one of these schools out of local authority control – into the hands of an outside organisation with a great track record – and give that new organisation the freedoms – over curriculum, over staffing, and freedom from bureaucratic control – which have been the precondition of success elsewhere?'

Alongside increasing the number of academies, Gove and his team also began working up plans to reboot the free school programme. Whereas academisation related to existing schools, Gove wanted to allow parents, faith groups and other organisations to set up their own facilities from scratch, with funding direct from central government. In the summer of 2008, he went on a research trip to Sweden, where free schools had been in operation since 1992. Speaking to The Spectator upon his return, Gove set out how the policy would work in practical terms. Free schools would receive from the government a set amount of money per pupil with which to operate, and how that money would be used would be down to the administrators. Higher staff salaries or a focus on a particular area of the curriculum would help introduce market forces into local education systems, and, in the eyes of a Thatcherite Conservative, that would lead to a rise in standards. 'In your neighbourhood, there will be a new school going out of its way to persuade you to send your children there. It will market itself on being able to generate better results, and it won't cost you an extra penny,' Gove said.[22]

In a sign that he would waste no time if the Tories won the next election, Gove promised to introduce an education reform bill in the very first Queen's speech of the new government. He also used the interview to expand on his personal motivations and offered up two definitions for the label of 'progressive' he had bestowed on himself. The first definition, 'someone who believes in a meritocratic society, tempered by an obligation towards the poorest', was essentially One Nation Conservatism, and at the time was seen to be the politics of David Cameron and his acolytes. The second definition offered up by Gove was far more radical, however: 'If you are a progressive, you are angered by unmerited hierarchies, by establishments that block progress, by cartels and producer interests that stand in the way of people being able to be the authors of their own life story.'[23] He added that a genuine progressive will 'deliberately seek to find these establishments and take them on'. These are not words you would associate with others in the Notting Hill set. The Camerons, Osbornes and Vaizeys of this world had no desire to smash up 'unmerited hierarchies'; they had, after all, done rather well out of the structure of society.

With such an intoxicating vision for how the country needed to change, perhaps Gove's political ambitions went higher than being the next Education Secretary? When asked if he had promised his wife that he would never run for leader, Gove 'throws his head back and laughs loudly', noted *The Spectator*. 'It's not as if she wrung the concession out of me at knifepoint,' he said.

> Look, I'd never run for leader because I know what the job entails.
> I know it would place an impossible burden on me and my family.
> And I told Sarah that if it ever becomes the case that the burden
> upon us is just intolerable, then I will have to take evasive action.

Careful to balance a radical shake-up of the schooling system with a conservative edge, Gove told a conference of head teachers in Brighton he wanted to see a more traditional approach to learning. He decried the pupil-centred learning approach as 'dethroning' teachers, and said:

> This misplaced ideology has let down generations of children ...
> It is an approach to education that has been called progressive,
> but in fact is anything but. It privileges temporary relevance over
> a permanent body of knowledge which should be passed on from
> generation to generation ... We need to tackle this misplaced
> ideology wherever it occurs.[24]

Another branch of Gove's political manoeuvres involved him en-suring the modernisation project had constant momentum. In an interview with the *Evening Standard* in August 2008, Gove claimed that the British public still viewed the Tories as 'unreformed and grumpy', and Cameron appealed to voters as he was a 'star centre forward' who 'is not just a Conservative like any other'.[25] It was a deliberate attempt to keep pushing the view that the party had changed from the days of Major and Hague: not only were the old guard not in charge any more but the new rulers held no truck with them.

His selective approach to attacking Labour saw him go as far as publicly speculating which members of the government could join a future Conservative administration. Work and Pensions Secretary James Purnell and Communities Secretary Hazel Blears were picked out for praise, but it was Schools Minister Lord (Andrew) Adonis who received the greatest testimonial. 'I have yet to find a speech of Andrew's outlining policies that I disagree with,' Gove told *The Observer*.[26]

Gove's indulgence in a game of Fantasy Cabinet reflected an increasing confidence that there would soon be a Conservative chairing the meetings in 10 Downing Street.

By the time the 2008 party conference in Birmingham came along, the Conservatives had been ahead in the polls for a year. The initial honeymoon bounce recorded by Brown had long since faded, and the economic constraints caused by the worldwide banking sector collapse were being laid at the door of the Downing Street incumbent. As well as outscoring Labour in the polls, the Tories were succeeding at the ballot box. In local council elections on 1 May 2008, the party gained control of twelve local authorities and saw its share of the vote rise to 44 per cent. Labour was pushed into third place on 24 per cent, behind the Lib Dems. The jewel in the crown was delivered by Boris Johnson, who defeated Labour's Ken Livingstone to become Mayor of London.

Going into 2009, it seemed the Tories were on course to return to government for the first time in thirteen years at the next election. The Brown government looked tired, bereft of ideas and ridden with infighting. The Conservatives had a fresher appearance – aided by virtue of being out of government since 1997 – and seemed to have rediscovered a creative edge and a sense of discipline in the ranks. Yet both parties, and their leaders, were about to face a crisis in the entire political class – a crisis in which Gove had played a major part.

CHAPTER 14

NOT A PENNY MORE,
NOT A PENNY LESS

O n 8 May 2009, the Telegraph began running the first of a steady stream of stories about MPs' expenses. The paper had obtained unredacted copies of claims dating from 2004 to 2008, and focused its initial coverage on the Labour Party. Three days later, and the Telegraph shifted to the Tories. In the gallery of six Tories splashed across the 11 May front page, Gove's face was first. '£7,000 on furnishings before a move' was the caption on top of the photo. The paper revealed that between December 2005 and April 2006, Gove had used the Additional Cost Allowance system to furnish the north Kensington home he had bought with Sarah Vine in 2002. The ACA was designed to help MPs claim back the costs of running second homes, and Gove decided his property needed a lot of money spent on it. The list of items he claimed for reads like the conveyor belt round from The Generation Game. There was a dishwasher (£454), a fridge freezer (£702), a cooker (£639), a toaster (£19.99), a Manchu cabinet (£493), a Loire table (£750, but he only received £600 back), a pair of elephant lamps (£134.50), a woven door mat (£30), Egyptian cotton bed linen (£243), eight coffee spoons and cake forks (£5.95 each) and a foam cot mattress from Toys R Us (£34.99) – despite children's equipment being banned under the rules. A total bill of £7,000 was run up, all charged to the taxpayer.[1] Having spruced up his north Kensington house, Gove seemed to decide it was now up to the sufficient standard required for it to be his main home. He still needed a place in the constituency, though, and 'flipped' his second home designation to a house in Elstead – at a cost to the taxpayer of £13,259 – in October 2006, as he had been unable to buy the house he was renting in Camberley. Between May 2005 and April 2008, Gove claimed £66,827 in second home expenses – more than his annual salary of £64,766. It wasn't just furnishings and moving costs claimed by Gove. He even put in a receipt worth more than £500 for a one-night stay for himself and his family at a hotel in his constituency when they were between house moves.[2]

David Cameron moved quickly to get ahead of the story and immediately ordered colleagues to pay back 'excessive' expense clams. 'People are right to be angry,' he added.[3] The Tory leader was keen to show that while the scandal affected politicians from all parties, he would lead the clean-up operation. He asked his chief of staff, Ed Llewellyn, and the party chief whip, Patrick McLoughlin, to set up an internal committee to decide which MPs had overstepped the mark. The penalty for not engaging with the process was immediate expulsion – but Cameron was under pressure to go further. Don Porter, the effective head of the voluntary branch of the Conservative Party, wrote to the leader to say that activists wanted scalps. Big ones. 'I believe you have to sack all those front-bench colleagues who have exploited the system. Anything less than this will ... leave our party tainted with the aura of sleaze once again.'[4]

It was not looking good for Gove. The shadow Education Secretary had instantly agreed to pay back the furnishings money, but that was no guarantee that he would keep his job. In a bid to lance the boil, Gove hastily arranged a public meeting in his constituency on Monday 18 May. The idea had been Cameron's but it was fully endorsed by Dominic Cummings. Ahead of the meeting, Gove's office had been inundated with calls and emails from angry constituents.[5] If that sentiment transferred itself to the meeting, it was difficult to see how Gove could survive as the Conservative candidate for Surrey Heath in the next election.

Thousands of constituents turned out to witness Gove's plea for forgiveness, which was issued appropriately enough in St Mary's Church, Camberley. National and local journalists joined the public to see if the famously polite and courteous Gove could charm his way out of the situation.

At just after 7.30 p.m., Gove began his case for the defence. 'I am here to apologise, explain and listen,' he began, before moving on the specifics of his claims. Regarding the spend of furniture, Gove said, 'I made an error of judgement. I should have considered more carefully when I was spending that money. Your money. And for that I unreservedly apologise.' But it wasn't all contrition. Gove vehemently denied the claim he had 'flipped' the designation of his main and second homes in order to maximise his expenses. The floor was then open for questions. One man who identified himself as 'flipping furious from Frimley' asked, 'Where, sir, was your moral compass when you booked a night at the Pennyhill Park hotel and spa?'[6]

'It was wrong,' Gove admitted. Calls were made for the MP to put himself up for reselection, or even quit entirely and trigger a by-election.[7] Yet, as the meeting wore on, it seemed the self-flagellation strategy was working. According to *The Guardian*:

When one angry ex-serviceman told Gove that during a surgery session the politician had talked to him about integrity and asked if he could not go back to work, there was a ripple of embarrassment. 'I have more integrity than you will ever have mate,' he said. A smattering of applause was hushed by collective tutting.[8]

At one point, laughter even broke out when a questioner pointed out that with his background in journalism, 'surely something should have told you that it was a bit naughty?' Gove allowed himself a smile.

By the end of the two-hour meeting, it seemed Gove had indeed done enough. One constituent said, 'He showed terrific contrition and people respect that. He's lanced a boil.'[9] Gove may have survived the public flogging, but there was still the possibility that Cameron could place his head on the chopping block. Luckily for Gove, he was one of the Prime Minister's key lieutenants, and far from being made an example of, he was afforded some protection. That was certainly the perception from some of the Tory old guard, who believed that colleagues not part of the inner circle faced the harshest punishments. Sir Peter Viggers, the Gosport MP who tried to claim for a duck house, and Douglas Hogg, MP for Sleaford and North Hykeham, who charged taxpayers for his moat-cleaning bill, were both placed under pressure not to contest the next election and subsequently announced they were not standing. The one member of Cameron's team to quit was Andrew MacKay, MP for Bracknell and a parliamentary aide to the Tory leader. MacKay and his wife Julie Kirkbride, MP for Bromsgrove, had alternately delegated the two properties they shared together as their first and second homes, and used public funds to pay for them both. After a bruising public meeting in his Bracknell constituency – adjacent to Gove in Surrey Heath – MacKay announced he was quitting as an MP at the next election. Gove and other shadow Cabinet members implicated in the expenses scandal including Francis Maude and

Andrew Lansley got to keep not only their seats in Parliament but their places at the top table. 'There are some very bruised feelings,' a senior backbencher told *The Times*, claiming that Cameron's inner circle 'were told that if they want a Cabinet career they should just get their chequebooks out and pay some of their expenses back'.[10]

Luckily for Gove, the repayment came before he lost his lucrative second career as a newspaper columnist. At the end of June 2009, Cameron decreed that all shadow Cabinet members had to give up any additional jobs in order focus on 'setting out our credentials as an alternative government'. That meant Gove had to say goodbye to effectively half of his earnings, with the £60,000-a-year columnist job at The Times now banned. To make things worse, the announcement came when Gove was battling a bout of swine flu. His final column appeared in January 2010, when he mused on timekeeping and why the 'uberposh' wear cream shirts instead of white. He signed off: 'You may have noticed there's an election campaign on and I have to march towards the sound of gunfire.'[11]

That gunfire was coming not only from the Labour opposition but from some in the educational establishment as well.

On 30 June 2009, Gove gave what could be considered to be the key speech articulating his vision for the country's education system. Speaking at the Royal Society of Arts, he harked back to his own upbringing to amplify the importance of good schooling:

> I know from my own experience that the opportunities I have enjoyed are entirely the consequence of the education I have been given. Perhaps I value education so much because it has given me so much – but what it has given me most is the chance to shape my own destiny. For generations of my family before me, life was a matter of dealing with the choices others made, living by a pattern others set. I, and those members of my generation who were

given the gift of knowledge by wonderful teachers, have been given the precious freedom to follow their own path.[12]

Gove's schooling, where he studied classic literature, poured over encyclopaedias and absorbed opera, was, in his mind, the right kind of education. It had, after all, saved him from life as a fish processor in Aberdeen and transported him to Oxford University. To him, every child should have that education, and it would help led to the opportunities he had.

He went on:

Every child should have the chance to be introduced to the best that has been thought, and written. To deny children the opportunity to extend their knowledge so they can appreciate, enjoy, and become familiar with the best of our civilisation is to perpetuate a very specific, and tragic, sort of deprivation. There is a peculiar, and to my mind, quite indefensible assumption among some that the only cultural experiences to which the young are entitled, or even open, are those which have a direct, and contemporary, relevance to their lives. So Carol Ann Duffy and drum 'n' bass are OK, but Austen and Eliot, Cicero and Wagner are out.

It wasn't just the classics from the world of art and literature which Gove defended, but the story of the United Kingdom:

A recent survey of students entering a Russell Group university to read history asked them to name the British general at Waterloo, the monarch during the Armada, Brunel's profession, a single nineteenth-century Prime Minister and the location of the Boer War. The survey found that just over one question in five was answered correctly. Almost twice as many students thought Nelson was in charge at the Battle of Waterloo as named the Iron Duke, while nine students thought it was Napoleon (or Napolian or Napoliun). Almost 90 per cent of the students could not name a single British Prime Minister from the nineteenth century.

This, of course, was information he had learned at Robert Gordon's College. It had helped him immensely, so why shouldn't it help every child? Why should those who do not attend private school miss out on a private school education? Why shouldn't poor children read Dickens? Why shouldn't working-class kids be taught about nineteenth-century wars? If they did, if they could gorge on centuries of art and wisdom, they too could rise from their backgrounds and become political biographers, leader writers at *The Times*, or a potential Cabinet minister. According to Gove, that was what schools should be focused on, not 'everything from promoting community cohesion to developing relationships with other public bodies, trusts, committees and panels'.

He reused many of the lines from that speech in his address to the 2009 Conservative Party conference in October. But whereas the Royal Society of Arts speech had focused on the problems in education caused by the Labour government ('schools are less places of teaching and learning and more community hubs from which a host of children's services can be delivered'), he used his conference address to attack the teaching establishment directly. The 'education establishment' had done more than 'squander talent', he said; it had also 'squandered money' and facilitated 'the entrenched culture of dumbing down'.

Such rhetoric did not sit well with those at which it was aimed, and a group of twenty-six head teachers penned a joint letter to *The Guardian* taking umbrage at Gove's accusations:

With the phrase 'we will tackle head-on the defeatism, the political correctness and the entrenched culture of dumbing down that is at the heart of our educational establishment', Gove lost the support of many headteachers, who are working tirelessly, often in the most challenging circumstances, for the young people of this country.[13]

It was the beginning of a battle between Gove and the educational establishment – which he would one day give a far more provocative name – that for many years seemed to be his defining moment in the minds of the public.

The latter part of 2009 saw Gove beginning the process of measuring up the curtains for what very well could be his new job. Ahead of the Conservative conference, he met with David Bell, the Permanent Secretary at the Department for Children, Schools and Families. Over a dinner at the City Inn in John Islip Street, Westminster, Gove talked Bell through what he wanted to achieve should he become the senior civil servant's new boss. No advisors were present, as the pair were keen to forge a personal relationship before getting down to the business of government – should the opportunity arise. Bell remembers that not a lot of what he heard from Gove came as a surprise, as so much of the party's policy was already in the public domain:

> Michael had been talking a lot about the free schools, curriculums and examinations, the expansion of academy status, a refocusing of the department away from the wider children's agenda that Ed Balls had been pursuing. We came up with some reasonable ideas on each of these fronts and that was good because it gave us a good basis for the early discussion.

The pair seemed to get on well, and Bell remembers being 'struck immediately ... by his intellectual range'. He adds, 'He was clearly a man who knew quite a bit about quite a lot of things. Of course, as we subsequently saw, he was not averse to sharing his knowledge widely. When I met him early on, I was impressed with him.'

The meetings carried on throughout 2009 and into 2010, and it wasn't all high-concept thinking that dominated the talks. Changing the name of the department from Children, Schools and Families was supposed to be a quick win, but the idea prompted more head-scratching than anticipated. 'I remember one of these slightly silly conversations we had with one of Michael's advisors when I said is it the Department *for* Education or the Department *of* Education?' says Bell. The team opted for the former.

To put into place the plans Gove and team were hammering out, there was the small matter of actually winning the next election. Heading into 2010, the Conservatives were consistently ahead in the opinion polls, but as the election grew nearer, the lead started to slip. The party's war room, based out of 30 Millbank, was split on whether to focus on attacking the perceived incompetence of Gordon Brown or to run a positive campaign extolling the virtues of the Conservatives' policy agenda. Gove was brought into the top team in February to help sharpen up attacks on Brown,[14] but Conservative support in the polls continued to fall, and by the time Brown officially called the election on 6 April, a YouGov survey for *The Sun* gave the Tories only an eight-point lead over Labour. An Ipsos MORI poll eleven months earlier had put the Conservatives twenty-two points ahead.

Against that backdrop, Gove held another meeting with Bell, who remembers the wannabe Education Secretary handing over 'a little list of things that he saw as his early priorities'. It was clear that Gove was not going to take time to settle into his new role – he wanted to hit the ground running.

The election campaign itself centred on the leaders of the three biggest parties going head to head in television debates – the first of their kind in British political history. Cameron, Brown and Liberal Democrat leader Nick Clegg would square off for the cameras three times over a two-week period. Clegg made the most of being the unknown – and therefore unblemished – candidate, and such was his success in the first debate on 15 April that his party topped a YouGov poll for *The Sun*. Cameron did better in the second debate, held on 22 April, and was widely seen to have 'won' the final contest on 29 April. Yet going into Election Day on 6 May, the Conservatives averaged a lead of seven points, nowhere near enough to deliver a majority in the House of Commons.

Whether Gove would be part of what could well be either a minority government or a historic coalition depended on whether the voters of Surrey Heath had forgiven him for his expenses claim. On the day of the election, Dominic Cummings drove Gove around the constituency in his Skoda to ensure that those who had said they would vote Conservative were actually on their way to the polling stations. At around 8 p.m., Gove sent a message to his wife to pass on the news that turnout seemed good and Surrey Heath was backing Cameron 'not just with its head, but its heart, soul and everything going'.[15]

At 10 p.m., the exit poll dropped, predicting that while the Conservatives would be the largest party in the new parliament with 307 seats, they would be nineteen short of a majority. The poll was almost spot on, with the Tories eventually winning 306 seats, Labour 258, and the Lib Dems fifty-seven. That left Cameron twenty seats short of what was needed to form a working majority. The Lib Dems were in the position of kingmakers.

In Surrey Heath, Gove's forgiveness was complete. The voters returned him to Parliament with an increased majority – 17,289, up from 10,845 in 2005. The 6.1 percentage point rise in his vote outstripped the 3.7 per cent swing the Tories experienced nationally. Yet while Gove was back in Parliament, it wasn't clear if he would find himself in government – or, if he did, what portfolio he would be given.

The Conservatives and Lib Dems began negotiations on whether to enter a coalition and, if so, what form it should take. If a formal arrangement was entered into, the Lib Dems would demand seats in Cabinet, and Education was one portfolio of interest. Alarm bells started to ring when the Lib Dems' shadow Education Secretary David Laws was put into his party's negotiating team, while Gove was cut out of the Conservatives'. As the talks between the two sides went on, Gove made a bold announcement. Appearing on the BBC's Andrew Marr Show on Sunday 9 May, he was asked if he would give up his seat at the Cabinet table to Laws. 'Yes,' he replied, adding:

David Laws, who's the Liberal Democrat Education spokesman, is someone who's – and I said this before the election result – thoughtful, flexible, someone who actually wants to improve our education system; and the ideas that he's put forward throughout this campaign, even though I don't agree with all of them, have been motivated by idealism.

Just to make sure he had heard correctly, Marr ended the interview by asking again, 'You ... would be prepared to concede, to give up your Cabinet seat to make this happen?' 'Yes,' came the one-word reply[16]

Gove's education team were in shock.[17] While it was obvious that Cabinet places would be part of the currency of the negotiations, to see your boss on the television openly conceding his position was a sobering moment. In truth, there was no danger of Gove being moved from the Education brief. Cameron knew the next government – in whichever form it eventually materialised – would be focused on getting to grips with the economy and reducing the spending deficit. In other words, there would be a lot of pain for a great many people across the country as the doctor administered the medicine. There needed to be some brightness in what would be a dark period, and education reform was seen as an area where Cameron could build a legacy. Gove was always, in his mind, the person to do it.[18]

On 11 May, with talks between Labour and Lib Dems completely broken down, Gordon Brown announced his resignation as Prime Minister and travelled to Buckingham Palace to tell the Queen she should ask David Cameron to form a government. The Conservative leader made his own trip to the palace an hour later and, although the coalition agreement with the Lib Dems had yet to be finalised, returned to Downing Street as Prime Minister. The Lib Dems signed off the coalition agreement later that night, and the next day, Cameron and Clegg held a joint press conference in the rose garden of 10 Downing Street to mark the first formal coalition government of the UK since the Second World War. The Lib Dems bagged themselves five Cabinet positions, with Clegg as Deputy Prime Minister, Vince Cable at Business, Chris Huhne at Energy and Climate Change, Danny Alexander in the Scotland Office, and David Laws as Chief Secretary to the Treasury.

Ahead of that press conference, Gove was summoned to Downing Street to meet his old friend, the new Prime Minister. Accompanied by Dominic Cummings, he entered one of the most famous buildings in the world, fully prepared to leave almost immediately and head over to his new office to begin work on the job he had spent three years preparing for. Cummings waited outside the room while Gove went in to get his appointment rubber-stamped. When

Gove emerged, there was not the delirium Cummings had expected on his friend's face. Instead, there was bad news. Gove was indeed off to the soon-to-be renamed Department for Children, Schools and Families, but Cummings would not be going with him. His appointment as Gove's special advisor had been blocked by Andy Coulson, the former News of the World editor who was now Cameron's director of communications. Coulson suspected that Cummings had leaked details of a meeting involving Gove, Cameron and George Osborne some three months earlier, and considered him too much of a liability to make the transition to government.[19]

Cameron's mind was made up and, with Cummings's blessing,[20] Gove left Downing Street and headed alone to the department's offices in Great Smith Street. Gove was now in government and was determined to hit the ground running – but within months he would fall flat on his face.

CHAPTER 15

THROUGH THE
LOOKING GLASS

Sir David Bell had enjoyed a more relaxed post-election week-end than he had anticipated. After hanging around the office on Friday 7 May 2010, the day after the general election, the Permanent Secretary at the soon-to-be Department for Education sent the vast majority of his staff home for the weekend as the coalition negotiations began. Far from the flurry of activity that he and his staff had predicted in the wake of a general election expected to produce a change of government, the office on Great Smith Street was relatively quiet. Instead of spending Sunday 9 May trimming budgets in the office, Sir David found himself cutting the grass at home. As he manoeuvred his mower across the lawn, he thought back to Michael Gove's interview on *The Andrew Marr Show* a few hours earlier. Was his offer to trade away the role of Education Secretary serious? In the lead-up to the election, Sir David had been wargaming how a Gove-led department would operate in its first few weeks and months. He had assumed the role of Gove in several exercises as he tried to get his department mentally prepared to serve a Conservative Education Secretary for the first time in thirteen years. In the wargaming exercise, some civil servants tried to talk 'Gove' out of certain decisions, such as abolishing a database of information on under-18s called ContactPoint, which had been designed to avoid a repeat of the failures of multiple institutions to prevent the murder of eight-year-old Victoria Climbié in 2000, who was tortured and killed by her great-aunt and her boyfriend. Sir David gave them short shrift. 'Be under no illusions: if Michael Gove walks through that door in May, you're going to have to shut this down,' he told them.

Reflecting on that period, Sir David says of his staff, 'It wasn't because they were being ideological, it was just "How could someone possibly do that?"'

He adds:

I, to be frank, underestimated the extent, not that people were party political or partisan, but having served the same government for a number of years people felt as if they understood the instincts of the Labour government. I think some civil servants found it a bit of a shock to find that the instincts were just different.

On Wednesday 12 May, it was confirmed that Gove would indeed be Sir David's new boss, and the Permanent Secretary waited by the door for him to arrive. 'Secretary of State, I'm seeing you five days later than expected,' said Sir David as he shook Gove's hand. Gove was still somewhat in shock that his arrival was without his right-hand man Dominic Cummings, but quickly made his way up to his new office.

After departing Downing Street, Cummings had put out a call to other members of Gove's education team to get down to the office and support the brand-new Cabinet minister. Policy wonk Sam Freedman and special advisor Elena Narozanski arrived on the scene, and the civil service sprang into action. Meetings were arranged and decisions were requested as the realities of being in charge of a department kicked in.

As Gove was sitting down at his desk in the Education Department, the man who had been rumoured to get the job in his place, David Laws, was settling into his role as the new Chief Secretary to the Treasury. On his desk was a letter from his Labour predecessor, Liam Byrne, which simply read: 'Dear Chief Secretary, I'm afraid there is no money. Kind regards – and good luck! Liam.' It was a stark reminder of the financial constraints facing the new government, and Gove was as aware of any minister of the need to find savings in his department's budget. But before he turned to number crunching, Gove wanted to give the department itself a makeover – or, indeed, a makeunder. As expected, the new-age-sounding Department for Children, Schools and Families was renamed the much more traditional Department for Education. Out went the rainbow logo and brightly coloured murals dotted around the office, and in came sepia pictures of school buildings. A coffee bar in the visitors' waiting room disappeared and was replaced by a sturdy desk.[1] Gove's own office was decorated with photographs of likely and unlikely figures. Margaret Thatcher, Theodore Roosevelt and Barack Obama found themselves alongside Lenin, Malcolm X and Martin Luther King. The Russian revolutionary had earned his place as by apparently having coined the phrase 'Education, education, education', while Malcolm X and Dr King reflected the new Secretary of State's vision of his role. 'I see education in the UK as a civil rights struggle,' Gove would later say.[2]

With the department's infrastructure starting to change, Gove began taking a hammer to some of Labour's legacy. As Sir David had predicted, ContactPoint was scrapped, as was the General Teaching Council for England – a quango set up in 2000 to improve standards in the profession. Yet it was one of Labour's boldest innovations in education – academies – which Gove wanted not only to protect but to nurture.

When the coalition government came to power, there were 203 academy schools in the UK. As we have seen, Gove was determined to dramatically increase that number in order to free schools from the grip of local authority control, and he wanted to start that process as soon as possible. 'Michael was absolutely determined to get the Academies Bill into law before the summer recess, so that took up a lot of our initial headspace thinking about how we could support the parliamentary process to make that happen,' remembers Sir David.

On 26 May, Gove wrote to the head teachers of every school in England, inviting them to become academies – including, for the first time, primaries and special schools. Those rated outstanding by the school inspectorate, Ofsted, would be fast-tracked through the process, and the first of the new academies were expected to be opened by September 2010. It was the biggest shake-up of the school system since 1965, when Labour Education Secretary Tony Crosland ruled that comprehensive schools should become the norm. The same day the head teachers received Gove's letter, the Academies Bill was presented to the House of Lords.

Gove may have been keen to push on with systematic reform, but, as with all departments, education was expected to deliver spending cuts. One area identified as ripe for culling was Building Schools for the Future, a £55 billion programme introduced by Labour. As we have seen, Gove had previously denied that the Conservatives would axe BSF, but that commitment was made in the pre-financial crash days of November 2007, and the mood music had now changed. The new Chancellor, George Osborne, was due to announce the results of a review of Whitehall spending in October, but with the DfE green-lighting multi-million-pound developments for schools on an almost weekly basis, the decision over BSF could not wait until the autumn. Gove and his advisors considered freezing the scheme until a proper assessment of the programme could be carried out, but it was argued that placing it in stasis would send out the signal it was going to be axed, so why not just pull the plug? Of around 1,400 schools going through the BSF process, 719 saw their improvement plans scrapped.

On 5 July, Gove delivered a statement to the Commons explaining his decision. He attacked BSF as being characterised by 'massive overspends, tragic delays, botched construction projects and needless bureaucracy'.

'Some councils that entered the process six years ago have only just started building new schools,' he said. 'Another project starting this year is three years behind schedule. By contrast, Hong Kong international airport, which was built on a barren rock in the South China Sea and can process 50 million passenger movements every year, took just six years to build from start to finish.'

Gove's focus on the incompetence of the scheme took an ironic twist thanks to his own performance. He irked Speaker John Bercow by overrunning the time allowed to deliver the statement, and had not provided MPs with a list of which projects had been axed and which were to go ahead.

Yet when Labour MP Stephen Twigg asked about schools in his Liverpool West Derby constituency, Gove told him that four were unaffected but five had had their developments axed. 'He's got a list!' shouted shadow Education Secretary Ed Balls as MPs began voicing their anger that while Gove knew what was happening with schools in their patches, they were in the dark. A stream of Labour MPs quizzed Gove about specific schools, but even he was unable to be certain about all of them.

It was a shambolic performance at the despatch box, but the

incompetence didn't end there. Not only had a list of schools affected been handed to the media before it was made available to MPs, but it contained numerous errors. Another list was published that evening, and then a third the next day, as the department struggled to put out accurate information. The effect was that twenty-five schools were told their redevelopment work was safe, when in fact their schemes were among those either facing the axe or up for discussion.

Gove was forced back to the Commons on 7 July to apologise to MPs for his handling of the announcement two days earlier. Before he wrote to the Speaker requesting the opportunity to set the record straight, Labour MP Tom Watson, whose West Bromwich East constituency housed nine schools that had been incorrectly told their redevelopments were going forward, grabbed a quick word with the Education Secretary. According to a source close to Gove, Watson said, 'Michael, anyone can make a mistake, so if you come back to the House of Commons to apologise, we'll be gentle with you.'

As Gove got to his feet to address a crowded House of Commons, it was clear that Watson's promise was a hollow one. Gove's apologies came thick and fast – sorry for not making the list of schools available at the start of the initial statement; sorry for publishing inaccurate information; sorry for considering a written apology to MPs before agreeing to make an appearance. 'Once again, Mr Speaker, I am grateful to you and to the whole House for granting me the opportunity to make this statement and, once again, to apologise unreservedly,' he concluded.

Shadow Schools minister Vernon Coaker tore into Gove, accusing him of facilitating 'chaos and confusion', and having to be dragged 'kicking and screaming' to the Commons to apologise. Gove adopted his most convincing Uriah Heep demeanour, repeatedly saying sorry for the errors. The opposition were having none of it, and the most forceful rebuke came from Watson. With his voice increasing in both anger and volume, the Labour MP said, 'He can embarrass himself, he can disgrace his party, but what is intolerable is that he has cynically raised the hopes of hundreds and thousands of families. You're a miserable pipsqueak of a man, Gove...'

The Commons erupted and the rest of Watson's attack was drowned out. John Bercow took to his feet to insist the Labour MP withdrew the term 'pipsqueak' – something Watson did 'out of deference' to the Speaker.

Gove again apologised, insisting, 'The mistake was mine and mine alone, and I am happy to acknowledge it.'

After just under thirty minutes, the grilling came to an end, and Gove escaped the chamber. As he left, veteran Conservative MP David Davis approached, and after using an Anglo-Saxon phrase to sum up the situation, insisted, 'You will be a better minister for this because you learn from your mistakes.'[83]

If Gove had hoped his fulsome apology would mark an end to the episode, he was mistaken. Another four errors were found in the latest list – its fourth incarnation – further adding to the sense of incompetence and also ensuring the story stayed in the media cycle. It was not looking good for Gove, and when members of his own party as well as the Lib Dems began speaking out publicly in opposition to the cancelling of the scheme, there was a growing sense that he had lost control. Gove's next appearance in the Commons was Education Questions, scheduled for Monday 12 July, and the BSF debacle was set to dominate what would be his third appearance in front of MPs on the issue in a week.

Gove arranged a meeting with David Cameron and George Osborne ahead of the session and spelt out the severity of situation. 'I might have to resign,' he told them. The Prime Minister and Chancellor were having none of it and told their old friend to stiffen his spine. With their advice ringing in his ears, Gove turned to an old ally to help navigate him the increasingly choppy waters.

Dominic Cummings was, of course, not supposed to be in the Department for Education. If had word got back to David Cameron that it was his former special advisor he had summoned into the offices on Great Smith Street, the PM's support for Gove might have evaporated. Having been snuck into the building, Cummings delivered advice typical of a man who seemed to take pleasure in antagonism: go on the attack. Sir David says, 'I remember Dominic saying, "Stop apologising, get out there and say why you're doing what you're doing for BSF."' With attack identified as the best form of defence, Gove began working his contacts in Fleet Street in an attempt to drum up some sympathetic coverage in the Sunday papers. According to one source, Cummings decided to shift the blame for the errors away from Gove and onto the body in charge of the BSF programme: Partnerships for Schools.

The *Sunday Times* was handed a 'government dossier' flagging up the £30 million annual cost of running the quango and the £216,000-a-year salary enjoyed by its chief executive, Tim Byles. The paper reported that 'Whitehall sources' were 'pinning blame' for the BSF debacle on Byles and his team, as it had 'had no full list of school projects available when Gove took office and that he received the list only 40 minutes before going to the Commons'. Journalists turned up on Byles's doorstep to quiz him over the claims of incompetence, and he later complained that he felt his phone had been hacked and had been receiving calls in which no one actually spoke to him.[4]

With Partnerships for Schools now taking some of the heat, Gove and his team spent the day before his next appearance in the Commons meticulously going through what would be the fifth

version of the list of schools facing changes to their BSF application status. Sir David remembers just how much pressure Gove was
under. Both men knew that if this list contained errors, Gove's reputation would take a serious dent. Cameron may not have sacked
him at that moment, but when the inevitable reshuffle occurred,
he would most likely face demotion. 'He'd never been Secretary of
State before and here he was a month on facing this – pardon my
French – shit-storm,' says Sir David, adding:

> I said to him, 'Michael this will be absolutely no consolation to
> you but I'm afraid there's something called the crisis merry-go-
> round in government and today sadly it's been you. It's much
> earlier in your term of office than you would have wanted and
> I certainly would have wanted, but you will look back on this
> period and you'll find that some other minister is in the spotlight.

An hour and a half before his make-or-break Commons appearance, Gove sent the new list over to his Labour opposite number
and all other MPs. A week on from his initial statement, he followed Cummings's advice to the letter and switched from injured
puppy to attack dog. After Balls spoke of the 'widespread anger'
over the decision to axe BSF, Gove shot back:

> He says that there was anger across the House. There was at the
> way in which the BSF project had been run by the right hon.
> Gentleman. There was justifiable anger at the way in which a
> project that was originally supposed to cost £45 billion ended up
> costing £55 billion, and it was shared by those who were shocked
> that under the previous government, one individual received
> £1.35 million in consultancy fees – money that should have gone
> to the front line. From the moment that I took office, everyone

involved in this process said to me, 'Make sure that you ensure that this faltering and failing project ends.' That is what I have done. I inherited a mess from the right hon. Gentleman, and we are clearing it up.

He continued in the same vein throughout the session and, with no additional errors flagged up, he left the chamber hoping his performance had done enough to save his reputation and, ultimately, his job.

Gove's team were furious with the civil service. For all his claim that the mistakes had been his and his alone, the Education Secretary had been badly let down by his officials. Byles later admitted that Partnership for Schools had not fully switched its systems from what the Labour government required to the needs of the new administration and so struggled to produced information on which schools had signed contracts on developments and which were still in the application stage. His warning that the initial list should be checked with local authorities to establish any errors was not passed on to Gove by DfE officials, and the Education Secretary was happy to let Partnership for Schools validate the data.

Byles was keen to pass some of the blame on to the DfE, but he admitted to MPs that the most high-profile cock-up – involving schools in Sandwell – was his quango's fault. 'It was made late at night, but it was our mistake and I take responsibility for it,' he told the Education Select Committee on 27 July. Byles also claimed his staff were working 'twenty-four hours a day for seven days a week for three weeks on the go' in order to get the data ready, painting a picture of unreasonable pressure from the DfE. Appearing in front of the same committee the next day, Sir David hit back at the suggestion: 'PfS said that it was checking the data all the way through, so I do not think that there is any question that there was some sort of last-minute, rushed process of checking the data.'

The select committee hearings seemed to take some of the pressure off Gove, especially with Sir David's admission that 'it was a mistake not to put to the Secretary of State the possibility of checking the data with local authorities. As Permanent Secretary, I am ultimately responsible for the policy advice that goes to the Secretary of State, so I take responsibility for that.' While the BSF row did rumble on, it was now more focused on the politics of cancelling rebuilding projects for 700 schools as opposed to the competence of those involved in implementing the decision. In the narrative of the state tightening its belt, it was much easier for Gove to defend the policy shift than its flawed execution.

If Gove thought his turn on the 'crisis merry-go-round' had come to end, the remainder of 2010 would leave him feeling dizzy. It seemed that all his plans and initiatives were met with hostility and cries of incompetence. The Academies Bill was rushed through Parliament at breakneck speed, receiving Royal Assent on 27 July – just two months after it was presented to the Lords. Ahead of the Bill reaching the Commons, Gove had talked up the desire in the education sector for schools to convert to academies. On 2 June, Gove claimed the response to his letter to head teachers inviting to them to convert their schools was 'overwhelming'. 'In just 1 week, over 1,100 schools have applied,'[5] he said. At the end of July, and with the Bill now law, the figure was revised down drastically – with just 153 applications received by the DfE.[6] While that figure rose to 181 by 1 September,[7] it was hardly a ringing endorsement for a policy which Gove had claimed would be welcomed by head teachers across England.

It was the same with free schools. At the beginning of June, Gove issued a rallying call for parents and other groups to begin submitting applications to set up new schools in their communities. Yet by September 2010 just sixteen projects had been approved,[8] and even that announcement began to unravel when a leaked civil service assessment of the applications ruled that 'a minority' of those schools would be in a position to appoint a head teacher by the December 2010 deadline, while others were struggling to have a site for the school ready by August 2011.[9]

Gove's reverse Midas touch even extended to his appearance at the Conservative Party conference in Birmingham. Ahead of his speech, he invited five guests to address party members from the main stage. One of those was Katharine Birbalsingh, a deputy head teacher at St Michael's and All Angels Academy in Camberwell, South London. Birbalsingh brought the conference to its feet after accusing schools of 'dumbing down' standards. Her employers weren't as happy with her intervention and told her to work from home for the rest of the week. She was soon looking for a new job.

Gove tried to seize back the initiative with his education White Paper 'The Importance of Teaching'. Published on 24 November, the document not only set out much of what Gove had spent the last three years preaching ('Education ... allows us all to become authors of our own life stories,' he wrote in the introduction), it also went further on his proposals to improve the standard of teaching in the classroom. Graduates with a 2:2 degree classification would no longer receive money for teacher training; the Teach First scheme which allowed trainer teachers to learn 'on the job' would be expanded; and it would become easier to sack substandard teachers. In a bid to encourage greater emphasis on 'traditional subjects', an English Baccalaureate was announced. Students with an A* to C grade in English, mathematics, the sciences, a modern or ancient foreign language and a humanity such as history or geography would get the award, and the achievement rate would be registered in school league tables. Alas for Gove, he was unable to set the bar particularly high when it came to his own abilities. When his statement was distributed for MPs to read in the Commons, the words 'coalition' and 'bureaucracy' were misspelt. His grammar wasn't much better, with one sentence 300 words in length.[10]

The White Paper itself received a scathing response from teaching unions. The main focus of their ire was the suggestion that poor-quality teachers were able to dodge getting sacked thanks to extensive red tape and a culture of tolerance.

Chris Keates, general secretary of the NASUWT union, said, 'We are today witnessing a vicious assault by the Secretary of State on teachers' commitment and professionalism,' while Dr Mary Bousted, general secretary of the Association of Teachers and Lecturers, said, 'Bit by bit Michael Gove is dismantling state education in England.'[11]

At the same time as the White Paper was produced, Gove was desperately trying to dampen down a row which had provoked anger far beyond the educational establishment. On 20 October, he wrote to Baroness Campbell, chair of the Youth Sport Trust, to inform her that funding for a £162 million national PE scheme was to be axed. Schools Sports Partnerships had been created by Labour in 2002, and eight years later some 450 were in operation across England. The partnerships used the ringfenced money to run PE classes in schools without any trained staff, and also to organise after-hours clubs, competitions and events. Gove felt the partnerships had done little to increase participation and it was far better to give schools extra money so head teachers could decide how to develop PE. However, the so-called Olympic initiative had a budget of only £10 million, far less than the partnerships' annual budget. The Youth Sport Trust described the decision as 'devastating', and by the end of November high-profile Olympic champions including Denise Lewis, Tessa Sanderson and Jason Queally wrote to David Cameron asking him to order a U-turn. 'The future health of all our children is at risk if you axe this funding,' they said.[12] Labour leader Ed Miliband picked up on the row during Prime Minister's Questions on 24 November, urging Cameron to overrule Gove. Cameron defended the decision, but a week later it appeared a U-turn was in the offing when he told MPs he was 'looking carefully' at Labour's concerns over the cuts. On 20 December, Gove confirmed a U-turn, with the partnerships now receiving funding until August 2011 instead of March, and schools able to continue funding the projects themselves after that date. As *The Guardian* reflected in 2012, 'It is quite something for a Conservative education secretary to rouse sporting heroes, parents, schoolchildren, head teachers and newspapers like the *Daily Mail* and *Daily Telegraph* into frustrated, uncomprehending opposition, but Gove managed it.'[13]

Having annoyed the sports world, Gove then turned his attention to one he was much more at home in: literature. Two days after the partnerships U-turn, it was announced that a charity set up to give free books to children in England would lose all £13 billion of its government funding from April 2011. BookTrust's chief executive Viv Bird was 'astounded and appalled' by the decision, saying, 'There was no dialogue. It was completely devastating.'[14]

As with the sports partnership decision, Gove soon found himself on the receiving end of a public backlash, as leading authors including Ian McEwan, Philip Pullman and poet laureate Carol Ann Duffy all spoke out against the plan. 'Sheer stupid vandalism, like smashing champagne bottles as a drunken undergraduate. It doesn't matter: someone else will clear it up. Well, if you miss the first years of a child's development, nothing can clear it up. It's gone. It won't happen. A whole generation will lose out,' said Pullman, while Duffy compared Gove to Ebenezer Scrooge.

With the story gaining traction over the Christmas holiday, Gove and his team spent 25 December in crisis management mode, trying to work out how they had managed to alienate some of the most popular figures in the country – again.

The U-turn was quicker this time, and on Boxing Day Gove called Bird to pledge that government funding would indeed continue after April, and a joint statement between DfE and Book-Trust was issued in a bid to diffuse the row.

One DfE insider blames a junior civil servant for the disaster, claiming that while axing BookTrust's funding had been discussed, it was not yet a firm policy and the letter had been prematurely sent to the charity. Regardless of who was responsible for the story, it meant that as 2010 came to an end, Gove was in danger of becoming known as the minister for U-turns. Such a reputation would severely hinder his chances of getting the educational establishment to back his more systemic changes to schooling, giving the impression that if heels were dug in and enough of a media storm generated, Gove would be for turning. He needed to get on the front foot; he needed some protection from the slings and arrows raining down on him; he needed someone to go out and fight his corner with the department, the educational establishment and the media. He needed Dominic Cummings, and in 2011 he got him back.

CHAPTER 16

LES ENFANTS TERRIBLES

On 21 January 2011, Andy Coulson quit as David Cameron's director of communications. The former *News of the World* editor was facing increasing scrutiny for his role in the phone-hacking scandal engulfing his former employer, and, having become the focus of media attention, his role as the Prime Minister's communications chief was compromised. He stepped down, and in 2014 he served just under five months in prison for conspiracy to intercept voicemails. With Coulson gone from Downing Street, Gove was finally able to appoint Cummings as his chief of staff. Within three hours of his first day, the returning special advisor was aghast at how the department operated:

> Between 8ish and 11ish, roughly every half hour officials knocked
> on the spad office door and explained a new cockup – we had
> accidentally closed an institution because we'd forgotten to renew
> a contract, the latest capital figures briefed to the media were out
> by miles, a procurement process had blown up, letters had gone
> out with all the wrong numbers in them (this happened maybe
> monthly over the three years I was there), and so on – meanwhile
> people were trying to organise the launch of the National Cur-
> riculum Review in documents full of typos and umpteen other

things were going wrong simultaneously. It seemed extraordinary at the time but soon it was normal.[1]

Cummings went in to see his boss to inform him of the 'horrors' he was witnessing, but as he filled Gove in, he noticed BBC News on a screen behind the Secretary of State. The ticker on the bottom claimed Gove was overseeing a 'new disaster' with another announcement.

Cummings said, 'Michael, we just agreed we weren't going to announce anything else, we're going dark until we get a grip of this madhouse, what the—'

Turning to look at the screen, Gove replied, 'I haven't authorised any new announcement and certainly not that. I haven't a clue what they're on about.'[2]

Frustration with the civil service was not just confined to Cummings. Henry de Zoete, Gove's media spad, was also taken aback by how the DfE operated. 'I naively assumed that the way the system would work would be that the Permanent Secretary would be sitting outside the Secretary of State's office, he'd be there every day barking orders making sure that what the minister wants get done,'[3] he said in 2018, adding:

> In fact, it's almost the opposite and the Permanent Secretary is based on the other side of the department, you see him kind of once a week for the occasional meeting and really what you have implementing what the Secretary of State wants is a private office of brilliant civil servants who are extremely committed but they are 25–35-year-old junior civil servants. You have effectively kind of mid-ranking civil servants saying to more senior civil servants, 'This is what you need to do and you need to make this happen and the paper you wrote isn't very good and the Secretary of State isn't very happy and you need to deliver this by X date and you've missed

that deadline.' That's very difficult for people who are mid-ranking to be telling people who they are going to be getting jobs off in a few years' time what to do and that system is geared up to not necessarily really deliver what the Secretary of State wants.[3]

As seen with the Building Schools for the Future episode, Permanent Secretary Sir David Bell was aware his civil servants were struggling to turn on a sixpence to provide their new boss with the level of service his Labour predecessor had enjoyed.

Yet Gove's team believed it was more than incompetence. Cummings in particular felt some in the department were actively trying to sabotage Gove's reforming agenda, and at times it was 'impossible to distinguish between institutionalised incompetence and hostile action'.[4]

So frustrated was Cummings that he gave this advice to anyone who had dealings with DfE:

Every process will be mismanaged unless it involves one of these officials [XYZ]. No priority you have will happen unless spads and private office make it a priority. Trust private office – they're the only reliable thing between you and disaster. Every set of figures will be wrong. Every financial model will be wrong. Every bit of legal advice will be wrong. Every procurement will blow up. Every contract process will have been mismanaged. Every announcement will go wrong unless Zoete [my fellow spad], Frayne [director of communications], or [names withheld to protect the innocent] is in charge – let them sort it out and never waste your time having meetings about communications.[5]

Yet throughout this incompetence, Gove maintained his legendary civility. James Frayne, brought in as the department's director of communications in February 2011, has no memory of his boss losing his temper with staff: 'I never once saw Gove do that, but he would have been well within his rights to have done so at times. With no ability to hire and fire, even the biggest mistakes can go unpunished. Shouting often seems like the only thing secretaries of state actually can do.'[6] That's not to say Gove did not have ways of making his displeasure obvious. One former civil servant remembers how Gove would bombard officials with a series of increasingly pointed questions if he was unhappy with the quality of information being presented to him.

With trust in DfE's civil servants severely languishing, Gove decided to circumvent official routes of communication for discussions with his key advisors. On 29 December 2010, Gove sent an email from the personal account of his wife – dubbed 'Mrs Blurt' – to five people, including Cummings, whom he continued to rely on for advice. Headed 'New Year Action Plan', the email set out themes for the first few weeks of 2011, including 'Reform Bearing Fruit On The Ground Week', 'Tackling Failure Week', 'Next Steps on Structural Reform Week' and 'Restoring Sanity Week'. Much of the email involved finding news angles through which to promote Gove's reforms.

The email also captured Gove's reaction to the impending start of a judicial review into the axing of the Building Schools for the Future policy, involving Waltham Forest Council, Kent County Council, Luton Borough Council, Nottingham City Council, Newham Council and Sandwell Council.

'AAAAAARGGGGGHHHH!!!!!!' was Gove's thought on the legal challenge.

The use of personal emails continued into 2011 and in February, Cummings – now in place as Gove's advisor – emailed De Zoete and copied in five Conservative Party staff, telling them he would 'not answer any further emails to my official DfE account'.[7]

The email went on: 'I will only answer things that come from gmail accounts from people who i know who they are. i suggest that you do the same in general but thats obv up to you guys – i can explain in person the reason for this.'[8]

Yet even using this method of communication did not stop the leaks. *Financial Times* journalist Chris Cook received copies of the emails and decided to see whether the department would front up about the use of personal accounts in the conduct of its work.

Cook began submitting requests under the Freedom of Information Act to see the emails he had already been leaked, but the DfE replied that it could not find any of the messages. In September 2011, the *FT* ran a front-page story on Gove and his advisors' use of private emails, revealing that the Information Commissioner was investigating them to see if they had broken the terms of the Freedom of Information Act. While the use of private emails is in itself not illegal, if the content of those communications relates to government business then the Act still applies, and the messages have to be considered for release to the public.

On 31 January 2012, Gove was grilled over the use of private email accounts during an appearance before the Education Select Committee. Labour MP Lisa Nandy was the most tenacious and blunt when it came to the matter. Three times she asked him, 'Have you or your advisors ever used private email accounts in order to conceal information from civil servants or the public?'

Gove repeated that he and his department had always followed Cabinet Office advice when it came to FOI requests, repeating a claim that he had been told that private emails were not covered by the Act, when in fact his own department's chief Freedom of Information officer had said they were. 'One of the things that I have found in government is that you will often find that there are different people who will have different interpretations of how things should be followed,' he argued.

He was then pressed on what steps his department had taken to prevent any more emails being deleted. Gove stuck to the line that since the Cabinet Office had not changed its advice, it was still working to that ruling – not to the Information Commissioner's 'view' – as he called it – that such emails were covered by FOI.

In March 2012, the scale of deletion of the emails came to light when the Media Standards Trust charity revealed that around 130 emails to and from Henry de Zoete had been destroyed. A DfE spokesman insisted the deletions were merely good housekeeping, adding, 'The act of deleting emails is not evidence of wrongdoing.'[9]

The email saga was just one example of how Gove and other members of his top team seemed determined to play by their own rules. Cummings in particular seemed nonplussed by notions of politeness and civility; Lib Dem minister David Laws noted in his diaries that 'Dom has a fairly fearsome reputation for playing the man, the ball and everything else'.[10] As part of his bid to get the department into shape, Cummings insisted that the five most senior officials in the DfE, including Sir David Bell, proofread all ministerial letters drafted by officials. According to Cummings, ministers were having to reject 'nine out of ten [letters] because of errors with basic facts, spelling, or grammar'.[11] He also took issue with the job-for-life culture of the civil service, demanding to know who would be replacing an official who had 'made mistakes that had cost the taxpayer many millions of pounds'.

'Dominic, you're a spad, you're not allowed even to discuss personnel matters,' came the reply from one the department's most senior officials.

Cummings retorted, 'Michael will certainly want to know what is happening with this official and so do I.'

Cummings later remembered the outcome: 'The official was, of course, not fired. He had an extended paid holiday then was promoted into a non-job for another few months before being pensioned off with a gong in the next honours list.'[12]

One civil servant who did leave DfE within months of Cummings's arrival was Sir David Bell. Having joined the department as Permanent Secretary in June 2007, Sir David planned to return to the world of education – he was a former head teacher – and in October 2011 announced his decision to leave the civil service. His resignation came at the same time as that of three other senior officials, prompting rumours of dissatisfaction at the top of the department as the motivation for the walkout. Sir David has always denied that suggestion and repeatedly insisted he had a good working relationship with Gove and his advisors. As he cleared his desk in December 2011 in preparation for his new role as Vice-Chancellor of the University of Reading, he came across the list of priorities that Gove had handed him during their meeting just before the general election. 'I was able to hand that list back to him and say, "We've done the things that you asked me to do a year and a half ago,"' he remembers.

Sir David's immediate replacement was Tom Jeffery, who would adopt a caretaker role until March 2012 when the permanent successor, Chris Wormald, could move over from the Cabinet Office. Jeffery may not have had a list of tasks to pass on, but he did have one matter to make Wormald aware of. In spring 2012, Cummings and the department's director of communications, James Frayne, were both named in a grievance complaint by a senior civil servant with twenty-seven years' experience. According to *The Independent*, 'Her complaint describes a "macho culture of intimidation, favouritism and 'laddism'" in Frayne's communications department, with Cummings singled out as "widely known to use obscene and intimidating language". The report records that Frayne denied swearing on a regular basis.'[13] An internal investigation – of which Gove repeatedly claimed he was not aware – found no disciplinary action was needed, but noted that the conduct of the pair had 'been perceived as intimidating'.[14] As well as the DfE inquiry, the civil servant also pushed for a tribunal – which would have seen evidence being heard in public – but the department agreed a settlement of £25,000 with the staff member.

It wasn't just those inside the department who would feel the wrath of Cummings's tongue. Journalists who crossed him were also given short shrift. One bone of contention was the activity of the Twitter account @ToryEducation. The account had been active since February 2010, initially describing itself as 'Conservative Education Press Officer Pantomime Villain of Leftie Education Folk', before later being amended to 'Pantomime villain of leftie education folk'. It was originally one of a number of accounts created by the official Conservative Twitter account, which claimed to be 'run by staff at Conservative party headquarters', although central office would later claim it had nothing to do with @ToryEducation.[15]

In September 2011, after the *FT*'s Chris Cook ran his first story on those in the DfE using private email accounts, the account labelled the journalist a 'stalker' and 'Walter Mitty'. The attacks turned to the *Observer*'s political editor Toby Helm in 2013, claiming he was a 'Labour stooge' and 'an activist – not a professional hack'. Cummings and De Zoete were suspected of posting through the account, an accusation with serious implications. Special advisors are not permitted to engage in personal attacks, and the content and tone of the tweets from @ToryEducation would have been a clear breach of the rules. *The Observer*'s editor, John Mulholland, wrote to Gove and Wormald asking them to investigate the account, and he also emailed Cummings and De Zoete to put the allegations to them directly. De Zoete replied with brevity: 'As I have already told Toby Helm I am not toryeducation or educationnews [an account Mulholland had incorrectly referenced when he asked for a response].' Cummings was more forceful with his reply. 'Have you lost the plot?' he asked Mulholland in one email, adding, 'What else are you going to invite me to "deny"? Am I secretly doing Rupert Murdoch's twittering while for Mossad on the side?' He also suggested Mulholland should 'confiscate Toby's phone, send Chris Cook a "How to boost your self esteem" book and stop sending such emails'.[16] Another journalist to receive one of Cummings' rants was *The Independent*'s Education Correspondent Richard Garner, who he suggested should 'speak to Chris Cook about a good therapist' after the journalist claimed he had suffered the 'wrath' of DfE advisors for his reporting.

If the actions of Gove's advisors were designed to facilitate a bunker mentality within the DfE, the Secretary of State himself was not averse to provoking some incoming enemy fire. After the slow start to his academy revolution, by January 2011 one in ten of all English secondary schools had changed status – double the number that had converted under the previous government. As well as the just over 200 schools that had shifted to academy status since Gove pushed his legislation through, a further 254 had applied. While Gove was celebrating, some in the education establishment believed schools were effectively being forced to become academies. Chris Keates, general secretary of the NASUWT, the largest teachers' union, said, 'The clear motivation for academy status is that most schools are being duped into believing that they will get extra money at a time when schools and education are facing savage cuts.'[17]

At NASUWT's annual conference in April 2011, the union passed a vote of no confidence in Gove, warning it had 'no confidence in the education policies of the coalition government'. The resolution said Gove's academies and free school policies were opening up education to the private sector, leading to 'inequality of educational entitlement, lack of public accountability and abuse of the system'. Gove was nonplussed. As his reforming hero Tony Blair had repeatedly argued, it was those in public sector institutions who had the most to lose who were the most resistant to change – and the changes Gove was pushing through directly threatened the powers of the unions. By allowing academies and free schools to set their own pay and reward schemes, the need for collective bargaining on a national scale was severely diminished. Ironically, it was the move away from collective bargaining which had seen Gove take to the picket line in 1989 while a trainee journalist for the *Aberdeen Press and Journal*. Now he was the one facilitating such a system.

With one teaching union calling on Gove to quit, the Education Secretary faced a decision. Did he retreat slightly in order to keep the education establishment onside, or did he carry on, knowing full well the other reforms he had planned would only cause further antagonism? The student of Blair was determined to go where no Blairite had gone before and, having set his controls for the heart of the sun, he chose to speed up, not retreat. As a Conservative, he had no financial or historical ties to the union movement, and he was, in his mind at least, able to finish the job that Blair had started. He was determined to defeat what was known around Whitehall as 'The Blob'.

That moniker had first been assigned to the education establishment not by Gove or his advisors but by Ronald Reagan's Education Secretary, William Bennett, in 1987. The term was imported to the UK by former Ofsted chief inspector Chris Woodhead, who used the insult in his 2002 book *Class War: The State of British Education*. Even before Gove entered government, he was urged to take on 'The Blob'. 'Michael Gove should not repeat the error of trying to defeat the Blob piecemeal. Only by blasting every part of the creature at once can he hope to destroy it,' wrote Dennis Sewell in *The Spectator* in January 2010.[18]

Gove needed little encouragement, and the 'Blob' insult soon began popping up in articles written by supportive columnists, such as Camilla Cavendish in *The Times* in June 2011 and Matthew d'Ancona in the *Sunday Telegraph* in June 2012. Not all in Whitehall appreciated the term, with one civil servant saying they 'hated all that',[19] but for Gove it summed up the enemy perfectly.

After hitting the institutional structure of The Blob through the academy and free school policies, Gove wanted to reform what was being taught in schools and how pupils' progress was assessed. In January 2011, he announced there would be a review of the national curriculum, carried out by an independent body of education experts headed by Tim Oates, director of assessment research and development at Cambridge Assessment. Gove's instruction to Oates was to 'trawl the curricula of the world's high performing countries, to collect core knowledge, and put it in the right order', according to another member of the body, Professor Andrew Pollard.[20]

Speaking to the BBC on the day the review was announced, Gove insisted it was for the panel to decide what a future curriculum should look like, saying, 'I'm not going to be coming up with any prescriptive lists, I just think there should be facts.' He went on: 'One of the problems that we have at the moment is that in the history curriculum we only have two names [of historical figures], in the geography curriculum the only country we mention is the UK – we don't mention a single other country, continent, river or city.'[21]

Teaching union leaders had no doubt in their minds about what the new curriculum would look like. After all, Gove had hardly hidden his desire for a more traditional form of education in classrooms across the country. As he told *The Times* before the 2010 election:

Most parents would rather their children had a traditional education, with children sitting in rows, learning the kings and queens of England, the great works of literature, proper mental arithmetic, algebra by the age of 11, modern foreign languages. That's the best training of the minds and that's how children will be able to compete.[22]

The NASUWT teaching union greeted the news by saying teachers 'want another curriculum review like a hole in the head'. General secretary Chris Keates described the review as 'pointless' as Gove had 'already determined that children should have a 1950s-style curriculum'.[23]

Even as the review was being carried out, Gove could not help but make his opinions known. In April 2011, he chastised the limits of the English Literature syllabus, complaining that not enough pupils were studying classic works of English literature from the nineteenth century. Writing in the *Telegraph*, he said:

> The curriculum suggests authors from Pope and Dryden to Trollope and Tennyson – but the English Literature GCSE only actually requires students to study four or five texts, including one novel. In exams more than 90 per cent of the answers on novels are on the same three works: *Of Mice and Men*, *Lord of the Flies* and *To Kill a Mockingbird*.[24]

It wasn't just a review of the curriculum that Gove set in train. In March 2011, he published a consultation on special educational needs, and in June there was a discussion paper on reforming teacher training. Gove also commissioned people from outside government to investigate different aspects of education. Darren Henley, managing director of Classic FM, was asked review music education; Clare Tickell, chief executive of the Action for Children charity, looked into Early Years Foundation Stage; and Alison Wolf from King's College London investigated the provision of vocational education. Gove was certainly keen on using experts to inform his policy making, and he was determined to move fast.

Yet for all the reviews being undertaken by DfE, it was the issue of pay that prompted the first strike action from teachers under Gove's tenure. Under reforms led by George Osborne in the Treasury, teachers were among public sector workers who would be required to pay more into their pension pots at a time of pay freeze as the government tried to get to grips with an ever-growing welfare budget. As well as the rise in contributions, the state pension age increase was sped up from sixty to sixty-five for women by 2018, and then to sixty-six for both sexes by 2020. The National Union of Teachers and the Association of Teachers and Lecturers elected to take part in a day of strike action on 30 June 2011, and leading up to the walkout Gove did little to placate those planning to join the picket lines. 'I do worry that taking industrial action, being on the picket line, being involved in this sort of militancy will actually mean that the respect in which teachers should be held is taken back a little bit,' he told the BBC's *Andrew Marr Show* the Sunday before the action.[25] His words did nothing to prevent the action and, on the day, 12,000 schools were either completely or partially closed as teachers walked out. Industrial action was carried out again on 30 November 2011, and ahead of the strikes Gove slipped into full newspaper columnist mode as he derided those preparing to walk out:

> Among those union leaders [calling for action] are people who fight hard for their members, and whom I respect. But there are also hardliners – militants itching for a fight. They want families to be inconvenienced. They want mothers to give up a day's work,

or to pay for expensive childcare, because schools will be closed. They want teachers and other public sector workers to lose a day's pay in the runup to Christmas. They want scenes of industrial strife on our TV screens, they want to make economic recovery harder, they want to provide a platform for confrontation, just when we all need to pull together.[26]

Gove's strong condemnation of the 'militants itching for a fight' showed a marked progression of his views on industrial action since taking to the picket line in Aberdeen in the late 1980s. The former journalist's participation in that strike had long been in the public domain, and Gove would use it as a cautionary tale as to why he was so opposed to such action. In September 2010, he claimed that, while he 'didn't think the dispute was a good idea', he backed the principle that underpinned the action: 'I don't think it was ignoble for the union to have argued that, when the majority believed that a house agreement was the right way forward, it should be maintained.'[27]

A year later, and having experienced strikes on his watch as Education Secretary, Gove was much less generous about the motivations of some of his former colleagues. He claimed the action at Aberdeen Journals was instigated because 'some people at the top of a union leadership wanted to prove a point'.[28] His comments provoked anger among some of those who had stood alongside him on the picket line. Mike Elrick, who would occasionally bump into Gove as the pair both lived and worked in London, was furious. 'How he misrepresented his time on strike over the years since then really destroyed any respect I had for him. I do think actually he was talking bollocks and he knows he was talking bollocks, but it suited his purposes when he was making those speeches at the time,' he says now.

Gove's rhetoric wasn't just alienating former comrades but those in the teaching industry too, and as time went on, it only got worse. At the Association of School and College Leaders conference in April 2012, he had a blunt message for head teachers who raised concerns about the sheer speed of change in the education sector: 'Lest anyone think we have reached a point where we should slacken the pace of reform – let me reassure them – we have to accelerate.' He later told journalists: 'If people say "It's all just a bit too much," my view is "Man up!"'[29]

In June 2012, Gove published his new draft curriculum for primary schools. Among the changes, nine-year-olds would be required to know their times tables up to 12x12, youngsters should read poetry aloud, and foreign language lessons should start from the age of seven. There was a greater insistence on teaching grammar and spelling, with the government providing a list of words children should master. No sooner had it been announced than the new curriculum was derided by experts – including those who had carried out a review of the national curriculum for Gove the previous year. Professor Andrew Pollard described the focus on spelling and rules of grammar as 'fatally flawed without parallel consideration of the needs of learners'. He argued that the new curriculum was far too prescriptive, and teachers 'need scope to exercise professional judgement'. He added:

> However, on the basis of the new National Curriculum proposals, they are to be faced by extremely detailed year-on-year specifications in mathematics, science and most of English. This is to be complemented by punitive inspection arrangements and tough new tests at 11. The new curriculum will preserve statutory breadth, we are told, but, whilst teaching of a foreign language is to be added, provision for the arts, humanities and physical

education is uncertain at this point. The constraining effects on the primary curriculum as a whole are likely to be profound and the preservation of breadth, balance and quality of experience will test even the most committed of teachers.[30]

Oates hit back, saying, 'Publishing content year by year is not some rigid straitjacket. There remains flexibility for schools in the scheduling of content.'[31]

The plan went out for consultation, and over the next year Gove was involved in running battles with those opposed to the changes.

It wasn't as if the Education Secretary was having a quiet time of it on other fronts. The row over pensions which had prompted the strikes in June and November 2011 rumbled on. In the autumn of 2012, the unions grew further incensed by a plan to link teachers' pay rises to their performances in the classroom. On 9 December 2012, the *Sunday Times* ran a front-page story claiming that the DfE had been put on a 'war footing' for the battle ahead. A department source was quoted as saying:

> A full national strike is regarded as a price worth paying to change the culture and break the destructive power of Keates and Blower. Resources are being moved internally to prepare for strikes. Lawyers are being discreetly spoken to. The best time to make this historic move is when the private sector is in big trouble and sympathy for unions is at its lowest. No amount of industrial action will persuade the DfE to change course while Gove is secretary of state.[32]

In his diary, Schools minister David Laws described the article as 'irritating', adding, 'It doesn't take very long to guess where this story has come from – Dom Cummings.'[33]

The new year brought another volley of criticism from 'The Blob', again focused on changes to the national curriculum. In February 2013, the DfE published its revised framework of study for twelve subjects, and it prompted an immediate backlash. Two years earlier, Gove had claimed he was not going to produce 'prescriptive lists' of what should and should not be part of the curriculum, but the history framework alone was incredibly detailed. Key Stage 1 pupils – those aged between five and seven – were required to learn about the 'concept of nation' and 'the lives of significant individuals in Britain's past who have contributed to our nation's achievements', such as Elizabeth Fry, Florence Nightingale or Christina Rossetti.

Children between the ages of seven and eleven would be required to learn about UK history from the Stone Age to the Glorious Revolution – taking in, among other things, Celtic culture, the Roman conquest, Viking settlements, Norman rule, the Crusades, the Plantagenets, the Hundred Year War, the Black Death, the Peasants' Revolt, the later Middle Ages, the War of the Roses, the Tudors, Shakespeare, the Great Plague, the Great Fire of London, and the Union of the Parliaments.

The pace didn't slacken when pupils reached secondary school, with the period from 1707 to the fall of the Berlin Wall in 1989 set out in the curriculum in great detail for students aged between eleven and fourteen.

After the draft plan was published, representatives from a host of historical societies penned a joint letter to *The Observer* complaining that the curriculum was 'far too narrowly and exclusively focused on British history to serve the needs of children growing up in the world today'.[34] Simon Schama, the well-known historian who had been drafted in by Gove to advise on reforming the curriculum, was blunt with his criticism, dubbing it 'insulting and offensive' and 'pedantic and utopian'. He added:

I would love also to bring Michael into a classroom and to do the entirety of not just the English but the English, Scottish and Irish Civil Wars in something like forty-five minutes. If you actually take the number of statutory, non-negotiable, indispensable items on the document that we now have and that all my friends out there are going to have to teach, that's what it comes down to! Whoosh, there was Disraeli! Whoosh, there was Gladstone! All whipping past one. The French Revolution, if it's lucky, may get a drive-by ten minutes!

There were some supporters of Gove's changes. David Starkey was one of fifteen leading historians to publicly back the reforms in a letter to *The Times*, arguing, 'It should be made possible for every pupil to take in the full narrative of our history throughout every century.'[35]

Yet even those who backed the principles behind the changes were critical of the framework, with noted historian Niall Ferguson warning it was 'much too prescriptive'.

'The 34 topics to be covered by pupils between the ages of seven and 14 already read a bit like chapter titles and, if there is one thing I hope we avoid, it is an official history textbook,' he warned.[36]

The criticism kept coming, and on 19 March 2013, 100 academics wrote a letter to *The Independent* attacking not just the history section of the new curriculum but the proposals for all subjects. The signatories, all either professors of education or members of university education departments, claimed, 'The proposed curriculum consists of endless lists of spellings, facts and rules. This mountain of data will not develop children's ability to think, including problem-solving, critical understanding and creativity.'[37]

Gove hit back with his most vicious attack yet on 'The Blob'. Writing in the *Mail on Sunday* five days later, the Education

Secretary labelled the academics 'The Enemies of Promise' as he accused them of being part of 'a set of politically motivated individuals who have been actively trying to prevent millions of our poorest children getting the education they need'. He went on:

> You would expect such people to value learning, revere knowledge and dedicate themselves to fighting ignorance. Sadly, they seem more interested in valuing Marxism, revering jargon and fighting excellence.
>
> They attacked the Coalition for our indefensibly reactionary drive to get more children to spell properly, use a wider vocabulary and learn their times tables. Expecting 11-year-olds to write grammatical sentences and use fractions in sums is apparently asking for 'too much too young' and will 'severely erode educational standards'.
>
> How can it erode educational standards to ask that, in their 11 years in school, children be given the opportunity to use the English language in all its range and beauty to communicate their thoughts and feelings with grace and precision? What planet are these people on?

He then argued that the size and power of the 'The Blob' had been underestimated, writing:

> In the past The Blob tended to operate by stealth, using its influence to control the quangos and committees which shaped policy. But The Blob has broken cover in the letters pages of the broadsheets because this Government is taking it on.
>
> We have abolished the quangos they controlled. We have given a majority of secondary schools academy status so they are free from the influence of The Blob's allies in local government. We

are moving teacher training away from university departments and into our best schools. And we are reforming our curriculum and exams to restore the rigour they abandoned.

The final paragraph summed up how he – and his advisors such as Cummings – viewed education reform: 'It's a battle in which you have to take sides.'[38]

A key part of any battle is knowing when to retreat, and when an updated framework was published in July 2013, the ambitious nature of the curriculum had been scaled down dramatically. Primary schools would be required to teach up to 1066, not 1707; there was space for topics from world history; and the overall framework was much less prescriptive. Much like the rows over sports funding and BookTrust, Gove had seemingly rowed back in the face of pressure from those with a high media profile.

The teaching unions clearly did not fit into that category. Even as the row over the curriculum changes was being fought, he was as defiant as ever when facing criticism from those working in England's school system. He rammed home his plan to continue with his education revolution during an appearance at the National Association of Head Teachers conference in Birmingham on 18 May 2013. 'If people find it stressful that I'm demanding higher standards, then I'm not going to stop demanding higher standards,' he insisted.

One of the most electrifying moments came when a head teacher with more than twenty years' experience took to the microphone to describe the current culture in the education world as 'one of bullying and fear'. She added:

You ask why head teachers are going down with stress and worrying, it's because they spend Monday, Tuesday, Wednesday, waiting for Ofsted [the school inspectors], not because they are not good schools, not because they can't do well, it depends on the people that come and what pressures they put on.

To gasps from the audience, Gove replied: 'If Ofsted is a cause of fear, then I'm grateful for your candour but I'm afraid we're going to have to part company.'

After one head teacher shouted, 'Are you leaving then?', Gove doubled down:

We wouldn't know what outstanding practice was around the country unless it were thanks to gifted inspectors taking the trouble to shine a light on what is good. If in your school you fear scrutiny, tell me what is wrong with that scrutiny? Do you think that the framework is wrong because there's a greater emphasis on children's achievement and attainment than ever before, a greater emphasis on leadership, a greater emphasis on behaviour? If there are specific concerns then I haven't heard them during the course of the last hour. What I have heard is repeated statements that the profession faces stress, but insufficient evidence of what can be done to do it. I'm interested in a constructive dialogue, but what I haven't heard sufficiently during the course of the last hour is a determination to be constructive. Critical, yes, but not constructive.[39]

This was Gove's Trotskyite zeal in action. Cummings's dealing with the press and Gove's relationship with teachers shared many similarities. Gove may have couched his attacks in softer language and more often with an air of exasperation than a howl of anger, but it came from the same place as Cummings's rage.

Reflecting on this period in 2018, former director-general of the

Association of Teachers and Lecturers Mary Bousted was clear
that the teaching profession also viewed the relationship with Gove
in those terms. She said:

> He would see any reasoned arguments about that as just opposition
> to his ideological position and he adopted the position that him,
> and only him and his close acolytes were in favour of poor children
> doing well at school, were in favour of poor children learning im-
> portant things. Once you adopt a sort of binary divide in that way,
> that you are on the crusade and everyone else is the infidel then you
> create completely unnecessary divisions and you don't bring the
> profession with you and that was in the end his biggest mistake.[40]

James Frayne, who quit as the Department of Education's director
of communications in 2012, believed it was an error on the part of
Gove and others to adopt such a stark attitude:

> Treating the teaching unions as if they were all reflective of the
> teaching union leadership was a mistake, because there's no
> doubt, there's no getting away from the fact that the leadership
> of the teaching unions at that time were just unfailingly opposi-
> tional to everything he was trying to do. I think probably he and
> we lumped all teachers into that category, which probably wasn't
> fair, and it's probably fair to say that even now when you talk to
> teachers there's still sort of residual irritation.[41]

As if moving schools away from local authority control and working
up a new curriculum weren't enough, Gove also had plans to reform
GCSEs and A levels. Yet this controversial move would provoke
the wrath not just of The Blob but of a group much closer to home:
the Liberal Democrats.

CHAPTER 17

CAT ON A HOT TIN ROOF

'This is self-evidently not policy which has been either discussed or agreed within the coalition government,' Nick Clegg told a journalist.[1] The Deputy Prime Minister was in Brazil, attending a UN conference on sustainable development, and was not expecting to have to pass comment on what would be the biggest shake-up of exams in nearly twenty-five years. On the morning of 21 June 2012, the *Daily Mail* ran a story which took Clegg and much of the government by surprise.[2] The paper had been leaked a plan to abolish GCSEs and bring back a two-tiered system of exams: O levels for the top pupils and CSEs for less academic students. The new system would be in place by 2014, with the first exams being taken two years later. Clegg was furious – not only with the policy but that it had been developed without the knowledge of him or any other Lib Dems. Despite being taken by surprise by the leak, Downing Street rowed in behind the plan, secure in the knowledge that while it would never get through Parliament as long as the party was in coalition, it was the sort of 'red-hot' Tory policy that would appeal to party members and core voters.[3]

Gove was more optimistic about getting the changes through, even in the tight timeframe he had set himself. One of those who would be helping him was David Laws, the Lib Dem MP who had been rumoured to be lined up for the Education Secretary role himself during the coalition negotiations. Laws gained a degree of notoriety when he was forced to quit the government in May 2010 after just seventeen days as Chief Secretary to the Treasury. The *Daily Telegraph* revealed Laws had claimed back £40,000 in expenses for renting a room in the house of his partner, James Lundie. Laws argued that he had painted Lundie as a landlord instead of a lover as he wanted to keep his sexuality private. The scandal saw him resign, but, as one of the key players in bringing the coalition together, he was tipped for a return to government. In September 2012, he was appointed Schools minister, along with a position in the Cabinet Office, and was also permitted to attend Cabinet meetings.

Laws's first role was to try to smooth relations between Clegg and Gove. The pair had initially got on well. Over a dinner near Clegg's house in Putney in the early days of the coalition, the Lib Dem leader was left with the same impression of Gove that many others shared during their initial interactions. 'I found him to be charm personified,' he said, adding, 'He was generous, witty, collegiate and very smart.'[4] However, as the coalition went on, Clegg found himself increasingly frustrated by both Gove and those around him – particularly Dominic Cummings. Two years of battles between Clegg and Gove began with a row over GCSE reform in 2012, quickly followed by a disagreement over the Education Secretary's decision to abolish the requirement for teachers in academy schools to have 'Qualified Teacher Status'. It was not just what Gove was doing but the fact that he had acted without consulting the government more widely that had infuriated Clegg.

It was into this increasing tension that Laws joined DfE in September 2012. It was a dramatic reshuffle, with Sarah Teather, Nick Gibb and Tim Loughton all departing, replaced by Laws, Edward

Timpson and Liz Truss – with Matthew Hancock having a joint role with the Department for Business, Innovation and Skills. Loughton was angry with his removal, and appearing before the Education Select Committee on 16 January 2013 he launched a savage attack on his former place of work:

> Most officials have never met the Secretary of State other than when he'll troop out a few chosen people for the New Year party, Mr Grace-like, tell us 'You've all done very well' then disappear. That's no way to run an important department. It is terribly anachronistic, terribly bureaucratic, terribly formal.[5]

That attack prompted a 'senior Department for Education source' to tell *The Spectator*, 'Loughton was a lazy incompetent narcissist obsessed only with self-promotion.'[6]

Those comments were deemed so strong that Gove was quizzed about them when he appeared before the Education Committee on 23 January, with Labour MP Ian Mearns referring to 'previous allegations about spads acting inappropriately' before asking, 'Are there elements working within the department that are out of control, Secretary of State?' Gove replied, 'No.'[7]

Loughton may not have been a fan of Gove's, but Laws, initially at least, was. The Education Secretary had been more polite about the Lib Dems than many of his Conservative colleagues, and when Laws had quit as Chief Secretary in 2010 Gove had given both public and private support. Laws would later describe Gove as 'amusing, intellectually impressive, thoughtful and never, ever dull'.[8] Gove's sense of fun ensured ministerial meetings were 'always entertaining', leading Laws to conclude: 'It was possible to disagree with Michael Gove. It was impossible to dislike him.'[9]

Clegg was struggling to hold the same view, but the pair seemed to patch things up when they reached a compromise over the GCSE reforms. A return to a two-tier system was shelved, and instead it was agreed there would be a new, tougher, qualification administered by just one examination board. Gove suggested calling it the English Baccalaureate Certificate – a name which would appeal to Tories as it had the word 'English', and to Lib Dems as it featured 'Baccalaureate'.[10] It was also agreed to delay the roll-out by a year, to come into force in autumn 2015.

Clegg and Gove visited the Burlington Danes Academy in west London to formally announce the new policy on 17 September 2012. Ebaccs, as the English Baccalaureate was to be known, would initially cover English, maths and science. Coursework was scrapped for English and maths, as Gove believed it only encouraged 'bite-size learning and spoon-feeding'.[11] Ebaccs in history, geography and languages would begin in 2016, with students taking the first exams two years later. Clegg insisted the changes to Gove's original proposal meant there would be no return to the two-tier system of O levels and CSEs, but the Education Secretary admitted that not all pupils would sit the Ebaccs and some would therefore leave school without any qualifications. 'We will make special – indeed, enhanced – provision, for these students with their schools required to produce a detailed record of their achievement in each curriculum area at sixteen, which will help them make progress subsequently – and we anticipate some will secure Ebacc certificates at the age of seventeen or eighteen,' he said.[12] That revelation prompted Christine Blower, general secretary of the National Union of Teachers, to dismiss Clegg's claim that he had had an influence on Gove's plans: 'What is being proposed here is blatantly a two-tier system,' she said. 'Pupils who do not gain Ebaccs will receive a record of achievement which will most certainly be seen to be of far less worth by employers and colleges.'[13]

Concerns about the practicality of getting the Ebaccs in place for autumn 2015 were raised by Ofqual, the exams watchdog. Speaking at the Headmasters' and Headmistresses' Conference in Belfast just over two weeks after Clegg and Gove's announcement, Ofqual's chief regulator, Glenys Stacey, said that key details about the qualifications – such as how much harder than GCSEs they should be and how much say exam boards would have over content – were still unclear.[14]

It wasn't just Ofqual who was in the dark about the detail. The shaky alliance established between Gove and Clegg was breaking down behind the scenes as it soon became clear that both sides had a different interpretation of what had been agreed. Gove and his team envisaged changing just a few GCSEs to Ebaccs, whereas Laws believed that if you were going to break the system, then all the qualifications needed to be replaced.[15] Gove didn't let such concerns slow him down, and on 17 October it was revealed that A levels were next up for reform, with a new 'Advanced Baccalaureate' being mooted. The qualification would see pupils taking a contrasting subject at AS level alongside A levels, meaning, for example, that a student studying maths and science for two years would also complete a one-year course in a language or humanities subject. A 5,000-word essay would also need to be completed in order to secure the qualification, which would then mark out a student for eligibility to a top university.

The concern about the sheer pace of change was highlighted by the Ofqual chief again in November, with a letter to Gove warning him that his ambitions for the Ebacc 'may exceed what is realistically achievable through a single assessment'.[16] The Education Select Committee lent its voice to the those raising concerns, with a report published in January 2013 warning the government was 'trying to do too much, too fast' and had not demonstrated how replacing GCSEs with Ebaccs would tackle underachievement or narrow the attainment gap.[17]

Even before the report was published, Gove had begun to realise the reforms were doomed and on Wednesday 30 January, Dominic Cummings told David Laws the new plan was to reform the existing GCSE programme – not replace it. Gove made the announcement in the Commons on Thursday 7 February, telling MPs:

> Last September, we outlined plans for changes to GCSE qualifications that were designed to address the grade inflation, dumbing down and loss of rigour in those examinations. We have consulted on those proposals and there is a consensus that the system needs to change. However, one of the proposals that I put forward was a bridge too far. My idea that we end the competition between exam boards to offer GCSEs in core academic qualifications and have just one wholly new exam in each subject was one reform too many at this time.[18]

Gove said he had decided 'not to make the best the enemy of the good' – a phrase he and others would find themselves repeating regarding a far greater challenge some years later – as he set out how the existing GCSEs would be reformed. From 2015, higher- and lower-tier papers would be scrapped, the vast majority of the assessments would take place at the end of the two years instead peppered throughout the course and there would be less reliance on coursework. The Advanced Baccalaureate was also dropped, with Gove promising there would be further reform in consultation with the schools and universities. In a leader article the next day, the *Daily Mail* came to Gove's defence, blaming 'militant teaching unions and Labour and Liberal Democrat MPs' responsible for sinking the 'new gold-standard Baccalaureate' and 'block[ing] a reform this country desperately needs if we are not to become economic also-rans'. The chief enemy of progress in the *Mail*'s eyes was the Deputy Prime Minister. 'Let's hope Mr Clegg, who enjoyed the best education money can buy, and who may send his own children to private school, can sleep at night,' the leader article thundered.[19]

The attack on Clegg came as the relationship between the Deputy Prime Minister and Gove plumbed new depths. On 2 December 2012, the *Mail on Sunday* ran a story claiming that Clegg had intervened to ensure BookTrust – the charity Gove had battled with two years earlier – received £12 million in funding from the Department for Education. The newspaper suggested Clegg's motivation for this move was because his wife, international lawyer Miriam González Durántez, was a supporter of the charity and months earlier had hosted a reception for BookTrust at Lancaster House. A spokeswoman for Clegg told the paper, 'Any suggestion of impropriety is completely wrong,' adding, 'Miriam has no role within the charity, beyond being supportive of its excellent work.' Yet while it was Gove who ultimately signed off on the grant, the DfE refused to issue a statement downplaying the story, with a spokesperson telling the paper, 'We have no comment.' Clegg was 'spitting blood' over the article, according to Laws,[20] and held Gove's advisors responsible for dragging his wife into the rough and tumble of politics. 'It was something the Deputy Prime Minister could never forgive or forget,' Laws later said.[21]

The relationship soured further when the Lib Dems sought to implement what would become one of their flagship policies: free school meals for infants. Gove had already taken an interest in the policy area following an Easter holiday to Marrakech in 2012, where he and his family stayed in the same villa as Henry Dimbleby, co-founder of fast food chain Leon. Dimbleby, son of veteran broadcaster David, had not met Gove before, but the pair found themselves in the same villa thanks to a mutual friend.[22] As Gove and Dimbleby drank cocktails by the pool, they discussed how to improve school meals, and in July 2012 it was announced that Dimbleby, along with his business partner John Vincent, would carry out an official review into the area. Published a year later, the School Food Plan recommended free school meals be extended to all primary school children as a means of ensuring youngsters were eating healthier food than often came in packed lunches.

Clegg and Laws were taken by this proposal, but after the plan was costed at £1.2 billion, they decided to scale down the proposal to cover just those in infant classes. When the Tory and Lib Dem top teams met in the run-up to the autumn Budget to decide on which policies to push, Cameron and Osborne agreed to support spending £600 million on the free school meals plan if their coalition partners backed a similar amount being set aside on tax breaks for married couples. On 9 September 2013, Laws met with Gove to tell him the Lib Dems were going to announce the policy at their autumn conference in a week's time. Knowing that Cummings was against the move – as he believed that directing schools, including academies, in this way was a violation of the principle of autonomy the Tories were keen to push – Laws asked Gove to keep the plan from his advisors. Gove replied, 'I support this. I know not everyone in government will agree with the policy, but I do. And I am happy with you working in private with officials on this over the next week. And – yes – I promise to tell no one, not even Dom!'[23]

The policy didn't leak, but the decision to hide it from Gove's top team provoked anger. When it came to trying to write into law that state-funded schools, including academies and free schools, had to provide the free meals using money provided by the government, Gove dragged his feet. On 7 November, Laws tried to confront Gove over why he was so opposed to the measure, but his attempt was nearly thwarted when the Education Secretary dashed out of the room into a toilet connected to his office. 'I was therefore left standing in his room alone, wondering both if the toilet had another exit and how long the Secretary of State was likely to be occupied,' Laws said. When Gove emerged, he argued that it was wrong to promise additional money to schools if the government could not deliver on it, and a further plan to hand over extra cash to improve kitchen facilities would divert money from other, more pressing, areas.[24]

Clegg was so exasperated with Gove's reluctance to put into law what the coalition government had agreed, he went directly to Cameron with his complaints. Over dinner on Wednesday 20 November, also attended by George Osborne and Danny Alexander, Clegg said he was more than happy to trade blows with Gove in public if that was what was needed to get him to put the free school meals policy into action. Cameron listened sympathetically and said he would try to talk Gove round.[25] Yet Gove, and those working alongside him, seemed determined to scupper the policy. As Clegg prepared to launch the scheme with a speech at a school in Lambeth two weeks later, Gove and Cummings told the Deputy Prime Minister that while he was able to announce an additional £70 million in funding from the Treasury to redevelop school kitchens, he was not allowed to pledge another £80 million which was due to be siphoned off from an unspent maintenance budget in the DfE. George Osborne's office was required to step in and send an email to Gove's office saying that the whole amount had been signed off by the Treasury and Downing Street, and a total of £150 million could indeed be announced.[26]

Gove's team hit back, and *The Guardian* was soon running a story claiming the Lib Dems were trying to fill a £200 million blackhole in the free school meals policy and were using money set aside to increase school places to plug the gap. Clegg's team responded with an extremely punchy quote: 'The DfE advisors are lying, going rogue, being hostile and talking bollocks.' Westminster's lobby journalists could hardly believe what they were witnessing, and Downing Street was soon required to step in. Cameron came down on the side of Clegg, with his spokesman telling reporters, 'The position is absolutely the one the DPM's office have set out.' Laws was so furious with Gove, the pair had a full-blown argument about the policy in the back of a ministerial car as they travelled together to the Commons for a vote later that day.[27]

The free schools meal debacle was one of the most public rows the coalition government had engaged in to date. At the centre of it was an Education Secretary who had been given leeway by Cameron to carry out his radical, reforming agenda virtually unhindered by Downing Street diktat, and a Deputy Prime Minister determined to ensure his party had a legacy in as many branches of government as possible. The pair actually shared a passion for education reform, and Clegg was initially supportive of Gove's policies as Education Secretary, but the more the Lib Dem leader tried to interfere in DfE, the more it rankled with Gove and his advisors – particularly Cummings. As Cameron remarked to Clegg during one bust up, 'The thing that you've got to remember with Michael is that he is basically a bit of a Maoist – he believes that the world makes progress through a process of creative destruction!'[28]

The irony of Gove and his advisors expressing frustration with outside interference is that the Education Secretary had no aversion to holding forth on policy areas beyond his department's remit. The Whitehall machine operates in straight lines, but outside of SW1 policies often cut across numerous departments and ministries. To ensure ministers aren't taken by surprise by any announcements, policies are sent to all members of the Cabinet for them to see if there are any implications for their departments. The majority of Cabinet ministers merely note these 'write-arounds' and only reply if it affects them. Not Gove. According to one former Cabinet minister, Gove would routinely send back his thoughts on a range of policies, suggesting improvements or raising questions. Nor were Gove's thoughts on subjects well beyond his brief confined to emails. One former Cabinet minister recalls Gove turning up to meetings having apparently 'swallowed a book' on whatever topics were on the agenda in order to ensure he could make a contribution. 'He would say things like, "Well, Cicero would say..."' his former colleague remembers, adding, 'He lives through being on the stage.' One of Gove's earliest interventions in a policy not related to education was to lead the opposition to a 5p levy on plastic bags. According to Cabinet sources, he spoke out against the policy when Environment Secretary Caroline Spelman proposed it in 2010. Chancellor George Osborne eventually rowed in behind his friend and blocked Spelman's attempts to include it in the 2012 Budget amid fears it would be seen as another increase in the cost of living.[29]

The Cameron–Osborne–Gove triad was a dominating force in Cabinet, but another former Secretary of State who witnessed the relationship up close believes Gove was very much the junior figure in the axis:

Michael always spoke at key moments and was indulged by Cameron and went on and on and on and didn't stop. Cameron treated him a bit like the younger brother really. He was great because he entertained them, so he was given rights of access, if you know what I mean, because he was entertaining, which Michael is.

It wasn't just Cameron and Osborne who were entertained by

Gove, but David Laws as well. The Lib Dem minister made numerous references in his diary to Gove's contributions at Cabinet and ministerial meetings in the Department for Education. On 11 September 2012, Laws noted: 'Michael Gove crackles and sparkles in a way that no other minister manages – he cannot say anything without saying it in an amusing and interesting way, and people always listen to him. Sometimes there's a risk that his flamboyance and style submerges the serious messages.'[30]

On 12 November 2013, Laws captured how Gove managed to torpedo an idea put forward by Early Years Minister Liz Truss.

Liz … made a slightly odd point proposing cutting grants for voluntary groups but expanding the budget for the Communications Department in the run-up to the general election. Michael said in his usual amusing way, 'Oh that's an interesting idea, Liz. So your proposition is that we should cut some of the charitable grants for vulnerable young people, and use the money to buy more DfE press officers?'[31]

Gove's confidence in dealing with his Cabinet and ministerial colleagues partly came as a result of his natural demeanour and partly because of the leeway afforded to him by Downing Street. Gove, along with Iain Duncan Smith at Work and Pensions and Andrew Lansley at Health, was one of the government's chief reformers, and Cameron was hoping he would provide the Tories with some positive stories to tell on the doorstep at the next election alongside the more sobering narrative of the austerity drive.

While Cameron, Osborne and Gove were instinctively in sync on virtually all issues facing the coalition – the need for austerity, support for military intervention in Libya in 2011, a desire for public service reform – there was one major area of disagreement: the EU.

In May 2012, Cameron cooked up the idea of pledging to hold an in/out referendum on the UK's membership of the EU in the next parliament, should the Conservatives win. The decision was taken in a pizza restaurant at O'Hare Airport in Chicago in a conversation with his chief of staff Ed Llewellyn and Foreign Secretary William Hague, with the latter convinced such a move would be the only way to end the decades-long obsession with Europe which had gripped the Tories. A sense that something had to be done over the EU had been growing since eighty-one Tories defied party orders and backed a Commons motion calling for a referendum in October 2011. The United Kingdom Independence Party, led by the charismatic Nigel Farage, was beginning to gain traction in opinion polls – at times equalling the support of the Lib Dems – and the Eurosceptic right of the Tory Party were sensing the public wanted a full-throated rejection of the EU project. The pro-EU Osborne was vehemently against the plan, repeatedly warning Cameron that a referendum of that nature would morph into an anti-establishment, anti-government vote, as well as splitting the Tory Party completely. The Chancellor's opposition to the referendum was echoed by Gove. Despite being the most Eurosceptic of the three by some distance, Gove believed the motivation for promising a referendum was all wrong. A source close to Gove later said, 'Throughout this time, Michael thought this whole thing was a recipe for disaster. What we're not doing is thinking through what Britain will be outside the EU, we're adopting a bunch of tactical strategies to stave off either UKIP's growth or our backbench problems.'[32] Gove joined Osborne in lobbying Cameron to pull away from pledging to hold a referendum, but there was another reason why the Education Secretary wanted to avoid the vote: he knew he might not be on the same side of the argument as his old friends. At the Conservative Party conference in October 2012, a relaxed Gove told journalists from the *Mail on Sunday* that he would vote to leave if the referendum was held on the current terms of membership. His revelation, influenced by the even more Eurosceptic Cummings, prompted the paper to run the front-page headline: 'Gove: We're ready to walk out on Europe'.[33]

Despite appearing to nail his colours to the mast, right up until Cameron made the referendum pledge in a speech on 23 January 2013 Gove was urging him to abandon the plan. 'You don't need to do this, you don't need to offer a referendum,' he wrote in an email to the Prime Minister. 'Don't worry, I know what I'm doing,' came the reply.[34] It was a response typical of Cameron, who never appeared to struggle under the weight of responsibility involved in occupying 10 Downing Street. Part of that breeziness was down to his natural demeanour, but part was down to his background. If Cameron appeared relaxed, it's because being Prime Minister was very much within the scope of the world into which he had been born. Conversely, Gove's freneticism in public life is a reflection of the notion that not many adopted sons of Aberdeen fish processors obtain high office – and who knows how long they will stay there for? It was because of this difference in background that Gove was so useful to Cameron and Osborne. As journalist Matthew d'Ancona, a friend of all three men, observed in his 2013 book *In It Together*, 'Like the comprehensive-educated [William] Hague, Gove was sometimes a much-needed ambassador from outside the west London Tory Demi-monde.'

While it was true that Gove – like Cameron and Osborne – had received a private school education and attended Oxford University, his background was fundamentally different from the Prime Minister and Chancellor. They were born into worlds where attending not just university but Oxbridge was expected, almost passé, whereas Gove was consistently breaking new ground in his family's story. As seen at the beginning of his career, whereas Cameron could benefit from mysterious phone calls advising people to give him a job in the Conservative Research Department, Gove had to return to Aberdeen to learn his craft as a journalist. He was not born into Cameron and Osborne's world; he had to work hard to be there. And once there, he was not going to squander any opportunities available to him. Not only that, but Gove's background meant that he was forced to wrestle with something Cameron and Osborne could happily ignore: failure. Not a fear of failure, but the consequences of failure. As Evelyn Waugh noted in his 1928 satire *Decline and Fall*, 'There's a blessed equity in the English social system ... that ensures the public school man against starvation.' The public school men in this context are Cameron, Osborne and Boris Johnson. They were born with not only a silver spoon in their mouths, but a permanent safety net under their feet. Gove was not. When he took risks, he had more to lose, be it the cold reality of financial consequences or an alienation from a social circle he had penetrated, not been born into. This differing perspective on life was recognised by Cameron and Osborne as a useful means for seeing how government policies were being interpreted outside of both Westminster and Notting Hill. It also meant that at a time when Cameron and Osborne were trying to play down their connections to rich-boy behaviour such as membership of the Bullingdon Club, at least one member of the clique had a suitable 'humble beginnings' story to put into the public domain. Gove was more than happy to give interviews and write articles focusing on his background throughout the coalition years, and would frequently discuss how it felt to be adopted, the sacrifices his parents had made to send him to Robert Gordon's College and the teachers who had inspired him.

It wasn't just Gove who would put personal details about his life into the public domain. Sarah Vine had no qualms about sharing with the world various aspects of the life of the Education Secretary.

In articles for *The Times* and, from 2013, the *Daily Mail*, Vine revealed countless nuggets of information about her husband. Thanks to Vine, the world knows that Gove had almost as many pictures of Margaret Thatcher in his office as of his family; he returned from a holiday in Austria with a pair of lederhosen-style swimming trunks; he worships the music of Richard Wagner in a manner comparable to 'the way your average 11-year-old girl is pro-One Direction'; he considers Angela Merkel 'as hot as Jennifer Lopez'; and he turned down appearing on *Desert Island Discs*. Incredibly, all of this information came from just one 167-word article published in the *Mail* in September 2013.[35]

Other tidbits liberally released by Mrs Gove include that her husband learned the ukulele to help cope with the stresses of being a Cabinet minister;[36] has an 'irrational aversion to houseplants and quiche';[37] and sings along to tunes by The Smiths when on car journeys.[38] Gove's battle with his weight also received a frequent airing, with Vine once complaining that her husband had shunned joining her on the sofa for a packet of Minstrels as part of an attempt at 'dropping two dress sizes in six weeks'.[39] He is also a frequent follower of the Atkins diet: 'I watch in amazement as, iron-willed, he forces down endless eggs and eschews all root vegetables,' Vine wrote in 2008. 'Never once does he fall off the wagon. He just doggedly does as he's told until he reaches his target weight.'[40] Gove even spent a week at a £2,500-a-week Austrian 'fat farm' in 2013 as he tried to shift an extra couple of stone he had put on since entering government.[41]

Vine was not afraid to get even more personal with some of her revelations. 'Is there anything more depressing in life than scheduled marital intercourse?' she wrote in an article in May 2015, adding, 'Especially when you're feeling about as allowing as last night's mashed potatoes (hang on: is that actually last night's potatoes on your jumper?). So you do the only sensible thing: wait until your partner has gone to bed, and the sound of his snoring starts, before creeping upstairs and sliding into bed next to him, taking care lest the poor fellow should wake and, you know, get ideas.'[42] It's little wonder that Gove's nickname for his wife is 'Mrs Blurt'.

As well as revealing snippets of information about her husband, Vine would also use her columns to provide a window on the pair's social circle – which just happened to include the Prime Minister and his wife. 'When David and Samantha Cameron moved into Downing Street, she was pregnant with my god-daughter, Florence,' Vine wrote in November 2013.

> I can remember then, watching the pair of them standing outside No 10, waving at the cameras and thinking, I really don't envy Samantha. Is there anything worse than having a baby in the full glare of publicity? In Samantha's case, the answer turned out to be yes: being photographed eight months pregnant standing next to Carla blooming Bruni. But once Florence was born, things got better. After all, Sam was a pro: Flo was her fourth baby, and she knew what to expect.[43]

It wasn't just the Prime Minister and his wife that Vine found herself socialising with, but an arguably even more powerful family. When media mogul Rupert Murdoch married model Jerry Hall in March 2016, Gove and Vine found themselves on the guest list. Gove met Murdoch shortly after joining *The Times* in 1996, with the pair coming into contact at various editorial lunches and conferences. The pair hit it off so well, there was speculation that Murdoch was keen for him to become editor of the paper, before eventually overlooking him and recruiting Robert Thomson in 2002. Gove never hid his admiration for Murdoch and, as we have seen, he launched a colourful defence of the *Times* proprietor when *The Guardian* launched an attack in 1999.[44]

In 2012, the pair's relationship came under intense scrutiny during the inquiry into media ethics chaired by Lord Justice Leveson. Gove and Murdoch were asked to explain meetings held after the former became Education Secretary in 2010. Between Gove's appointment and July 2011, the pair had met six times, but there had also been three further meetings involving the Education Secretary and Rebekah Brooks, chief executive officer of Murdoch's News International. Of particular interest to the inquiry was a visit to a site in Newham, east London in November 2010, when Gove, along with Brooks and London Mayor Boris Johnson, discussed the possibility of Murdoch's company investing in an academy in the area. The project had come to nothing, with Gove claiming it was most likely because the department was not willing to stump up additional funds to help build the school.[45] The very fact that Gove had been in discussion with Murdoch's people over having his company become involved in the education sector added fuel to the fire that the Education Secretary – if not the entire government – was too close to the Murdoch empire. In typical Gove fashion, he used his appearance before the Leveson Inquiry on 29 May 2012 to launch a full-throated defence of his former boss, describing him as a 'force of nature, a phenomenon, a great man. I enjoyed meeting him as a journalist, I subsequently enjoyed meeting him when I was a politician.'[46] The Murdoch-owned press was equally generous in its praise of Gove, with a leader in *The Sun* in May 2014 proclaiming, 'Michael Gove is possibly the best Education Secretary in living memory.'[47]

However, Gove was not the only Cabinet minister receiving praise from the UK's most-read newspaper that day. 'Theresa May never talks about her ambition to be Tory leader but she is one of the top contenders,' noted *The Sun*'s columnist Trevor Kavanagh. Within a matter of weeks, Gove and May would be engaged in a ferocious public row – and one of them would no longer be in post.

CHAPTER 18

DECLINE AND FALL

A s resignation letters go, it was hardly conventional. A 250-page screed touching on genetics, philosophy, energy, space, Thucydides and Dostoevsky – all under the title 'Some thoughts on education and political priorities'.[48] But then, Dominic Cummings was never a conventional employee of the Department for Education. He announced he was leaving his role as special advisor to Michael Gove in September 2013,[49] just as his mind-bending essay was published. When the news was made public, he told *The Independent* he was considering helping free schools develop and wanted to work on education matters 'outside politics'.[50] His departure, set for January 2014, came at a time when it seemed like Gove's education reforms were, if not quite Mission: Accomplished, no longer seen as Mission: Impossible. In November 2013, David Cameron's chief political strategist, Lynton Crosby, paid Gove and his advisors a visit with some positive news. Whereas in most countries education was seen as the natural property of the political left, Crosby's polling data showed that in the UK this territory was up for grabs. As such, the narrative around Gove's school reforms would play an important role in the 2015 general election campaign. Yet even this positive news, together with the departure of Cummings, did little to quell Gove's seemingly insatiable desire for confrontations.

The end of January 2014 saw the Education Secretary lock horns with Sir Michael Wilshaw, the chief inspector of schools. Sir Michael was angry about a growing number of attacks on Ofsted from right-wing think tanks, and he believed they were being directed by people inside the DfE. He claimed the motivation for the criticism was that Ofsted had recently instructed two free schools to close and deemed several others to be failing following inspections. 'I am spitting blood over this and I want it to stop,' he said. Asked whether he wanted Gove to call off the attack dogs, he replied, 'Absolutely,' adding, 'It does nothing for his drive or our drive to raise standards in schools. I was never intimidated as a head teacher and I do not intend to be intimidated as a chief inspector.'[51] Sir Michael tried to couch his attack in terms that Gove and his allies would understand: 'I am concerned the Blob, the orthodoxy that Michael Gove criticises very heavily, will be replaced by another Blob, which wants children to be lectured for six hours a day in serried ranks.'

Gove's relationship with Ofsted was already in a rocky patch before Sir Michael's intervention. The Education Secretary had decided not to renew the contract of the organisation's chair, Labour peer Baroness Morgan. She was convinced her axing after three years in the post was because 'of an absolutely determined effort from No. 10 that Conservative supporters will be appointed to public bodies'.[52] Gove claimed to David Laws that while he had told Dame Sally she wasn't being reappointed for political reasons, the truth was he did not believe she was up to the job and wanted to spare her feelings.[53]

Even if that was his motivation, it meant that Gove was once again facing public criticism – and this time from figures who were supportive of his education reform programme. On 4 February 2014, the *Times* columnist Rachel Sylvester perfectly summed up the corner into which Gove had backed himself: 'What is it about

Michael Gove? He's the politest and cleverest member of the Cabinet, but he keeps making enemies.' Referring to the treatment of Dame Sally, Sylvester said, 'If her appointment in 2010 symbolised a non-tribal approach, then her dismissal represents the dismantling of Mr Gove's big tent. It is unfortunate that the sacking also coincides with a whispering campaign against Sir Michael Wilshaw, the Chief Inspector of Schools, who shares the Education Secretary's traditionalist instincts.' Her article concluded, 'Mr Gove has shown he has the strength to take on his enemies. If he wants to secure his revolution he must now also make some friends.'[54]

The advice went unheeded, and later that day he found himself shouting down a Conservative colleague – junior defence minister Anna Soubry. Gove had long been exercised about the Ministry of Defence subsidising combined cadet forces in private schools but not in state schools. He had raised the issue with Defence Secretary Philip Hammond, but the situation remained unchanged. According to David Laws, Gove let rip with an 'astonishing rant' at Soubry at a meeting in the Education Department:

He leant forward aggressively and shouted very loudly: 'Anna. I am sorry. It... is... totally unacceptable... for this situation to continue. How can we possibly justify as a government the fact that we are spending tens of millions of pounds on subsidising private school pupils to be in cadet forces when poor children in the state-funded system have to pay for this themselves or don't get it at all? IT IS UN–ACC–EPTABLE! WE HAVE GOT TO DO SOMETHING ABOUT THIS. I AM FURIOUS.[55]

That skirmish with Soubry was as nothing compared to the battle he was about to enter into with the Home Secretary, Theresa May. From the very beginning of the coalition government, the pair had clashed over policy. May was the most passionate supporter of Cameron's promise to reduce net migration to below 100,000 a year, whereas Gove felt the measures needed to reach that goal – such as making it more difficult for non-EU citizens to settle in the UK – would harm the economy. Their disagreement over substance was exasperated by conflicting political styles. Whereas Gove viewed politics in the manner of the board games he so enjoyed playing at school – and continued to play into his adulthood – May operated in straighter lines. She was not part of any set, Notting Hill or otherwise, and sought to build alliances through her work as Home Secretary, not at dining societies. Both were enthusiastic contributors at Cabinet meetings, but whereas Gove would take pleasure in referencing great works of literature, philosophical thinkers or the latest cultural zeitgeist, May's interventions would be markedly less flamboyant.

One Cabinet minister remembers:

He was always at odds with Theresa because he and the Chancellor, the two of them, and I think the Prime Minister was a fellow traveller, used to oppose her endlessly on the migration stuff all the time because they wanted much more liberal migration. She was quite the opposite. I remember he used to wind her up a lot, it was quite funny. There would be lots of nodding and winking between the three of them – like silly schoolboys, really.

Gove was not afraid to make his dissatisfaction with May more overt. One Cabinet colleague remembers an incident when Gove tore into May for giving a speech interpreted as an early pitch to set herself up as a successor to David Cameron. 'It was so uncomfortable to watch,' the source says, adding, 'It felt like a domestic abuse episode.'

May gave as good as she got, and one witness described how after Gove made some 'slightly provocative and not terribly well considered remarks' about a paper she had prepared for a meeting, she let rip: 'What she could have done is just brush them aside, but she leapt on it. She went off the handle. David Cameron just stared,' according to the account.[56]

Gove was by no means the only Cabinet colleague May came to blows with. George Osborne, Nick Clegg and Kenneth Clarke were just some of the others she found herself feuding with as the coalition rumbled on. Yet it was a clash with Gove over the anti-radicalisation of young Muslims that would prove the most explosive. The Education Secretary had, of course, more than a passing interest in counter-terrorism and how to combat Islamist fundamentalism. His position on the Extremism Task Force gave him the opportunity to make his views known, and he frequently found himself crossing swords not just with May, but with Communities Secretary Eric Pickles and Faith and Communities minister Baroness Sayeeda Warsi. One proposal to come from Gove was to regulate madrassas, prompting David Laws to record in his diary:

> Even the right-wing Tories such as Theresa May, Chris Grayling and Eric Pickles looked a bit shocked, and Baroness Warsi was distinctly unimpressed and asked Michael whether she could have a list of all the members of the Muslim community the DfE had consulted. She obviously knew that we had consulted nobody. Michael was quick to admit this, which did create an impression that his proposals had been rather cobbled together.[57]

Gove's lengthy and at times aggressive interventions in the Extremism Task Force meetings led Pickles to deliver a blunt put-down on 20 November 2013: 'Michael, I object to your hectoring behaviour.

Shut up for a minute and let me speak.'[58] Warsi would later compare Gove's views on Muslims to those espoused by US President Donald Trump, saying, 'If Michael had been left to run this [anti-extremism] policy in the way he would run it, we would be seeing the kind of things that we're now seeing in the White House.'[59] Warsi also went on to claim that Gove's concerns that a sizeable minority of Muslims were sympathetic to fundamentalism, as noted in *Celsius 7/7*, influenced Cameron's approach to tackling fundamentalism. 'I sometimes joke that Michael Gove radicalised David Cameron,' she said in 2018, adding, 'In private conversations [I know that David] had some concerns about some of the extreme views that Michael had but over time [Gove] influenced a lot of his views.'[60]

In 2014, reports began seeping into the media of an apparent plot by Muslim fundamentalists to destabilise and then take over schools in Birmingham – dubbed 'Operation Trojan Horse'. The DfE had first been made aware of concerns of the Islamisation of schools in Birmingham in 2010, when Tim Boyes, head teacher of Queensbridge School in the city, gave a three-hour presentation to Schools minister Lord (Jonathan) Hill setting out his fears.[61] Gove was not aware of the meeting, and no warning or concerns were filtered up the chain. The issue came back on the agenda at the end of 2013, when an anonymous 'Trojan Horse' letter was sent to Birmingham City Council and the DfE claiming the existence of a plot to impose a more hardline Muslim ethos on schools.[62] Both organisations, along with the Education Funding Authority, began investigating the claims, and in March 2014 Gove ordered Ofsted to inspect fifteen schools in the city. In April, he tasked the former National Co-ordinator for Counter Terrorism Peter Clarke, supported by a specialist Extremist Unit he had set up in the DfE, to look into the suggestion that twenty-five Birmingham schools had been targeted by Islamist fundamentalists.

Gove viewed the allegations as a vindication of his warnings that the Home Office had been too soft on fundamentalism, and he used a lunch at *The Times* at the beginning of June to directly attack May's department. 'Cabinet at war over extremists in schools' was the headline on the paper's 4 June edition, with reports from a 'senior source' – later revealed to be Gove – saying:

> The education secretary is convinced that a small group of extremists has infiltrated schools in the city with tactics similar to those used by the Militant Tendency in the Labour Party in the 1980s ... Mr Gove blames their influence on a reluctance within Whitehall, especially in the Home Office, to confront extremism unless it develops into terrorism and believes that a robust response is needed to 'drain the swamp'.

The Times contacted May's special advisor Fiona Cunningham for a response, and she found herself not just defending her boss but also her partner, Charles Farr. Farr was the head of the Office for Security and Counter Terrorism (OSCT), located within the Home Office, and was slammed by Gove for only wanting to take on extremists when they become violent, a policy described as 'just beating back the crocodiles that come close to the boat rather than draining the swamp'. Cunningham hit back with a punchy quote, trying to turn attention onto Gove's conduct: 'Why is the DfE wanting to blame other people for information they had in 2010? Lord knows what more they have overlooked on the subject of the protection of kids in state schools? It scares me.'

Cunningham decided those words weren't enough, and a letter which had been sent from May to Gove asking why the Education Secretary had not investigated the matter when his department had been made aware of the concerns in 2010 was published on the Home Office website. Just to make sure journalists were aware, Cunningham sent a tweet from the official Home Office account linking to the letter.[63]

Cameron was furious. Two of his leading Cabinet ministers were having a turf war in public – and they had completely overshadowed the latest Queen's Speech. He ordered Cabinet Secretary Sir Jeremy Heywood to investigate the events, and within days the civil servant gave Cameron his report. Gove was ordered to apologise to both May and Farr for his briefing to *The Times*, but it was May who initially suffered the most, as Cunningham was encouraged to resign for her response and the publication of the letter – both breaches of the ministerial code.

A subsequent investigation by DfE Permanent Secretary Chris Wormald found no examples of direct warnings of 'extremism' being ignored or officials acting inappropriately in the department. However, Wormald did conclude that 'the Department has lacked inquisitiveness about this issue, and that procedures could have been tighter than they were … There is a marked contrast between, for example, how the Department responds to reports of child protection issues and how it has historically responded to reports of potential extremism.'[64]

The 'Trojan Horse' plot itself turned out to be bogus, and in March 2015 a report from the Education Select Committee concluded, 'No evidence of extremism or radicalisation, apart from a single isolated incident, was found by any of the inquiries and there was no evidence of a sustained plot nor of a similar situation pertaining elsewhere in the country.'[65]

Gove may have survived the row with May, but it was hardly the only fire that needed putting out. Arsonist-in-chief remained Dominic Cummings, who, now freed from what little constraint he felt while working at the DfE, was in full attack mode. When asked about his views of Nick Clegg for a piece in the *Sunday Times* in April 2014, Cummings described him as 'the worst kind of modern MP'. He added:

He is self-obsessed, sanctimonious and so dishonest he finds the words truth and lies have ceased to have any objective meaning, and he treats taxpayers' money with contempt. He won't do the hard work to get policy right – all he cares about is his image. He is a revolting character. And I say that after spending 15 years at Westminster.[66]

Having taken aim at the Deputy Prime Minister, Cummings then let rip at the man in charge: David Cameron. 'As Bismarck said about Napoleon III, Cameron is a sphinx without a riddle – he bumbles from one shambles to another without the slightest sense of purpose,' Cummings said in an interview with *The Times* in June 2014. 'Everyone is trying to find the secret of David Cameron, but he is what he appears to be. He had a picture of Macmillan on his wall – that's all you need to know.'[67]

Yet it wasn't rows with May, bust-ups with Clegg or Cummings's machine-gunning of Downing Street that caused Cameron to seriously ponder Gove's future in his top team. Lynton Crosby, who had so pepped up the Education Secretary at the end of 2013, was about to deliver a fatal blow to his time in the post. In a meeting with Cameron ahead of a Cabinet reshuffle planned for July 2014, Crosby told the Prime Minister that teachers and parents viewed Gove as 'toxic'.[68] Cameron realised his old friend would have to be moved out of the job he so loved, but he had no cause for concern about how Gove would take the news. The pair had had two previous conversations which led Cameron to believe that Gove would understand the reasons for his reshuffle. Gove had told Cameron that if he was ever a liability as Education Secretary, he would understand if he was axed from the post. A second conversation had taken place in which Gove told Cameron he would be happy to take over as Chief Whip from Sir George Young, who had announced in November 2013 that he would stand down at the next election. With these conversations in his mind, Cameron invited Gove into Downing Street for a drink on Wednesday 9 July and told him of his plan.

To Cameron's slight surprise, Gove was initially not overly sold on the idea. After leaving No. 10, Gove called Cameron to say he would indeed make the switch from Education Secretary to Chief Whip. But the next day Gove began to panic. He loved his role as Education Secretary, and he knew that, however it was spun, a move to Chief Whip would be seen as a demotion. Not just that, but militant teaching unions, antagonistic academics, uncooperative civil servants and resentful colleagues would all see it as a scalp. On Friday 11 July, Gove phoned Cameron to tell him the deal was off: he didn't want to be moved from Education. An hour later, while he was on a train to Dorset, he received a phone call from Sir George Young, the man he was supposed to be replacing in the Whips' Office. 'If I were you, Michael, I would take the job,' was the advice, with a strong hint that if Gove refused to take the position of Chief Whip, Cameron would go the whole hog and kick him out of the Cabinet completely. Just to reinforce the point, Sir George made it clear that he had rarely seen Cameron so angry. Facing the possibility of being kicked out of not just the DfE but frontline politics altogether, Gove agreed to the move. On Tuesday 15 July, the reshuffle was carried out, and Gove's axing as Education Secretary was the biggest shock of the day. He was replaced by Nicky Morgan, who immediately vowed to adopt a different tone to her predecessor.[69]

The implications of Gove's sacking were both immediate and long-term. A direct consequence of the move was that he had just taken a salary cut of £35,000, by virtue of the fact that the Chief Whip is not an official Cabinet position. That sort of money may have not dented the coffers of Cameron or Osborne, but for the Gove family it made a difference. In a sign of how little the Prime Minister had factored the financial impact into his decision, Gove was initially unsure if he would be taking the cut. A less obvious implication was the immediate damage to Gove and Cameron's relationship. After Gove had U-turned on his U-turn about whether to take the job as Chief Whip, Cameron considered the matter over. As a mutual friend later said, 'David just kept smiling and assumed if they didn't talk about it that everything would be fine.'[70] Explaining the move in Downing Street on the day of the reshuffle, Cameron sought to smother Gove in praise:

> I can tell you, if you are Prime Minister, the Chief Whip is one of the most important jobs in government. I wanted one of my big hitters, one of my real stars, one of my great brains, someone who has done extraordinary things for education in this country, to do that job, to deliver the government's programme, to help secure the future for our country. I am pleased that he is doing that job. He will do it brilliantly.[71]

Gove gave a slightly less focused analysis of his shift from Education to Chief Whip, telling the *PM* programme on BBC Radio 4: 'Demotion, emotion, promotion, locomotion, I don't know how you would describe this move, though move it is, all I would say is that it's a privilege to serve.'

The reaction from the commentariat was to be expected. *The Times* described Gove's move from Education as a 'mistake',[72] while the

Daily Mail described it as 'the sad day David Cameron ran up the white flag in the battle to prevent yet another generation of Britain's children from being let down by our underperforming schools system'.[73] *The Guardian*'s political editor, Patrick Wintour, questioned why Gove had been axed but Iain Duncan Smith – whose reforms in Welfare were far less successful than his counterpart's in Education – remained in post.[74] One thing all these comment pieces and analyses had in common was the narrative that Gove had become 'toxic' to parents and teachers. Downing Street wanted to make it clear that Gove's departure was Cameron following the orders of Lynton Crosby to get 'the barnacles off the boat' ahead of the 2015 general election. 'Michael is the King of the Barnacles,' one senior figure told *The Guardian*,[75] while another said Cameron was 'deeply pissed off' with Gove because of the Trojan Horse row and the attacks from Cummings: 'The party wants to run a highly disciplined election campaign – there can be no place for a rogue elephant.'[76] As if to prove the point, Dominic Cummings greeted the sacking by painting it as a victory for those establishment voices opposed to Gove's reforms: 'We got away with subverting every W/hall & No10 process, & it took DC 4 yrs to surrender.'[77]

Gove later claimed he could 'entirely understand what happened' and insisted he 'wasn't badly treated'. However, a sense of anger at just how easily Cameron cut him adrift entered Gove's psyche, and he later said, 'I would like to think that I would have, if I'd been in the PM's shoes, said to Lynton, "I'm not going to make calculations like that, and these are things I believe in and we're going to go into the general election fighting full-throatedly for them."'[78]

The teaching unions were, as expected, delighted to see the back of Gove. The National Union of Teachers, who had once labelled him a 'demented Dalek on speed who wants to exterminate anything good in education', said it was clear Gove had 'lost the support of the profession and parents for justifiable reasons'. Mary Bousted, general secretary of the Association of Teachers and Lecturers, was equally delighted at his sacking: 'Time after time he has chased newspaper headlines rather than engage with teachers,' she said, adding, 'The dismantling of the structures which support schools, the antagonism which he displayed to the teaching profession and the increasing evidence of chaos in the bodies he established has led Cameron to one conclusion – Gove is more of a liability than an asset.'[79]

The most prescient analysis of Gove's sacking came from Max Hastings. Indeed, Sarah Vine's only public response to her husband's demotion was to retweet Hastings's *Daily Mail* column, in which he described the move as 'worse than a crime'. Hastings concluded, 'The Prime Minister has done a bad day's work, and will surely live to regret it.'[80] Cameron would, in a way he could not yet imagine.

With Gove no longer Education Secretary, the teaching establishment was able to finally take a breath and survey just what had happened to the sector after four years of almost constant reforms. When Gove took his seat in the DfE in May 2010, 11 per cent of secondary schools and no primary schools were academies. By the end of 2013/14, 57 per cent of secondary schools and 11 per cent of primaries were academies. By the end of October 2014, 252 free schools had opened, with a further 111 pencilled in.[81] The trends only continued one way, and by January 2018, 72 per cent of all secondary schools were academies or free schools, as were 27 per cent of primary schools.[82] Gove had successfully, and it seems permanently, remoulded the institutions that deliver secondary education, with primary undergoing a more gradual shift. Yet the key question is: did he manage to create thousands of Robert Gordon's Colleges across the country, with state-funded schools matching the academic excellence of the independent sector? According to a 2017 report by the Education Policy Institute think tank (chaired by former Schools minister David Laws), 'academies do not provide an automatic solution to school improvement'.[83] The report finds that 'the structure of the school is less meaningful to the outcomes of pupils than what is happening within those schools', although it seems that schools that were doing well before 2010 thrived even more once they converted to academies. 'The academies that were rated as "outstanding" by Ofsted in the latest inspection prior to June 2010 – when the Academies Act was passed – improved pupils' attainment by almost one grade in each of two subjects,' the report notes.

As we have seen, Gove was not just concerned with the institutional arrangements of schools: he wanted to send a message from the top of government that traditional education was very much back in fashion. His desire to redraw the national curriculum, particularly in history and English, was evidence of this, but it also exposed a contradiction at the heart of his thinking. Gove espoused autonomy for schools and teachers, and yet from his desk in Whitehall he was happy to prescribe in great detail what should be taught and when. The curriculum didn't even apply to academy schools, so Gove was effectively attempting to create lesson plans for those working in institutions who had not bought into his academisation vision. Teachers had to earn the right to be left alone. Even when they did convert to academies, Gove was still keen to exert an influence, be it through reforms to GCSEs and A levels or sending every school a copy of the King James Bible in 2012. The latter scheme was funded by philanthropists, and every copy bore the inscription 'presented by the Secretary of State for Education' on the spine.[84] Gove wanted teachers to be left to run schools but, seemingly, only if they were doing it in the way that matched his vision – and that vision was a clear echo of the education he had received, the education that had taken him from a life of processing fish in Aberdeen Harbour to Oxford University, the BBC, *The Times* and the Cabinet. At times, it seemed Gove did not want to take on just 'The Blob' but the entire cultural elite, which he perceived was playing down Britain's 'island story' out of a misplaced sense of shame. At the beginning of 2014, as preparations began to mark the centenary of the start of the First World War, the then Education Secretary penned an article for the *Daily Mail* attacking Cambridge historian Sir Richard Evans for arguing that those who enlisted in 2014 were not fighting to defend freedom.

'Richard Evans may hold a professorship,' Gove wrote, 'but these arguments, like the interpretations of "Oh! What a Lovely War" and *Blackadder*, are more reflective of the attitude of an undergraduate cynic playing to the gallery in a Cambridge Footlights revue rather than a sober academic contributing to a proper historical debate.'[85]

Regardless of whether Gove had a point, the seemingly insatiable desire to insert himself into any argument only added to the sense he would happily build a road just so he could cross it to start a fight.

Gove's fighting skills would now be utilised in the Whips' Office, but he suffered an embarrassing defeat on his very first day, thanks to a combination of his own politeness, Labour MP Bill Esterson and a toilet.

CHAPTER 19

CRIME AND PUNISHMENT

The division bells rang out across the parliamentary estate, in-
forming MPs that the eight-minute window to get into the
voting lobbies was underway. Labour MP Alison McGovern was
pushing to allow the Office for Budget Responsibility to audit the
manifestos of parties in the run-up to the general election and had
called a vote on the matter.

The new Chief Whip, on his first day in the role, was relaxed
about the vote. A little too relaxed, it turned out. Having paid a
visit to a cubicle in the toilet in one of the voting lobbies, Michael
Gove struck up a conversation with Labour's Bill Esterson, who
was also using the facilities. 'He stopped to apologise to me for
missing our select committee appearance that morning because of
his change of job – he was due to talk to us about our inquiry on
extremism in Birmingham schools,' said Esterson.[1] Having made
his apologies, Gove walked out of the toilets and realised a vote was
taking place. Worse than that, he was in the wrong voting lobby
and could be about to vote against his own government. He rushed
out just before the doors were locked, but it was too late for him to
register a vote against the plan. The government lost by 203 votes to
sixteen. Labour had great fun with the error, with shadow Leader
of the House Angela Eagle claiming the next day, 'Mr Gove hasn't

had the most auspicious of starts. Yesterday, he not only lost his first vote but he managed to get stuck in the toilet in the wrong lobby.'[2]

Gove managed to avoid any more toilet-related debacles, but his brief period as Chief Whip was not a happy one. The party whose discipline he was now responsible for was frustrated after four years of coalition with the Lib Dems. UKIP had won the European Parliament elections in May 2014, and many in the party were concerned that, even with the referendum pledge, Nigel Farage's 'People's Army' could inflict real damage at the next general election. That feeling only increased when Clacton MP Douglas Carswell announced on 28 August that he was defecting from the Conservatives to UKIP, with Rochester and Strood MP Mark Reckless making the same journey a month later. Both men triggered by-elections in order to get a mandate from the voters for their moves, and Carswell romped home comfortably in Clacton with 60 per cent of the vote.

Heading into the Rochester and Strood by-election, scheduled for 20 November 2014, the Tories were under pressure to stem the tide of defections. Reckless's seat was not as naturally 'UKIP-friendly' as Clacton, and the Conservatives calculated that while a defeat would be unwelcome, if the size of the majority could be kept low enough it would deter others thinking of jumping ship. With the UK's relationship with the EU front and centre of the political discourse, the Tories were highly sensitive over any measure which could be seen to further the UKIP claim that too many powers were being transferred from Britain to Brussels. In the run-up to the by-election, MPs were set to vote on retaining thirty-five police and justice directives emanating from Brussels – including the European Arrest Warrant (EAW). The regulation requires EU member states to transfer citizens without trial to another country in the bloc if there is a suspicion that a crime has been committed.

Home Secretary Theresa May was a supporter of the EAW and lobbied hard for David Cameron to order MPs to vote in favour of keeping the UK signed up. A group of Eurosceptic Tories were opposed to the EAW, believing it made it too easy for UK citizens to be deported on trumped-up charges. A sizeable rebellion was on the cards.

The vote was set to take place on Monday 10 November – ten days before the Rochester and Strood by-election. The Conservatives found themselves trying to push through a measure that was essentially pro-EU at a time when they were trying to convince voters they were actually a Eurosceptic party. A ruse was cooked up whereby MPs would get a vote on eleven of the thirty-five measures the UK was planning to opt in on, but not the EAW itself. The government would take the passing of the eleven as a go-ahead for retaining the warrant.

Labour's shadow Home Secretary Yvette Cooper spotted the sleight of hand, and said:

> They took it out because they wanted to minimise the rebellion. They wanted to tell journalists that it was a vote on the European Arrest Warrant, but tell the backbenchers not to worry because they were only voting on prisoner transfer arrangements instead. They wanted to pretend to Parliament that this was a vote on a package of thirty-five measures, yet let their MPs fend off UKIP in their constituencies by claiming that they never voted for the most controversial plans.[3]

If the plan had been designed to help avoid a Commons bust-up, it failed. Conservative MP Jacob Rees-Mogg described it as 'an outrageous abuse of parliamentary proceedings', adding 'This approach is fundamentally underhand.' Bill Cash, the veteran Tory

Eurosceptic and chair of the European Scrutiny Committee, was equally angry: 'This is a disgraceful way of going about a very, very important matter. It is tainted with chicanery, it is not the way this Parliament should be treated.'The vitriol directed at Gove and Theresa May from the government backbenchers was stark, with BBC Parliament reporter Mark D'Arcy labelling it 'the most extraordinary tangle I've ever seen [the] Commons get into'.[4] The anger and panic was captured by documentary maker Michael Cockerill, who had received special permission to film inside Parliament for the four-part series *Inside the Commons*. His footage shows Gove in frantic discussions with May on the government frontbench as Tory backbenchers rain down criticism, and then in consultation with Speaker John Bercow as the Home Secretary filibustered after Labour called a surprise vote on stopping the entire debate to allow a new one to be convened explicitly on the EAW. Whips were ordered to track down Conservative MPs who were off the estate to ensure they were back in Parliament to vote, including David Cameron, who had gone to the plush Lord Mayor's dinner at Mansion House. The Prime Minister did not have time to change, and so walked through the voting lobby wearing his full white tie regalia. The government defeated Labour's ploy by 272 to 229 – with twenty-five Tories voting against.[5] On the main motion itself, the Tory rebellion increased to thirty-seven – but as the measure had the backing of Labour, it sailed through by 464 votes to thirty-eight. In terms of a whipping operation, it had not quite been a disaster, but Gove had certainly played his part in the undue panic sweeping through the government. As an avid reader of Robert Caro's tomes on US President Lyndon B. Johnson, himself a former Senate majority whip, Gove would have been well aware of the first rule of politics: learn to count.

The practicalities of the job may not have played to Gove's

strengths, but he did enjoy the symbolism of the role. To mark the 10th anniversary of the political gossip blog Guido Fawkes, Gove recorded a video message from his office to be played at a celebratory dinner. 'Here in the Whips' Office, the black book is no longer where the real secrets are kept. Is it perhaps the Guido Fawkes website instead?' he said before channelling his inner Francis Urquhart: 'You might think that; I couldn't possible comment.'[6]

While that video message had a clear purpose, another clip he recorded in October 2014 was slightly more mysterious. James Delingpole, the conservative columnist and writer, recorded a strange one-question interview with Gove while in his country garden. The Chief Whip was asked what his favourite moment was from the television series *Game of Thrones* and responded:

My favourite character ... is undoubtedly Tyrion Lannister. The moment I love most is when he leads what's apparently a hopeless charge of his troops in defence of King's Landing against the forces of Stannis Baratheon. You see there that this misshapen dwarf, reviled throughout his life, thought in the eyes of some to be a toxic figure, can at last rally a small band of loyal followers.[7]

The use of the word 'toxic' is most telling. Gove was well aware that it was the adjective briefed out to journalists by Downing Street as the reason for his dismissal from Education, and it revealed that Gove was still clearly harbouring a grudge. However, the *Game of Thrones* character he most identifies with does not have ambitions to sit on the Iron Throne himself; Tyrion Lannister is presented as someone who is unappreciated for the sacrifices he has made in defence of his family and its legacy.

Like Tyrion, Gove was not someone who kept his views to himself. The role of Chief Whip was traditionally a silent one, with the occupier shunning interviews and media interventions in order to remain in the shadows. Such behaviour was the antithesis of Gove's natural state, and Cameron – as part of the sugar on the bitter pill of demotion – allowed Gove to keep up media appearances. Yet without a policy book to promote, some of the vim and vigour associated with the man disappeared. He took part in two LBC radio phone-ins – one on 5 February 2015 and the other on 3 March – in a bid to keep his profile high. He launched a staunch defence of Boris Johnson's abilities when asked what role the soon to be former London Mayor should be given if he was re-elected to Parliament in the upcoming election. 'Because of his personality, because it's attractive, because he wonderfully gives the impression that he's never taking anything too seriously, people underestimate the fact that he is actually one of the smartest people in British public life, one of the most intelligent, one of the most thoughtful,' said Gove. Other questions focused on whether ISIL was worse than Saddam Hussein, what it was like working with the Lib Dems and whether the Tories would make an EU referendum a red line if another coalition needed to be negotiated after the next election. He was also quizzed about his smartwatch after it had been revealed that during a recent Cabinet meeting he had attempted to open an email on the device and accidentally began playing a Beyoncé song on his phone via Bluetooth. 'I could actually feel my face going beetroot red,' he told LBC presenter Iain Dale about the incident.

Gove's time as Chief Whip lasted just ten months. On 7 May 2015, the Conservatives recorded a surprise victory in the general election. A collapse in support for the Lib Dems handed David Cameron an effective majority of twelve in the House of Commons. The electoral breakthrough threatened by UKIP failed to materialise, with only Douglas Carswell in Clacton winning a seat for Nigel Farage's so-called People's Army. With a full slate of

Cabinet seats to fill, Cameron decided Gove was ready for a return to the very top of government and appointed him Justice Secretary. He replaced Chris Grayling, who was demoted to Leader of the Commons. The legal world held its breath, wondering what kind of Justice minister Gove would be. He had made little comment on the sector before taking up the position, but his articles in *The Times* in the later 1990s suggested he could take a rather hardline approach. After all, he had advocated the return of the death penalty, and in 1996 had argued that the Tories had not been tough enough on law and order. 'While Margaret Thatcher's ministers won the economic arguments, they were more muted on social matters. The consequence was a rising crime rate, a sense that politicians were detached from their concerns and a waning in respect for the justice system,' he wrote.[8] It took Gove more than six weeks to set out his vision for the UK justice system, and in his first speech he adopted a 'One Nation' approach to his new department, arguing that 'justice cannot be blind to the fact that while resources are rationed at one end of our justice system, rewards are growing at the other end'. The main thrust of the speech was that those at the top of the profession should do more 'to help protect access to justice for all'.

'Many of our leading law firms have committed to give twenty-five hours pro bono on average per fee earner each year. That is welcome, but much more needs to be done,' he said.[9]

This redistribution – Gove wasn't clear whether it should be of time or resources or both – was a political philosophy more in keeping with Ed Miliband than Margaret Thatcher, and indicated that the new Justice Secretary might just be different from what was expected.

Reacting to the speech, law firms flagged up not just the fact many of them did carry out pro bono work, but also that the government was cutting legal aid fees paid to solicitors by 8.75 per cent

– a move the Law Society warned could threaten the survival of the criminal justice system as it currently operated.[10] The cut had been planned by Grayling, but Gove signed it off on 10 June 2015.

However, in September, the Justice Secretary had a change of heart. After a summer spent locked in negotiations with the Criminal Law Solicitors' Association and the London Criminal Courts Solicitors' Association, Gove announced the cut would be suspended.[11] In January 2016, Gove confirmed it would be suspended for another year and also announced a row-back on plans to slash the number of firms paid to do criminal legal aid work.[12]

It wasn't just legal aid changes that Gove abandoned. In July, the new Justice Secretary took issue with the activities of the Ministry of Justice's commercial division. Set up by Chris Grayling in 2013, Just Solutions International exported UK expertise in prison design and management to the world. Like much of Grayling's work as Justice Secretary, it met with controversy; its dealings with regimes with poor human rights records came in for particular criticism. Gove wanted not just to close the division down but also to cancel an existing contract signed with Saudi Arabia. Foreign Secretary Philip Hammond was opposed to the move, fearing it would damage diplomatic relations with a country that had provided useful intelligence in the fight against terrorism. In a memo circulated to members of the National Security Council, Gove argued the moral case for cancelling the £5.9 million deal, claiming the UK should not be assisting a regime which uses beheading, crucifixion, stoning and lashing to punish its people. Hammond felt Gove's approach was 'naive', and a Whitehall source told *The Times*: 'There was a robust exchange of views. The Ministry of Justice had human rights concerns; the Foreign Office felt this would have far bigger ramifications.'[13]

It initially seemed Hammond had emerged victorious from the

battle, with David Cameron backing the judgement of his Foreign Secretary, and on 10 September Gove was only able to announce the closure of Just Solutions international[14] and not the cancelling of the Saudi Arabia contract. Yet a month later, on 13 October, it was confirmed the deal was off, with a Downing Street spokeswoman saying:

> This bid to provide the additional training to Saudi Arabia has been reviewed and the government has decided that it won't be proceeding with the bid. The review has been ongoing following the decision that was announced earlier in September to close down the Just Solutions International branch of the Ministry of Justice that was providing some of these services.[15]

It was a victory for Gove, who soon began to find himself feted by the liberal commentariat as he repealed numerous policies instigated by his predecessor. As well as the legal aid changes and prison training contracts, Gove lifted restrictions on the number of books prisoners could keep in their cells and cancelled the building of £100 million 'secure college' jail designed to hold 320 teenage offenders.

While many subscribers to the conservative ideology believe humans are not only imperfect but imperfectible, Gove argued that it was worth a try. In a speech on 17 July 2015 entitled 'The treasure in the heart of man – making prisons work', the Justice Secretary focused on rehabilitation as he hit out at the fact that 45 per cent of adult prisoners reoffend within a year of release: 'No government serious about building one nation, no minister concerned with greater social justice, can be anything other than horrified by our persistent failure to reduce reoffending,' he warned.[16]

His solution related to both the body and soul. The prison estate, derided by Gove as 'out-of-date, overcrowded and in far too many cases insanitary and inadequate' needed to be revamped – or in some cases knocked down completely to destroy the 'dark corners that facilitate bullying, drug-taking and violence'. He continued, 'Unless offenders are kept safe and secure, in decent surroundings, free from violence, disorder and drugs, then we cannot begin to prepare them for a better, more moral, life.'[17]

The soul aspect of his plan to reduce reoffending came from an understanding of who the people in prison were:

> Prisoners come – disproportionately – from backgrounds where they were deprived of proper parenting, where the home they first grew up in was violent, where they spent time in care, where they experienced disrupted and difficult schooling, where they failed to get the qualifications necessary to succeed in life and where they got drawn into drug-taking. Three quarters of young offenders had an absent father, one third had an absent mother, two fifths have been on the child protection register because they were at risk of abuse and neglect.[17]

Gove's solution saw him plundering ideas from his time as Education Secretary. He wanted to give prison governors more autonomy over how to structure the institutions they managed, but with a greater emphasis on helping prisoners benefit from education – even linking studying to a reduction in sentences. 'I am attracted to the idea of earned release for those offenders who make a commitment to serious educational activity, who show by their changed attitude that they wish to contribute to society and who work hard to acquire proper qualifications which are externally validated and respected by employers,' he said.[18]

The speech was received well by media outlets who had often

derided his work as Education Secretary. Gove had brought 'an inquiring mind and humane instincts to this sensitive job' opined *The Independent*, concluding, 'Michael Gove may prove to be a great reforming Justice Secretary.'[19] Will Hutton, writing in *The Observer*, argued that Gove's speech had thrown a challenge to the British left for how they would solve the 'crisis' in UK prisons, saying, 'One-nation Toryism, genuinely delivered, could marginalise Labour for decades.'[20] Even Kevin Maguire in the *Daily Mirror* managed to squeeze out some praise: 'Credit where it's due to Justice Secretary Michael Gove for vowing to improve prisons instead of running jails as finishing schools for criminals.'[21]

As in Education, Gove was keen to move fast to bring about institutional reform in the sector he was now responsible for. But unlike his previous policy role, he had not had three years to prepare for being in a position to make changes. As a consequence, he appeared to be a much more engaging figure with interested parties in the justice system than he had been with their equivalents in the education establishment. Frances Crook, chief executive of the Howard League for Penal Reform, admitted in 2018 that she had been pleasantly surprised by Gove's actions, as well as his style:

> With his track record at Education, we expected an ideologue, but of course he had come into Education with a blueprint. Because he was appointed in Justice without knowing that was going to happen, he came in open-minded, so he behaved in a completely different way. He didn't have a vision of what he wanted to do. He had a moral compass, but not a plan of action.[22]

In order to create a plan, Gove followed the formula he had honed in Education of seeking to learn best practice from other countries. In September 2015, he travelled to Texas to see first-hand measures introduced to reduce reoffending. He was followed on his trip by BBC's *Panorama* programme, who captured on camera the tie-wearing Oxford graduate engaging with repeat offenders in Texas about measures deterring them from a life of crime. He was particularly taken with Judge Bobby Francis, described by Ian Birrell, the journalist who accompanied Gove, as:

> A typical Texan republican who wears cowboy boots, owns scores of guns and has an office filled with skins of animals he has shot. Unlike most judges, Francis swears freely in court and banters with offenders about sports games. His court sessions are like a cross between group therapy and a reality television show, with applause for people doing well and small prizes for star performers.[23]

Gove looked on as 'Judge Bobby' quizzed the offenders on why they hadn't turned up for court dates, and, speaking to a man battling crystal meth addiction afterwards, he put forward his own theory as to why the judge's relaxed but no-nonsense approach was helping to keep people on the straight and narrow. 'Listening to Judge Bobby, it seemed like he was the father that lots of people in this courtroom never had,' said Gove. 'He's my "Daddy Francis", that's what I call him, I call him my Daddy,' came the reply from the middle-aged Texan, who added, 'He cares. It's just like a man taking care of a little kid that their dad don't want.'[24]

The visit further compounded a view Gove had formed long before he entered politics: that role models are essential for people from challenging backgrounds. His memory of being inspired by the teachers at Robert Gordon's College had fuelled much of his educational reforms, and he wanted to replicate the strong leadership model of schooling through his academy programme. Yet the role models that Gove admired were not those who offered empathy to those who were facing struggles, but those who set out a clear path towards success. This emphasis on paternalism is a key factor in understanding Gove's motivations.

But this focus on the perpetrators of crimes was not to everyone's liking. With Gove's previous support for old-fashioned justice measures like the death penalty, some of the Tory right had expected him to be a Justice Secretary more in keeping with traditional Conservative views. Having seen the focus on redemption and reform, Shipley MP Philip Davies could stand it no more and in the Commons on 26 January 2016 he told Gove he had 'gone native in record time' and was 'hanging off every word that is said by the Howard League for Penal Reform'.

'When will [the Secretary of State] get back his mojo and actually put the victims of crime at the heart of what he is doing?' Davies asked.

Speaking from the despatch box, Gove made no apology for his direction of travel:

> I am not sure that Labour Members would agree with the suggestion that I have become a sandal-wearing, muesli-munching vegan vaguester. I think that they would probably say that I am the same red-in-tooth-and-claw blue Tory that I always have been. And it's because I'm a Conservative, I believe in the rule of law as the foundation stone of our civilisation. It is because I am a Conservative that I believe that evil must be punished; but it is also because I am a Conservative, and a Christian, that I believe in redemption, and I think that the purpose of our prison system and our criminal law is to keep people safe by making people better.[25]

In March 2016, Gove announced that he would be bringing forward a Prisons Reform Bill to put into practice much of what he'd been preaching during his ten months as Justice Secretary. Prison buildings dating back to the Victorian era would be closed and sold off, league tables for jails would be introduced and failing institutions would be taken over by more successful counterparts.[26] The Bill was announced in the Queen's Speech on 18 May 2016, but Gove never had the opportunity to put his reforms into action. Instead, he placed himself at the centre of one of the most brutal and dramatic betrayals in UK political history.

CHAPTER 20

WAR AND PEACE

'**Q**uaking in our boots about Dominic Cummings. Not.'[1] It was a message that would come back to haunt its sender. Craig Oliver, the former BBC News editor appointed Downing Street's director of communications in 2011, was relaxed about the latest career move of his old sparring partner. Cummings had never liked Oliver and was happy to lump him in with the No. 10 'muppets' the former Department for Education advisor so derided during his time working for Michael Gove. The catalyst for Oliver's text message, sent to a Westminster journalist, was the news that Cummings was going to be heading up the campaign strategy for the Out campaign in the upcoming EU referendum. Cummings had been lobbied to take the role by leading Eurosceptics in Westminster within days of Cameron's surprise victory in the 2015 election. Matthew Elliott, the founder of the small-state campaign group the Taxpayers' Alliance, had been tasked by Conservative MEP Daniel Hannan and other key players to assemble a team capable of beating not just the government machine but the more anarchic group of Eurosceptics being assembled by UKIP leader Nigel Farage and his colourful leading donor Arron Banks. Cummings's Euroscepticism, his organisational nous and his ruthlessness marked him out as the top candidate. Vote Leave was launched on 9 October 2015, complete with the campaign slogan 'Vote Leave, Take Control' and the claim that the UK's departure from the EU would return £350 million a week to the Treasury.

In Downing Street, work was taking place on keeping the UK in the European Union. The Stronger In campaign officially kicked off on 12 October 2015, with former Marks & Spencer boss Lord Rose as chairman. On 10 November, Cameron set out his priorities for his renegotiation of the terms of the UK's membership of the EU in a speech at Chatham House. His four key goals were to protect the single market for Britain and others outside the Eurozone; write 'competitiveness into the DNA' of the whole European Union; exempt Britain from an ever-closer union; and tackle abuses to the right to freedom of movement and enable the UK to control migration from the EU.[2] It was that last point that would prove central to the referendum campaign, and in the run-up to the speech Michael Gove warned his old friend of its importance:

> Everyone's telling you what you must get out of the renegotiation in order to please them. For me, the big problem is that, fundamentally, laws are made which we cannot change. But speaking as your friend and your advisor, not just Michael Gove, you lose unless you get a good deal on migration. That's the critical thing.[3]

That conversation should have alerted Cameron that Gove was unlikely to back him in the upcoming referendum, as the issue of sovereignty goes to the heart of the European Union. The organisation is fundamentally an exercise in pooling sovereignty, and if someone believes the pre-eminence of national Parliaments is more important than any degree of federalism, it is hard to see how some tweaks to the UK's membership rules would sate those concerns. Yet Cameron believed Gove could be won over to backing the UK remaining in the EU, with the Justice Secretary himself seemingly sending out mixed messages. On 18 December, as rumours swirled over whether a Cabinet minister was about to resign in order to back Leave, Gove appeared on BBC Radio 4's *The World at One*. He was asked if he was subject of the rumours, and his denial was so strong that it prompted the belief in Downing Street that he would back Cameron when it came to the crunch: 'No … I'm confident he can secure a deal … where our interests are safeguarded,' he said.[4]

Gove and other Eurosceptic Cabinet ministers were keeping their powder dry while Cameron underwent the renegotiation, but a cabal of Tory MPs were working hard to ensure there was a suitable vehicle for them to join should they decide to support the Leave campaign. The MPs involved in Vote Leave were the usual Tory Eurosceptics, with Bernard Jenkin, Owen Paterson and Steve Baker helping to get the plane off the ground. But once it was in flight, Cummings seized control of the bombing command. Using his years of studying the Eurosceptic landscape, he knew exactly how to attack the pro-Brussels enemy. On 9 November, two students from the London School of Economics were tasked with disrupting David Cameron's speech to the Confederation of British Industry (CBI) conference at Grosvenor House in Mayfair. As the PM was addressing the gathering of the country's leading CEOs, the pair stood up and began chanting, 'CBI: voice of Brussels!' as they unfurled a banner with the same message. The guerrilla tactics were picked up by the broadcast media and successfully overshadowed the PM's speech extolling the government's economic policy.

Conservative MPs involved with Vote Leave were furious. Attacking the CBI in an attempt to undermine the pro-EU business voice was fine, but embarrassing their party leader was not a tactic they could agree with. Cummings was held responsible, but instead of backing off, he doubled down. As well as undermining any attempt for businesses to form a unified pro-EU voice in the campaign, he wanted to attack the credibility of Downing Street. At the beginning of December 2015, Cummings briefed the *Mail on Sunday* that even if Cameron was to come out for Leave in the referendum, he would not play a part in the official campaign as he was 'toxic on this issue'. Wellingborough MP Peter Bone and his ally Tom Pursglove, MP for Corby, were so furious with Cummings's behaviour and subsequent refusal to apologise that they quit Vote Leave and set up their own campaign group, Grassroots Out. Still Cummings would not change his methods of attack, and in January 2016, with Cameron's negotiations nearing their end point, a coup was launched against him. Orchestrated by Bernard Jenkin and Matthew Elliott, Cummings was summoned to a meeting in 55 Tufton Street, the home of numerous right-leaning think tanks, and told by members of the Vote Leave board that he was going to be shifted from head of campaigning to a consultancy role. Cummings scuppered the attempted coup by simply refusing to go. Not only that, he pointed out that many of the leading figures in the campaign would also quit in protest, leaving Vote Leave flying without an engine. Such a decimation of the operation could lead to the Nigel Farage-backed Grassroots Out winning designation as the official Leave campaign, which would in turn – in the mind of Cummings – see the referendum come down to Cameron *v.* Farage, a contest he feared the Prime Minister would win. Cummings knew his departure would not only see crucial people walk away from Vote Leave; it might also scupper the chances of high-profile politicians joining. Cummings knew Gove would be coming over but was unable to tell those trying to oust him, as he had promised not to divulge the Justice Secretary's intentions. 'I had a trump card to play but I couldn't play it,' he later said. 'I couldn't overtly say, "No one knows this, apart from me and Michael's wife."'[5]

While Cummings was certain Gove was going to come out for Leave, Cameron was still determined to convince his friend to fall into line. One of the perks of being Prime Minister is the use of the Chequers country home in Buckinghamshire. The Grade I listed building has been used by Prime Ministers to host visiting dignitaries, crunch Cabinet meetings and informal gatherings since it was given to the nation by Sir Arthur Lee in 1917. David Cameron certainly made use of the estate, and in December 2014 it hosted Samantha Cameron's very belated 40th birthday party (she was by then forty-three), complete with a temporary dancefloor installed in the Great Hall and Ibiza DJ Sarah HB providing the soundtrack. On 31 December 2015, another get-together was organised, this time to mark the New Year. Among the guests were Michael Gove and his wife Sarah and, as the conversation turned to the year ahead, the impending referendum was discussed. Vine knew her husband was seriously considering backing Leave. One of the tell-tale signs of Gove preparing to make a big decision is his mass consumption of literature related to the subject. The dressing table on her husband's side of the bed had become weighed down with books such as David Butler and Uwe Kitzinger's analysis of the 1975 referendum, and Roger Bootle's *The Trouble With Europe*.[6] Yet when she was asked by Samantha Cameron about her husband's likely course of action, Vine was uncharacteristically circumspect. A friend of Samantha later said her conversation with Vine left her 'with a very strong impression that Michael would back Remain'.[7] Vine herself would later admit that in conversations with the Prime Minister himself, 'I had not been entirely transparent – mostly because I genuinely wasn't sure which way Michael was going to go, but also because, being frightfully middle-class about it all, I didn't want to start a row.'[8]

Cameron knew Gove was wavering but genuinely believed he

was in play for backing Remain. The Prime Minister deployed Gove's old friends to help persuade the Justice Secretary to side with the vast majority of the one-time Notting Hill set. Osborne held conversations with him both before and after Christmas 2015, Nick Boles was tapped up to pile on the pressure, and a chance encounter with Ed Vaizey on a train saw the Prime Minister promise the long-serving Culture minister a job in Cabinet if he could get Gove to back Remain.[9]

It was against this pressured backdrop that Gove received a text message from the *Daily Mail* journalist Andrew Pierce on 25 January. Pierce had been tipped off about the coup and told Gove that Cummings was about to be sacked by Vote Leave. Gove realised the implications of such a move – the collapse of Vote Leave, the rise of Farage, the likelihood that the Leave campaign would be dominated by immigration to an unpalatable degree – and he leapt into action. For once, it was Gove carrying out crisis management on behalf of Cummings. He rang his former special advisor to establish what was going on and then called Bernard Jenkin, Steve Baker and Peter Cruddas, the Conservative treasurer bankrolling Vote Leave. As Tim Shipman notes in his book *All Out War*, 'To each of them he delivered the same message: "Look, I haven't declared yet, but you won't have a chance of winning if you get rid of Dom." The subtext, unstated, was that if Cummings was to go they would have little chance of securing Gove's support.'[10]

It wasn't just Gove's support that was up for grabs. Under pressure from Leader of the Commons Chris Grayling and Northern Ireland Secretary Theresa Villiers, Cameron agreed to suspend collective ministerial responsibility over the referendum issue. All members of the government would be able to campaign for whichever side of the issue they wanted. While the decision helped keep Cameron's Cabinet together, it removed a possible way of keeping

Gove onside. Since being appointed Justice Secretary after the election, Gove had been reenergised, particularly as he delved deeper into the issue of prison reform. 'I could see the fire that had been extinguished when he left the Department of Education re-kindled in his belly,' wrote Vine. 'He had his political mojo back, and he was happy for the first time in ages.'[11] Had Cameron not suspended collective ministerial responsibility, campaigning for the UK to leave the EU would have meant Gove resigning from the Cabinet and exiling himself to the back benches. Cameron's decision meant that Gove did not have to make that choice. (Although had the Prime Minister not given a free vote on the referendum, it is plausible that party discipline would have broken down in a dramatic fashion.)

With a constitutional barrier to him supporting Leave removed, Gove was faced with an agonising decision: stay loyal to his principles or stay loyal to his friends. He canvassed opinion from friends and former colleagues, including Steve Hilton and Daniel Finkelstein among others. One of those he spoke to remembers:

> My translation of it, to be honest, was he was already thinking to himself, 'I'm going to have to support Leave but I don't want to. If I don't do this, it will make an idiot of me for who I am, and what will I ever be able to say about anything?'

While Gove was wrestling with the decision, Cameron was still hoping to bounce him into backing Remain. Ahead of a speech the Prime Minister was due to give on 8 February regarding the government's prison reform programme, Cameron's chief of staff Ed Llewellyn called Gove to explain the obvious issue. No matter what Cameron said in the speech, the only thing journalists would want to know was whether the Secretary of State responsible for implementing the reforms supported the government's EU policy.

Gove was asked to make a statement saying he backed Cameron. 'Sorry, I can't do that, I'm genuinely torn,' said Gove.[12]

Having tried to get Gove's friends to persuade him and then issued orders to get him to fall into line, Cameron finally made a direct, personal appeal on 9 February. In the flat above 11 Downing Street, Cameron and Osborne set out in blunt terms why Gove must not back Leave in the referendum: it would be the end of the modernisers. 'You know if I lose, then it will destroy me. You can't do this,' said Cameron, with more of a matter-of-fact manner than a pleading tone.[13] Osborne, who tried to make the case for the UK staying in the EU for geopolitical reasons, also fell back on factional reasons for backing Remain: 'If Dave loses, then the party will be in the hands of the people we've been trying to argue out of their traditional prejudices.'[14] Gove was exasperated. He had warned Cameron way back in 2012 that calling a referendum on the UK's EU membership was an unnecessary risk. 'I'd put my feelings in a box, and now the box has been opened,' he told Cameron. 'My feelings on this have been unleashed. And it's just incredible difficult for me. If I take a particular view to row in behind you, then everyone will know it's insincere.'[15]

Gove needed to clear his head, so he headed back to Aberdeen to see his family. The Cabinet minister and close friend of the Prime Minister was back in the house where he had been an ambitious, precocious schoolboy. And that schoolboy had seen his father sell up the business that had been started by his father before him as a result of policies coming from Brussels. Gove had what Cameron and Osborne did not have: an emotional response to the EU formed by a childhood experience. When he returned to London, he again canvassed opinion, this time from his three special advisors, Henry Cook, Henry Newman and Beth Armstrong. They all told him the same thing: if you back the PM, people will know it is out of loyalty and not out of conviction, and your credibility will be shot. 'You will forever be seen as a Jeeves figure, a stooge, someone who is a wholly owned subsidiary of Cameron Inc., not an independent political act.'[16]

Gove had to back Leave. He had no choice, and, despite suggestions to the contrary, he was acting out of loyalty. It was a loyalty to the boy who had fought his way up from an unremarkable house at the top of a hill in Aberdeen to president of the Oxford Union, to an accomplished journalist for the BBC and *The Times*, to the Houses of Parliament, to the Cabinet table and, now, Lord Chancellor. Gove had achieved all of this on his own merit. Yes, he had received an expensive education, and yes, he had had parents who had supported and nurtured him, but that should not detract from the remarkable journey he had undertaken, and all on his own terms. His engine for that journey had been the books he had read and the ideas he had considered – and that is what he returned to at the moment of decision. It would have been disloyal of Gove to put all of that to one side just to fall into line behind Cameron. And for what? A quiet life? Deference to his friend? Cameron had told Gove that he would be destroyed if he lost the referendum, but did Cameron consider that Gove might be destroyed when he sacked him from Education? Did Cameron, in the moment when Lynton Crosby labelled Gove as 'toxic', pick loyalty over pragmatism and launch a defence of his old friend? Did Cameron, when Gove explicitly told him that he didn't want to move from Education to the Whips' Office, let sentiment or loyalty change his decision? A former Cabinet minister who worked with both men says:

> It just showed you that Cameron was ruthless enough when the moment came: 'Away you go.' When the boot was on the other foot, it's a bit rich for Cameron to turn around and say he was

stabbed in the back when in fact he was the more recent stabber. He sends his man to the gulag, where he stays for about a year before he's moved off to Justice.

On 16 February, three days before Cameron travelled to Brussels to sign off the renegotiation, Gove met with Osborne and revealed he was 'almost certain' to back Brexit. An earlier conversation involving the two men and Cameron had seen Gove promise not to lobby other ministers to join the Leave campaign, and he also subsequently pledged not to tear into the renegotiation when it was finally presented to Cabinet. However, there is some dispute over whether Gove made a promise to maintain a low profile in the upcoming referendum campaign. One ally of Cameron later claimed that Gove said, 'I'm going to take a back seat. I'll be on their side, but I won't be involved.'[17] But someone close to the Justice Secretary denied he had ever been so explicit and said it was Gove's legendary politeness that caused the confusion. 'Michael's so very polite that when he says "Yes" he means "No" but he thinks the manner in which he says it indicates the underlying intent,' the source said.[18] Quite why Cameron thought Gove would play a low-key role in Vote Leave, even if he had given a form of assurance, is a mystery. This was a man who in the middle of battling the education establishment decided to pick an argument about the merits of the First World War. This was someone who when he was Chief Whip – a post historically noted for its occupant disappearing from view in order to pull strings behind the scenes – was appearing on radio phone-ins and giving speeches. This was someone who having been sacked as Education Secretary not long after riling up a Cabinet colleague with a row over Islamist extremism in schools decided to pick a fight with the Foreign Secretary over a prison training contract with Saudi Arabia within weeks of being brought back into the top team. Gove instinctively could not avoid a fight. It is possible that Cameron may have thought that with him, Gove would be different. Those who observed the two up close believes Cameron saw Gove as entertaining younger brother: 'Michael played court jester in a sense to the king and that was how he was perceived – then the court jester suddenly discovered one of his rattles was in fact a knife.'

Cameron and Osborne had expended much effort on trying to get Gove to fall in line. Part of their motivation was that, despite those claims that he was 'toxic' less than two years earlier, they realised that Gove was an effective and articulate communicator who would hand a credibility boost to a Leave campaign, whose most high-profile figure thus far was Nigel Farage. The other reason they were keen to keep him onside was because he was seen as a gateway drug for many of those unsure which way to fall. Business Secretary Sajid Javid and Environment Secretary Liz Truss were two that Downing Street had particular concerns over, and, while they were hardly household names, the greater the number of Cabinet ministers backing Leave, the harder it would be for Cameron to convince the public that remaining in the EU was the best course of action for the country. As it was, Gove did not help anyone from the Cabinet make the journey to Leave, but he was instrumental in convincing one of the biggest beasts of all to join the fray: Boris Johnson.

Johnson was seeing out his second term as London Mayor when the referendum manoeuvres began. Having been re-elected to the Commons in the 2015 election as MP for Uxbridge and South Ruislip, there was an expectation that once he left City Hall in May 2016 he would find himself in Cameron's Cabinet. Before the 2015 election, Johnson approached Cameron and Osborne and offered to spearhead the renegotiation with Brussels ahead of the referendum. The pair refused, believing Johnson would set the bar too high and any changes subsequently agreed would seem inconsequential. As 2015 wore on, and Johnson saw the limited ambition of Cameron's renegotiation aims, he became increasingly open to the idea of backing Leave. Yet, unlike Gove, he did not have that emotional connection with the Brexit cause. His reasons for advocating withdrawal from the EU were tied up much more with the failures of Brussels to reform than with an instinctive and intrinsic antipathy towards the project. Oliver Letwin, Chancellor of the Duchy of Lancaster, was given responsibility for winning over Johnson, and on 16 February he called Johnson to give more details on Cameron's renegotiation. After picking up the phone, Johnson told Letwin he was going to put him on loudspeaker as 'I've got the Lord Chancellor here'.[19] Gove and his wife, Sarah, along with the owner of the *London Evening Standard*, Evgeny Lebedev, had been invited over to Johnson's Islington home for dinner and, of course, to discuss the referendum campaign. As Vine later recounted, 'Michael and Boris leaned into the iPhone, Boris firing questions at it, Michael making listening noises. I, too, listened dutifully for a few minutes, but it really was a very lawyerly conversation, and the aroma rising from the slow-roasted shoulder of lamb was getting to me. I tucked in.'[20] Johnson and Gove spent the whole night chewing over not just the lamb but the conundrum of party loyalty versus sincerely held beliefs. Much alcohol was consumed in the process as the conversation flowed.[21]

The next morning, Johnson – looking even more dishevelled than normal – visited Cameron in Downing Street for a one-on-one chat. A heated conversation took place, with the Prime Minister reportedly offering Johnson any job in the Cabinet he wanted except Chancellor. Johnson left the meeting telling the waiting media that 'no deal' had been struck by the pair over the referendum. On Thursday 18 February, Gove began preparing his statement setting out his reasons for backing Leave in the referendum. Osborne tried one more time to get him to change his mind, but Gove told him he was '99 per cent' certain he would vote Leave. The Chancellor asked if there was anything he could do to encourage that 1 per cent of Gove leaning to Remain. 'No,' came the answer.[22] Gove had made his mind up. On Friday 19 February, as Cameron thrashed out the details of a renegotiation of the terms of the UK's EU membership in Brussels, the news leaked out to the BBC and the Huffington Post that Gove was going to back Leave. The Justice Secretary was baffled as to how the news got out, and his team insists they had not briefed journalists about his plan. There were suspicions that Downing Street had leaked the news in order to get it out before Cameron formally presented the renegotiated agreement the next day – which No. 10 denied. Either way, it meant that Cameron was fielding questions about Gove in a press conference later that evening. 'Michael is one of my closest and oldest friends, but he has wanted to get Britain to pull out the EU for about thirty years ... I am disappointed but I am not surprised.'[23]

The next day, 20 February, saw the UK hold its first Saturday Cabinet meeting since the Falklands crisis. As ministers made their way to the Cabinet Room, Iain Duncan Smith collared Gove to let him know that the others from the top team set to campaign for Leave – himself, Theresa Villiers, Chris Grayling, John Whittingdale and Priti Patel – were going straight from Downing Street to Vote Leave's HQ for a photoshoot after the meeting. Cameron kicked off the Cabinet meeting, and after Osborne and Theresa May spoke, Gove told the Prime Minister that he could not support the deal and with a 'heavy heart' he had to be 'true to my convictions and my country'.[24]

When the meeting broke up, Cameron left through the front door of Downing Street to tell reporters that the referendum would take place on 23 June. Gove and the other five Leave-backing Cabinet members went out the back door and made their way over to Vote Leave's HQ, with the Justice Secretary hopping in Villiers's car. Once inside, the six posed for photographs with Vote Leave staff members to show that finally the cavalry had arrived. All eyes were now on Johnson and, having spent that day in his Oxfordshire home drafting two articles for the *Telegraph* – one on why he was voting Remain, one on why he was backing Leave – he finally showed his hand on Sunday 21 February. He texted Cameron at around 4.45 p.m. to tell him his decision, and ten minutes later walked out of his London home to inform the media that he was indeed supporting Leave. The teams were assembled, and the battle could begin.

Any hopes Cameron had that Gove would play a low-key role in Vote Leave were dashed within weeks of him joining. At the beginning of March, Gove was appointed co-convener of the Vote Leave board, alongside Labour MP Gisela Stuart, with the Justice Secretary having responsibility for chairing the campaign committee. Even before that announcement, Gove had found himself in the headlines for a story relating to arguably the most sacred institution of all: the monarchy.

'Queen backs Brexit' screamed *The Sun*'s front page on 9 March. The extraordinary claim was based on an account of a conversation between Queen Elizabeth and Nick Clegg at a lunch at Windsor Castle during the coalition years. According to a 'senior source': 'People who heard their conversation were left in no doubt at all about the Queen's views on European integration. It was really something, and it went on for quite a while. The EU is clearly something Her Majesty feels passionately about.'[25] Clegg did not initially shoot down the story, claiming instead that he had 'absolutely no recollection' of the incident.

Bringing the resolutely apolitical monarch into the Brexit debate was a bold move, and the search was on for the source. Hacks deduced that the lunch in question took place in April 2011, and others present included Welsh Secretary Cheryl Gillan, Lib Dem justice minister Lord McNally and then Education Secretary Michael Gove. Gove was under the microscope for breaching what would be the most sacred bond of trust between the monarch and MPs. When asked if he was the source, Gove told reporters, 'I don't how *The Sun* got all its information.' That 'all' was telling and suggested that the Justice Secretary had at provided at least some of the intelligence. The heat on Gove only increased when the *Mail on Sunday* discovered that Gove had lunched with *The Sun*'s proprietor, Rupert Murdoch, days before the story broke. He spent an anxious Sunday wondering if the newspaper was going to make that revelation front and centre of its coverage, but instead it splashed on David Laws's book about being a minister in the coalition government. It was a strange turn of events that Gove was relieved to see a front page quoting the Prime Minister as saying he was 'nuts'.[26]

Regardless of whether Gove was responsible for all, some or none of the story about the Queen's Euroscepticism appearing in *The Sun*, it was a further indication – if any were needed – that Vote Leave were not going to play by the conventional rules of war. Whereas Downing Street refused to sanction any blue-on-blue attacks by the official Remain campaign Stronger In, Cummings had no problem causing maximum destruction to anyone he deemed to be in his way. The fundamental difference between the two camps was that while Cameron and Craig Oliver were mindful of how to reunite a divided Conservative Party after the referendum, Cummings was not thinking about the post-campaign landscape at all. Indeed, should the Conservative Party become collateral damage in the process of winning the referendum, all the better as far as Cummings was concerned.

Gove was more than happy to follow Cummings's lead when it came to campaign tactics. 'Michael's approach all the way through was "I want to help you guys win, and I'll do what you tell me to do,"' Cummings later recounted.[27] Against the backdrop of this encouragement, Gove fired up his old debating contest mojo, making interventions that went far beyond what could be deemed as measured. In a speech on 19 April, Gove argued that Brexit could spark 'the democratic liberation of a whole continent'[28] as he compared the EU to the Austro-Hungarian Empire, Russia under Nicholas II, and the final days of Rome.[29] In an interview on *The Andrew Marr Show* on 8 May, Gove tore into the credibility of organisations such as the IMF, the OECD and the World Bank, warning that Brexit would leave the UK worse off:

Well, many of these organisations were wrong in the past about the single currency. They were cheerleaders for our entry into the euro, and we were told at the time that if we stayed outside the single currency, the City of London would be devastated and our economy would go backwards. Actually, the opposite was the case. And the truth is that these organisations are led by politicians and bureaucrats primarily.[30]

Cummings wanted more from Gove and Johnson. He wanted them to go harder on uncontrolled EU immigration, on the amount of money the UK paid to Brussels and on how that cash could be spent on the NHS.

The moment that caused the pair to agree with Cummings's demand to 'pick up a baseball bat and smash David Cameron and George Osborne over the head' was when, on 18 May, *The Sun* ran a story that Johnson's wife, Marina Wheeler, was rumoured to be the QC caught in a 'drunken clinch' with another lawyer at Waterloo

Station the year before. The story made it clear the rumours were false and said they were part of a 'Remain smear' against Johnson and had been doing the rounds at Westminster drinks parties. It was believed the rumours originated from Downing Street – something Nos 10 and 11 denied – and Cummings later remembered that Johnson and Gove were both livid about the story, with Gove saying, 'What No. 10 has done is deplorable. I assume David and George don't know about this. But this must be stopped and this is why we must win.'[31]

With Gove and Johnson now even more determined to win a victory at all costs, Vote Leave began to deploy what Cummings believed was a key argument: the prospect of Turkey joining the EU. On 20 May, a video was released juxtaposing a fight in the Turkish Parliament with footage of Cameron from 2010 saying: 'I want to pave the road from Ankara to Brussels.' Repeated at the beginning and end of the video was a simple message: 'David Cameron cannot be trusted on Turkey.'

The video was released as Gove gave a speech warning that the UK's population could increase by 5.2 million by 2030 thanks to five new countries joining the EU within four years. 'The idea of asking the NHS to look after a new group of patients equivalent in size to four Birminghams is clearly unsustainable. Free movement on that scale will have huge consequences for the NHS,' he said, sticking keenly to the Cummings playbook of linking the UK's membership of the EU to the national health care system.[32]

As a member of the UK government, Gove knew full well that the likelihood of Albania, Montenegro, Serbia, Macedonia and Turkey joining the EU by 2020 was extremely low, even if it was technically possible. Turkey in particular was likely to have to wait decades before becoming a full member, and the UK had a veto on such a move. Yet in his desire to win the referendum, Gove, who had previously accused Home Secretary Theresa May of being obsessed with cutting immigration to the detriment of the UK's economy and international standing, was willing to play any card Cummings handed him.

With Gove backing the Turkey strategy, Vote Leave went even further two days later. A statement released by the campaign on Sunday 22 May presented Turkish membership as a threat to UK security. It read:

> Since the birthrate in Turkey is so high, we can expect to see an additional million people added to the UK population from Turkey alone within eight years. This will not only increase the strain on Britain's public services, but it will also create a number of threats to UK security. Crime is far higher in Turkey than the UK. Gun ownership is also more widespread. Because of the EU's free movement laws, the government will not be able to exclude Turkish criminals from entering the UK.[33]

An image released the same day showed a picture of a UK passport acting as a door, with footprints walking through it. 'Turkey (population 76 million) is joining the EU', read the text.

The immigration button was pushed again four days later, when the 'baseball bat' was wielded over the government's repeated failure to hit its target of reducing net migration below 100,000 a year. On 26 May, figures from the Office for National Statistics showed that net migration had hit 330,000 in 2015, with half of that number relating to the EU. It was the perfect set-up for what would be a game-changing letter from Johnson and Gove. Drafted by Cummings and Vote Leave's head of communications, Paul Stephenson, the letter to Cameron would attack the Prime Minister for repeatedly making the immigration pledge despite knowing full well he was unable to deliver it while signed up to the EU's rules on free movement of people. 'This promise is plainly not achievable as long as the UK is a member of the EU and the failure to keep it is corrosive of public trust in politics,' read the killer line, which Cummings claims was written by Johnson himself.[34] Gove recognised that such an attack was 'quite strong',[35] but even after the letter was toned down, the line remained. It appeared in the *Sunday Times* on 29 May underneath the headline 'Boris and Gove lash Cameron on immigration'. One of Cameron's aides would later describe the letter as the 'turning point in the campaign' and, reflecting on it after the campaign, Gove admitted it was a moment when the campaign became a full-blown contact sport: 'I don't think we committed any professional fouls, but I think there were a few times where we went in quite hard and the shoulder-charge was quite aggressive – but it's a campaign.'[36] Having bluntly set out why Cameron's immigration target was so damaging, Vote Leave decided to present an alternative policy platform. On 1 June, Gove, Johnson and Employment Minister Priti Patel presented a joint declaration stating that after Brexit, the UK would adopt an Australian-style points-based immigration system. 'Class sizes will rise and [NHS] waiting lists will lengthen if we don't tackle free movement,' the statement warned, as the Leave campaigners promised that 'by the next general election, we will create a genuine Australian-style points-based immigration system'. Gove had made the complete transition from reluctant Leaver to energetic campaigner and now seemed to be putting together a manifesto for a government in waiting. But he was still seen as very much the secondary figure in the Leave campaign compared to Johnson, who appeared to be the Prime Minister in waiting. On 3 June, that perception began to shift.

Faisal Islam was pumped up. The Sky News political editor had struggled to find his groove since taking on the job in

September 2014. Replacing Adam Boulton, who was staying on as editor-at-large, was a daunting task for anyone, but coming in at the fag-end of the coalition government after covering economics for *Channel 4 News* presented its own challenges. The 2016 referendum was Islam's chance to show he had got to grips with one of the biggest jobs in political journalism. When David Cameron sat down opposite him in the Sky studios in Osterley, west London on 2 June for a one-on-one interview, it wasn't just the Prime Minister under scrutiny. Islam had spent three weeks preparing for the interview, and it showed. He was punchy, well-briefed and entertaining. Cameron held his own answering questions about migration and the economy, and both men received plaudits for their performances. The next night, it was Michael Gove's turn.

The Justice Secretary had been reluctant to take part and felt that as Boris Johnson was the frontman of Vote Leave, it should really have been his platform. Gove was worried that while he would be able to handle Islam's scrutiny, the second half of the show, which involved questions from a studio audience, would be trickier. He was, after all, 'toxic' with the public. However, allies of the now former London Mayor were worried that his involvement would reduce it to a simple 'Cameron *v*. Boris' narrative, and others in Vote Leave wanted to ensure they had a range of figures in the public eye putting forward the case for Brexit. Sarah Vine was particularly worried, asking her husband, 'Why the hell are you doing it?' during a discussion at the Goves' house with some of the campaign team. 'Well, who else is there?' he replied.

Yet Gove was not feeling as nervous as he would have done had it not been for a slightly surreal incident at the FA Cup final less than two weeks earlier. Despite being a season ticket holder at Queens Park Rangers, Gove went along to the final with his Chelsea-supporting son to watch Manchester United take on Crystal Palace.

According to someone who has been to subsequent games with him, Gove is a strange man to watch football with. 'He stares intently at the game, as if he's trying to work it out. You can't really talk to him as he's just so focused,' the source says. On 21 May, as United came from behind to beat Palace 2–1, some fans did manage to get Gove's attention. Manchester United fans repeatedly came up to him to say thank you for his Brexit stance. 'The people are with us,' he told his Vote Leave colleagues after the match. There is, of course, a sizeable difference between getting pats on the back from Manchester United fans during the Cup final and facing a potentially hostile television studio audience in west London, but that small incident made Gove believe that perhaps the campaign he was involved in was connecting with people in a way the commentariat weren't fully understanding.

At just after 8 p.m. on 3 June, Sky News presenter Kay Burley welcomed viewers to the debate and handed over to Islam. 'Mr Gove, you're a man with a dream,' began Islam. 'Exactly how many independent economic authorities share your dream of Britain outside the EU? Can you name a single one?'

Gove replied by claiming that the very institutions warning against Brexit were the same ones who had advocated the UK joining the euro and failed to predict the financial crash. He was clearly nervous, speaking quickly and with his voice pitched slightly higher than normal. Islam kept pressing that no economic experts were on his side of the argument, prompting Gove to utter a line which could come back to haunt him long after the referendum campaign was over.

Gove: I think the people in this country have had enough of experts with... er...

Islam: They've had enough of experts? The people of this country have had enough of experts?

Gove: ...from organisations with acronyms saying they know what is best and getting it consistently wrong.

Islam labelled Gove's dismissal of 'experts' as not just the politics of Donald Trump, but 'Oxbridge Trump'. That accusation seemed to stir something in Gove, and he decided to emulate the then US presidential candidate's style even more keenly. When asked to justify his suggestion that the EU was not working for more than half of the people in the UK, Gove delved back into his past.

Gove: I know myself from my own background, I know that the European Union depresses employment and destroys job. My father had a fishing business in Aberdeen destroyed by the European Union and the Common Fisheries Policy. The European Union has hollowed out communities across this country. It has also contributed to lower salaries for working people and it has also ensured that young people in this country don't have the opportunities to get the entry-level jobs that we heard about last night. You can say that their concerns don't matter, you can dismiss the concerns...

Islam: I didn't say that.

Gove: You were dismissing my father's example. You can dismiss the claims of working people. You are on the side, Faisal, of the elites, I am on the side of the people.

Much of the audience applauded and cheered the attack on Islam, but it was a low blow. As a former journalist of some standing, Gove knew Islam was doing his job by asking searching questions and putting him under scrutiny. But, like Trump, Gove was trying to undermine that scrutiny by discrediting the media. As if the Trump emulation weren't obvious enough, Gove ended the session with

Islam by repeating the presidential candidate's catchphrase from the television show *The Apprentice*: 'I think it's time that we said to people who are incapable of acknowledging that they've ever got anything wrong, I'm sorry, you've had your day, unelected, unaccountable elites, I'm afraid it's time to say, you're fired. We're going to take back control.'

Having won much of the studio audience over during his clash with Islam, Gove faced their questions next. In true politician fashion, he avoided engaging with much of the substance put to him, and instead constructed a straw man argument which UKIP leader Nigel Farage had been parading for a number of years: 'Many of those who are arguing that we should remain are trying to frighten you by saying that it would be impossible for Britain to succeed. They're saying that Britain is too small, too poor and we're all too stupid for Britain to succeed on the outside. I comprehensively reject that.'

The audience session ended with a question not about the referendum, but about the aftermath: 'Mr Gove, you and Boris have led the Leave campaign. When Mr Cameron steps down in the future, are you considering a leadership bid?'

Gove was emphatic in his response: 'I'm absolutely not. The one thing I can tell you is there are lots of talented people who could be Prime Minister after David Cameron, but count me out.'

After that exchange, the show came to an end, and as Islam and Burley said goodbye to viewers, Gove began shaking hands with audience members. He had not just survived but thrived – but at what cost? The man who was known and respected for his intellectual approach to situations, who valued rigour in analysis, who was infamously polite, had resorted to personal attacks on a journalist, dismissed the value of 'experts' (even if his comments were directed purely at those 'from organisations with acronyms' who sometimes get things wrong), and backed up bold assertions with personal anecdotes instead of empirical evidence. This Michael Gove was unrecognisable to his old friend David Cameron, who was 'pretty contemptuous' of his style in the debate, an aide recalled.[37]

However, it was not completely without precedent. Gove's old English teacher Mike Duncan had sometimes warned him before a debating competition, 'Your judgement's gone out of the window here.' Here was that tendency writ large, enabled and emboldened by the influence of Cummings.

Gove's performance was deemed a success, but his reference to his father's business piqued the interest of journalists. Gove had claimed to have seen the business 'go to the wall' because of the European Union. The truth was, of course, that Ernest Gove had sold the company as a going concern, not folded it as it was collapsing.

The Guardian's Scotland editor, Severin Carrell, decided to check out the claim, and contacted Gove Sr. Ernest told him:

It wasn't any hardship or things like that. I just decided to call it a day and sold up my business and went on to work with someone else. [I] couldn't see any future in it, that type of thing, the business that I had, so I wasn't going to go into all the trouble of having hardship. I just decided to sell up and get a job with someone else. That was all.[38]

The story was published on 15 June, the same day Gove took part in another televised debate – this time a special *Question Time* show on BBC One. The programme's host, David Dimbleby, put to Gove his father's words. 'My dad was rung up by a reporter from *The Guardian* who tried to put words into his mouth,' Gove claimed, adding that his father had always been clear to him that 'the business he invested so much care and time in had to close as a result of the Commons Fisheries Policy'.

As he went on, his voice slipped from the usual clipped tone to a more earthy Aberdeen accent: 'I know what my dad went through when I was a schoolboy and I don't think that *The Guardian* or anyone else should belittle his suffering or try to get a 79-year-old man to serve their agenda instead of agreeing and being proud of what his son does.' Gove looked as if he was about to lose control of his emotions as his voice caught on the final words of his sentence. Once again there was the attempt to discredit a media organisation for asking questions, and an emotional reaction to the EU which Johnson and Cameron were unable to invoke. It earned him a sustained round of applause. In the next statement, he again echoed Trump as he claimed that leaving the EU would 'allow this country to become great again'.

Gove did not feature in the other television debates. Boris Johnson, Andrea Leadsom and Gisela Stuart represented Vote Leave in an ITV clash, and the same trio were deployed again at an event at Wembley Arena two days before the referendum itself. He was, however, deployed on the final *Andrew Marr Show* before the vote. It was a key slot and would help set the tone for the campaign as it entered its final few days. The appearance took on even more gravitas because of the events of Thursday 16 June. Labour MP Jo Cox was assassinated while on the way to a surgery meeting in her Yorkshire constituency of Batley and Spen. Her murderer, Thomas Mair, shouted out, 'This is for Britain', 'Keep Britain independent', and 'Put Britain first' as he shot her three times and repeatedly stabbed her. It was the first assassination of a sitting MP in the UK since the IRA murdered the Conservative Ian Gow in 1990. All campaigning in the referendum was halted, and attention quickly focused on a campaign poster Nigel Farage had unveiled in the hours before Cox's death. Over a photograph of refugees crossing into Croatia from Slovenia the previous summer were the words

'Breaking Point – the EU has failed us all' and 'We must break free of the EU and take back control of our borders'. It was branded 'disgusting' by SNP leader Nicola Sturgeon, while Labour's Yvette Cooper accused Leave campaigners of 'exploiting the misery of the Syrian refugee crisis in the most dishonest and immoral way'.[39] The juxtaposition of that poster with the murder of Cox a few hours later prompted anger at the negative campaigning tactics of Farage and, by implication, the whole Leave campaign. Appearing on *Marr*, Gove said that when he saw the poster he 'shuddered', and he went on to claim he was 'pro-migration'. Marr hit back with the claims Vote Leave had made about Turkey:

> 'Since the birth rate in Turkey is so high we can expect to see an additional million people added to the UK population from Turkey alone within eight years. Crime is far higher, gun owner-ship,' and so forth. That sounds a bit like that's 'the other', those are threats, those people out there. Are you totally happy with the tone of that kind of statement?

Gove replied, 'Yes, because I think it's important to stress that when we're thinking about the enlargement of the European Union, it's the official European Union policy to accelerate Turkey's accession to the EU.'

Despite criticising the Farage poster, Gove made no attempt to tone down or distance himself from Vote Leave's focus on Turkey, even in the aftermath of Jo Cox's death. A senior member of the Vote Leave team says he has no recollections of Gove speaking out against the Turkey campaign strategy. Yet two years later, in an interview with his former *Times* colleague Tom Baldwin for the latter's book *Ctrl Alt Del: How Politics and the Media Crashed Our Democracy*, Gove appeared to show some regret. Baldwin writes:

I ask Gove if he was entirely comfortable making claims that appealed to some very low sentiments. He pauses for a long time. Eventually, he replies: 'I know what you mean, yes. If it had been left entirely to me the Leave campaign would have [had] a slightly different feel. I would have to go back and look at everything I said and think whether that was the right response at the right time. There is a sense at the back of my mind that we didn't get everything absolutely right. It's a difficult one.'[40]

On Thursday 23 June, voters went to the polls in the EU referendum. Gove spent that evening having dinner with his wife, his advisor Henry Newman, television presenter Kirstie Allsopp and Henry Dimbleby – the man Gove had commissioned in 2012 to look into improving school dinners. He sloped off to bed at around 10.30 p.m., and by all accounts slept soundly until he was called by another aide – Henry Cook – at 4.45 a.m. to give him the news he had not been expecting: 'I don't know if you've seen the news, but it's good news – we've won.' For a man known for his eloquence, Gove kept his reply perfunctory: 'I suppose I had better get up.'[41] Some 17.4 million people – 52 per cent of those who turned out – voted to leave the EU. The Remain campaign secured 16.1 million.

At 7.50 a.m., he received another phone call, this time from the Prime Minister: 'Michael, congratulations, it's a clear and unambiguous victory, well done.'[42] Cameron signed off, not telling Gove what he was planning to announce in his 8.15 a.m. press conference. Now at the Vote Leave office, the Justice Secretary watched on television as Cameron walked out of Downing Street accompanied by his wife and told the nation he was resigning as Prime Minister. Three hours later, and it was Gove's turn to face the cameras, alongside Boris Johnson and Gisela Stuart. The three – and the two Tories in particular – were keen not to appear triumphant at the victory. That was easiest for Gove, who having just seen Cameron stand down as Prime Minister was in the mood to celebrate.

Yet politics moves quickly, and within hours of Cameron announcing he was standing down Gove was involved in discussions over who should be his successor. The events of the next seven days would come to redefine the view of Gove among the party and the country at large.

Boris Johnson had been worried that Gove might have his eyes on the top job in the weeks leading up to the referendum – and not without reason. Gove himself confided to Cummings that he was worried his supporters would urge him to run against Johnson, but Cummings talked him out of it and urged him to do a deal with the former London Mayor. On 24 June, having given the sombre press conference in Vote Leave HQ, the pair began discussions on the race to succeed Cameron. Johnson asked for Gove's support, but he did not get an unequivocal guarantee from the man who had helped him get elected as president of the Oxford Union some thirty years earlier. 'I'm pretty certain I'm going to back you, but I just need to think about this over the next twenty-four hours,' Gove said.[43]

As Gove had predicted, the lobbying for him to stand instead of Johnson began. It was not just his advisors, but his friend Nick Boles, Justice Minister Dominic Raab and three Cabinet ministers – including Chris Grayling and Philip Hammond – all pressed him to throw his hat into the ring. Gove was reluctant, and on Saturday 25 June he called Johnson to let him know he would back him. Later that day, Gove met up with his advisors in Cummings's Islington home to tell them he was definitely not standing. Cummings had vowed not to play a role in the leadership contest itself, as, having recently become a father for the first time, he was looking forward to taking back control of his home life. However, once the leadership contest was over, Cummings planned, he would work for the new government, with Johnson as Prime Minister and Gove as Chancellor and chief Brexit negotiator. Crucially, Cummings would be given licence to reform the civil service – an institution he had long railed against. These demands were put to Johnson and his team via a conference call that evening, along with an attempt to find jobs for the various aides and advisors both men had around them. Tensions started to develop on both camps, with each wanting their own people in key positions. On Sunday 26 June, the two teams met at Johnson's home in Thame, Oxfordshire. Here, the differences between the camps became even more apparent, with Gove's team updating spreadsheets of which MPs would back the ticket and wanting to drill down into detail, while Johnson's gang seemed to be more in favour of relaxing around the barbecue.

With disenchantment already seeping into the 'dream ticket', Gove himself began to get cold feet. On Monday 27 June, as Iceland beat England in the first knockout round of Euro 2016, he told Cummings and other advisors he wasn't sure he wanted to be Chancellor and also take on the additional responsibility of the Brexit negotiations and reforming the civil service. Cummings reassured Gove that he would do all the heavy lifting on the Whitehall shake-up. In order to nail down exactly what role he and his teams would have in a Johnson premiership, a meeting was suggested involving Gove and Cummings on one side and Johnson and his close advisor Lynton Crosby on the other. Ahead of the meeting, Vine decided to send her husband an email stiffening his spine. Alas, as she went to write Henry Newman's name in the cc box, she accidentally selected the email address of a Tom Newman – a public relations worker who was not sympathetic to Gove's politics. The email was leaked to Sky News, who published it a day later:

Very important that we focus on the individual obstacles and thoroughly overcome them before moving to the next. I really think Michael needs to have a Henry or a Beth [Gove's special advisors] with him for this morning's critical meetings.

One simple message: You MUST have SPECIFIC assurances from Boris OTHERWISE you cannot guarantee your support. The details can be worked out later on, but without that you have no leverage.

Crucially, the membership will not have the necessary reassurance to back Boris, neither will Dacre/Murdoch, who instinctively dislike Boris but trust your ability enough to support a Boris Gove ticket.

Do not concede any ground. Be your stubborn best.
GOOD LUCK.

The meeting with Gove, Cummings, Johnson and Crosby did not turn out as planned, as Tory MP Ben Wallace – co-running Johnson's campaign – also showed up and was surprised to see Cummings present, as he had been told that the former Vote Leave campaign chief was sitting out the leadership election. More distrust and disagreement between the camps developed when the teams began sharing lists of which MPs they had tapped up to get support, and Gove's camp discovered they had recruited far more than Johnson's.

The day things moved from disorganised to farcical was Wednesday 29 June. Johnson was due to appear before a cabal of Remainer Tory MPs to set out why he and Gove should be given the keys to Downing Street, but he pulled out just half an hour beforehand, fearing an ambush from supporters of Theresa May, who was seen as his main rival in the election. A far more serious problem manifested itself when Energy minister Andrea Leadsom, with whom Johnson had shared a stage on two occasions during the referendum campaign, began making noises that she would run for the leadership if she was not given a big job in government – preferably Chancellor. Johnson and Gove met with Leadsom to establish what post she would take in exchange for supporting the duo, and she said either Chancellor or Deputy Prime Minister with responsibility for Brexit negotiations. After mulling it over with Lynton Crosby, it was agreed to guarantee Leadsom one of those jobs once Johnson was in Downing Street. Leadsom was promised an offer in writing by eight o'clock that evening along with a tweet from Johnson's Twitter account confirming the deal and that she would be one of the leading lights of his administration.

There then followed a bizarre series of events more in keeping with an Ealing comedy than a group of people who wanted to run the country.

The night began with a party at the headquarters of advertising company M&C Saatchi. Johnson and Leadsom were both present but did not speak to each other. Johnson then went on to a party at the Hurlingham Club in west London which, given recent events, had morphed into a farewell event for David Cameron. Gove was also in attendance and Leadsom was supposed to be present, having reserved a table. Nick Boles, who had spent much of the day trying to get Johnson to write his speech ahead of his leadership launch scheduled for the next day, texted Leadsom to ask where she was and if she wanted a picture of the note promising her a spot at the top of Johnson's team. She did not reply. Johnson then texted Gove setting out a form of words for the tweet announcing Leadsom was on board, but he didn't reply either. Either way, the activity all took place past the 8 p.m. deadline Leadsom had insisted upon, to give her time to get her own nomination papers in for the leader-ship contest should Johnson renege on his promise. With no letter delivered or tweet sent, Leadsom assumed the deal was off. When

Gove returned home later that evening, he called Leadsom, who told him she was now running for leader. Gove was furious and, on the advice of his wife and Simone Finn – his ex-girlfriend who was friends with Vine and over for dinner that evening – he summoned his advisors to discuss what to do about a campaign that was struggling to get even the basics right.

One of those ordered to join him in his Ladbroke Grove home was Nick Boles. The Grantham MP had left the Hurlingham Club party with Johnson and travelled with him by taxi to his home to finally get the leadership speech finished. During the journey, Boles took control of Johnson's mobile phone so he the former London Mayor could focus on his speech. Boles discovered a text from Leadsom, saying that in the absence of a public endorsement of the deal, she would now be filing her own nomination papers. He told Johnson there had been a 'cock-up' about the tweet,[44] and Johnson instructed Boles to reply, asking Leadsom whether she wanted the tweet sent now or in the morning. Johnson has subsequently been adamant that Boles did not tell him Leadsom was going to stand herself, and the reply sent by Boles does not mention Leadsom's own ambitions: 'Sorry, my cockup. I told Boles about the letter, not about the tweet. We can do the tweet now or tomorrow first thing as you prefer.'[45]

At 12.30 a.m., having tried to help Johnson write his speech, Boles left the leadership candidate to it and jumped in a taxi to Gove's house. Upon arrival, Boles found that Gove had already reached the point where he could not back Johnson. All the qualities Johnson seemed to have adopted, or at least done a good impression of understanding the importance of, during the referendum campaign had completely disappeared. Message discipline, organisation, taking advice, working to deadlines. All gone. Leopards do not change their spots, of course, but sometimes they can at least camouflage them for a while. Yet, as the discipline of the Vote Leave campaign evaporated, Johnson reverted to type. It was a type undoubtedly popular with the public, but Gove was not considering that factor as the clock neared 1 a.m. on the morning of Thursday 30 June. He was considering whether this man could be Prime Minister.

Gove thought back to his own experiences working closely with a Prime Minister. He remembered seeing the security services rushing in, clearing the room and telling Cameron he had to make an instant decision on whether to give the go-ahead to have someone killed. Could Johnson handle that level of pressure and responsibility? Could he be that decisive? He wasn't even able to coordinate giving a piece of paper to Andrea Leadsom and sending a tweet. Having just returned from a party where Cameron's virtues had been extolled by speaker after speaker, Gove came to the conclusion Johnson was not in that league and that he should not be Prime Minister. He decided to withdraw his support. Having made that mental leap, it was not too difficult to surmise who should in fact succeed Cameron at 10 Downing Street. Theresa May had backed Remain in the referendum and so questions marks stood over the form of Brexit she would seek to deliver. Having never been a Cabinet minister, Andrea Leadsom was too inexperienced to hit the ground running at a time when the country would need what one might call strong and stable leadership. After talking it over for around an hour, the answer was obvious: Gove himself would have to stand.

Vine, who was beginning to earn a reputation as a Lady Macbeth figure thanks to the 'be your stubborn best' email, supported her husband's decision, but she was not the driving force behind it. In the week since the referendum, she had been keen to ensure Gove was not exploited by Johnson in the negotiations over Cabinet posts and backroom staff, but she was not strongly lobbying for him to stand himself. Indeed, her contributions to the debate tended to be much more practical, such as whether she would want to live in Downing Street. Yet by the end of that night, she was completely behind her husband's decision.

According to one friend of the Goves': 'The real Lady Macbeth figure was Boles.' Gove's old friend was arguably more exasperated with Johnson's behaviour than anyone, and he had been lobbying for Gove to stand from the very beginning. Cummings in particular believes Boles manipulated the events of that night to ensure the Leadsom–Johnson deal died. 'Boles pulled a fast one. Both got suckered by a scumbag and didn't know what they were dealing with,' Cummings later said, adding, 'Michael would trust Boles completely. It would not occur to Michael that Boles would invent shit.'[46] Despite repeated requests, Boles refused to be interviewed for this book.

At around 1.30 a.m., Gove's advisor Henry Cook called Cummings to tell him of the plan. Cummings, who was preparing to go on holiday the next day, advised him, and everyone else, to sleep on it. They did, but the morning light of Thursday 30 June did not prompt a change of heart. Gove's team snapped into action. After a conference call with his advisors, including his old ally from Education Henry de Zoete and Vote Leave alumnus Paul Stephenson, the team began contacting MPs they believed would back the plan to arrange a meeting in Gove's Commons office for 9 a.m.

Before the meeting, Gove called Johnson to deliver the news but was unable to get through. He instead rang Lynton Crosby and said, 'I'm standing.'

'Standing for what, mate? What do you mean you're fucking standing?' Crosby replied with his distinctive Australian accent.

'I'm standing to be leader of the party and Prime Minister,' Gove clarified.

Having told Team Boris of his decision, Gove faced the MPs gathered in his office: Suella Braverman (then Fernandes), Dominic Raab, Nick Gibb, Oliver Dowden, Rishi Sunak, Jacob Rees-Mogg, Robert Jenrick, John Hayes and Ed Vaizey. Vaizey was the most enthusiastic about Gove's announcement, and it was only Oliver Dowden who said he needed to think about whether he could make the switch from Johnson to Gove (in the end, he supported Theresa May). With a cabal of MPs onside, an email was sent to the Westminster lobby journalists at 9.02 a.m., as they were all gathered for Theresa May's official leadership bid launch at the Royal United Services Institute in Whitehall. 'I have come, reluctantly, to the conclusion that Boris cannot provide the leadership or build the team for the task ahead. I have, therefore, decided to put my name forward for the leadership,' read his statement. If Gove didn't want to make his decision seem like a brutal political assassination, that statement was the wrong way to go about it. With the news out there, Gove's team began ringing round MPs to gauge support. While they hit the phones, a television screen carried live footage of Johnson's leadership bid speech. Except it wasn't a leadership bid speech. It was a concession of defeat. Having set out what the next Prime Minister needed to do to make the UK thrive in a post-Brexit world, Johnson said, 'Having consulted colleagues and in view of the circumstances in Parliament, I have concluded that person cannot be me.' Gove's team were shocked. They had not expected Johnson to pull out of the race. Initially, they believed this could benefit them, as Gove was now the most high-profile Leave campaigner in the contest. That feeling soon dissipated as the realisation dawned that Gove was being seen as a combination of Macbeth and Brutus.

On 1 July, Gove formally launched his leadership campaign at the headquarters of the Policy Exchange think tank he had helped establish. Gove's speech was almost 5,000 words long and knocked together in twenty-four hours, a contrast to Johnson's struggle to pull together 1,500 words over the course of a week. The key theme was 'change' – with the word and its variants mentioned twenty-eight times. It was the passage reflecting on why he was standing which prompted the most interest. 'I never thought I'd ever be in this position,' he said, adding, 'I did not want it; indeed, I did almost everything not to be a candidate for the leadership of this party.'

After claiming he had no 'charisma' or 'glamour', he took a brief tour of those he had slain to reach this position who were often associated with those descriptions. It was 'a wrench' to part company with David Cameron in the EU referendum, he said, while 'for all Boris's formidable talents', Johnson was 'not the right person' for the task ahead. 'I had to stand up for my convictions. I had to stand up for a different course for this country. I had to stand for the leadership of this party.'

In the run-up to the launch, Gove was put through his paces by his team as they tried to anticipate what questions he would face from the media. It was during this session that Gove made a startling admission. According to someone with intimate knowledge of the event, Gove was asked if he had ever taken drugs. 'Yes, cocaine,' he replied. Gove was instructed not to give that answer in public and told instead to fall back on the words David Cameron had used when he was running for leader, namely that politicians are entitled to a private life before entering politics. There had long been rumours in Westminster that Gove had taken the drug while working at *The Times*, but the claims had never been reported. The fact that Gove – who at the time was Justice Secretary and Lord Chancellor – was seemingly prepared to go public with this information would have marked the first time a candidate for the highest office in the land admitted taking a Class A drug.

Having faced the media, it was now Gove's turn to put himself before MPs at the first hustings event since the close of nominations. He braced himself for a rough ride. Johnson's supporters had made no secret of their feelings about the person who had brought down the man they believed should be king. Rossendale and Darwen MP Jake Berry tweeted, 'There is a very deep pit reserved in Hell for such as he. #Gove', and then followed it up with: 'I do not for one moment resile from my opinion that as a traitor Gove leaves Judas Iscariot standing. #Gove'. Wyre and Preston North MP Ben Wallace, Johnson's campaign manager, decided his thoughts should not be restricted by Twitter's 140-character limit and penned an article for the *Telegraph*. 'Michael seems to have an emotional need to gossip, particularly when drink is taken, as it all too often seemed to be,' he wrote, before claiming Gove would pose a security risk: 'UK citizens deserve to know that when they go to sleep at night their secrets and their nation's secrets aren't shared in the newspaper column of the prime minister's wife the next day, or traded away with newspaper proprietors over fine wine.'[47]

As it was, when Theresa May, Andrea Leadsom, Liam Fox and Stephen Crabb all joined Gove on Monday 4 July to put their case to MPs as to why they should be Prime Minister, Gove wasn't asked any questions about Johnson. He survived the first ballot, held a day later, winning forty-eight votes. Fox was eliminated, having secured just sixteen backers, while Crabb withdrew, having picked up only thirty-four votes. Both men announced they would be backing May in the next round.

With Leadsom on sixty-six votes – eighteen ahead of Gove – and the two now ex-candidates supporting May, who had pulled in 165, it seemed unlikely that Gove would make it to the final two and therefore go through to the ballot of activists. Boles decided to adopt, on Gove's behalf but without his knowledge, a self-flagellation strategy, and sent a text to MPs who were supporting May asking them to switch support to his man in order to keep Leadsom off the final ballot. 'Michael doesn't mind spending two months taking a good thrashing from Theresa if that is what it takes, but in the party's interest and the national interest surely we must all work together to stop AL?' read part of the message.[48] When it came to the second hustings, held on Wednesday 6 July, Gove was confronted by MPs over the text from Boles. He claimed he had not sanctioned such a message, but it further added to the perception that Gove was willing to use underhand tactics to get into Downing Street.

Another intervention which helped May but hindered Gove came from Conservative veteran Ken Clarke. In 2001, Gove had warned about the dangers to the future of the Tory Party if Clarke was to win the leadership ahead of Michael Portillo. Some fifteen years later, and Clarke returned the compliment ten-fold, warning that Gove was a threat to global stability. As the former Chancellor sat down for an interview with Sky News, he did not realise an off-air conversation he was having with his old colleague Sir Malcolm Rifkind was being recorded. Speaking about Gove, Clarke said:

> I remember being in a discussion once about something we should do in somewhere like Syria or Iraq, and he was so wild that I remember exchanging looks with Liam Fox, who's much more right-wing than me ... Liam was raising eyebrows and I think with Michael as Prime Minister we'd go to war with at least three countries at once.[49]

If that contribution did no favours for Gove, Clarke's assessment of Theresa May as a 'bloody difficult woman' actually gave the Home Secretary an unofficial campaigning slogan which won her respect from MPs.

When the next ballot was held on 7 July, Gove actually saw his support fall from forty-eight to forty-six, while Leadsom secured eighty-four votes and May won well over half the party with 199 backers. In a two-week period, Gove had helped bring about the resignation of David Cameron, thwarted Boris Johnson's ambitions to be Prime Minister, and burned through any reputation he had as someone who could be trusted, in a doomed attempt to win the top job for himself. Matters only got worse a week later. The leadership contest never made it as far as a ballot of party members, as Leadsom withdrew from the race on Monday 11 July. She had been widely criticised for an interview she had given to *The Times*, published two days earlier, in which she discussed how being a mother 'means you have a very real stake in the future of our country' – unlike, she implied, the childless Theresa May. With Leadsom out, May was the new Prime Minister and, as such, would be choosing a new Cabinet. On Thursday 14 July, Gove was summoned to Downing Street to be told that, unlike new Foreign Secretary Boris Johnson, he would not be part of her top team. After telling him she wanted to make room for new faces, May said, 'One of the things that's very important is loyalty, and after the last few weeks I've been speaking to people in the party... I wouldn't say that you could never come back, but you need to take a period on the back benches in order to demonstrate loyalty.'[50]

Gove told May he understood, congratulated her again on her victory and left Downing Street to prepare for life on the back benches. He was not alone. George Osborne, Nicky Morgan, Oliver Letwin, John Whittingdale, Ed Vaizey and Dominic Raab were also all out of the government. Within a year, one of them would not only return but play a vital role in keeping May as Prime Minister.

CHAPTER 21

A MOVEABLE FEAST

Having led his country out of the European Union, caused the resignation of the Prime Minister, scuppered the chances of the leading figure to be his successor and then stood for the premiership himself, there was perhaps not a lot of new ground for Michael Gove to break in 2016. But as it was only July when Theresa May sacked him as Justice Secretary, he needed to find something to fill his now emptier-than-expected diary. Growing a beard appeared to be the first order of business – an act which frees up more time than it takes up – and in mid-August Gove was snapped returning home from a run with scruffy grey hair on his chin and a thinner red moustache barely covering his top lip. Sarah Vine revealed her husband – now set free from being in high demand for media appearances – was 'very much enjoying his new hipster look'.[1]

With his political career on pause, Gove returned to his first profession to supplement his earnings as a backbench MP. In October, he rejoined *The Times* as a columnist and book reviewer, and his years at the top of the political game had seen his value increase dramatically. When he left *The Times* in 2009, he was paid £60,000 a year. His new pay cheque was £150,000 a year for eight hours' work a week.

He used one of his first columns to re-run the Brexit campaign, claiming it was a 'victory secured against the weight of City money, the strength of the political establishment and the expectations of nearly every expert commentator in SW1',[2] while a subsequent article blasted Bank of England Governor Mark Carney as 'neither always infallible nor truly independent' and hit out Carney's elevation to a 'special realm of near-divinity' by some commentators.[3] Later columns detailed support for Theresa May's 'Brexit means Brexit' approach to the upcoming negotiations with the EU, and a love for Ed Balls, his former opposite number when he was the Tories' Education spokesman, who, having lost his seat in the 2015 general election, was now an enthusiastic contestant on *Strictly Come Dancing*.

Gove's contribution to *The Times* was not restricted to his weekly column and book reviews. He attended meetings of the paper's politics team, which involved other columnists and leader writers, such as Daniel Finkelstein, to get a feel for how the paper was planning to cover upcoming issues. One source said Gove attended 'three or four' of these meetings and was 'always quite careful with what he said'. 'You don't say anything in front of Danny Finkelstein you don't think might not go back to Downing Street,' the source added.

If Gove thought he was going to take home his sizeable pay cheque without doing some actual reporting, he was wrong, and in November he was sent by editor John Witherow to the United States to feed back on the final days of the 2016 presidential election. His first despatch was from North Carolina, where he attended a rally for Republican nominee Donald Trump. 'Donald J. Trump does everything big. Except humility,' opened the double-page spread. He then went on to list the reasons why Trump was so flawed:

He's an intemperate, bullying, foul-mouthed panderer with no experience of public service, no record of charitable endeavour and no intention of paying his taxes. What is astonishing is not that a man with such an enormous ego and so few accomplishments should think he could be president. It is that so many Americans, in full knowledge of all his flaws, will still vote for him.[4]

After experiencing 'The Donald' in full flow, Gove took in a Hillary Clinton rally in Florida which was overshadowed by a literal storm as well the figurative political one being conjured up by her rival. Having noted that he saw only white faces in the crowd at Trump's event, Gove reflected on the diversity of Clinton's supporters:

> Just as the Trump rally was mono-ethnically white to a painful degree, so at the Clinton rally a different, more diverse, but in its own way, equally polarised crowd was in evidence. It was the classic old-school liberal Democratic universe – African-American and Hispanic, public sector and non-profit, teachers union members and LGBT activists. If there was a gun-owning, country and western-listening, southern Baptist in the audience he would have been a very lonely man.

Gove said this inability to reach out beyond the Democrats base voters should worry Clinton, but concluded:

'I still think that Mrs Clinton will win. The shape of the electoral college, population change and superior ground organisation should work in her favour.'[5]

Had Gove been proved right, he would have missed out on the most high-profile interview of his career. After Trump was crowned President-elect following the vote on 8 November, Gove suggested to Rebekah Brooks, head of News UK, that an interview with the next occupier of the White House should be pursued. Negotiations were carried out and Trump agreed to a fifteen-minute chat with

Gove and another fifteen-minute interview with Kai Diekmann, former chief editor of the German newspaper *Bild*.

Gove flew over to New York on Friday 13 January and after meeting up with Diekmann the pair agreed to combine their two fifteen-minute slots into one thirty-minute interview in order to get as much out of Trump as they could. As it was, the President-elect spent an hour in conversation with the pair, and Gove got the topline from the interview he wanted. Splashed across *The Times* on Monday 16 January was the headline: 'I'll do a deal with Britain' above a picture of Trump at his desk in Trump Tower.

The interview itself was decidedly softball, and the headline story came from more of a vague promise from Trump than a detailed policy statement:

Gove: So do you think we will be able to get a trade deal between the US and the UK quite quickly?
Trump: Absolutely, very quickly. I'm a big fan of the UK, uh, we're gonna work very hard to get it done quickly and done properly – good for both sides.

The interview ended with Trump ribbing Gove for not being as prescient about his presidential victory as Nigel Farage: 'Well, how is our Nigel doing? I like him, I think he's a great guy, I think he's a very good guy and he was very supportive. He'd go around the US – he was saying Trump's gonna win. He was one of the earliest people that said Trump was gonna win. So, he's gotta feel for it. Michael, you should've written that we were gonna win.'

Gove tried to make up for his lack of faith by giving Trump a copy of *Celsius 7/7*. 'That's fantastic – how to fight terrorism, I can use that,' replied Trump.

Aside from his forays back into the life of a newspaper hack, Gove did still have work to do as an MP. With Theresa May's request for him to 'demonstrate loyalty' ringing his ears, he set about becoming the very model of a loyal backbencher. In the Commons chamber, he made interventions supporting Health Secretary Jeremy Hunt, Brexit Secretary David Davis and Education Secretary Justine Greening. He even came to the defence of Boris Johnson when the Foreign Secretary sparked criticism by accusing the French President, François Hollande, of wanting to 'administer punishment beatings' in the manner of 'some World War Two movie' to the UK for wanting to 'escape' the EU. Gove took to Twitter to say: 'People "offended" by The Foreign Secretary's comments today are humourless, deliberately obtuse, snowflakes – it's a witty metaphor'.

As part of his rehabilitation, Gove seemed to take inspiration from his favourite television show, *Game of Thrones*. In one episode, Cersei Lannister is forced to walk naked through the streets to atone for her sins while crowds jeer. Thankfully, Gove only adopted this strategy in a metaphorical sense. He cooperated with books written about his role in the Brexit campaign and betrayal of Johnson and told a journalist sent to interview him for *The Times* that she could 'ask me anything'.[6] His most personal reflections came in an edition of the BBC show *Fern Britton Meets...* in December 2016. Of his ill-fated bid to be Prime Minister, Gove admitted:

> The way in which I declared my stand for the leadership, I shouldn't have done it that way. As I look back on that time, I think that there were mistakes that I made. I also think that my initial instinct that I was not the best person to put themselves forward as a potential prime minister – well, most of my colleagues agreed.

On May, the person he had mocked, berated and clashed with,

Gove concluded that sacking him from the Cabinet 'was the right thing to do'.

'To be honest, if I'd been in her shoes I would have sacked me too,' he said.

The programme featured contributions from Gove's mother, his former English teacher Mike Duncan and, most revealingly, his wife, Sarah. When asked about the state of the friendship with the Camerons, Vine said, 'I haven't spoken to them since before the referendum.' She then paused, shrugged and added, 'So that's it, we haven't had any communication. My door's always open, but that's where we are at the moment.'

Gove said that while it was difficult to quantify the damage his campaigning for Leave had done to his friendship with the Camerons, 'It's put a significant strain, absolutely, on it.'

Cameron appeared unwilling to make any advances towards reconciliation, joking in the summer of 2018 that he was so behind in writing his memoirs that 'Michael Gove is still one of the good guys'.[7] The animosity goes deeper than just Gove being the butt of Cameron's jokes, according to one friend of the former Prime Minister. 'Cameron has used the words "dead to me" in private conversations,' the source reveals.

It's not just with Cameron that Gove has damaged a friendship. One person who was close enough to him as to say, 'If something happened to him, I'd go round and look after their kids,' admits that they now only speak 'from time to time'.

'I miss my friend and I didn't know what to do about it very much,' the source says, adding, 'But I can't get away from the fact that he's one of the principal architects of something that I think is extremely damaging to this country.'

With his 'walk of shame' strategy in full swing, together with a ready abundance of praise for the government, Gove was showing that he had indeed been rehabilitated and he was ready to serve in any capacity should May decide to bring him back from political exile. In an ironic twist, it was the Prime Minister's own moment of hubris that saw Gove return to the top of UK politics.

CHAPTER 22

YOU ONLY LIVE TWICE

In a volatile political world, there are some constants. The voters of Surrey Heath electing a Conservative MP is one of them, and in the general election on Thursday 8 June 2017, Michael Gove was chosen once again to be their representative in Parliament. He picked up 37,118 votes, 4,536 more than in 2015 and 12,476 more than when he was first elected in 2005. Gove's majority increased by 139 to 24,943 and he took home 64.2 per cent of the vote. His popularity in the country may have taken a hit in the two years since the previous election, but support from his constituents had never been higher.

Not all Conservatives were celebrating, though. Theresa May's gamble on calling a general election to increase her slim governing majority had backfired dramatically. The election result saw her lose the Tories' Commons majority of seventeen, leaving her twelve short of a majority. After striking a deal with the Democratic Unionist Party, in which the party's ten MPs would vote with the Conservatives, she was able to cling on as Prime Minister, but she was a severely weakened figure.

On Sunday 11 June, Gove was in his constituency when he got an unexpected phone call from Downing Street. Indeed, it was so unexpected, when the voice on the end of the line said they were from

'Switch' – the name for the Downing Street switchboard – Gove thought it was a practical joke. He was told the Prime Minister wanted to see him, and, still feeling slightly concerned he was the victim of a prank, Gove got in his car and drove from Surrey Heath to central London. Unable to find anywhere to park near Downing Street, Gove completed his journey to Westminster on the London Underground and was relieved to see a member of the Downing Street staff waiting for him. It wasn't a hoax after all. He waited in No. 10 for about thirty minutes before being ushered in to see the Prime Minister. 'Michael, I would like you to rejoin the government, it's a Cabinet post, Secretary of State for Environment. I understand you're very interested in the area,' said May. 'Yes!' he replied. It was a brief conversation with May eleven months earlier that had ended his Cabinet career, and now an even briefer conversation saw it return. After agreeing to take on the position as Secretary of State for Environment, Food and Rural Affairs, Gove met with Downing Street's head of propriety and ethics, who asked if he was a vegetarian. 'No,' came the slightly surprised reply.

Much like his appointment as Justice Secretary, Gove found himself leading a department to which he had previously given little thought. He emulated his approach at Justice and sought as wide a range of opinions as possible as soon as he sat down at his desk. Craig Bennett, chief executive of Friends of the Earth, did not expect to get a phone call from the new Secretary of State. Usually, it was the big boys of the environmental lobby that received attention first, with the National Trust and RSPB getting a direct chat with the new person in charge. As Bennett was sitting in his office, his PA came in to tell him that Gove's office had been in touch and wanted to speak with him imminently. 'Sure enough, half an hour later we were talking on the phone,' said Bennett, adding, 'He was very engaged, and listening very carefully to the things I was saying and the questions I was asking of him.'[1]

Gove's desire to harvest the opinions of experts ensured he was soon winning praise from unlikely sources. *Guardian* journalist George Monbiot, a passionate advocate for environmental reform, almost couldn't believe what he was hearing when Gove gave a speech warning of 'the fundamental eradication of soil fertility'.[2] 'This is amazing,' he tweeted. 'One by one, @michaelgove is saying the things I've waited years for an environment secretary to say.'[3]

Gove's appointment as Defra Secretary came at a time when the government was desperate to find a narrative beyond Brexit. The general election result heralded a sharp decline in support for the party among younger voters, with the age at which a person became most likely to back the Conservatives rising to forty-seven. The PM's director of communications Robbie Gibb – brother of junior Education minister Nick Gibb – identified the environment as an area the Tories could zone in on to generate some positive headlines. 'Robbie Gibb wants to make the Tory Party the animal welfare party,' one senior Tory said in 2017.[4] The combination of an enthusiastic Secretary of State and a Downing Street operation happy to let him off the leash meant that within months of his appointment, environmental issues were rising to the top of the agenda. By December 2017, Gove had announced the introduction of CCTV in all slaughterhouses, a proposed ban on bee-killing pesticides, reintroducing beavers into the UK, making the sale of products with microbeads illegal, and a ban on ivory sales.

The Defra Secretary had 'certainly hit the ground running', according to David Bowles, head of public affairs at the RSPCA. 'Defra has gone from being one of the more looney departments to one of the most important,' said Bowles in December 2017, adding, 'He is the most accessible Secretary of State we have had in a decade – he's always open to address and evaluate the evidence.'[5]

Gove's flurry of activity when he took over the role was not all down to his own work, though. Many of the policies he announced had been in gestation in the department for months, if not years. A Defra source revealed that policies such as CCTV in slaughterhouses and banning microbeads had almost been made public by Gove's predecessor, Andrea Leadsom. 'Andrea nearly had the CCTV policy signed off just before the election. Good policy ideas have been around the department for several years but have not been able to get across the line,' they said, adding, 'Gove's a big hitter, a big figure in government.'[6]

Friends of the Earth's Craig Bennett agreed that Gove's reputation and ability ensured he was able to get ideas out of the department that had been languishing for a while. He said:

> My perspective is there's always an incredible sort of bottleneck of good ideas, bad ideas, whatever, coming from the civil service but ultimately there's a bottleneck and most of them don't see the light of day until a minister comes along that decides to push them through and make them happen. Things like the 25-year environment plan, launched by Theresa May, pulled together really under Michael Gove. Well, that's been being developed for years and years, it's not like it suddenly happened under Michael Gove's watch. But what I think is interesting is he's the first Environment minister we've had in the last few years that's managed to pull it over the finishing line and make it happen.[7]

Gove may have been winning plaudits for his work in the department, but his return to government saw him sitting across the Cabinet table from someone who could well have taken pleasure in him failing upon his return to frontline politics. It had been less than a year since Gove had spectacularly betrayed Boris Johnson, and now the two were having to work together again. In the aftermath of the election disaster, the rumour mill was rife that Johnson would challenge May for the party leadership. He dampened the suggestion by sending a WhatsApp group of Conservative MPs a list of reasons why May should continue in the role. The first MP to reply was Gove, saying, 'Boris is right.'[8] That exchange took place just hours before Gove rejoined the Cabinet. After his appointment was made public, another message from Johnson arrived on Gove's phone. This one was not sent to a group but to Gove personally, and it congratulated him on his return to frontline politics.

While the pair never had a proper clear-the-air chat, relations began to thaw as the Brexit negotiations progressed. As the two frontmen of Vote Leave, Gove and Johnson had staked their reputations on the UK thriving outside the EU and understandably took a keen interest in the talks between London and Brussels. On 22 September 2017, Theresa May travelled to Florence to set out how she believed the negotiations – which had begun in earnest after the general election – should progress. It was her first major speech on Brexit since an address at Lancaster House on 17 January 2017, in which a bullish Prime Minister declared it would be an act of 'calamitous self-harm' for the EU to seek a deal that 'punishes Britain'. She continued, 'While I am confident that this scenario need never arise – while I am sure a positive agreement can be reached – I am equally clear that no deal for Britain is better than a bad deal for Britain.'[9] Nine months on, and with the parliamentary arithmetic no longer in her favour, May adopted a more collaborative approach. She argued that both sides in the talks shared a 'profound sense of responsibility' to negotiate a good deal, as 'the only beneficiaries would be those who reject our values and oppose our interests'.

May ruled out striking a trade deal which mirrored the one signed between the EU and Canada – quickly becoming the option of choice for many Brexiteers – because it would 'represent such a restriction on our mutual market access that it would benefit neither of our economies'.[10]

May recognised that the government and business community needed time to implement any deal that was agreed, and she proposed a two-year period after 29 March 2019 during which the UK's trading relationship with the EU would be virtually unchanged. Free movement of people would continue, and the UK would follow all EU rules. However, the UK would have no representation in the EU's political structures and would not take part in the 2019 European elections. At no point in her speech did May repeat her belief that no deal was better than a bad deal.

Gove and Johnson were concerned. While they welcomed the more positive tone of the speech compared to the address made at Lancaster House, they worried that the implementation period plan could be used by those inside the Cabinet who opposed Brexit to stretch out negotiations and undermine the UK's negotiating stance. Gove in particular was well aware of the ability of institutions to dilute radical structural shifts – and Brexit was the most radical policy he had ever been involved in.

In the wake of the speech, Johnson and Gove sat down together, shared a bottle of Merlot and crafted a letter setting out their concerns. It was intended to be seen only by May and her chief of staff Gavin Barwell and was framed as Gove and Johnson offering to help the Prime Minister refine and promote the Brexit strategy she had set out in Florence. The letter began, 'Firstly, can we congratulate you on the steps you have taken to ensure we leave the EU in a smooth and orderly fashion? Your excellent Florence speech landed well. Your leadership gives us the chance to move forward in a determined way.'

With the niceties dispensed with, the pair set out their concerns. The implementation period needed a specific end date 'to shape expectations', with 30 June 2021 suggested. 'There should be no question of the UK implementing new EU rules during this period – or any European Court of Justice jurisdiction on any new rules,' they continued, adding, 'Clarifying that particular issue in the minds of colleagues who have not yet internalised that logic would help.' That swipe at their Cabinet colleagues was followed by a more direct criticism over a lack of preparation for a no-deal Brexit:

> We are profoundly worried that in some parts of government the current preparations are not proceeding with anything like sufficient energy. We have heard it argued by some that we cannot start preparations on the basis of 'no deal' because that would undermine our obligation of 'sincere cooperation' with the EU. If taken seriously, that would leave us over a barrel in 2021.[11]

The most controversial section in the letter related to who should be responsible for preparing the civil service for Brexit. In theory, this fell within the remit of the Department for Exiting the European Union, but Gove and Johnson wanted to see an Implementation Task Force set up in Downing Street to oversee this work.

May, aware of her political weakness thanks to the election result and a disastrous autumn conference performance in which she lost her voice during her keynote speech, recognised that any deal struck with the EU would now effectively have to be signed off by Johnson and Gove. In November 2017, she decided to bring the Environment Secretary into the heart of her Brexit planning by adding him to a special 'War Cabinet' of ministers who considered the government's negotiation strategy. On the committee were two colleagues Gove had had run-ins with since his return to the Cabinet five months earlier: Chancellor Philip Hammond and International Trade Secretary Liam Fox. Hammond and Gove had butted heads before, of course, with Gove angry at Hammond's failure to reform the funding of the cadet system when he was Defence Secretary, but now the pair had a more fundamental disagreement.

One of Gove's primary motivations for Brexit was to see the UK fishing industry escape the grip of the EU's Common Fisheries Policy, which saw Brussels dictate how many fish could be caught in Britain's coastal waters and by whom. Thanks to his Aberdeen background, opposition to the policy formed the emotional centre of Gove's Euroscepticism. As if it needed compounding any further, a viewing of the Christopher Nolan film *Dunkirk* in the summer of 2017 hardened his motivation to deliver a Brexit that would benefit the UK fishing industry. 'This shows why we should care for our fishing industry – it was there in our hour of need,' Gove told a colleague in Defra after seeing how 850 private boats, many of them fishing vessels, sailed across the Channel to help rescue 340,000 Allied forces from France in 1940.[12] One colleague in Defra recalls that Gove would often say, 'I need to be able to look my dad in the eye over this.'[13]

Hammond took a much more dispassionate approach, as befitted his nickname of 'Spreadsheet Phil' – a man who liked to be aware of where every last penny was being spent. Hammond recognised that fishing rights would be a powerful card to play in the negotiations with the EU, and access to coastal waters could be traded in exchange for a deal favourable for the UK's financial sector. The pair had a heated exchange over the issue during a meeting in August 2017, with Gove insisting it should be down to the UK and the UK alone who fishes in the country's waters.

Gove's clash with Liam Fox also centred on Brexit. In the summer of 2017, chlorine-washed chicken suddenly became a cause célèbre. Back in 1997, the EU had banned meat washed in chlorine – a practice which is common in the United States – being sold in the trading bloc. As the UK began exploring a post-Brexit trade deal with the US, campaign groups raised concerns that Britain was about to lower its food hygiene standards in order to cut a deal with Washington. In a visit to America at the end of July 2017, a clearly frustrated Fox accused the British media of being 'obsessed with chlorine-washed chickens', something he believed was 'a detail of the very end-stage of one sector of a potential free trade agreement'.[14] To Gove, who was trying to push the Tories as the party of animal welfare, the debate went beyond a mere 'detail' of a trade deal. On the BBC Radio 4's *Today* programme on 26 July, he was asked bluntly, 'Yes to chlorinated chickens, or no?'

'No,' he replied instantly, adding, 'I've made it perfectly clear, and indeed this is something on which all members of the government are agreed, we are not going to dilute our high animal welfare standards or our high environmental standards in pursuit of any trade deal.'

The debate around future trade deals and the role of chlorinated chicken within them was still very much taking place in the abstract, as the UK had yet to agree a departure deal with the EU. When the negotiations began in June 2017, it was agreed that citizens' rights, the financial settlement – known as the 'divorce bill' – and the Northern Irish border would all need to be settled first before talks could turn to the future trading relationship between the UK and the EU. The original plan was to have these talks – dubbed 'Phase One' – completed by the end of October 2017, to allow the talks to progress to the future relationship. As became typical with the Brexit negotiations, the deadline was missed, and the discussions rolled on into November. A scheduled summit on 15 December was then identified as the meeting at which 'sufficient progress' in the

Phase One talks would be signed off by EU leaders, but as the new deadline approached, there seemed to be no breakthrough on the divorce bill or the Irish border question. On the divorce bill, figures as high as £88 billion were floated in the press – largely thanks to mischief making from the European Commission – but the UK seemed prepared to go only as high as £18 billion.[15] In a bid to break the deadlock, the Cabinet agreed to sign off a settlement of £39 billion. That left the issue of how to avoid a hard border between Northern Ireland and the Republic if a trade deal was not ready to be implemented by the time the UK left the EU. It was agreed that a 'backstop' arrangement would be needed, although May had to tear up an initial plan for customs union and single market rules to only apply to Northern Ireland after outrage from the DUP. Instead, the UK pledged to 'maintain full alignment' with the single market and customs union rules that prevented a hard border being created. May also vowed there would be 'no new regulatory barriers' between Northern Ireland and the rest of the UK – unless agreed by the devolved assembly in Stormont.

With the DUP now on board, Gove was tasked with selling what had been agreed to the public. Before sitting down to pen an article for the Saturday 9 December edition of the *Telegraph*, he spoke with May's advisors in Downing Street to ensure he had the correct interpretation of the agreement. As Gove saw it, as long as the UK and Ireland reached the same end point in key areas – such as agricultural standards – the British government would be free to diverge from the actual regulations. Having received those assurances from Downing Street, he filed his article containing the passage:

At the end of the two-year transition period the UK will be able to pass laws that strengthen our economy and enhance our environment, with full freedom to diverge from EU law on the single market and customs union. If the British people dislike the arrangement that we have negotiated with the EU, the agreement will allow a future government to diverge.[16]

Gove wasn't the only Cabinet minister who was given the impression that what had been negotiated was more of an aspiration that a solid guarantee. Appearing on the BBC's *Andrew Marr Show* the day after Gove's article was published, Brexit Secretary David Davis described the agreement as 'much more a statement of intent than it was a legally enforceable thing'.

That interpretation was not shared by EU heads of state, in particular the Irish Taoiseach Leo Varadkar, with his spokesman telling reporters, 'The agreement sets out the parameters for further talks. I am confident that the political guarantees in this are rock solid.'[17]

With Phase One seemingly over, the focus turned to the next stage of the talks: namely, what exactly did the UK want its future relationship with the EU to be? May organised a get-together of her Brexit committee at Chequers on 23 February 2018 to thrash out just how closely aligned the UK should be with the EU once it left the bloc. A presentation from the government's chief Brexit negotiator Olly Robbins set out the UK's four key goals for the next round of talks with the EU: to maintain mutual recognition of standards for goods; to make a public commitment to keep British standards as high as those in the EU; to keep rules and regulations 'substantially similar'; and to create a dispute resolution mechanism which had no role for the European Court of Justice.[18] These four tents won the approval of the sub-committee. Gove, Johnson and others who wanted to see the UK gain the freedom to diverge from EU rules in order to strike new free trade deals believed the plan offered the necessary elasticity. Hammond, Amber Rudd and Greg

Clark, who all favoured a close relationship with Brussels to protect existing industries, believed the plan would actually keep the UK aligned to most of the EU's rules. It was a fudge, summed up by one Cabinet source who told the *Sunday Times*, 'The main question, "What can we diverge on and when?" hasn't been properly discussed or explored.'[19]

After the Chequers away-day, Gove's attention shifted once again to the issue at the heart of his Euroscepticism. A week after the summit, he travelled to Scotland for meetings with the Scottish Conservative leader Ruth Davidson around the role of fishing in a post-Brexit transition period. The prospect of still being in thrall to the Common Fisheries Policy (CFP) at a time when Britain did not have a seat at the table was unpalatable to say the least. The Environment Secretary was keenly aware that the promise of imminent freedom from Brussels' rules had been made to the Scottish fishing industry during the 2017 general election, and it was no coincidence that the mini-resurgence of Scottish Conservatism in that vote – which saw the number of Scottish Tory MPs rise from one to thirteen – had been fuelled by votes in coastal constituencies.

David Duguid, who overturned a 14,339 SNP majority to win the north-east seat of Banff and Buchan, was one of those Tories who had centred their election campaigns on the UK withdrawing from the CFP. 'It is clear that the industry does not want, nor does it need, a two-year transition period,' he said in February 2018, adding, 'The best option … is for a nine-month bridging period that will see the UK take its seat at the 2019 end-of-year fisheries negotiations as an independent coastal state.'[20] Gove was in close contact with Ruth Davidson over this issue, and against the backdrop of Scotland beating England 25–13 at Murrayfield during the 2018 Six Nations, the pair held talks with the Scottish Fishermen's Federation to take on board their concerns over another two years of the CFP.

Yet despite Gove's lobbying – supported by Davidson, Johnson and Scottish Secretary David Mundell, there was no carve-out for fishing in the implementation period agreed between the UK and Brussels on 19 March. Gove did not even bother to hide his anger, and speaking in the Commons on 20 March he said, 'As someone whose father was a fish merchant and whose grandparents went to sea to fish, I completely understand how fishing communities feel about the situation at the moment, and I share their disappointment.'[21] Unfortunately for Gove, 'disappointment' was not a strong enough word for some of his Scottish colleagues. Douglas Ross, MP for Moray, said it would be 'easier to get someone to drink a pint of sick than try to sell this as a success' and warned he would vote against any final Brexit deal that 'does not deliver, unequivocally, full control over fish stocks and vessel access'.[22]

Gove's close collaboration with Ruth Davidson over the fishing issue cemented a burgeoning friendship between the two Scots. While they had been on opposite sides of the referendum debate, Gove had spent time campaigning in Scotland in the 2017 general election campaign, with Davidson recognising that a benefit of Brexit was the UK's escape from the CFP. Later that year, the two would help to launch a new Conservative-focused think tank called Onward, with both giving speeches at a reception in the Churchill Room in Westminster. Gove's attempt at humour fell slightly flat when he claimed he was the Ike Turner to Davidson's Tina – perhaps unaware that Ike was a self-confessed domestic abuser.[23]

Gove's appearance at the launch of Onward was part of a blitz of speeches on the think tank circuit in the spring of 2018. On 15 May, he spoke at Centre for Policy Studies reception to launch a collection of essays titled *New Blue: Ideas for a New Generation*. In his remarks, Gove called on his party to stop making 'tired arguments' about the economic disaster of Venezuela as they sought to win back young voters tempted by the policies of Jeremy Corbyn. He said:

> It's not enough if we make the case, as we have to, for free markets, for liberal economics, for choice, for personal autonomy, simply to rely on a few tired arguments about what's happened in Venezuela, heart-rending though the fate of that country is – or to say that we need to recapture the arguments of the 1980s, heroic as that decade was.[24]

He expanded on his call for new ideas three weeks later in a speech to the Policy Exchange think tank, painting a vivid picture of why so many younger voters were suspicious of capitalism and did not see how it worked for them. 'Economic power has been concentrated in the hands of a few, and crony capitalists have rigged the system in their favour and against the rest of us,' he claimed. He went on to argue that the Conservatives needed to support the disrupters and entrepreneurs. 'Competition and innovation drive up standards for all,' he said, 'but they most benefit the outsiders and the excluded, who are discriminated against by those who benefit from maintaining the status quo.'[25]

Yet his most memorable performance that spring was not at a think tank or a drinks reception, but at the 30th birthday party of the Conservative Party's communications director, Carrie Symonds. Held in north London in March 2018, the soirée attracted a host of the party's leading figures, including then Communities Secretary Sajid Javid and Foreign Secretary Boris Johnson – who it was later revealed was in a relationship with Symonds. Gove had a special present prepared – not for the birthday girl, but for Johnson. He decided to whip out a skill he usually reserved for dinner parties: rapping. It was not Gove's first attempt at rapping in public – in

2014, he attempted to impress some schoolchildren by reciting part of 'Wham Rap!' – but this time he had gone the extra mile. Having seen a performance of the musical *Hamilton* during a trip to New York in 2016, he decided to recreate the opening number for the party guests. A backing track was put on, and his special advisor Henry Newman clicked his fingers to keep him in time. Wearing a purple jumper and corduroy trousers, Gove began rapping, but with lyrics he had composed himself. Instead of singing about American founding father Alexander Hamilton, he rapped about Boris Johnson:

The million-pound NHS funder
A golden wonder, bought us out of the EU blunder...
By fighting like thunder, by blowing enemies asunder.
Which is why Vote Leave made *him* top gunner.
And everyday Remain complained and people said his career was destroyed
Inside he knew the country needed freedom and that was going to be the place he would lead them.
And then a referendum came, the BBC and *Guardian* thought they had inflicted pain...
And Craig Oliver [boos from the guests] knew you better than to play the game.
Well, the word got around that kid was our man
We got to get him to lead the fight to save our land, get our liberation, don't forget from whence he came.
The world's gonna know your name... what's your name...
My name is Alexander B. Johnson
And there were a million votes we won, making Britain great, that's my fate, that's my fate.

While most found it hilarious, Johnson looked on perplexed.[26]

Away from Broadway musicals, there was the matter of Brexit to deal with. Having been forced to compromise on fishing, Gove soon found himself being pushed into a direction he did not want to go on the UK's post-Brexit customs arrangements. Two options were put forward by May for consideration – both designed to prevent the creation of a hard border on the island of Ireland. The customs partnership plan, favoured by May, would see the UK collect tariffs on imports on behalf of the EU and then dispense rebates to businesses if the goods stayed in the UK. Gove was opposed to the plan, describing it as 'completely bonkers' at a dinner of a group of Conservative MPs at the end of April. He was joined in opposition by Boris Johnson, David Davis and Liam Fox, and ahead of a crunch meeting of the Brexit subcommittee on Wednesday 2 May, the four met for drinks in the flat of the Foreign Secretary to discuss how best to kill the plan. At the meeting itself, it was Sajid Javid, the recently appointed Home Secretary, who dealt the most devastating blow to the plan, and he was supported by Defence Secretary Gavin Williamson. With the pair adding their voices to those of Gove, Johnson, Davis and Fox, the opponents to the plan were victorious. While May did not put the matter to a vote, Johnson repeatedly said, 'Six–five! Six–five!' to underline that his side of the argument was victorious.

The anti-partnership group favoured the second option proposed by May: maximum facilitation. This plan would see the UK completely free from the EU's customs union and would rely on technology to create as frictionless a border as possible with the bloc. Opponents of 'max fac' believed it would ultimately require customs checks on the Irish border, breaking a promise to avoid new infrastructure on the frontier.

Yet May refused to allow her preferred customs plan to die and took the unusual step of splitting up her sub-committee into two smaller groups, each tasked with analysing the strengths and weaknesses of one of the proposals. Gove joined Fox and Cabinet Office minister David Lidington to work on the customs partnership model, with Davis, Business Secretary Greg Clark and Northern Ireland Secretary Karen Bradley looking at max fac. The groups met only a handful of times and were fundamentally unproductive. Indeed, Gove was so frustrated with the process that he physically tore up the civil service summary of the discussions in a meeting at the end of June after finding his concerns had been downplayed.

The frustration over May's lack of desire to negotiate a clean break with Brussels reached a tipping point when she held another get-together at Chequers on Friday 6 July. This time, the whole Cabinet decamped to the Buckinghamshire country estate for what was billed as the meeting where the government would finally settle the question of just what sort of relationship it wanted with the EU after Brexit. They were presented with a plan to effectively stay in the single market for goods, underpinned by the UK agreeing to sign up to a 'common rulebook' to ensure that regulations brought in by Brussels were echoed in Britain. This model would help prevent a border being created in Northern Ireland, but it would also limit what the UK could offer in terms of trade deals with third countries. Johnson was not happy and told May her plan was 'a big turd',[27] while David Davis and Liam Fox also expressed concerns. Gove was conflicted. The proposal put forward by May was not what he had been fighting for. He wanted the UK to be free from Brussels' rules, not continue to follow them without even having a seat at the table. His options seemed to be: resign in protest or stay in the Cabinet and try to influence the direction of the negotiations going forward. Quitting was the riskiest option, as there was no way of knowing if his resignation would be the first domino to fall in a sequence which could end up with May being ousted as Prime

Minister, only to be replaced by an even more Remain-focused leader, or even trigger a general election that could see Jeremy Corbyn get the keys to Downing Street. However, Gove's influence on the Brexit talks had been pretty thin. There was no carve-out for fishing in the implementation period, and his opposition to May's customs partnership plan had seemed to make little difference, as it was back once again before the Cabinet at Chequers. At about 3.15 p.m., Gove made his contribution. He said he preferred to have a looser, Canada-style free trade deal with the EU and again called for the government to step up its no-deal preparations to help strengthen its negotiating hand. However, despite his reservations, he decided to publicly support the plan and called on others to back it. The deciding factor in Gove's mind was that May's deal got the UK out of the European Union. It wasn't perfect, it needed improvements, but it did deliver Brexit. Gove was living the maxim 'don't let the perfect be the enemy of the good', as he clung to the belief that getting the UK out of the EU would help quell the growing appetite for another referendum on the issue. It was a school of thought he would cling to again and again over the coming months.

On Sunday 8 July, Gove was sent onto *The Andrew Marr Show* to defend the Chequers plan. 'Is this what people voted for?' Marr asked, bluntly. Gove replied:

> Yes, we'll be outside freedom of movement. That was a critical part of the promise that we made during the course of the referendum campaign. We'll be outside the Common Agricultural Policy, outside the Common Fisheries Policy. Over a huge swathe of our economy we will have the autonomy to decide what's in our best interests. We will also have a free trade agreement between the UK and the EU that will work in the interests of business. We'll also be outside the formal legal structures of the

European Union. We will no longer have the European Court of Justice having direct control over what happens in this country, and we will no longer have membership of the Common Foreign Security Policy. We'll also be outside the justice and home affairs pillar, which has been part of the EU as well. So all of these structures, we're outside. That's what people voted for. This honours that vote.

Yet it didn't take much probing from Marr to get to the heart of Gove's frustrations with the plan. When asked if this was everything he hoped for, Gove replied, 'No, but then I'm a realist.' The Environment Secretary agreed the plan was essentially a 'common market for goods' but contested the idea that the 'common rulebook' turned the UK into vassal state, as some of his Brexit-backing colleagues had warned.

It is the case in any trade agreement that there's an agreement about common rules and standards right at the beginning. Now, if one country wants to diverge from that agreement, of course they have the sovereign ability to do so. But that means the other country can say, 'Well, you're no longer accepting those common rules, so therefore we have the right, you know, to say, to erect a barrier.' But that is no different from any trade agreement between any two sovereign entities. And the big difference is this: that Britain has the right, the British Parliament and British politicians have the right, if they believe that something is not in our interest, to say no. That was not a right that we had in the European Union.

Gove was keen to accentuate the positives, and it was telling that almost exactly a year after Theresa May had instructed him to learn about the importance of loyalty, he was the minister sent out on her behalf to defend the controversial proposal.

Yet, as good a job as Gove tried to do to keep the Cabinet together, both at Chequers and on *Marr*, his endeavours failed. At around 10.30 that evening, Gove was informed that David Davis was about to quit in protest at the agreement. Boris Johnson followed the next day, and rumours began circulating that a vote of no confidence would be triggered in May's leadership by disgruntled Conservative MPs. Johnson's departure signalled the end of the rapprochement with Gove, and he used his resignation speech in the Commons on Wednesday 18 July to launch a thinly veiled attack on the Environment Secretary: 'It is absolute nonsense to imagine, as I fear some of my colleagues do, that we can somehow afford to make a botched treaty now and then break and reset the bone later on. We have seen even in these talks how the supposedly provisional becomes eternal.'[28]

Gove's decision to offer support for May's plan did not mean he was going to simply roll over and accept that it could not be changed. In September 2018, he joined with other Chequers-sceptics in the formation of what became known as the Pizza Club. Hosted by Commons leader Andrea Leadsom in her spacious office just behind the Speaker's chair, the meetings saw Gove join with Liam Fox, Esther McVey, Chris Grayling, Penny Mordaunt, Sajid Javid and Gavin Williamson to discuss the progress of the negotiations and coordinate opposition to any developments. While the gatherings became known for the cuisine served, the first get-together did not actually see any pizzas delivered, and it was only when a snap of discarded takeaway pizza boxes was sent to the *Mail on Sunday* in October that the moniker stuck. One source says that Gove often stuck a slightly ambiguous figure during discussions at meetings of the club. 'His Brexit position was never entirely clear,' the insider reports.

Yet it was not Johnson, Davis or the Pizza Club that killed off the Chequers plan, but the EU. At a meeting of EU leaders in Salzburg on 20 September, May's post-Brexit vision was wholeheartedly rejected. European Council President Donald Tusk was blunt as he said the EU were 'not ready to compromise'[29] over what would effectively be splitting the four freedoms of the single market: goods, capital, labour and services.

The Chequers plan may have been dead, but any potential agreement on the structure of the UK's future relationship with the EU would have been meaningless in any case unless the two sides could first agree a withdrawal plan. The most contentious point remained how to avoid a hard border on the island of Ireland in the case of no trade agreement being in place at the end of the transition period. The EU wanted this 'backstop' to lock Northern Ireland into the customs union and large parts of the single market in order to facilitate frictionless trade across the frontier. Such an arrangement would see Northern Ireland in a separate customs and regulatory regime to Britain, effectively creating a border down the Irish Sea. This was unacceptable to the UK, and in February 2018 May told the Commons that no Prime Minister could ever sign up to such an arrangement. May's solution was to commit the whole of the UK to remaining in the EU's custom union after 2020 if a trade deal wasn't ready to be implemented – but only for a limited time. The EU pushed back, arguing that if the backstop had a time limit, it wasn't really a backstop, and signing up to the customs union didn't solve the regulatory issues brought about by the UK no longer being part of the single market.

On 14 November 2018, the UK and EU agreed a draft deal aimed at bringing the Brexit negotiations to an end and solving the backstop conundrum. The UK would stay in the EU's custom union once the implementation period ended if no trade deal had been agreed which would keep the Irish border invisible. Northern Ireland would also follow single market rules on areas such as agriculture and the environment. The UK would not be able to unilaterally exit this arrangement, and the only certain way to end it would be by signing a trade deal. Even if alternative arrangements were made to keep the border invisible, the UK would have to ask an arbitration panel to rule in its favour that the new arrangements protected the integrity of the single market and customs union. Another way out of the backstop was by suggesting that the EU was not acting in good faith in the trade negotiations – essentially accusing Brussels of dragging out the talks to keep the UK locked into its rules and regulations. Again, this would be ruled on by an independent panel, and proving such a motivation by the EU would be incredibly difficult. Conservative Brexiteers reacted with fury to the backstop protocol, believing that far from the UK leaving tentacles of Brussels, the country was about to be enveloped by them even more tightly – and this time with no say over the rules and regulations the country would be abiding by. Like Chequers, the plan provoked resignations from the Cabinet. On 15 November, Dominic Raab, the man who had replaced David Davis as Brexit Secretary in July, resigned, and he was soon followed by Work and Pensions Secretary Esther McVey.

The Cabinet was on the verge of disintegrating. May summoned Gove for a crisis meeting, desperate to keep him on board. If he followed Raab and McVey out of the door, her premiership could well be over. Tory MPs were already putting in letters to the chairman of the Conservatives' backbench 1922 committee demanding a vote of no confidence in her leadership, and she needed to stop the bleeding from her Cabinet to stem the flow of letters. May made a bold move and offered Gove the job of Brexit Secretary. Gove made an even bolder move and turned it down. He told May he would only accept the role if she let him go back to the EU and demand negotiations were reopened on the withdrawal agreement, as in its current form there was no way it would get through Parliament. May said no, leaving Gove in a tricky situation. He had just told the Prime Minister he disagreed with her central Brexit plan, so how could he stay in the Cabinet? Gove agonised over whether to quit, and friends say that when he went to bed that night he was fully prepared to resign. The next morning, he decided, once again, that it was better to be inside the tent than outside. Two key factors influenced his thinking. Firstly, as the withdrawal agreement would not make it through Parliament in its current form, he could still have some influence on whatever came next in the negotiations. Secondly, he was enjoying his work as Environment Secretary – a department which was set to get a new lease of life once the UK was free of the Common Fisheries Policy and the Common Agricultural Policy. There was, however, another reason bubbling along just under the surface. If he had quit, it could well have led to May's defenestration. Having helped to bring about the demise of David Cameron and then so spectacularly thwarted Boris Johnson's bid to be PM, a fatal move against another leading Conservative would have once again opened him up to the charge of disloyalty. Gove had spent a year in the political wilderness – he did not want to spend so much as another day there. He stayed in the Cabinet, determined to get Brexit over the line in whatever form necessary.

The first opportunity for MPs to agree to May's Brexit plan was scheduled for Tuesday 11 December, and five days of debate were set aside in the run-up to the vote. With the opposition parties vowing to vote against the plan, May was relying on her own MPs and the DUP to bring it over the line, but as the debate went on, and MP after MP gave speeches setting out why they would not be backing the deal, it became increasingly clear the government was headed for a large defeat. On Monday 10 December, Gove was once again asked to resume his role as defender-in-chief of the government's plans. Appearing on BBC Radio 4's *Today* programme, he was asked if the vote was 'definitely, 100 per cent going to happen'. 'Yes,' he replied, later adding, 'The vote is going ahead.' Less than four hours later, it was pulled. Following a conference call with her Cabinet, May finally came to the realisation that the deal as it currently stood would not get through the Commons. She resolved to go back to Brussels to secure guarantees that the UK would not be trapped in the backstop indefinitely. The abandonment of the vote finally snapped the patience of her harshest critics, and a vote of no confidence in her leadership was triggered when the threshold of forty-eight Tory MPs formally requesting a ballot was met on 11 December. The vote was held the next day, and Gove publicly backed May to continue as Prime Minister.

While the votes were being counted in Parliament, Gove went to the Christmas drinks party of an old friend: Rupert Murdoch. The media mogul was hosting showbiz stars and senior politicians in his swanky flat in the St James's area of London. At just after 9 p.m., Gove sat down next to Murdoch on a sofa to watch the result of the no-confidence ballot, announced on television by Sir Graham Brady, chairman of the 1922 committee. Not wanting to let the Environment Secretary siphon off all the attention from one of the most powerful men in the media, Health Secretary Matt Hancock awkwardly perched behind the pair as the results came in. May had survived, winning by 200 votes to 117. Gove was relieved, and after leaving Murdoch's party he travelled to the 5 Hertford Street private members' club in Mayfair to compete in a poker tournament with Richmond Park MP Zac Goldsmith. At just before midnight, he re-emerged, £250 better off.

The vote on May's Brexit deal was rescheduled for Tuesday 15

January. As with the abortive vote in December, five days of debate were scheduled, with Gove opening the fourth day. He began his statement with a personal message. On Christmas Eve, his fourteen-year-old son William had tripped over their Christmas tree and fallen through the plate-glass French windows at the family home in Ladbroke Grove. The accident resulted in a 10-centimetre-long gash on his shoulder that was so deep the boy's bone and tissue could be seen. Vine rushed home from a nearby shop to be confronted with a hallway 'looking distinctly Quentin Tarantino', such was the amount of blood that had been lost. Gove sprinted from the Tube station to his house in order to take care of William, who was taken by ambulance to Chelsea and Westminster Hospital, where he was 'stitched up a treat', according to Vine.[30]

Reflecting on the incident in the Commons, Gove said:

I am very, very grateful to Members on both sides of the House, from all parties, who very kindly contacted me or sent messages over the course of the Christmas holidays following my son's accident. I am very grateful for the kind words that many sent. My son is recovering well, and I just wanted to register my appreciation.

Turning his attention to the Brexit debate, Gove once again clung to his favoured maxim:

All of us might have a perfect version of Brexit – a change here, an alteration there – but we all have to accept our responsibility next Tuesday to decide whether we are going to honour that verdict. Are we going to make the perfect the enemy of the good? Are we going to put our own interpretation of what Brexit should be ahead of the votes of 17.4 million people, ahead of the interests of everyone in this country who has a job, and ahead of the clearly expressed democratic will of the British people? Are we going to endanger their future by either seeking to overturn that mandate or rejecting this agreement and entering what the Prime Minister has suggested would be uncharted waters? As I pointed out earlier, if we reject this agreement – the current course on which Parliament is set – and have no deal, Britain will of course prosper eventually but it is undeniably the case, because the facts on the ground demonstrate it, that our citizens and constituents will face economic turbulence and damage. That is why, after long reflection, I have decided that we must back this agreement. We must ensure that the British people's vote is honoured, that their futures are safeguarded and that Britain can embrace the opportunities that our people deserve. That is why I commend this agreement to the House.[31]

Gove's defence of the deal mattered naught, and even with a letter signed by European Commission President Donald Tusk and European Council President Jean-Claude Juncker promising the EU would 'work speedily' on agreeing a measure to replace the backstop, the government was still facing a sizeable defeat. On Tuesday 15 January, the Brexit plan was defeated by 432 votes to 202. It was the largest defeat of a government in Parliament in UK history.[32] With May reeling from sheer scale of the defeat, Labour leader Jeremy Corbyn pressed for a no-confidence vote in the government. May had no choice but to agree, and it was scheduled for the very next day. If the government lost the vote, the country would be on course for a general election. The stakes could not have been higher.

Before the vote itself, there would be a six-hour debate on whether the government had the support of the Commons. Corbyn would open the debate, with a response from the Prime Minister, and Labour's deputy leader Tom Watson would close it for the opposition. May knew she needed an accomplished orator to close the debate for the government side and decided to hand the responsibility to Gove. He was told that morning that he would be the final speaker and immediately pulled together his aides to begin drafting a speech. Gove decided the best form of defence would be attack, and he planned to centre his speech not on the record of the government but on the prospect of Jeremy Corbyn becoming Prime Minister. National security was identified as Corbyn's weak spot, and Gove began putting thoughts on paper. As the debate went on, Gove sat himself on the government front bench, listening to interventions from across the House and making notes on Commons paper. At 6.40 p.m., the Chamber began to fill up as Tom Watson delivered Labour's final assault on the government. The party's deputy leader adopted a 'more in sadness than anger' approach to his speech, saying he felt sorry for May and that her failures had not come through 'lack of effort or dedication' but through a lack of compromise. 'At every turn, she has chosen division over unity. She has not tried to bring the 17 million people who voted Leave and the 16 million people who voted Remain together,' he said. Watson concluded his remarks by pointing at his Tory opponents as he said that 'everyone in this Chamber ... knows in their heart that this Prime Minister is not capable of getting a deal through'.

Lifting his voice, Watson said, 'Government members know it. They know that we know they know it, and the country knows it. That is why we must act. That is why we need something new. That is why we need a general election. I commend this motion to the House.'[33]

Labour MPs cheered wildly and waved their order papers, but as that wave of noise crashed down on their Conservative opponents, another cheer came back to meet it. Gove had got to his feet, and

Conservative MPs were determined to give him a platform of noise from which to launch his attack. Gove stood, his hands gripping the edge of the despatch box, staring intently at his opponents like a boxer preparing for a bout. The cacophony of rival cheers and jeers crashed together over his head, while the Prime Minister, sitting to his left, looked on. Labour MPs began to laugh as the man Watson had once described as a 'miserable pipsqueak of a man' tried to look intimidating. As the noise died down, Gove began, not with a roar as his demeanour suggested, but by displaying his legendary politeness. He paid tribute to MPs from across the Commons for their contribution to the debate, rattling through fourteen names in quick succession. Then came the first jab at Corbyn. Gove thanked John Woodcock, the Barrow and Furness MP who had quit Labour in July 2018. An outspoken critic of Corbyn, Woodcock had told the Commons he would not be supporting his former party's no-confidence motion as he believed the Labour leader was 'unfit to lead the country'. Banging the despatch box and then pointing in the direction of Corbyn, Gove said, 'It takes courage – and he has it, having been elected on a Labour mandate and representing working-class people – to say that the leader of the party that he joined as a boy is not fit to be Prime Minister. He speaks for his constituents, and he speaks for the country.' The Conservative benches cheered. Gove was now in his stride and decided to drill down further into the fundamental split in the Labour Party: the competence of Jeremy Corbyn as leader. He turned to Watson, and, after saying the deputy leader had spoken well, he picked up on one glaring omission from his remarks: 'He did not once mention in his speech the Leader of the Opposition or why he should be Prime Minister.'

Watson looked glum, while Corbyn briefly looked up from a piece of paper he was reading, as if he'd overheard a row on a train and was wondering what all the fuss was about. Gove continued:

I have a lot of time for the honourable gentleman, and we have several things in common: we have both lost weight recently – him much more so; we are both friends of Israel – him much more so; and we both recognise that the right hon. Member for Islington North is about the worst possible person to lead the Labour Party – him much more so.

And so Gove went on punching the bruise. After boasting about the government meeting NATO's requirement for 2 per cent of GDP to be spent on defence, Gove said Corbyn wanted the UK to leave NATO, abolish its nuclear weapons and adopt the Costa Rica approach to defence and scrap the army.

If the Leader of the Opposition cannot support our fighting men and women, who does he support? Who does he stand beside? It was fascinating to discover that he was there when a wreath was laid to commemorate those who were involved in the massacre of Israeli athletes at the Munich Olympics. He says he was present but not involved. 'Present but not involved' sums him up when it comes to national security. When this House voted to bomb the fascists of ISIS after an inspirational speech by the right hon. Member for Leeds Central [Hilary Benn], sixty-six Labour Members, including the hon. Member for West Bromwich East [Tom Watson], voted with this government to defeat fascism. I am afraid the Leader of the Opposition was not with us. In fighting fascism, he was present but not involved.

With the adrenaline pumping, Gove paced around the despatch box in a style reminiscent of his days as president of the Oxford Union. Attempts by MPs to intervene were dismissed with a flick of the hand and a curt 'no' as Gove claimed that Corbyn's inability to stand up to Russian President Vladimir Putin over the Salisbury poisonings and fascists in Syria meant he would certainly not be able to 'stand up for us in European negotiations'.

Labour MPs were silent, with the exception of a handful of Corbyn's supporters shouting out 'Shame' as Gove tore into the party leader. Danielle Rowley, MP for Midlothian, tried to get the bout stopped by complaining to Speaker John Bercow, but he was having none of it and allowed Gove to continue.

Having attacked what Corbyn would do as Prime Minister, Gove turned to his record as Labour leader:

> Why is it that a Labour Member of Parliament needs armed protection at her own party conference? Why is it that nearly half of female Labour MPs wrote to the Leader of the Opposition to say that he was not standing up against the vilification and the abuse that they received online which had been carried out in his name? If he cannot protect his own Members of Parliament, if he cannot protect the proud traditions of the Labour Party, how can he possibly protect this country?

Conservative MPs sitting behind Gove were buoyed. After months of having their own divisions brutally and relentlessly exposed, it was Labour's turn to be humiliated. As Gove's speech went on, many Tories seemed to physically grow in stature, as his words breathed life back into bodies that had been deflated and crushed by the constant Brexit bickering.

As the clock struck 7 p.m., Gove concluded his speech – but so powerful was the adrenaline, he accidentally began commending the motion of no confidence instead of opposing it. As Bercow tried to bring the House to order, Gove sat down to huge cheers from Conservative MPs. Frontbenchers patted him on the back, including Theresa May. The government won the vote by 325 votes to 306.

Michael Gove, the man who was 'toxic', the man who betrayed Boris Johnson, the man who had been despatched to the political wilderness, the man who was flogging a Brexit deal which many of them disagreed with, had, at this most critical moment, brought the Conservative Party back together. Since coming back to the Cabinet in June 2017 he had demonstrated loyalty, ingenuity and temperance. He had retained his reforming zeal but curbed his destructive tendencies. He had learned the importance of balancing a drive for perfection with the art of the possible. His political rehabilitation was complete.

CHAPTER 23

THE END OF THE AFFAIR

Michael Gove's concluding speech in the no-confidence debate cemented his position as one of the most accomplished politicians in Parliament, but it did not kick-start a renaissance for Theresa May's dying premiership. The government tried to pass its Brexit deal for a second time on 12 March, and again Gove was required to speak from the despatch box. May had lost her voice – an all too frequent occurrence for someone who was required to speak in public on a regular basis – and at the end of that morning's Cabinet meeting he was asked by May's chief of staff Gavin Barwell to prepare himself to open the debate. The government was defeated again, this time by 391 votes to 242. A third attempt to pass the deal – this time without the section outlining the future relationship between the UK and EU – occurred on 29 March, the day the UK was supposed to leave the EU, but this was also defeated by 344 to 286 votes. May then committed to holding cross-party talks with Labour in an attempt to find an agreement that could pass through the Commons. Gove played a key role in the talks, but after almost seven weeks of negotiations they broke down without agreement. May's last throw of the dice was to propose bringing the withdrawal agreement for a fourth time, but this time with an option for MPs to vote in favour of another referendum on the UK's EU membership.

This was too far for the Pizza Club, who held a meeting in Andrea Leadsom's office on Wednesday 22 May – the day after May had set out the plan in a speech – to discuss their options. Gove was in attendance as Leadsom announced to the group that, as Leader of the Commons, she could not bring forward legislation which she so fundamentally disagreed with. That evening, she announced her resignation from Cabinet. By Friday 24 May, it was all over for the Prime Minister. Home Secretary Sajid Javid and Foreign Secretary Jeremy Hunt made it clear to May that she needed to rethink her plan, and, facing the disintegration of her Cabinet, May announced that she was stepping down as Prime Minister, with the contest to replace her beginning on 10 June. Even before she made her emotional statement in Downing Street, a number of Conservatives had already said they would stand in a leadership contest, with Boris Johnson, Esther McVey and Rory Stewart all making their ambitions clear. With her resignation confirmed, Jeremy Hunt, Matt Hancock, Andrea Leadsom and Dominic Raab announced that they too would all be standing.

Gove had been preparing for May's departure for many months. He began being talked about as a possible future leader in the summer of 2018, when Conservative Party donor Crispin Odey, a hedge fund manager who had backed Leave in the referendum, called for new thinking at the top of the party. 'I would go to Gove,' he said. 'He's the only minister who is still being a minister. Michael has got lots of attributes that make him a non-traditional Tory. He is very aware that he has to appeal not just to the wealthy, but also more broadly. I don't think May can carry Brexit through any more.'[1]

Gove tried to play down suggestions that he might take another crack at becoming party leader in December 2018, but he did not rule it out completely. Asked during an interview on BBC Radio 4's

Today programme on 10 December if he would consider standing again, he said, 'I think it's extremely unlikely that I will ever be in that position,' before adding, 'You never know, if Boris Johnson nominated me for the leadership and Philip Hammond seconded, I might think again, but it's extremely unlikely that that scenario would ever happen.'

Yet as May's Brexit deal was repeatedly voted down by MPs, Gove came to the realisation that not only would her premiership soon be over but Brexit itself was under threat. He became convinced that when the extension granted by the EU to enable the UK to ratify the withdrawal agreement came to an end on 31 October, Parliament would be left with a stark choice: no deal or revoke Article 50 – and feared MPs would opt for the latter. Watching some of those who had campaigned the longest for the UK to leave the EU repeatedly vote down the deal reminded Gove of Oscar Wilde's *The Ballad of Reading Gaol*: 'Yet each man kills the thing he loves.'

Gove decided to start testing the water to see if he should be preparing a leadership bid for when May finally relinquished office. Treasury minister Mel Stride was tasked with organising dinners with MPs to find out what they would be looking for from the next party leader – in terms of both style and substance. Stride had already created a WhatsApp group called Deep Blue, a name chosen to reflect the moderate right agenda being pursued. MPs were added to the group and then invited to dinners with Stride, including some at his three-storey townhouse in Chelsea. Initially, Gove's name wasn't mentioned in the conversations, leading some MPs to believe that Stride was preparing the ground for Foreign Secretary Jeremy Hunt, or even for his own tilt at the leadership. As anger over May's negotiations with Labour intensified throughout April, the dinners became a more overt forum for promoting Gove, and the Environment Secretary himself began attending.

Upon arriving at Stride's house, MPs would gather in the living room and be served drinks by Stride's three young daughters. One attendee said this helped 'lighten the mood' as it disarmed the usually cynical politicians. The group would then be shown into the dining room, where Stride's wife would serve a home-cooked meal – another personal touch which created a relaxed atmosphere. The conversation would then switch to discussions about the state of the party before, inevitably, turning to the race to succeed May.

Gove would then set out his pitch, playing up his experience running three government departments, claiming it was evidence that he could bring fresh ideas to the top job. One MP says that at the dinner they attended – just three days before May announced she was resigning – Gove put forward two specific ideas: extra money for primary schools, and the creation of a new branch of the police force to deal purely with cybercrime. 'Gove said the normal police are overwhelmed by cybercrime, so he wanted to create a version of the British Transport Police but just for cybercrime.'

It was not just Gove supporters at the dinner, and one attendee who was more hostile to the Environment Secretary was blunt with their question: 'How can we trust you after you stabbed Boris in the back?' Gove replied, 'I don't see it as stabbing people in the back, I was trying to do the public a service.' Another questioner delivered an equally forthright question: 'Aren't you a bit toxic with the public? Don't people see you as a speccy git?' Gove laughed and acknowledged that while he was 'not the most photogenic', he had been the face of the Vote Leave campaign in the EU referendum, which won 17.1 million votes.

Finally, Gove was asked what was the worst thing he had ever done – a nod to the question asked to Theresa May in the 2017 general election campaign. May had said, to widespread derision, that her greatest indiscretion was running through fields of wheat as a child. Gove was a lot more cagey: 'I can't tell you too much because somebody is writing a book about me, but I did used to make prank phone calls.'

It wasn't just dinners where Gove would hold court. At the beginning of May 2018, Stride organised a question-and-answer session at the Surprise pub in Chelsea. Some forty-six MPs turned up to quiz Gove, who talked up his years of government experience and his record for competence. While he did not make the point explicitly, the contrast with Dominic Raab, who had served in the Cabinet for just four months, and Boris Johnson, who had made numerous gaffes as Foreign Secretary, was clear.

Having canvassed opinion, stress-tested the arguments and built up cabal of followers, Gove made his move on Sunday 26 May. He stepped out of the front door of his Ladbroke Grove home to deliver the following message to the waiting journalists: 'I can confirm that I will be putting my name forward to be Prime Minister of this country. I believe I'm ready to unite the Conservative and Unionist Party, ready to deliver Brexit and ready to lead this great country.'

He was entering a crowded field. As well as the seven candidates already declared – Stewart, McVey, Johnson, Hunt, Hancock, Leadsom and Raab – a slew of other MPs put themselves forward in the subsequent days. Home Secretary Sajid Javid, junior Brexit minister James Cleverly, Housing minister Kit Malthouse, former Universities minister Sam Gyimah and ex-Chief Whip Mark Harper all announced their candidacies in the following days, swelling the field to thirteen contenders. Nominations were set to open on 10 June, and, in a bid to avoid the contest dragging on for weeks, the committee of Conservative backbenchers responsible for organising the parliamentary part of the election introduced new rules. Candidates would need the support of eight MPs to get on to the ballot, instead of the previously required two. In the first ballot, any candidate getting fewer than seventeen votes would be eliminated, and in the second round, hopefuls needed to get more than thirty-three votes to proceed. Facing the new rules, Gyimah, Cleverly and Malthouse dropped out of the race, feeling they were unable to generate the required support needed before nominations opened. While those campaigns were failing to get going, Gove's own bid was gaining momentum. His successor as Education Secretary, Nicky Morgan, announced she was backing him on 2 June, and further endorsements trickled out in the following days. Tom Tugendhat, the respected chair of the Foreign Affairs Select Committee, Energy minister Claire Perry and Skills minister Anne Milton all endorsed Gove. Ironically for the man who had played such a key role in helping Vote Leave win the referendum, Gove struggled to get heavyweight Brexiteers to back him. Kemi Badenoch, the Saffron Walden MP elected to the Commons in 2017, was one vocal Leaver to endorse Gove, as was the colourful figure of Michael Fabricant. Yet the hard-core Brexiteers were staying away, instead splitting their support between Raab and Johnson. Gove's stock with the hard Leave faction of Tory MPs known as the European Research Group (ERG) had been falling steadily since the Chequers plan was created the previous summer. Mark Francois, the bullish vice-chair of the ERG, went as far as to call into question Gove's desire to leave the EU at all. 'The new Prime Minister will be a proper Brexiteer, which Michael Gove, in my opinion, is not,' said Francois, the day after Gove had said he was 'not wedded' to the UK leaving the EU on 31 October if extra time was needed to secure a deal.[2]

On Friday 7 June, Gove found himself facing another issue which threatened to derail his leadership bid. The *Daily Mail* secured the rights to publish extracts from this book, and his confession to an aide in 2016 that he had previously taken cocaine was going to be front and centre of the paper's coverage. The paper went to Gove for comment that evening, and he was advised by his wife to tell the truth. 'I had no hesitation. Just be honest, I told him. Tell the truth on television, rather than shy away or dodge questions,' she wrote in her column for the *Mail* five days later.[3] Gove followed her advice and issued a statement to the paper: 'I took drugs on several occasions at social events more than twenty years ago. At the time I was a young journalist. It was a mistake. I look back and I think, I wish I hadn't done that.'

After he had given the statement to the *Mail*, MPs on Gove's leadership team were told the details of the story that was about to break and were advised to prepare themselves for calls from journalists. The news of Gove's confession swept through Westminster, and even before the *Mail* had gone to print, journalists from *The Sun*, the *Daily Telegraph*, the BBC and ITV were all aware of the story, and ringing up Gove's team and the author of this book for more information. When the front pages of Saturday 8 June were published, the impact of the story, fuelled by Gove's admission, was clear. 'Gove: My cocaine confession' was the headline on the *Mail*, while *The Sun*, the *Daily Telegraph*, the *Daily Mirror* and the *Daily Express* all carried the story on their front pages.

The story gained more traction the following day, when the *Mail on Sunday* ran a story claiming that cocaine had been taken at a party in Gove's flat in Mayfair on 27 December 1999 – just hours after he had written a column for *The Times* decrying middle-class drug takers. His article set out the reasons Gove did not support a relaxation of drug laws, as he criticised journalists who called for reform out of a sense of guilt as they themselves took illegal substances. 'There is no greater sin in journalistic eyes than hypocrisy,' Gove argued. He went on:

> Middle-class professionals may be able to live with, manage and
> control drug use much as they have grown used to managing

adultery. But it is a little less easy to cope with the consequences of illegal drug use, or family breakdown, in South Shields than it is in south Hampstead. If elites, for the comfort of their own consciences, say an activity is fine when the costs for others are much less easy to bear, then what's virtuous about that?[4]

The source who spoke to the *Mail* did not say whether Gove had taken the drug at the party that night but claimed he must have known the Class A drug was being indulged in by some present. 'It wasn't that people were doing it in the open on the sofas, but it would be hard for him not to have been aware of what was going on,' said the guest. A spokesperson for Gove told the *Mail on Sunday* that the Environment Secretary had 'no recollection of a party on that date'.[5]

The story had now evolved from one about poor judgement to one of hypocrisy – a potentially fatal charge to be levelled at a politician. On Sunday 9 June, Gove appeared on the BBC's *Andrew Marr Show* not only to explain his Brexit plan but to face questions over his past drug use. 'Do you accept that you committed a crime?' asked Marr. 'Yes, it was a crime. It was a mistake. I deeply regret it,' replied Gove.

Marr asked how many times Gove had taken the drug – 'Several occasions,' came the reply – and then was even blunter: 'Was it a habit?'

'No, I don't believe it was. It was a mistake and it was a mistake that I deeply regret,' said Gove.

Marr then pushed Gove on whether he had lied on the visa waiver form which travellers from the UK need to complete when visiting the United States.

Gove: I don't believe that I've ever on any occasion failed to tell the truth about this when asked directly and one of the things of course—

Marr: But it would be on the form. I mean, you would have to say yes or no and if you'd said yes you could be banned for life from entering the United States.

Gove: I think it is the case that if I were elected the Prime Minister of this country then of course it would be the case that I would be able to go to the United States. And I think that it's foolish to suggest otherwise.

With the Marr interview over, Gove returned to his preparations for his official leadership campaign launch, set to be held the next day in Millbank Tower, Westminster.

If Gove had hoped that the Marr interview would see a line drawn under the cocaine story, he was soon disappointed. On Monday 10 June, the story was still dominating front pages, with *The Times* headline reading 'Gove pleads for second chance over cocaine use', *The Guardian* describing his leadership campaign as 'on the brink' and the *Mirror* dubbing Gove a 'cocaine hypocrite'. Even worse for the leadership contender was the news that Work and Pensions Secretary Amber Rudd – a leading figure in the One Nation grouping of Tory MPs – had declared her support for Jeremy Hunt in the battle for Downing Street. Hunt's campaign received another boost when Defence Secretary Penny Mordaunt – one of the few Brexiteers in the Cabinet – also gave her backing to the Foreign Secretary.

At just before 3 p.m. on Monday 10 June, journalists and Gove supporters gathered in the Sky Bar at the top of Millbank Tower, next to the river Thames. On a clear day, the views of London are spectacular, but it was perhaps fitting that instead of glorious June sunshine, the sky was filled with storm clouds. With the media pack in situ, Gove took the stage. The backdrop displayed the words the contender hoped would convince MPs and party members to back him: 'Unite. Deliver. Lead.' Addressing the packed room, which included his wife Sarah, Gove did not mention the cocaine revelation in his speech. Instead, he focused on his backstory, his record running the Education, Justice and Environment departments, and his vision for the future. He hit out at a policy floated by Johnson's camp that would see tax cuts for those earning between £50,000 and £80,000, saying, 'One thing I will never do as Prime Minister is to use our tax and benefits system to give the already wealthy another tax cut.' He repeated the claim that he had 'led from the front' in the Vote Leave campaign, saying he had been 'tested in battle'.[6]

The speech was delivered without notes and was an accomplished and energetic performance. The journalists in the room would not let the cocaine story die, however, and BBC *Newsnight*'s Nick Watt – who had worked with Gove at *The Times* in the 1990s – delivered a stark assessment of his former colleague's campaign:

> In your heart of hearts you must know your campaign is in real trouble because when you were a prominent figure, not an MP but a prominent figure, twenty years ago you thought it was OK in a London dinner party to break the law by snorting cocaine and then when you were in government and you were at the pinnacle of the criminal justice system as Lord Chancellor you sent the people that gave you that cocaine to jail and those people often came from very underprivileged backgrounds. Is your problem not [that] in your party and in your country that there's revulsion at that double standard?

Gove replied:

> Thank you, Nick. I explained both to the *Daily Mail* and also in a twenty-minute interview with Andrew Marr yesterday my regret

at my past mistakes. But one of the consequences of having had the chance to reflect on my mistakes is that when I was Justice Secretary I was determined to ensure that those people who had fallen into the net of the criminal justice system were given all of the support, the help and the care they needed in order to achieve redemption and to enjoy a second chance. I take my responsibilities in government incredibly seriously and I would ask anyone to judge me on the basis on what I did as a reformer at the Department of Justice in order to ensure that we find that treasure in the heart of every man.

The first test of whether MPs would give Gove a shot at redemption came three days later, on Thursday 13 June, in the first round of voting. Johnson topped the poll, with the support of 114 MPs. Second was Hunt with forty-three, while Gove came in third with thirty-seven votes. His team were relieved, as while they had not picked up any more supporters than expected, they had also not lost any. The ballots continued throughout the next week, with Gove finishing third in rounds two and three. The final day of voting was Thursday 20 June, with two ballots scheduled. The first of the day saw Gove creep into the all-important second-place position with sixty-one votes, two ahead of Hunt. Home Secretary Sajid Javid was eliminated, and the thirty-four MPs who backed him in that round were now up for grabs. The results of the final ballot were announced at just after 6 p.m. Johnson secured 160 votes, an increase of just three on his performance earlier in the day. Gove had seventy-five, but Hunt returned to his position in second place with seventy-seven votes. Gove was out. There were immediately suggestions – denied by members of the team – that the Johnson camp had lent votes to Hunt to ensure that Gove was kept off the ballot. These suspicious weren't shared by everyone in the Gove camp, however. 'Of course,' said one supporter when asked if it was a 'stitch-up', while another said, 'Doesn't look like it' when asked the same question. Speaking to the media, Mel Stride, who had worked so hard to sound out potential supporters of Gove, said he believed the cocaine revelation had impacted the campaign. 'It stalled us and meant momentum was lost at that time,' he said.[7] Another member of Gove's top team believes that while the cocaine admission was a factor early on in the contest, the repercussions of his decision to betray Johnson in the leadership race three years earlier were still having an impact. 'The argument from Hunt's team that talked about the psychodrama about 2016 and how they didn't want the party to be dragged through the mud – that was a powerful message,' the source said. The sense that Johnson had got revenge for the 2016 betrayal was played out on the front pages of many of the next day's newspapers, with the *Daily Telegraph*'s headline 'Boris exacts his revenge as Gove is squeezed out' echoed by other outlets.

Gove issued a message of goodwill to the final two candidates, who would go off to spend a month campaigning across the UK to win the support of Conservative Party members. The Environment Secretary returned to his day job, unsure of what role – if any – he would play in the next Prime Minister's government. His dream of holding that office himself had been thwarted for the second time in three years, and he may yet have to console himself with being added to the long list of politicians frequently categorised as the best Prime Ministers the UK never had. As a biographer of Michael Portillo, who is occasionally included on that list, he will appreciate the company in which he finds himself. However, given the volatility of UK politics, it is impossible to say if the 2019 leadership contest will prove to be the final opportunity for Gove to achieve his ambition. The man in a hurry could still be the future of the right.

ENDNOTES

CHAPTER 1

1 http://www.aberdeen-harbour.co.uk/article/timeline/
2 *Aberdeen Press and Journal*, 24 May 1975
3 *Aberdeen Press and Journal*, 14 February 1976
4 *Fern Britton Meets Michael Gove*, BBC One, 12 December 2016
5 Ibid.
6 http://www.dailymail.co.uk/news/article-2057850/Michael-Gove-describes-adoption-transformed-life.html
7 *The Times*, 24 July 1998, p. 19
8 http://www.dailymail.co.uk/news/article-2057850/Michael-Gove-describes-adoption-transformed-life.html
9 *The Times*, 24 July 1998
10 http://www.dailymail.co.uk/debate/election/article-1268403/MICHAEL-GOVE-My-birth-mother-knows-I-Ill-try-track-down.html
11 https://www.newstatesman.com/education/2010/09/gove-8220-parents-school
12 *The Times*, 24 July 1998, p. 19
13 https://www.dailyrecord.co.uk/news/uk-world-news/parents-reveal-new-education-secretarys-1059101
14 http://www.dailymail.co.uk/news/article-2057850/Michael-Gove-describes-adoption-transformed-life.html
15 Ibid.
16 Ibid.
17 https://www.dailyrecord.co.uk/news/uk-world-news/parents-reveal-new-education-secretarys-1059101 b
18 *Fern Britton Meets Michael Gove*, op. cit.
19 http://www.dailymail.co.uk/news/article-2619230/Teachers-like-Ann-Maguire-transform-lives-Im-proof-Education-Secretary-MICHAEL-GOVE-pays-emotional-tribute-teachers-took-life-care-Oxford.html
20 Ibid.
21 https://www.theguardian.com/politics/2012/oct/05/michael-gove-next-tory-leader
22 https://www.thetimes.co.uk/article/the-teenage-gove-was-bright-inquiring-and-actually-rather-popular-says-old-english-master-tjx5xcjholb
23 http://www.dailymail.co.uk/news/article-2619230/Teachers-like-Ann-Maguire-transform-lives-Im-proof-Education-Secretary-MICHAEL-GOVE-pays-emotional-tribute-teachers-took-life-care-Oxford.html
24 Ibid.

25 Ibid.
26 *The Times*, 25 July 1998
27 https://www.dailyrecord.co.uk/news/uk-world-news/parents-reveal-new-education-secretarys-1059101
28 Ibid.
29 https://www.dailymail.co.uk/debate/article-2281373/He-belted-school-says-wifes-boss-confesses-best-Education-Minister-years-Im-Mr-Blurt-PM.html
30 https://www.bbc.co.uk/news/education-20034101

CHAPTER 2

1   https://www.theguardian.com/politics/2010/jan/30/thatcher-honorary-degree-refused-oxford
2   https://www.apnews.com/2ac49f542c3ea67941556cf5d89d0928
3   *The Times*, 2 February 1985
4   https://www.theguardian.com/politics/2012/oct/05/michael-gove-next-tory-leader
5   Andrew Gimson, *Boris: The Adventures of Boris Johnson* (Simon & Schuster, 2016)
6   Ibid.
7   Ibid.
8   Ibid.
9   Ibid.
10 Ibid.
11 Private interview
12 Private interview
13 http://www.samiraahmed.co.uk/michael-gove-on-educational-elitism-a-flashback-to-oxford-1988/
14 Ibid.
15 Ibid.
16 Ibid.
17 Ibid.
18 *The Times*, 14 February 1997
19 Ibid.
20 https://www.dailymail.co.uk/news/article-1063366/Top-Tory-Michael-Gove-bed-Oxford-romp.html
21 Ibid.
22 https://www.dailymail.co.uk/debate/article-2281373/He-belted-school-says-wifes-boss-confesses-best-Education-Minister-years-Im-Mr-Blurt-PM.html
23 https://www.independent.co.uk/news/uk/politics/gove-hague-and-johnson-feature-in-tales-of-oxford-hijinx-found-in-student-newspaper-8459177.html
24 https://www.dailymail.co.uk/debate/article-2281373/He-belted-school-says-wifes-boss-confesses-best-Education-Minister-years-Im-Mr-Blurt-PM.html
25 https://www.dailyrecord.co.uk/news/politics/cringeworthy-video-emerges-young-michael-8348131
26 https://www.dailymail.co.uk/debate/article-2281373/He-belted-school-says-wifes-boss-confesses-best-Education-Minister-years-Im-Mr-Blurt-PM.html
27 *Democrat and Chronicle*, 14 April 1988
28 Private information

CHAPTER 3

1   https://www.bbc.co.uk/news/av/uk-scotland-29376057/aberdeen-journals-strike-25-years-on
2   Gimson, op. cit.
3   Michael Ashcroft and Isabel Oakeshott, *Call Me Dave* (Biteback Publishing, 2016), p. 75
4   Ibid., pp. 79–80

5   https://www.newstatesman.com/education/2010/09/gove-8220-parents-school
6   https://www.theguardian.com/media/2005/jan/31/pressandpublishing.politicsandthemedia
7   Ibid.
8   Private information
9   Private interview
10   https://www.telegraph.co.uk/education/8964253/Michael-Gove-faces-new-questions-about-what-he-did-with-a-traffic-cone.html
11   https://www.dailymail.co.uk/news/article-1284300/The-Cone-Secretary--young-Michael-Gove-fell-foul-law.html
12   *The Observer*, 20 August 1989
13   https://www.bbc.co.uk/news/av/uk-scotland-29376057/aberdeen-journals-strike-25-years-on
14   *The Guardian*, 24 February 1990
15   https://www.theguardian.com/politics/2012/oct/05/michael-gove-next-tory-leader
16   https://www.youtube.com/watch?v=-vhYIZTtIhU
17   http://thesettledwill.blogspot.com/2014/10/a-strike-like-no-others-25-years-on.html

CHAPTER 4
1   https://www.independent.co.uk/news/people/obituary-bob-cryer-1369763.html
2   Private interview
3   Michael Ashcroft and Isabel Oakeshott, op. cit., p. 42
4   Ibid., p. 66
5   Francis Elliott and James Hanning, *Cameron: Practically a Conservative* (Fourth Estate, 2012), p. 10
6   https://www.theguardian.com/politics/2009/oct/04/david-cameron-bullingdon-club
7   https://www.dailymail.co.uk/news/article-2268550/Throwing-scrambled-egg-love-rival-Michael-Gove-earned-VERY-saucy-nickname-Oxford.html
8   Private interview
9   Private information
10   Private interview
11   http://www.bbc.co.uk/archive/gay_rights/12016.shtml

CHAPTER 5
1   *A Stab in the Dark*, Channel 4, 5 June 1992
2   https://www.theguardian.com/politics/commentisfree/2016/jul/05/the-tv-show-i-made-with-michael-gove-still-gives-me-nightmares
3   https://www.comedy.co.uk/podcasts/richard_herring_edinburgh/2013_02_david_baddiel_katie_mulgrew/
4   https://twitter.com/Baddiel/status/750288122903162884
5   https://www.theguardian.com/politics/commentisfree/2016/jul/05/the-tv-show-i-made-with-michael-gove-still-gives-me-nightmares
6   *A Stab in the Dark*, Channel 4, 5 June 1992
7   https://www.theguardian.com/politics/commentisfree/2016/jul/05/the-tv-show-i-made-with-michael-gove-still-gives-me-nightmares
8   Ibid.
9   https://www.comedy.co.uk/podcasts/richard_herring_edinburgh/2013_02_david_baddiel_katie_mulgrew/
10   https://www.youtube.com/watch?v=5osLS2T-zzc
11   *A Stab in the Dark*, Channel 4, 5 June 1992
12   Ibid.
13   *A Stab in the Dark*, Channel 4, 12 June 1992
14   Ibid.
15   Ibid.

16 *A Stab in the Dark*, Channel 4, 19 June 1992
17 *A Stab in the Dark*, Channel 4, 31 July 1992
18 *A Stab in the Dark*, Channel 4, 10 July 1992
19 *A Stab in the Dark*, Channel 4, 26 June 1992
20 Ibid.
21 *A Stab in the Dark*, Channel 4, 7 August 1992
22 *A Stab in the Dark*, Channel 4, 3 July 1992
23 *A Stab in the Dark*, Channel 4, 24 July 1992
24 *A Stab in the Dark*, Channel 4, 7 August 1992
25 *A Stab in the Dark*, Channel 4, 24 July 1992
26 *A Stab in the Dark*, Channel 4, 26 June 1992
27 *A Stab in the Dark*, Channel 4, 17 July 1992
28 https://www.theguardian.com/politics/commentisfree/2016/jul/05/the-tv-show-i-made-with-michael-gove-still-gives-me-nightmares
29 https://www.independent.co.uk/arts-entertainment/television-hard-lessons-from-the-auto-cue-david-sexton-on-problems-met-by-presenters-samaritans-1539471.html
30 *The Stage*, 31 December 1992
31 *The Times*, 8 January 1999
32 https://www.newstatesman.com/blogs/the-staggers/2010/07/gove-dark-stab-baddiel-footage
33 https://www.theguardian.com/politics/commentisfree/2016/jul/05/the-tv-show-i-made-with-michael-gove-still-gives-me-nightmares

CHAPTER 6

1 https://www.bbc.co.uk/programmes/profiles/k6FxLL1ZJKytnkmpTjZs67/john-humphrys
2 *The Times*, 19 February 1997
3 https://www.telegraph.co.uk/news/celebritynews/8432731/Sir-Christopher-Lees-film-co-star-Michael-Gove-was-a-natural-school-chaplain.html
4 http://zeitgeist-diagram.com/index.php/interviews/7-the-history-man-interview-with-director-justin-hardy
5 https://www.empireonline.com/movies/feast-midnight/review/
6 https://www.dailymail.co.uk/news/article-3122076/My-obsession-Britt-Ekland-s-nude-derriere-starred-film-chum-Christopher-Lee-Lord-Chancellor-MICHAEL-GOVE.html
7 Ibid.
8 Ibid.
9 Private information
10 *The Guardian*, 19 August 1994
11 *The Guardian*, 17 October 1994
12 *The Guardian*, 22 February 1995
13 Ibid.
14 Michael Gove, *Michael Portillo: The Future of the Right* (Fourth Estate, 1995), p. 319
15 Ibid., p. 305
16 Ibid., p. 86
17 https://www.independent.co.uk/news/diary-5424804.html
18 *The Guardian*, 28 February 1997
19 *The Times*, 19 October 1995
20 *Sunday Times*, 8 October 1995
21 *The Guardian*, 4 October 1995
22 https://www.independent.co.uk/arts-entertainment/books/the-pain-from-spain-1538690.html
23 Private information
24 *The Times*, 9 September 1999
25 *The Times*, 10 September 1999

26 Portillo, op. cit., p. 48
27 Ibid., p. 71
28 Ibid., p. 305
29 *The Times*, 29 December 1998
30 *The Guardian*, 11 January 2001

CHAPTER 7

1 *A Stab in the Dark*, Channel 4, 12 June 1992
2 *The Times*, 10 February 1996
3 *The Times*, 11 July 1996
4 *The Times*, 19 October 1996
5 *The Times*, 10 February 1997
6 *The Times*, 14 June 1996
7 *The Times*, 1 February 1996
8 *The Times*, 14 March 1997
9 *The Times*, 1 April 1997
10 Ibid.
11 *The Times*, 31 May 1996 and 27 September 1996
12 *The Times*, 4 February 1997
13 Francis Elliott and James Hanning, *Cameron: The Rise of the New Conservative* (Fourth Estate, 2007), p. 142
14 Michael Ashcroft and Isabel Oakeshott, op. cit., p. 111
15 Francis Elliott and James Hanning (2007), op. cit., p. 169
16 *The Times*, 23 December 1996
17 *The Times*, 2 April 1997
18 *The Times*, 22 October 1996
19 *The Times*, 18 March 1997
20 *The Times*, 29 April 1997
21 Private interview
22 *The Times*, 2 May 1997

CHAPTER 8

1 http://www.johnmajorarchive.org.uk/1990-1997/mr-majors-resignation-statement-2-may-1997/
2 *The Times*, 3 May 1997
3 http://www.bbc.co.uk/news/special/politics97/leadership/review.shtml
4 Michael Crick, *In Search Of Michael Howard* (Simon & Schuster, 2005), p. 369
5 *The Times*, 24 September 1997
6 http://labour-uncut.co.uk/2012/06/21/the-night-michael-gove-nearly-joined-the-labour-party/
7 http://www.ukpol.co.uk/michael-portillo-1997-speech-to-centre-for-policy-studies/
8 *The Times*, 11 October 1997
9 *The Times*, 26 June 1998
10 *The Times*, 22 December 1998
11 *The Times* (Times 2), 1 May 2013

CHAPTER 9

1 *The Times*, 21 January 2004
2 https://www.tatler.com/article/sarah-vine-interview-exclusive
3 *The Times*, 21 January 2004
4 https://www.dailymail.co.uk/debate/article-6390995/SARAH-VINE-dream-having-nightmare-doing-all.html

5 https://www.tatler.com/article/sarah-vine-interview-exclusive
6 *The Times* (Times 2), 1 May 2013
7 https://www.dailymail.co.uk/femail/article-2414560/Dieting-hair-fall-Men-zone--I-busy-hiding-bald-patch--Introducing-honest-mischievous-irresistibly-funny-SARAH-VINE.html
8 *The Times*, 8 February 2012
9 *The Times*, 13 January 2009
10 https://www.dailymail.co.uk/debate/article-3653588/SARAH-VINE-d-voted-Remain-d-burn-ballot-paper-bullies-scaremongers.html
11 https://www.dailymail.co.uk/femail/article-2414560/Dieting-hair-fall-Men-zone--I-busy-hiding-bald-patch--Introducing-honest-mischievous-irresistibly-funny-SARAH-VINE.html
12 Ibid.
13 *The Times*, 5 May 2006
14 Ibid.
15 https://www.tatler.com/article/sarah-vine-interview-exclusive
16 https://www.dailymail.co.uk/debate/article-2573444/SARAH-VINE-Why-Ive-chosen-send-daughter-state-school.html
17 https://www.theguardian.com/education/2014/mar/07/sarah-vine-miracle-state-education
18 https://www.dailymail.co.uk/debate/article-3044336/Love-hair-ladies-one-day-like-endure-agony-losing-writes-SARAH-VINE.html
19 Ibid.
20 *The Times*, 5 May 2006
21 https://www.dailymail.co.uk/femail/article-2414560/Dieting-hair-fall-Men-zone--I-busy-hiding-bald-patch--Introducing-honest-mischievous-irresistibly-funny-SARAH-VINE.html
22 https://www.dailymail.co.uk/debate/article-2573444/SARAH-VINE-Why-Ive-chosen-send-daughter-state-school.html
23 Ibid.
24 https://www.dailymail.co.uk/femail/article-2414560/Dieting-hair-fall-Men-zone--I-busy-hiding-bald-patch--Introducing-honest-mischievous-irresistibly-funny-SARAH-VINE.html
25 https://www.tatler.com/article/sarah-vine-interview-exclusive
26 Ibid.
27 https://www.dailymail.co.uk/femail/article-2414560/Dieting-hair-fall-Men-zone--I-busy-hiding-bald-patch--Introducing-honest-mischievous-irresistibly-funny-SARAH-VINE.html
28 https://www.tatler.com/article/sarah-vine-interview-exclusive
29 Ibid.
30 *The Times*, 19 February 2008
31 https://www.theguardian.com/politics/2016/jul/02/sarah-vine-daily-mail-columnist-and-driving-force-behind-goves-pm-dream
32 https://www.tatler.com/article/sarah-vine-interview-exclusive
33 Ibid.
34 https://www.dailymail.co.uk/debate/article-2504851/SARAH-VINE-My-woman-war-whats-society.html
35 *The Times*, 12 December 1998
36 *The Times*, 12 January 1999
37 Michael Ashcroft, *Dirty Politics, Dirty Times* (Biteback Publishing, 2009), p. 92
38 *The Times*, 13 July 1999
39 https://www.ft.com/content/4593dcb3-a960-344b-92b9-5f232743bbd3
40 Michael Ashcroft, op. cit., p. 145

41 *The Times*, 9 December 1999

42 *The Times*, 4 April 2000

43 *The Guardian*, 26 January 2000

44 *The Times*, 28 March 1997

45 *The Times*, 12 May 1998

46 https://www.irishtimes.com/news/relatives-of-ira-victims-gather-to-support-yes-vote-1.152794

47 Ibid.

48 Michael Gove, 'The Price of Peace' (Centre for Policy Studies, 2000)

49 Ibid.

50 Ibid.

51 Ibid.

52 Ibid.

53 Ibid.

54 https://www.independent.co.uk/news/uk/politics/hague-adviser-quits-nasty-tories-710993.html

55 *The Times*, 16 June 2009

56 *The Times*, 12 February 1999

57 *The Times*, 17 February 1999

58 Ibid.

59 *The Times*, 3 October 2000

60 Ibid.

61 *The Times*, 10 May 2001

62 *The Times*, 4 October 2000

63 *The Times*, 10 October 2000

64 *The Times*, 5 October 2000

65 *The Times*, 10 October 2000

66 Ibid.

67 *The Times*, 27 February 2001

68 *The Times*, 27 February 2001

CHAPTER 10

1   https://www.dailymail.co.uk/femail/article-2414560/Dieting-hair-fall-Men-zone--I-busy-hiding-bald-patch--Introducing-honest-mischievous-irresistibly-funny-SARAH-VINE.html

2   https://www.theguardian.com/politics/2001/jun/08/election2001.conservatives

3   *The Times*, 9 June 2001

4   *The Times*, 12 June 2001

5   Andrew Gimson, op. cit.

6   *The Times*, 1 September 2001

7   *The Times*, 17 July 2001

8   Private interview

9   Private information

10 Private interview

11 *The Times*, 18 July 2001

12 Private interview

13 *The Times*, 8 May 2002

14 Ibid.

15 *The Observer*, 23 September 2001

16 Private interview

17 Private interview

18 *The Times*, 25 August 1998

19 *The Times*, 20 February 2001
20 *The Times*, 14 September 2001
21 https://www.dailymail.co.uk/debate/article-3461103/The-torture-watching-husband-
22 https://www.gq-magazine.co.uk/article/caitlin-moran-how-to-build-a-girl-interview
23 *The Times*, 8 May 2002
24 https://www.thetimes.co.uk/article/atticus-gove-is-ready-for-take-off-as-he-beats-his-bete-noire-5xp0prqq9xs
25 Justine Greening, 'A wholly healthy Britain?' in *A Blue Tomorrow* (Politico's, 2001), p. 198
26 *The Guardian*, 8 October 2001
27 *The Guardian*, 23 November 2001

CHAPTER 11

1 https://www.conservativehome.com/thetorydiary/2014/05/a-profile-of-dominic-cummings-friend-of-gove-and-enemy-of-clegg.html
2 Ibid.
3 *The Times*, 3 November 1999
4 *The Guardian*, 10 March 2000
5 *The Times*, 31 May 2001
6 *The Times*, 7 September 2001
7 https://www.telegraph.co.uk/news/uknews/1364683/We-must-change-to-survive-say-Tory-webmasters.html
8 https://www.telegraph.co.uk/news/uknews/1383518/Gay-Tory-who-aims-to-modernise-party.html
9 *The Times*, 29 April 2002
10 https://www.theguardian.com/media/2001/apr/27/pressandpublishing.thetimes
11 https://www.telegraph.co.uk/news/uknews/1385645/Changing-Times-ahead-as-editor-quits-after-10-years.html
12 https://www.theguardian.com/media/2002/feb/25/newsinternational.mondaymediasection
13 *The Times*, 29 May 2002
14 http://news.bbc.co.uk/1/hi/programmes/newsnight/review/3051798.stm
15 *The Times*, 21 September 2002
16 *The Independent*, 5 June 2002
17 *The Guardian*, 6 June 2002
18 *The Observer*, 6 October 2002
19 Ibid.
20 https://www.theguardian.com/politics/2002/oct/15/davidcameron.politicalcolumnists
21 *The Times*, 7 May 2005
22 https://www.pressgazette.co.uk/times-promotes-gove-to-boost-saturday/
23 Francis Elliott and James Hanning (2007), op. cit., p. 245
24 *The Times*, 12 August 2003
25 *The Times*, 22 February 2003
26 *The Observer*, 2 November 2003
27 *The Guardian*, 5 November 2003
28 *The Times*, 7 December 2005
29 https://www.theguardian.com/politics/2004/apr/09/uk.conservatives
30 https://www.telegraph.co.uk/news/uknews/1465579/Surrey-Heath-members-believe-that-their-money-ought-to-be-able-to-buy-a-future-prime-minister.html
31 Ibid.
32 Ibid.
33 *The Times*, 6 July 2004
34 https://www.theguardian.com/media/2005/jan/31/pressandpublishing.politicsandthemedia
35 *The Times*, 29 October 2004

36 https://www.politico.eu/blogs/on-media/2016/07/michael-goves-next-move-write-the-book-hes-been-promising-for-years-brexit-theresa-may-levenson-henry-st-john/
37 *Sunday Times*, 12 November 2004
38 https://www.telegraph.co.uk/news/1481883/Howard-Why-Britain-must-set-quotas-on-immigration.html
39 *The Times*, 22 March 2005
40 *The Times*, 30 April 2005
41 Private interview
42 *The Times*, 7 May 2005
43 https://www.theguardian.com/politics/2005/may/13/uk.election2005
44 *The Times*, 7 May 2005

CHAPTER 12

1   https://www.theguardian.com/politics/2005/may/06/election2005.comment
2   https://publications.parliament.uk/pa/cm200506/cmhansrd/vo050607/debtext/50607-21.htm#50607-21_spnew0
3   Francis Elliott and James Hanning (2007), op. cit., p. 262
4   Ibid., p. 265
5   Michael Ashcroft and Isabel Oakeshott, op. cit., p. 235
6   https://www.theguardian.com/politics/2005/jun/29/speeches.conservatives
7   http://archive.spectator.co.uk/article/27th-august-2005/6/why-david-cameron-has-decided-to-copy-tony-blair
8   http://www.ukpol.co.uk/david-cameron-2005-speech-to-launch-leadership-bid/
9   *The Times*, 4 October 2005
10 Michael Ashcroft and Isabel Oakeshott, op. cit., p. 251
11 *The Times*, 4 November 2005
12 *The Times*, 27 May 2006
13 https://publications.parliament.uk/pa/cm200506/cmhansrd/vo060524/halltext/60524h0010.htm
14 https://publications.parliament.uk/pa/cm200607/cmhansrd/cm070516/debtext/70516-0006.htm
15 https://publications.parliament.uk/pa/cm200607/cmhansrd/cm070522/debtext/70522-0004.htm#07052290000002
16 https://webarchive.nationalarchives.gov.uk/20140122190743/http:/www.levesoninquiry.org.uk/wp-content/uploads/2012/05/Witness-Statement-of-Michael-Gove-MP.pdf
17 Michael Gove, *Celsius 7/7* (Weidenfeld & Nicolson, 2006), p. 42
18 Ibid., p. 43
19 Ibid., p. 36
20 Ibid., p. 112
21 Ibid., p. 56
22 Ibid., p. 92
23 Ibid., p. 131
24 Ibid., p. 136
25 Ibid., p. 138
26 https://www.evernote.com/shard/s350/client/snv?noteGuid=2824657b-270b-4d9f-8d6d-c0121efcc3db&noteKey=704af79337e788c6&sn=https%3A%2F%2Fwww.evernote.com%2Fshard%2Fs350%2Fsh%2F2824657b-270b-4d9f-8d6d-c0121efcc3db%2F704af79337e788c6&title=Killer%2BReview%2Bof%2BGove%2527s%2BGod%2BAwful%2Bbook
27 https://www.telegraph.co.uk/culture/books/3654434/Democracy-is-the-solution.html
28 https://conservativehome.blogs.com/books/2006/09/celsius_77.html
29 https://highprofiles.info/interview/michael-gove/

30 https://conservativehome.blogs.com/books/2006/09/celsius_77.html
31 https://web.archive.org/web/20070927021649/http://www.stephenpollard.net/002929.html
32 https://www.telegraph.co.uk/news/uknews/1537211/Ministers-take-leaf-out-of-Torys-book.html
33 Private information

CHAPTER 13

1   https://www.telegraph.co.uk/news/uknews/1551714/David-Willetts-speech-on-grammar-schools.html
2   *The Times*, 17 May 2007
3   http://news.bbc.co.uk/1/hi/uk_politics/6679005.stm
4   *The Times*, 22 May 2007
5   http://news.bbc.co.uk/1/hi/uk_politics/6679005.stm
6   *The Times*, 12 June 2001
7   *The Times*, 15 July 2003
8   *The Times*, 21 January 2003
9   https://hansard.parliament.uk/Commons/2007-07-10/debates/07071034000004/ChildrenSchoolsAndFamilies#contribution-07071034000191
10 Ibid.
11 https://www.theguardian.com/commentisfree/2007/jul/01/comment.conservatives
12 https://www.dailymail.co.uk/news/article-528759/In-Daves-groovy-new-Tories-youre-youre---The-Green-Chip-Club.html
13 Ibid.
14 https://conservative-speeches.sayit.mysociety.org/speech/599789
15 https://www.conservativehome.com/thetorydiary/2014/05/a-profile-of-dominic-cummings-friend-of-gove-and-enemy-of-clegg.html
16 https://publications.parliament.uk/pa/cm200708/cmhansrd/cm071121/debtext/71121-0004.htm
17 Ibid.
18 *The Spectator*, 23 February 2008
19 *The Spectator*, 1 March 2008
20 https://www.theguardian.com/politics/2010/oct/01/gove-interview-reforms-education
21 *The Times*, 20 March 2008
22 *The Spectator*, 27 September 2008
23 Ibid.
24 *The Guardian*, 9 May 2008
25 *Evening Standard*, 16 August 2008
26 *The Observer*, 28 September 2008

CHAPTER 14

1   https://www.telegraph.co.uk/news/newstopics/mps-expenses/5305434/Michael-Gove-flipped-homes-MPs-expenses.html
    https://mpsallowances.parliament.uk/mpslordsandoffices/hocallowances/allowances-by-mp/michael-gove/Michael_Gove_0506_ACA.pdf
2   Ibid.
3   *Daily Telegraph*, 12 May 2009
4   Michael Ashcroft and Isabel Oakeshott, op. cit., p. 309
5   *Sunday Telegraph*, 17 May 2009
6   *The Guardian*, 19 May 2009
7   https://www.getsurrey.co.uk/news/local-news/mp-michael-gove-faces-expenses-4824257
8   *The Guardian*, 19 May 2009
9   Ibid.
10 *The Times*, 13 July 2009
11 *The Times*, 11 January 2010

12 https://www.academia.edu/30273661/WHAT_IS_EDUCATION_FOR_Speech_by_Michael_Gove_MP_to_the_RSA
13 *The Guardian*, 12 October 2009
14 Dennis Kavanagh and Philip Cowley, *The British General Election of 2010* (Palgrave Macmillan, 2010), p. 133
15 *The Times*, 8 May 2010
16 http://news.bbc.co.uk/1/hi/programmes/andrew_marr_show/8670887.stm
17 Private information
18 Matthew d'Ancona, *In It Together: The Inside Story of the Coalition Government* (Viking, 2013), p. 27
19 https://www.independent.co.uk/news/education/education-news/dump-fing-everyone-the-inside-story-of-how-michael-gove-s-vicious-attack-dogs-are-terrorising-the-8497626.html
20 Private information

CHAPTER 15

1 Mike Finn (ed.) *The Gove Legacy: Education in Britain after the Coalition* (Palgrave Macmillan, 2015), pp. 15–16
2 https://www.ft.com/content/ebe8018c-aa45-11e3-8497-00144feab7de
3 *The Andrew Marr Show*, BBC One, 27 November 2016
4 https://www.bbc.co.uk/news/education-14249341
5 https://www.gov.uk/government/news/over-1000-schools-apply-for-academy-freedoms
6 https://www.theguardian.com/education/2010/jul/29/michael-gove-academies-schools-claims
7 https://www.nao.org.uk/wp-content/uploads/2010/09/1011288.pdf
8 https://www.bbc.co.uk/news/uk-11197827
9 https://www.theguardian.com/education/2010/oct/06/most-free-schools-behind-schedule
10 *The Times*, Thursday 25 November
11 https://www.dailymail.co.uk/news/article-1332802/Michael-Goves-education-reform-Trendy-teaching-focus-traditional-subjects.html
12 https://www.bbc.co.uk/news/uk-politics-11879062
13 https://www.theguardian.com/education/2012/aug/06/michael-gove-own-goal-school-sports
14 https://www.theguardian.com/books/2010/dec/26/booktrust-funding-cut-pullman-motion

CHAPTER 16

1 https://dominiccummings.com/2014/10/30/the-hollow-men-ii-some-reflections-on-westminster-and-whitehall-dysfunction/
2 Ibid.
3 *Gove in Government*, BBC Radio 4, 24 June 2018
4 https://dominiccummings.com/2014/10/30/the-hollow-men-ii-some-reflections-on-westminster-and-whitehall-dysfunction/
5 Ibid.
6 https://www.totalpolitics.com/articles/opinion/james-frayne-truth-about-working-michael-gove
7 *Financial Times*, 19 September 2011
8 Ibid.
9 https://www.huffingtonpost.co.uk/2012/03/03/michael-gove-government-emails-henry-de-zoete_n_1318380.html
10 David Laws, *Coalition Diaries 2012–2015* (Biteback Publishing, 2017), pp. 25–6
11 https://dominiccummings.com/2014/10/30/the-hollow-men-ii-some-reflections-on-westminster-and-whitehall-dysfunction/
12 Ibid.
13 https://www.independent.co.uk/news/education/education-news/dump-fing-everyone-the-inside-story-of-how-michael-gove-s-vicious-attack-dogs-are-terrorising-the-8497626.html

14 https://www.theguardian.com/politics/2013/feb/09/michael-gove-bullying-claims-payout1
15 http://liberalconspiracy.org/2013/04/18/the-full-story-of-michael-goves-depart-ment-and-the-curious-toryeducation-account/
16 https://www.whatdotheyknow.com/request/149778/response/383207/attach/html/3/FOI%20Mr%20Bosch%20results.pdf.html
17 https://www.theguardian.com/education/2011/jan/06/one-in-ten-schools-is-academy
18 https://www.spectator.co.uk/2010/01/michael-gove-vs-the-blob/
19 Private information
20 https://ioelondonblog.wordpress.com/2012/06/12/proposed-primary-curriculum-what-about-the-pupils/
21 https://www.bbc.co.uk/news/education-12227491
22 *The Times*, 6 March 2010
23 https://www.bbc.co.uk/news/education-12227491
24 *Daily Telegraph*, 1 April 2011
25 http://news.bbc.co.uk/1/mobile/programmes/andrew_marr_show/9523011.stm
26 https://www.theguardian.com/society/2011/nov/28/striking-workers-employers-notice-gove
27 https://www.newstatesman.com/education/2010/09/gove-8220-parents-school
28 https://www.huffingtonpost.co.uk/2011/11/28/michael-gove-launches-attack-union-bosses_n_1115780.html
29 https://www.bbc.co.uk/news/education-17481888
30 https://ioelondonblog.wordpress.com/2012/06/12/proposed-primary-curriculum-what-about-the-pupils/
31 https://www.theguardian.com/education/2012/jun/12/michael-gove-curriculum-attacked-adviser
32 *Sunday Times*, 9 December 2012
33 David Laws, op. cit., p. 68
34 *The Observer*, 16 February 2013
35 https://www.bbc.co.uk/news/education-21600298
36 https://www.theguardian.com/commentisfree/2013/feb/15/history-teaching-curriculum-gove-right
37 *The Independent*, 19 March 2013
38 *Mail on Sunday*, 24 March 2013
39 https://www.bbc.co.uk/news/education-22558756
40 *Gove in Government*, BBC Radio 4, 24 June 2018
41 Ibid.

CHAPTER 17

1 https://www.bbc.co.uk/news/uk-politics-18539463
2 David Laws, op. cit., p. 5
3 https://www.theguardian.com/politics/2012/jun/21/nick-clegg-michael-gove-exams
4 https://www.theguardian.com/politics/2016/sep/05/nick-clegg-michael-gove-lib-dem-coalition-idealogue
5 https://www.mirror.co.uk/news/uk-news/michael-gove-blasted-by-conservative-col-league-1544330
6 https://blogs.spectator.co.uk/2013/01/loughton-vs-dfe/
7 https://www.theguardian.com/politics/2013/feb/09/michael-gove-bullying-claims-payout1
8 David Laws, *Coalition: The Inside Story of the Conservative–Liberal Democrat Coalition Govern-ment* (Biteback Publishing, 2016), p. 211
9 Ibid., p. 213
10 Ibid., p. 219
11 https://www.theguardian.com/education/2012/sep/17/gcse-exams-replaced-ebacc-michael-gove
12 Ibid.
13 https://www.theguardian.com/education/2012/sep/17/gcse-ebacc-michael-gove

14 *The Times*, 4 October 2012

15 David Laws (2016), op. cit., p. 220

16 https://www.theguardian.com/politics/2013/feb/07/michael-gove-gcse-replacement

17 https://www.parliament.uk/documents/commons-committees/Education/EIGHTH-RE-PORT-GCSEs-to-ECBs-Reform-HC-808.pdf

18 https://hansard.parliament.uk/commons/2013-02-07/debates/13020759000004/CurriculumAndExamReform

19 *Daily Mail*, 8 February 2013

20 David Laws (2017), op. cit., p. 62

21 David Laws (2016), op. cit., p. 298

22 https://www.thecaterer.com/articles/344467/leons-henry-dimbleby-insists-review-of-school-meals-isnt-driven-by-money

23 David Laws (2016), op. cit., p. 340

24 David Laws (2017), op. cit., pp. 207–8

25 Ibid., p. 214

26 Ibid., p. 226

27 Ibid., pp. 226–8

28 David Laws (2016), op. cit., p. 368

29 https://www.independent.co.uk/news/uk/politics/osborne-defies-pm-and-blocks-plastic-bag-tax-7878755.html

30 David Laws (2017), op. cit., p. 27

31 David Laws (2017), op. cit., p. 210

32 Tim Shipman, *All Out War: The Full Story of How Brexit Sank Britain's Political Class* (William Collins, 2016), p. 10

33 *Mail on Sunday*, 14 October 2012

34 Tim Shipman, op. cit., p. 11

35 https://www.dailymail.co.uk/debate/article-2431009/SARAH-VINE-What-twerk-tells-pornification-children.html

36 *Sunday Times*, 5 May 2013

37 https://www.dailymail.co.uk/debate/article-3461103/The-torture-watching-husband-choose-beliefs-old-friend-PM-Daily-Mail-columnist-SARAH-VINE-s-intensely-personal-ac-count-momentous-decision.html

38 https://www.thesun.co.uk/news/1375607/how-the-adopted-son-of-an-aberdeen-fish-mer-chant-is-now-tipped-to-be-the-new-pm/

39 *The Times*, 11 January 2012

40 *The Times*, 27 December 2008

41 https://www.dailymail.co.uk/news/article-2436701/Goves-2-500-fat-farm-makeover-Its-auf-wiedersehn-flab-Education-Secretary-loses-2st-Austrian-spa.html

42 *Daily Mail*, 21 May 2015

43 *Daily Mail*, 9 November 2013

44 *The Times*, 12 January 1999

45 https://webarchive.nationalarchives.gov.uk/20140122190743/http://www.levesoninquiry.org.uk/wp-content/uploads/2012/05/Witness-Statement-of-Michael-Gove-MP.pdf

46 https://www.theguardian.com/media/2012/may/29/michael-gove-rupert-murdoch

47 *The Sun*, 26 May 2014

CHAPTER 18

48 https://static.guim.co.uk/ni/1381763590219/-Some-thoughts-on-education.pdf

49 Private information

50 https://www.independent.co.uk/news/uk/politics/michael-goves-controversial-adviser-dominic-cummings-quits-to-open-new-free-school-8864909.html

51 *Sunday Times*, 26 January 2014

52 https://www.bbc.co.uk/news/education-25997102
53 David Laws (2017), op. cit., p. 256
54 *The Times*, 4 February 2014
55 David Laws (2017), op. cit., p. 258
56 https://www.theguardian.com/politics/2013/sep/27/theresa-may-tories
57 David Laws (2017), op. cit., p. 148
58 David Laws (2017), op. cit., p. 214
59 https://inews.co.uk/news/long-reads/baroness-warsi-interview-islam-muslims-michael-gove/
60 https://www.businessinsider.com/islamophobia-scandal-conservative-party-goes-right-up-to-the-top-baroness-warsi-interview-2018-6?r=US&IR=T
61 https://www.theguardian.com/world/2017/sep/01/trojan-horse-the-real-story-behind-the-fake-islamic-plot-to-take-over-schools
62 https://publications.parliament.uk/pa/cm201415/cmselect/cmeduc/473/47305.htm
63 https://www.channel4.com/news/operation-trojan-horse-extremism-radicalisation-schools
64 https://assets.publishing.service.gov.uk/government/uploads/system/uploads/attachment_data/file/396211/Review_into_possible_warnings_to_DfE_relating_to_extremism_in_Birmingham_schools.pdf
65 https://publications.parliament.uk/pa/cm201415/cmselect/cmeduc/473/47303.htm
66 *Sunday Times*, 27 April 2014
67 *The Times*, 16 June 2014
68 https://www.telegraph.co.uk/news/politics/11609570/Secrets-of-the-Tories-election-war-room.html
69 David Laws (2017), op. cit., p. 357
70 Tim Shipman, op. cit., p. 151
71 https://www.theguardian.com/politics/2014/jul/15/cameron-sacks-toxic-gove-promotes-women-reshuffle
72 *The Times*, 16 July 2014
73 *Daily Mail*, 16 July 2014
74 https://www.theguardian.com/politics/2014/jul/15/tale-of-two-careers-michael-gove-iain-duncan-smith
75 https://www.theguardian.com/politics/2014/jul/15/cameron-barnacles-trouble-tory-right
76 https://www.theguardian.com/politics/2014/jul/15/cameron-sacks-toxic-gove-promotes-women-reshuffle
77 Ibid.
78 Tim Shipman, op. cit., p. 151
79 https://www.telegraph.co.uk/education/educationnews/10968144/Cabinet-reshuffle-teachers-hail-Michael-Goves-departure.html
80 https://www.dailymail.co.uk/debate/article-2693693/A-shabby-days-work-Cameron-live-regret.html
81 https://publications.parliament.uk/pa/cm201415/cmselect/cmeduc/258/25804.htm
82 https://www.nao.org.uk/wp-content/uploads/2018/02/Converting-maintained-schools-to-academies-Summary.pdf
83 https://epi.org.uk/wp-content/uploads/2017/07/EPI_-Impact_of_Academies_Consolidated_Report-.pdf
84 https://www.theguardian.com/politics/2012/may/15/michael-gove-king-james-bible
85 https://www.dailymail.co.uk/news/article-2532923/Michael-Gove-blasts-Blackadder-myths-First-World-War-spread-television-sit-coms-left-wing-academics.html

CHAPTER 19

1 https://www.politics.co.uk/news/2014/07/17/flushing-out-the-truth-here-s-how-michael-gove-got-stuck-in

2 https://www.theguardian.com/politics/2014/jul/17/michael-gove-stuck-toilet-commons-chief-whip

3 https://hansard.parliament.uk/Commons/2014-11-10/debates/14111019000001/CriminalLaw

4 https://twitter.com/DArcyTiP/status/531901621316624387

5 Anne Marie Morris recorded a positive abstention by voting both for and against the motion.

6 https://order-order.com/2014/10/22/michael-gove-at-gf10/

7 https://www.theguardian.com/politics/2014/oct/16/michael-gove-tyrion-lannister-game-of-thrones-video

8 *The Times*, 16 November 1996

9 https://www.gov.uk/government/speeches/what-does-a-one-nation-justice-policy-look-like

10 https://www.theguardian.com/law/2015/jun/10/legal-aid-fees-to-be-cut-by-875-confirms-ministry-of-justice

11 https://www.theguardian.com/law/2015/sep/18/michael-gove-legal-aid-fee-criminal-solicitors

12 https://www.bbc.co.uk/news/uk-35432581

13 *The Times*, 13 October 2015

14 https://www.theguardian.com/uk-news/2015/sep/10/michael-gove-close-just-solutions-international-ministry-of-justice-commercial

15 https://www.theguardian.com/world/2015/oct/13/uk-ditches-plan-to-bid-for-saudi-arabia-prisons-contract

16 https://www.gov.uk/government/speeches/the-treasure-in-the-heart-of-man-making-prisons-work

17 Ibid.

18 Ibid.

19 *The Independent*, 18 July 2015

20 *The Observer*, 19 July 2015

21 *Daily Mirror*, 20 July 2015

22 *Gove in Government*, BBC Radio 4, 24 June 2018

23 https://www.dailymail.co.uk/news/article-3267742/Has-depraved-Texan-gangster-convinced-Gove-jails-extraordinary-encounter-UK-s-Justice-Secretary-reformed-hoodlum-revolutionise-penal-policy-let-criminals-streets.html

24 BBC *Panorama*, 12 October 2015

25 https://publications.parliament.uk/pa/cm201516/cmhansrd/cm160126/debtext/160126-0001.htm

26 https://www.theguardian.com/society/2016/mar/16/michael-gove-announces-plans-for-reform-prisons

CHAPTER 20

1 *Sunday Times*, 23 August 2015

2 https://www.itv.com/news/2015-11-10/if-we-vote-to-leave-we-will-leave-david-camerons-eu-warning-as-he-sets-out-reform-demands/

3 Tim Shipman, op. cit., p. 145

4 *The World at One*, BBC Radio 4, 18 December 2015

5 Harry Mount, *Summer Madness: How Brexit Split the Tories, Destroyed Labour and Divided the Country* (Biteback Publishing, 2016), p. 94

6 https://www.dailymail.co.uk/debate/article-3461103/The-torture-watching-husband-choose-beliefs-old-friend-PM-Daily-Mail-columnist-SARAH-VINE-s-intensely-personal-account-momentous-decision.html

7 Tim Shipman, op. cit., p. 147

8 https://www.dailymail.co.uk/debate/article-3461103/The-torture-watching-husband-choose-beliefs-old-friend-PM-Daily-Mail-columnist-SARAH-VINE-s-intensely-personal-account-momentous-decision.html

9 Private information

10 Tim Shipman, op. cit., pp. 109–10

11 https://www.dailymail.co.uk/debate/article-3461103/The-torture-watching-husband-choose-beliefs-old-friend-PM-Daily-Mail-columnist-SARAH-VINE-s-intensely-personal-account-momentous-decision.html

12 Owen Bennett, *The Brexit Club: The Inside Story of the Leave Campaign's Shock Victory* (Biteback Publishing, 2016), p. 200

13 Tim Shipman, op. cit., p. 149

14 Ibid., p. 150

15 Ibid., p. 150

16 Ibid., pp. 148–9

17 Ibid., p. 153

18 Ibid., p. 153

19 Owen Bennett, op. cit., p. 202

20 https://www.dailymail.co.uk/debate/article-3461103/The-torture-watching-husband-choose-beliefs-old-friend-PM-Daily-Mail-columnist-SARAH-VINE-s-intensely-personal-account-momentous-decision.html

21 Tim Shipman, op. cit., p. 162

22 Owen Bennett, op. cit., p. 203

23 https://www.theguardian.com/politics/2016/feb/20/cameron-set-to-name-eu-referendum-date-after-cabinet-meeting

24 Tim Shipman, op. cit., p. 165

25 https://www.thesun.co.uk/news/1078504/revealed-queen-backs-brexit-as-alleged-eu-bust-up-with-ex-deputy-pm-emerges/

26 *Mail on Sunday*, 13 March 2016

27 Harry Mount, op. cit., p. 101

28 https://www.theguardian.com/politics/2016/apr/19/brexit-could-spark-democratic-liberation-of-continent-says-gove

29 https://blogs.spectator.co.uk/2016/04/why-i-think-brexit-is-the-right-choice/

30 http://news.bbc.co.uk/1/shared/bsp/hi/pdfs/08051604.pdf

31 Harry Mount, op. cit., p. 105

32 https://www.theguardian.com/politics/2016/may/20/eu-immigrant-influx-michael-gove-nhs-unsustainable

33 https://www.theguardian.com/politics/2016/may/21/vote-leave-prejudice-turkey-eu-security-threat

34 Harry Mount, op. cit., p. 106

35 Tim Shipman, op. cit., p. 284

36 Ibid., p. 284

37 Tim Shipman, op. cit., p. 325

38 https://www.theguardian.com/politics/2016/jun/15/michael-gove-father-company-eu-policies-fish-processing-aberdeen

39 https://www.theguardian.com/politics/2016/jun/16/nigel-farage-defends-ukip-breaking-point-poster-queue-of-migrants

40 Tom Baldwin, *Ctrl Alt Delete: How Politics and the Media Crashed Our Democracy* (C. Hurst & Co., 2018), p. 211

41 Owen Bennett, op. cit., p. 333

42 Tim Shipman, op. cit., p. 445

43 Ibid., p. 482

44 Harry Mount, op. cit., p. 167

45 Ibid., p. 167

46 Ibid., p. 174

47 https://www.telegraph.co.uk/news/2016/07/03/michael-gove-has-an-emotional-need-to-gossip-particularly-when-d/

48 Harry Mount, op. cit., p. 188
49 https://www.youtube.com/watch?v=ipWiD2EyDbA
50 Tim Shipman, op. cit., p. 572

CHAPTER 21

1 https://www.dailymail.co.uk/debate/article-3744431/SARAH-VINE-needy-men-try-steal-limelight.html
2 *The Times*, 14 October 2016
3 *The Times*, 21 October 2016
4 *The Times*, 5 November 2016
5 *The Times*, 7 November 2016
6 *The Times*, 8 October 2016
7 https://www.thesun.co.uk/news/7121220/david-cameron-michael-gove-memoir-jibe/

CHAPTER 22

1 *Gove in Government*, BBC Radio 4, 24 June 2018
2 https://www.theguardian.com/environment/2017/oct/24/uk-30-40-years-away-eradication-soil-fertility-warns-michael-gove
3 https://twitter.com/GeorgeMonbiot/status/922845169380151297?ref_src=twsrc%5Etfw%7Ctwcamp%5Etweetembed%7Ctwterm%5E922845169380151297&ref_url=https%3A%2F%2Fwww.huffingtonpost.co.uk%2Fentry%2Fmichael-gove-tories-animals-defra_uk_5a39274ce4b0fc99878ed555
4 https://www.huffingtonpost.co.uk/entry/michael-gove-tories-animals-defra_uk_5a39274ce-4b0fc99878ed555
5 Ibid.
6 Ibid.
7 *Gove in Government*, BBC Radio 4, 24 June 2018
8 *Sunday Express*, 11 June 2017
9 https://www.gov.uk/government/speeches/the-governments-negotiating-objectives-for-exiting-the-eu-pm-speech
10 https://www.gov.uk/government/speeches/pms-florence-speech-a-new-era-of-cooperation-and-partnership-between-the-uk-and-the-eu
11 *Mail on Sunday*, 12 November 2017
12 https://www.huffingtonpost.co.uk/entry/michael-gove-tories-animals-defra_uk_5a39274ce-4b0fc99878ed555
13 Private information
14 https://www.theguardian.com/politics/2017/jul/24/us-chlorinated-chicken-not-ruled-out-by-no-10-in-pursuit-of-trade-deals
15 https://www.telegraph.co.uk/news/2017/10/18/britains-20bn-brexit-divorce-bill-offer-peanuts-says-european/
https://www.theguardian.com/politics/2017/nov/29/brexit-divorce-bill-how-much-is-it-and-what-is-it-for
16 *Daily Telegraph*, 9 December 2017
17 *The Times*, 11 December 2017
18 *Sunday Times*, 25 February 2018
19 Ibid.
20 *Daily Telegraph*, 2 February 2018
21 https://hansard.parliament.uk/Commons/2018-03-20/debates/FE048CAA-4B4B-429E-9AFD-DE4A48786248/LeavingTheEUFisheriesManagement
22 https://www.politicshome.com/news/uk/political-parties/conservative-party/theresa-may/news/93765/scottish-tory-mp-brexit-fishing
23 https://www.mirror.co.uk/news/politics/michael-gove-joked-meghan-markles-12574652

24 https://www.huffingtonpost.co.uk/entry/michael-gove-venezuala-conservatives-young-votes_uk_5afb2d79e4b09a94524cab31

25 https://www.huffingtonpost.co.uk/entry/michael-gove-capitalism-crony-reform_uk_5b-17fa56e4b0599bc6df5e00

26 Private information

27 *Sunday Times*, 18 July 2018

28 https://hansard.parliament.uk/Commons/2018-07-18/debates/C599EEE1-D863-4AC9-87B3-35DA3A3EAFEE/PersonalStatement

29 https://www.theguardian.com/politics/2018/sep/20/donald-tusk-demands-answer-to-irish-border-question-next-month

30 https://www.dailymail.co.uk/debate/article-6529243/SARAH-VINE-learned-REAL-LY-matters-Christmas.html

31 https://hansard.parliament.uk/Commons/2019-01-10/debates/159740E3-991B-4DF4-A29C-D04B2F1CE10F/EuropeanUnion(Withdrawal)Act

32 https://www.bbc.co.uk/news/uk-46879887

33 https://hansard.parliament.uk/commons/2019-01-16/debates/D130C27B-C328-48F8-B596-03F05BF2EF8A/NoConfidenceInHerMajestySGovernment

CHAPTER 23

1 https://www.theguardian.com/politics/2018/jun/02/replace-theresa-may-with-michael-gove-tory-donor-says-brexit-uk-news?CMP=aff_1432&utm_content=The+Independent&awc=5795_1559121507_a622419644f1aaaf43428f66ee2da15d

2 https://talkradio.co.uk/news/mark-francois-gove-not-proper-brexiteer-19060631242

3 https://www.dailymail.co.uk/news/article-7129687/SARAH-VINE-opens-heart-Michael-Goves-cocaine-past.html

4 *The Times*, 28 December 1999

5 https://www.dailymail.co.uk/news/article-7119791/Michael-Gove-hosted-cocaine-fuelled-party-London-flat-hours-condemning-Class-drug.html

6 https://www.theguardian.com/politics/2019/jun/10/gove-launches-tory-leadership-campaign-after-drug-revelations

7 https://inews.co.uk/news/politics/tory-leadership-contest-michael-gove-cocaine-row/